INTERNATIONAL
PROPAGANDA
AND
COMMUNICATIONS

INTERNATIONAL PROPAGANDA AND COMMUNICATIONS

General Editor:

DR. CHRISTOPHER H. STERLING
Temple University

Editorial Advisory Board:

DR. MORRIS JANOWITZ
University of Chicago
DR. JOHN M. KITTROSS
Temple University
DR. BRUCE LANNES SMITH
Michigan State University

International News
and the Press

AN ANNOTATED BIBLIOGRAPHY

Compiled by
RALPH O. NAFZIGER

ARNO PRESS
A New York Times Company
New York • 1972

Reprint Edition 1972 by Arno Press Inc.

Reprinted from a copy in The University of
Illinois Library

International Propaganda and Communications
ISBN for complete set: 0-405-04740-1
See last pages of this volume for titles.

Manufactured in the United States of America

Library of Congress Cataloging in Publication Data

Nafziger, Ralph O
    International news and the press.

    (International propaganda and communications)
    Reprint of the 1940 ed.
    1. Press--Bibliography. 2. Journalism--
Bibliography. 3. Foreign news--Bibliography.
I. Title. II. Series.
Z6940.N16 1972   016.07   72-4675
ISBN 0-405-04759-2

International News
and the Press

International News and the Press

Communications, Organization of News-Gathering, International Affairs and the Foreign Press

AN ANNOTATED BIBLIOGRAPHY

Compiled by

RALPH O. NAFZIGER

Department of Journalism, University of Minnesota

THE H. W. WILSON COMPANY

NEW YORK   1940

FOREWORD

While we have become acutely aware of the effects of propaganda in domestic and international affairs and of the importance of news reports transmitted from the far-flung and often disturbed corners of the globe, few scholars and not many publicists have seriously studied the communication agencies which carry propagandistic symbols and various forms of intelligence from point to point on the world's surface. The multiplication of the techniques and the extension of the radius of communication have long been a matter of interest and concern to Foreign Offices and to the defense services of various countries. Rulers and the military from the dawn of history had never slighted communications in the maintenance of power. Newspapers and news-gathering agencies from the first were regardful of the importance of quick transmission of intelligence; in fact, the press historically has fostered the improvement and extension of the facilities of communication. Business men from the days of the fifteenth century merchants were acutely aware that accurate information of events and a knowledge of the sentiments of other peoples, were of importance if mutual benefits were to be enjoyed on both sides of a great land or water barrier.

But while these groups possess intimate understanding of the facilities which transmit diplomatic, commercial, news and propagandistic intelligence, scholars themselves have not in many cases familiarized themselves with either the physical multiplicity of the communication network, the agencies which make use of the communication web for the carrying of various forms of intelligence, the nationalistic control of communications, or the full consequences of use and control of these vital symbol-carriers.

True, they have occupied themselves with the political and social changes that followed the remaking of the map sociologically, psychologically and economically when distance was telescoped by the coming of mechanical communication agencies. The contraction of the globe meant to them such things as the development of a world opinion, or the transmission of culture patterns from one national state or geographic area to another, or the spreading of propaganda and the consequent creation of nationalistic fears and hates or even hopes. They have studied the symbols that pass over communication channels.

Nevertheless, there is much work still to be done. No really thorough-going understanding of today's political and social problems is possible, and especially is this true in the international area, without a more competent and painstaking analysis of the impact of modern communications on the social scheme of things than scholarship has given us to date. The advent of the principle of the transmission of information by electrical energy coincided with the broadening of the base of political power and literacy in the great states of the world. The interchange of information among all classes of people had consequences that are known to every reputable social scientist. And yet no really penetrating study of these consequences has fully taken account of the role of communication agencies in this picture.

Dr. Ralph O. Nafziger's bibliography should be welcomed as a useful tool for scholars who wish to advance the frontiers of knowledge and understanding of the part communication plays in the life of societies and nations and, on a broader scale, it will help to implement the studies of nationalism and internationalism in their various aspects. Dr. Nafziger has not concerned himself solely with a selection of materials on the systems of communication, the relationship of communications to transportation, commerce, the press, and the military services, but he has had the good judgment to include other sections closely related to the foregoing.

Up to the present, it has seemed important for social scientists, professors of journalism, publicists, and other interested persons to study single communication agencies, such as the newspaper, the radio or the motion picture, or to observe the government's relationships with one or another of these agencies of mass impression, or to tackle some minor aspect of a wider problem. While this has given us excellent studies, the method has been in some ways a disservice to scholarship. While it may be impossible for one single authority to unify the problem of the social consequences of the inter-action of communication agencies on the whole of life, nevertheless it is high time that investigators come to the understanding that single threads run through all subject matter bearing on the communication problem.

To be more specific, there is little advantage in studying aspects of nationalism without grasping the fact that the government and its economic structure, press, news-gathering organizations, cable, radio and telephone companies, and even the foreign correspondent are not separate patches in the national fabric. Occasionally, this truism becomes fairly obvious even to casual students, as, for example, when Sir Arthur Willert warned the British nation in 1937 that in his opinion the British news-gathering services had a more effective role to play alongside their own government in resisting the organized, subsidized foreign competition of ministries of propaganda and rival news services. More strikingly, this undramatic unity of nation and communication agencies came to the fore with the appointment in 1938 of a Commission, headed by Sir Robert Vansittart, to coordinate the "propaganda" agencies of Great Britain. In short, scholars now will find that it is necessary to gain an "over-view" conception of the broad field of communications if they are to make significant contributions in the narrower areas of this subject.

Dr. Nafziger provides in this volume citations of the best materials on communications, news-gathering, foreign correspondence, the press and world affairs, war and press, the foreign press and other subject matter. The scholar who hasn't yet familiarized himself with a constructed area may till the smaller garden by referring to references cited in this book. The seeds for his crop are here. The investigator who prefers, however, to develop an integrated area, can bring together the individual plots into a more fertile and more expansive contribution to knowledge.

RALPH D. CASEY
Chairman, Department of Journalism
University of Minnesota

PREFACE [1]

Considerable attention is being given today by educators, statesmen and the public to the methods and forces which shape foreign news dispatches in their passage from sources to newspaper pages. Strangely enough, few careful case studies or objective analyses with a view to shedding more light on this important and complex problem have been attempted.

SCOPE

One handicap to investigators of these problems is the lack of a guide to the literature on the subject. A few notable publications such as Riegel's *Mobilizing for Chaos* and Desmond's *The Press and World Affairs* are valuable guideposts. Memoirs of all sorts, numerous popular books and magazine articles by correspondents and other observers in foreign countries, brief attempts to account for the fundamental differences in the newspaper press of various countries and the effect which these differences have on international news communications have appeared in print. Government documents, proceedings and publications of international organizations, occasional studies in journals devoted to research, and a continuous stream of articles in newspapermen's journals chronicling the experiences of foreign correspondents and developments in the relationship of press and government throughout the world offer an opportunity to piece together fragmentary and episodic bits into patterns and backgrounds against which historical and case studies can be developed. Trends manifested in these patterns, despite serious gaps, offer an excellent perspective for the student of the press and foreign affairs.

SOURCES AND ACKNOWLEDGMENTS

This volume is an attempt to bring together and to classify titles of documents, books, pamphlets, magazine articles, and studies dealing with the subject of international news communications and the foreign press. A mimeographed edition representing a collection of references, which I had assembled over a period of years for my own use because no bibliography on the subject had appeared in print, was issued in the summer of 1937 by the Burgess Publishing Company of Minneapolis. With the assistance of the University of Minnesota and the Work Projects Administration, this new volume is made possible. All of the entries in the original bibliography have been rechecked, the material has been brought up to date, and annotations have been added.

Materials were drawn from the Library of Congress lists, the *Readers' Guide* and several equivalents in foreign languages, the International Index to Periodicals, newspapermen's journals in the United States and foreign countries, publishers' lists, my private collection of titles and a

[1] Published by the University of Minnesota as a report on Official Project No. 65-1-71-140, Sub-project No. 248, conducted under the auspices of the Work Projects Administration.

number of miscellaneous sources including friends and correspondents to whom I am gratefully indebted for valuable suggestions. Collections in the libraries of the University of Minnesota, the University of Wisconsin and the Wisconsin State Historical Society were also consulted. No attempt was made to include entries in bibliographies such as Lasswell, Casey and Smith's *Propaganda and Promotional Activities*, Karl Bömer's *Internationale Bibliographie des Zeitungswesens*, Rudolf Löwenthal's *Western Literature on Chinese Journalism* and the inclusive lists which have appeared in recent years in the bibliographic sections of the *Journalism Quarterly*. Moreover, titles were restricted to those which can be obtained in American libraries.

I wish to express my thanks particularly to Joseph R. Buckwald, Miss Margaret Cameron, Miss Emily L. Wier and Willis S. Wykoff for assistance in the laborious task of bringing together and editing this volume. Without the pledge of their help I should not have undertaken this revision.

R. O. N.

CONTENTS

PART II. THE FOREIGN PRESS

INTRODUCTION

THE STUDY OF WORLD NEWS COMMUNICATIONS

Despite competition today between newspapers and new agencies of mass impression, the public still depends largely on the newspaper press for its day-to-day and week-by-week information on foreign affairs. Moreover, the sources of information, and in large measure the channels upon which these agencies depend for their news, are identical.

The limited number of channels leading from the sources of foreign news to immense readership in America today—to the citizens who are called upon from time to time to decide the course of action which the country is to take—has made the press a vital factor in modern government and diplomacy. Whether a state is democratic or totalitarian, the manner in which news communications are operated and controlled, affects the outlook of the people on foreign affairs.

The publicity given to these and similar problems as a consequence of the first World War, and the importance which has been attached since then to the newspaper press by statesmen, and by the "Ins" and the "Outs" struggling for power in countries throughout the world, has stimulated widespread interest in the relationship of the press and foreign affairs. The flood of brief descriptions and extensive comments on the subject has served largely, however, to show the need for analyses of specific cases and basic trends.

Problems which are assumed to be new to the press in one country are often similar to those in other countries; indeed, have often been solved in other countries. Customs and unique experiences of a people account for basic differences in the newspapers of various countries. What seem to be sudden changes in news-gathering methods and in the relationships of press and government are usually steps in a long-time series of developments. Consequently an examination of the literature, including accounts in popular journals, offers an approach to pertinent topics and background materials.

Thus war correspondents were regarded a century ago as interlopers in situations which were the concern exclusively of military men and government officials. Efforts to restrict the operations of the correspondents led to an accumulation of experience which gradually formalized the limitations imposed on them, and led governments either to use the correspondents to bolster up national policies or actually to absorb them into the army as an important and legitimate branch of the armed services.

Similarly, censorship and official propaganda have been the rule in the world, and the democratic concept of freedom of press, nebulous at its boundaries but distinguishable at the core, has been the exception which has been suffered at times in a number of countries and well established in only a few.

A study of the serious limitations which always have been placed in the way of reporters and agencies who have sought to gather foreign news shows that simple explanations for problems of international news–gathering, and time-honored clichés and generalizations concerning the objectivity of foreign news reports serve mainly to confuse the reading public. Moreover, if the prevailing assumption that the impact of news from abroad is an important factor in international understanding is true, then the need for careful study of this entire field is important and urgent.

It is necessary, of course, that the human beings who gather and who edit news from abroad should be exceptionally able and dependable, for often a single man stationed at an important news source is the eyes and ears for millions of readers. Moreover, the wholesome demand for interpretative reports has resulted in conspicuous instances in which good reporters have turned special pleaders, identifying themselves with the game of diplomats and the promotion of Great Causes. The evidence is strong, however, that no matter how intelligent and able the correspondents and editors are, they are often hedged in by carefully guarded impediments which allow the newspaperman little part in the process of selecting the news which shall appear in the public press. New and expanded channels of communication make it much easier to disseminate news quickly throughout the world than was true a generation ago. Communication agencies today can transmit many times the volume of news which they are called upon to carry. The amount and quality of foreign news has doubtless improved greatly decade by decade for a century, particularly in the press of the United States. But improved facilities for distributing objective news often become improved facilities for distributing distorted news, and the opening of new channels of international news communication stimulates the wider application of age-old methods for controlling or canalizing the news. Nations, like individuals and institutions, follow the natural inclination to put their best foot forward.

COMMUNICATION CHANNELS

Communications in the broad sense are fundamental to the existence and maintenance of empires and nations. They are fundamental to commerce, national defense and politics. Social and political relationships, carried on by the exchange of information, by discussion, understandings and agreements are influenced and shaped by communicative acts.

News communications, as a part of newspaper processes, necessarily share in these communicative activities and functions. They contribute, particularly through the cumulative effects of the information which they carry and disseminate, to the attitudes and opinions of society and to the understandings which serve individuals and peoples as bases for their decisions and attachments.

The factors which shape the news at its springs, and the symbols by which the news at the source is expressed, are powerful influences. The controls exercised over the communication channels and arteries in the world such as the telegraph, cables, telephone and radio likewise con-

tribute their share to the nature and tendency of the news. The process
of selection and the symbols used at the receiving end of the news may
also determine the tendency of news dispatches. However accurate the
news facts are which survive this sifting process, their incompleteness
may affect greatly the understanding of the total news event which the
news reading public achieves. Each of these points in the news communications channel is, therefore, worthy of investigation in any case
study of foreign news reporting.

In modern times, the systematic gathering of news has paralleled
the discovery and growth of communication lines. Widespread demand
for news and the development of means for distributing it speedily depended, of course, on the growth of printing processes, quantity production of paper, the rise of universal education and other factors, but efficient organization for procuring and disseminating news awaited the
coming of proper physical means for transmitting information. Travel-
ers and singers could carry a certain amount of information despite poor
roads. Letter exchanges among cloisters, messenger services between
cities and among princelings, merchants, and army leaders as developed
by the Hanseatic News League and the cities of Augsburg, Nürnberg,
Venice, Antwerp and others, and the exchange of news in coffee houses
and reading rooms, were in keeping with the facilities of the times. The
rise of professional news agents was stimulated by the improvements in
the postal services which were eventually regarded as a public need and
a public service. But the development was slow. Widespread censorship in the seventeenth and eighteenth centuries was a strong check on
the growth of systematic news gathering. In the early nineteenth century
the use of newly devised light signals and the use of carrier pigeons
helped somewhat, coincidental with the demand for political news arising
out of the ferment created by the French revolution. It remained, however, for the coming of electrical transmission of news—the telegraph—
to remove the numerous physical hindrances to exchange of information
within and among the countries of the world. The telegraph stimulated
immediately the growth of news-gathering agencies which have persisted
and expanded to the present day.

Within a few decades after the telegraph had developed from a
laboratory novelty into a practical means of transmitting information,
continents were linked in the late 50's and the 60's· of the nineteenth
century by submarine cables. The importance which statesmen, as well
as newspapermen and traders, attached to the land and submarine telegraph is demonstrated by the succession of controversies, agreements,
and competitive enterprises in the establishment of wire networks which
followed immediately upon the successful completion of the early cable
lines. Moreover, the connection with empire and colonial expansion is
shown by the expansion decade by decade of land and ocean telegraph
along the very routes which the armed forces of empires, the colony
builders, and the commercial and financial interests were following. In
the wake of these vanguards came the news-gatherers.

The first transoceanic cable route was built across the Atlantic.
Another cable system was laid from northern Europe and past Gibraltar
into the Mediterranean and on into the Red Sea, the Indian Ocean and

the Pacific. Connecting lines along the east and west coasts of Africa were shortly in service. Alternate land routes were constructed from Europe into the Middle and Near East to the Persian Gulf, and across Russia and Siberia to the Pacific, meeting there with cables to Japan and to points along the coast of China. The network expanded from points in Europe to South America and from the United States to Central and South America. When the United States at the close of the nineteenth century turned her attention dramatically to the Far East, American commercial interests and the government culminated negotiations over a trans-Pacific cable route with agreements which shortly led to the construction of cable lines from the United States to Asia.

The needs of her expanding empire, her extensive commercial and financial interests and her defence forces, account, perhaps, for the far-sighted manner in which Great Britain quickly took the leadership in the construction of world-wide communication routes. Early in the twentieth century British cable interests were greater than those of all other nationals combined. Moreover, her news-gatherers literally supplied the world with international news. "News of British origin," to use a euphemism, had almost no competition in the welter of world trade, world politics and world news. How Great Britain was in a position to isolate her enemies during the first World War from virtually all routes of international news communication is common knowledge. How during the 20's and the early 30's her statesmen and press were alarmed by the encroachments on her hitherto undisputed leadership as the world's purveyor of news, resulting from the increasing use of a new agency—the radio—by upstart European competitors, and from the amazing expansion and enterprise manifested by American press associations, is another story which has never been told in detail.

The entire picture is, at present, undergoing profound change. Who owns the communication channels along which the news of the world flows? The answer to this question has a significant bearing on the relationship of press and foreign affairs. What country, or whose nationals, supplies most of the world's news? This is likewise important.

Whoever controls the main news centers of the world, or the "bottle-necks" of world news, is in a position, as has been true in the past, to exercise extraordinary influence on the tendency of the news, particularly in times of crises. For that reason the status of the communications system must be studied in connection with the organization for gathering foreign news at the source and for distributing and editing it at home.

FOREIGN NEWS GATHERING

A study of prevailing systems of gathering and exchanging foreign news offers an opportunity to isolate fundamental problems involved in reporting and publishing foreign news. For more than a century there have been mainly two means of collecting and distributing world news. Newspapers with strong financial resources and superior equipment develop their own staffs for gathering foreign news. This method is open only to a few newspapers. No more than five in the United States have found it feasible to adopt it. Even these newspapers, despite a foreign service budget in one case of about $500,000, find it necessary to supplement their reports with other news services. And $500,000 is, of course, more than the total operating budget of most newspapers.

Under the second method international transoceanic news arteries are used, and the enterprise is financed by contributions from hundreds of clients or member newspapers. The Associated Press, United Press, Reuter and Havas are examples of these news-gathering associations. This is the most economical and successful means which has been devised for collecting and distributing world news. It is the logical means of using the ever-expanding network of telegraph, submarine cable, radio, and telephone.

Despite the successes achieved by a universal use of this system of press associations for reporting foreign news, it has given rise to many criticisms. A few may be mentioned by way of illustration:

1. By dominating the field of international reporting the press associations have assumed tremendous power and great responsibility. They select for the editors the news which they believe is important, interesting, or desired by their clients.

2. In consequence of nationalism and the desire of all nations to maintain a "good press" in the world, the tendency has been to slant the news toward the ideas, aims and interpretations of the country in which the press association operates. Rarely is an "international point of view" uncolored by specific national points of view possible.

3. The press associations have, therefore, become handy instruments of national policy. Obviously the press associations in most countries of the world must get along with the government of the country in which they are established.

4. In only a few countries in the world is it possible to maintain an adequate, profitable news-gathering agency without some form of subsidy from large business interests or the government. Newspapers in only a few countries are financially in a position to maintain an independent world-wide news-gathering agency.

5. In all cases, the tremendous cost of gathering foreign news compels the press associations to enter into exchange agreements whereby some of the news, at least, is gathered cooperatively. This method, logical and necessary though it may be, opens up numerous gaps through which tendentious news from purely national viewpoints may be funneled.

6. The press associations are dependent on the communication agencies such as telegraph, submarine cable, telephone, radio, which are in most cases owned, controlled or supervised by governments. The press associations have developed parallel with the development of communication systems. Given the British empire with a communications system encircling the globe, a far-sighted government inclined to cooperate actively with the press associations, a huge pool of capital which can finance extensive and costly news-gathering ventures, and a powerful navy to safeguard the arteries of international news communications, and you have an ideal arrangement for the press relations of that empire. Given China, Turkey, Italy, Spain, Japan and any number of other countries and you have inevitably a situation in which the national press associations must lean heavily on the government or on other press associations which are in control of the world's news arteries.

Despite these criticisms, however, champions of the press associations and the foreign news services of individual newspapers are in a position to emphasize the striking improvements which have been achieved in the services of the large news-gathering organizations. American newspapers particularly are proud of the leadership which their correspondents have won throughout the world in recent decades.

Newspapermen urge critics to approach the examination of worldwide news distribution from the perspective of history. Granted faults in the operation of international news communications, each decade for a century has witnessed consistent progress and improvement, and the tendency toward full and objective reports—still necessarily short of the ideal goal—is continuing year by year.

The coming of the telegraph in the second quarter of the nineteenth century stimulated the rise and rapid growth of the modern news-gathering associations such as the Associated Press in America, Reuter in England, Havas in France, the old Wolff agency in Germany and scores of others. But long before the nineteenth century there were various kinds of correspondence bureaus or news-gathering and disseminating agencies which set a pattern for the organizations which grew up in the last century. Historians have told this story, but it is important to remember that these little bureaus were usually linked with business and finance, or with the courts of various princelings in central Europe.

The Hanseatic News League in the 12th and 13th centuries is an example. Augsburg, Nürnberg, Venice, Antwerp and other trading centers needed news services and developed them. The system of correspondence operated by the House of Fugger in the sixteenth century is common knowledge. So also, Lloyds of London, and Rothschilds spreading out from Frankfurt a.M., required some form of news agency.

In the late sixteenth century Nürnberg received weekly letters from Venice, Antwerp, Cologne, sometimes from Prague, Breslau, Frankfurt, and other cities and redistributed them. Each of these points served as collecting centers for other parts of the world. From Antwerp came news of the Netherlands, France, England, Denmark. Rome took care of Italian states, Spain, southern France; Venice, the Orient.

Occasional news letters printed in the fifteenth century were succeeded by annual collections of news in the sixteenth century, then semi-annual issues, and in the early seventeenth century by weekly sheets in Augsburg, Strassburg, London, and elsewhere.

In time the center of this activity was destined to shift from postmasters and merchants to news bureaus and press associations. At any rate, business interests set the ball rolling. Exchanges, banks, merchants needed news, brought to them as swiftly as possible.

Likewise the various courts, members of the nobility, defense forces, and educated people stimulated the development of systematic news-gathering. The Bavarian, Hessian, Saxony court news services were in full operation in the sixteenth and seventeenth century. The princes meeting in Regensburg, 1575 to arrange for a regularized news exchange, involved Brandenburg-Ansbach, Bavaria, Mainz, Palsgrave, Mecklenburg, Hesse, Würtemburg, Magdeburg. In 1727 Prussia connected the various news bureaus in that monarchy for the service of the state.

By the early part of the nineteenth century business interests and governments had laid the groundwork for the telegraphic news agencies. To be sure there was little change from the seventeenth to the beginning of the nineteenth century in the methods of news-gathering despite the development of the printing press. Technical advances were few, improvements in the speed with which news was carried were limited in number despite the employment of semaphore systems like the Chappé

method, and the use of carrier pigeons. Censorship and the impoverish-
ment of Central Europe were serious hindrances, particularly to the
dissemination of political news, which, stimulated by the French Revolution, began to compete definitely with market news early in the nineteenth century.

It is the second quarter of the nineteenth century with which we are
particularly concerned, because within a decade, centering in the 40's,
the big press associations of today got their start.

The first of the modern agencies to raise its head above the level of
the little correspondence bureaus—by taking advantage of electrical
transmission facilities and by employing various astute business methods
—was the Havas agency of France. Charles Havas, who as a youth
had employed his talents on a Parisian paper sympathetic to Napoleon
Bonaparte, and with the eclipse of Napoleon had himself sunk into
oblivion for a number of years, was a linguist. During the years in
which he served as translator for commercial news services he had developed ideas for a news-gathering agency of his own. In 1835 he had
started his new undertaking after consolidating two correspondence
bureaus which specialized in translations from foreign newspapers. For
several years the Havas agency did a modest business of collecting and
disseminating news. Subventions from Louis Philippe helped somewhat. In the 40's the business forged ahead when Havas began to employ carrier pigeons, particularly on the route from London to Paris.
Havas continued to make himself acceptable to the French government,
and thereby to secure a virtual monopoly in France. Critics complained
in 1840 that French papers had developed a stifling uniformity, particularly in their articles dealing with foreign events.

After the telegraph had developed into a usable network in Europe,
Havas set out on an expansionist movement which has continued to
the present day. The coming of speedier communications, however,
stimulated two of his co-workers to leave him for enterprises of their
own. Israel J. Beer, who later became Baron Reuter, was one of them.
Reuter had been a bank clerk and had become interested in news services. He first set up his business in Aix-la-Chapelle in 1848, then moved
to Brussels. Disturbances throughout Central Europe, the completion
of a submarine cable across the English Channel, and an astute eye for
business led him to transfer his headquarters to London in 1851. At
first the London newspapers would have nothing to do with him. He
struggled along with a commercial service for merchants and financiers.
A series of notable "scoops" won him recognition by the London press
late in the 50's, and from then on his success was assured. Good business man that he was, he made his agency mean much to Great Britain,
and in turn British trade and commerce and the British government
helped him to develop a press association unique in the world's history.
His news services and private financial undertakings went hand in hand.
Before the century had ended Reuter agents were in every corner of
the world. No other agency could compete with it on equal terms. The
British agency was literally furnishing the world with international news,
and as has been maintained by many observers, its outlook on world
affairs.

The second coworker of Havas who left the French agency in 1848 was Bernhard Wolff. He, like his two friends, was a linguist. He had studied medicine in his youth and had begun his news-gathering activities by becoming a translator of medical treatises. He left the service of Havas to become editor on April 1, 1848 of the *Nationale Zeitung* of Berlin, a paper with liberal leanings like many others which began operations during that eventful year. This was the year in which the famous *Kölnische Zeitung* and others sprang up in the German states, to be followed within a few years by such papers as the *Frankfurter Zeitung*. The liberal revolution was short, to be sure, but long enough to develop a great many able editors and notable newspaper enterprises.

Wolff made use at once of the new telegraph system, for transmitting commercial news at first and political news by 1855. Frontiers of German states were everywhere, however, reaction was back in government, and wire rates were very high (3 Thalers, 10 silver Groschen from Cologne to Berlin, 13 Thalers from St. Petersburg to Berlin), whereupon Wolff decided to offer his dispatches to business firms and to other newspapers. With this the Wolff Telegraphic Bureau began. In Bremen, Frankfurt, Hamburg, Dresden, and Leipzig were competing bureaus which Wolff gradually absorbed or with which he entered into satisfactory exchange agreements.

The biggest threat to Wolff was, however, the enterprising Reuter service. Reuter had broken into German territory by way of Hanover and was attempting in the early 60's to buy up small German agencies. Reuter, with his fast-expanding interests and strong financial backing, would doubtless have run the Wolff agency into the ground had not the latter got the support of the Prussian government in its fight against the foreign invader.

These steps are important because they are typical and because they helped to shape the course of today's press associations. Early preoccupation with business news and business enterprises is one common characteristic of these organizations. The remarkable facility of Havas, Wolff, and Reuter to "cuddle up"—for expediency or self-protection—to governments in power was another common tendency. That none of these pioneers was primarily an editor wedded to a cause or eager for self-expression in news articles and editorials, is also an interesting sidelight. None was a Horace Greeley, eager to find acceptance for viewpoints expressed in prolific writings. None was a Godkin with a zeal for promoting social, economic and political ideas and ideals. They were more like Woolworth, or the early Rockefeller, or Huntington and Stanford, or as was true of Reuter in later years—a Marshall Field or a Selfridge. They were news merchants, eager to promote their businesses, eager to get along for strategic reasons with the governments under whom they operated. Since readers couldn't or wouldn't pay for the cost of collecting the news which they read, the books had to be balanced with contributions from other sources. The Stefani agency of Italy, wedded to thé unification policy of Cavour, was an exception, as were also the American press associations which grew, unhampered by government interference, out of the enterprise of newspaper publishers. Nevertheless, these *were* exceptions, and not the rule.

The move by Wolff in 1865 to get support from the Prussian government is, therefore, a case in point. One of Wolff's associates, Richard Wentzel the business manager, consulted with an influential member of the King's court, who in turn conferred with Bismarck. Wentzel sent a brief of Wolff's case against Reuter to the king, and on March 4, 1865, a cabinet memorandum assured a loan in behalf of the government of 300,000 Thalers, and 200,000 Thalers for the Continental Telegraph Co., which Wolff managed. Funds were supplied by a group of Berlin bankers, including Bleichröder. A limited stock company was formed, although Wolff remained as a director until 1871, and from then on Berlin bankers and the government were in close touch with the leading German news agency.

The fight with Reuter continued through the years, but while Wolff was never able to compete fully with the British organization it did in consequence of the financial support which it received from the bankers squeeze its big competitor out of Germany. From 1867 to 1870 Wolff fought Reuter over news channels from the United States. Reuter demanded a big price for its American service, whereupon Wolff made an agreement with the Western Associated Press which then centered in Chicago, for an independent report. In 1870, however, the big agencies agreed to enter into definite arrangements for systematizing the exchange of their news reports. Havas, Reuter and Wolff made a contract to this effect and each in turn entered into agreements with the smaller national agencies in their orbits. This was the origin of the famous "ring combination" or international cartel, anathema to patriots in countries outside of the British Empire and the United States and boon to the interests of the few big agencies, which thereby extended their domination of international news channels. The agreement of 1870 was to continue for 20 years. At the end of that time it was twice extended with some alterations to 1903, when an inclusive series of contracts was entered into which revealed the widespread ramifications of the system.

Each of the contracting parties was to have a monopoly of newsgathering and news distribution in prescribed areas which the others were not to violate. Each was to make available to the others their daily news reports. Wolff was to operate or to cooperate with the smaller agencies in the Scandinavian countries, in St. Petersburg, Austria, Hungary, a part of Switzerland, the German colonies, and a part of the Balkans.

Havas was to cover France and her colonies, Italy, Spain, Portugal, Belgium, Turkey, Rumania, Serbia, and most of South America.

The Associated Press of the United States, which had been reorganized and strengthened in 1901, had as its exclusive sphere of interest this country and her possessions, Canada, Mexico, Central America.

Reuter took in most of the rest of the world, including her Empire and possessions, Holland, the entire Near East and Far East, Africa aside from colonies owned by the other parties to the contracts, the Dutch East Indies, part of the Balkans, and part of South America. Thus Reuter got the lion's share.

Before long, criticisms of Wolff reached print in German magazines and newspapers and on the floor of the Reichstag. Germany, her champions insisted, was getting a bad press in the world because of the Ring Combination. The Wolff reports were accessible to Reuter and Havas, to be sure, but these agencies were not under compulsion to send them in entirety through their news channels to newspapers in their spheres of influence. A member of the Reichstag, Sudekum, in 1905 criticized the close connection of Wolff with the government, insisting that the agency was virtually a mouthpiece for Chancellor Von Bülow. For three decades this criticism continued in Germany, and similar attacks were made on press associations in Japan, Italy and other "have-nots."

Actually Havas, Reuter or Wolff make little or no profit from sales of their general news reports. Havas, which includes the government among its important paying clients, reaps a harvest from its advertising business. Reuter has various business investments. Wolff made money on its speedy financial and market news service, to which bourse circles and the banks subscribed. It made money on its dispatch transmission service for business firms through the preferential wire rates it enjoyed and the business code which it used. It also profited by its multiple-message service through which one telegram could be dispatched at special rates to many addresses throughout the world.

When the Hitler regime came into power, the effects on the German press agencies was inevitable. Wolff and the Telegraph Union were merged into an official agency which frankly became a tool in the hands of government officials. The new Deutsches Nachrichten Büro continued to exchange news with the other agencies, but it sought to achieve —with little more success than was won by the efforts of Wolff in former years—to establish for itself a real place in the sun among its big rivals. It did establish stronger independent bureaus of correspondence in the Americas—Washington, Los Angeles, Rio de Janeiro, Santiago (Chile), Mexico City, and many others in other continents. Its work was supplemented by renewed efforts to put life into the cheap or free Transocean news service by wireless. It did become a nuisance to Reuter and a menace in the eyes of such British publicists and publicity men as Sir Arthur Willert, but it won few additional paying newspaper clients in the world.

Other factors, aside from the organization of DNB, loosened the bonds of the Ring Combination after the World War. The cables had been the foundation upon which this cartel stood. Radio messages, which crossed international boundaries without permission, without the need for expensive wire-laying projects, and despite navies in time of war, was one of these factors. Moreover, other new press associations like the United Press in America had taken advantage of the Ring Combination by entering any and all private hunting grounds—such as South America—to establish its bureaus and to sell its products to new clients. This agency promoted its interests by contending that it operated independently of governments and foreign agencies.

Despite the tendency to lessen the hold of the Ring Combination on news-gathering, several century-old problems still remain unsolved:

1. Gathering and distributing of political news, with a few exceptions, is not a profit-making enterprise without some form of subsidy.
2. By compulsion or for the sake of expediency, most of the world's press associations are dependent for their existence on the governments or the banks of the countries in which they operate. No one has discovered a means of establishing a press association for gathering the news of the world which can operate independently of governments and banks, except in a few countries like the United States where a large number of newspapers are in a position to pay higher assessments to their press associations than can newspapers elsewhere in the world.
3. Exchange of news among the news agencies is virtually a necessary part of the system.
4. Newspaper readers must still use discrimination by comparing reports from various news sources, observing sources, channels and dates.

The nature of the news-gathering organizations, at any rate, has an important bearing on the world's news communication system. The great press associations of today are equipped to supply inclusive daily reports of foreign news. The energy which they expend in an effort to increase their usefulness to newspaper readers is limited, of course, by the obstacles which prevent them from observing or otherwise arriving at the facts.

FOREIGN NEWS EDITING

An uncommon amount of criticism is levelled, especially in time of crisis, at the nature of foreign dispatches in the newspaper press. Each day the news of the world jumps with explosive force at the reader from the pages of the press. Front pages crackle with urgent reports from abroad, but much of this news is incomplete, contradictory, and confusing. Moreover, editors and publishers have neglected to take readers into their confidence by explaining to them frankly the impediments that exist to free and independent reporting of the news, and critics have been quick to charge that the press itself is responsible for the incompleteness of foreign dispatches. This failure of the press to explain its position is often the result of a notion among publishers that to admit inability, for good and sufficient reasons, to produce news which is 99 per cent objective and true is analogous to the situation in which a grocer would be if he explained that every third or fourth egg in his supply is contaminated. The press has failed to point out to the public that the reader cannot forego the mental effort of reading the news with discrimination by comparing reports from various sources, by observing sources, channels, datelines, and by sifting through his own mind the reports which signalize news events.

During the course of the present war more has been done, without a doubt, than heretofore to warn readers against censorship and to explain the limitations which news-gatherers face. Writers, far more generally than was true during the first World War, have contended that the news *is* complex and confusing at times, and for good reason. Edwin L. James [1] of *The New York Times* and others argue that much of the

---

[1] How Muddling Through Makes More Muddling, *The New York Times*, p.E3, October 9, 1938.

news is confusing and illogical because the official news sources are confused and illogical. Was the press misleading or did it lie when in September 1938 it published articles based on an "authoritative statement" to the effect that Britain would fight if Germany invaded Czechoslovakia, and a few days later quoted Premier Chamberlain when he expressed a contrary viewpoint? Did the press mislead the public when it cited Czech authorities to the effect that Czechoslovakia would fight if invaded? Did the press fool the public by printing articles from Berlin during the first week in November 1937 which stated that Germany was proposing to mediate the Sino-Japanese conflict, followed hours later by denials from the Far East? Was it poor reporting when the American press published statements from London to the effect that the Czechs were ready to accede to Germany's demands, together with statements from Prague insisting that the reports from London were false? Should the press, when it has no means of investigating the facts independently of government officials, refuse to publish completely contradictory statements from official London and Berlin sources concerning the results of a big air battle between British and German air fleets? Is it possible that news articles from abroad are often inconsistent and muddy because the expressed policy of foreign nations is often inconsistent, illogical, opportunistic, unclear, changeable? Is there good evidence showing that the press, which is in a position to foster hostility or understanding between nations through the cumulative effect of tendentious news articles published over a period of time has, by reporting and commenting independently upon diplomatic negotiations, created a worse mess in specific instances of world politics than have the diplomats? Is there good evidence to show that the press influences public opinion throughout the world independently of the governments which furnish the news? Does the press create or lead public opinion regarding foreign affairs, or does it merely follow the lead of governments and mirror their activities?

The lengths to which governments have gone to assure "cooperation" of the press in promoting official foreign policy by creating government press bureaus, ministries of information or ministries of propaganda is common knowledge. Authoritarian states have also been leaders in advancing the cause of press treaties or "press non-aggression pacts" under which governments which are parties to the bilateral or multilateral agreements would undertake to develop a "basis of mutual respect and understanding" by eliminating from the press criticism and attacks on foreign governments and their leaders. Aside from efforts which were made during the conferences of press experts under the auspices of the League of Nations from 1926 to 1933, German officials during the Hitler regime have pressed this formula most energetically. Following Hitler's Reichstag speech of January 30, 1937, for example, German leaders such as Otto Dietrich, Reich press chief, appealed to the world for a "press peace." Dr. Dietrich is reported to have said on one occasion:[2]

How peaceful the world would be today if newspapers everywhere would not only talk peace but also keep the peace themselves. The press could easily achieve miracles in the political lives of peoples if such a general truce were proclaimed and lived up to.

[2] *The New York Times*, p. 10, March 8, 1938.

The relations of press and government, particularly during crises, have also been commented upon on a number of occasions by Premier Chamberlain, who has consistently urged restraint by the press when it reports foreign news. In an address to the House of Commons on August 29, 1939 Mr. Chamberlain explained that it was not in the public interest to announce the contents of the notes which had been exchanged with the German government regarding the Polish question. The inference was drawn by the press that if the notes were made public the government would be committed to the policies which were enunciated in the notes, thereby preventing "flexibility" of policy. If the press in its daily reports of the negotiations accurately demonstrated sudden shifts in policy, or reflected inconsistency in a sequence of diplomatic maneuvers, did it thereby mislead the public?

Countless other illustrations could be cited to show the far-reaching questions which result from an examination of the relationship between the press and foreign affairs. That the press, in its efforts to report the news of the world, has a bearing on the course of world politics and on the social values which are widely promoted or to which people cling, is generally accepted as a fact. The ramifications of these effects and what, in specific cases, lies behind them is a field which is virtually unexplored.

The pervasiveness of the press, and the attention which men in high places have paid to it, has given it credit for exerting great force and power. But what are the facts? What adequate examples are available to permit generalizations?

RALPH O. NAFZIGER

Minneapolis
May, 1940

International News and the Press

PART I. INTERNATIONAL NEWS

I. COMMUNICATIONS

See also
Propaganda—Channels, p.50; World War, 1914
—News Transmission, p.88; Second World
War, 1939—Communications, p.103.

A. HISTORY AND ANALYSIS

Albion, Robert Greenhalgh
Communication revolution. American Historical Review. 37:718-20. July 1932
    The communication revolution was a distinct development and should not be considered a phase of the industrial revolution.

Anderson, Paul Y.
The Radio Corporation in the news. Nation. 130:9-10. Jan. 1, 1930
    Remarks on a proposal to merge transoceanic cable and radio systems and the domestic telegraph lines in one gigantic communications monopoly.

Archambault, G. H.
Phone supplanting wire in Europe. Editor and Publisher. 67:viii. Apr. 13, 1935

Arnold, H. D. See Page, Arthur W. jt. auth.

Brooks, Sydney
Development of Pan American communications; telephony and telegraphy by radio, cable and wire. il. Pan American Magazine. 43:407-14. Dec. 1930
    Telephony and telegraphy by radio, cable and wireless telegraphy as aids to international relations.

Brown, Frank James
The cable and wireless communications of the world. 153p. London, New York: Sir I. Pitman and Sons, 1930
    "A survey of international communications by cable and wireless, containing chapters on cable and wireless finance."
    An authoritative source book.

Clark, George Norman
Unifying the world. 116p. (Handbooks on International Relations) New York: Harcourt, Brace and Co., 1920
    Modern methods of communication; communications, national and international; effects of war and commerce on communications; international politics and communications.

Clark, Keith
International communications; the American attitude. 261p. New York: Columbia Univ. Press; London: P. S. King and Son, 1931
    The universal postal, international telegraph, submarine cables and international radio unions. Historical development and international negotiations.

Communications plan disputed. Newsweek. 3:29. Mar. 10, 1934

Crane, Charles E.
Mobilizing news. Scientific American. 112:134-5. Feb. 6, 1915

Fayle, C. Ernest. See Wright, Charles, jt. auth.

Fellner, Frederick Vincent de
Communications in the Far East. 362p. London: P. S. King and Son, 1934
    The center of gravity of economic forces shifted from the Atlantic to the Pacific following the World War. Expansion of transportation and communication facilities followed as a result of this change.

First land wireless newspaper. Scientific American. 88:298. Apr. 18, 1903
    The first daily newspaper dispatches received by wireless at station established March 25, 1903 at Avalon, Santa Catalina Island.

Griffith, Capt. Glyn. See Worsley, Frank Arthur, jt. auth.

Gross, Gerald C. See Herring, James M. jt. auth.

Harlow, Alvin F.
Old wires and new waves. 548p. New York, London: D. Appleton-Century, 1936
    The history of the telegraph, telephone and wireless.

Herring, James M. and Gross, Gerald C.
Telecommunications. 544p. New York: McGraw-Hill, 1936
    A thorough discussion of the economics and regulations of communication agencies.

Hodges, Charles
The background of international relations. 743p. New York: John Wiley and Sons, 1931
    World communications, public opinion and the press are discussed in several chapters.

Mills, John
Some universal principles of communication. Scientific Monthly. 29:553-60. July 1929
Technical discourse involving the mechanics of electrical communication.

Nagle, P. E. D.
International communications and the International Telegraph Convention. St. Petersburg. 1875; Lisbon, 1908. 68p. Washington: Government Printing Office, 1923

Page, Arthur W.; Arnold, H. D.; and others
Modern communications. 182p. Boston: Houghton Mifflin, 1932
The importance of modern communications and the part played by research in telegraphy, telephony, speech, hearing.

Pew, Marlen
Twenty-five millions for news. Editor and Publisher. 67:78, 248, 252. July 21, 1934

Rice, Stuart A. See Willey, Malcolm M., jt. auth.

Richardson, James D., comp.
A compilation of the messages and papers of the Presidents, 1789-1902. Washington: Bureau of National Literature and Art. 1897-1902
What American Presidents had to say during the 19th century regarding official attitudes towards communications. Presidents Grant, Hayes and Theodore Roosevelt are particularly important in this connection.

Riegel, Oscar W.
Mobilizing for chaos. 231p. New Haven: Yale Univ. Press, 1934
How censorship of the news has been achieved by governments of the world through control over newspaper correspondents and communications.

The Seizure of the wires. Literary Digest. 59:17-18. Dec. 28, 1918
Editorial opinions, pro and con, as to the wisdom of federal control of American communication agencies.

Sharpe, Eugene Webster
International news communications. 43p. (Univ. of Missouri Bulletin, Journalism Series, no. 45) Columbia, Mo.: 1927

Shoup, G. Stanley
The control of international cable and radio communications. Congressional Digest. 9:107-9. Apr. 1930
The dominant role Great Britain plays in the control of international cable and radio communications.

Towers, Walter K.
From beacon fire to radio. 302p. New York, London: Harper, 1924

United States. Bureau of the Census
Census of electrical industries: telephones and telegraphs. v.1-3. Washington: Bureau of the Census, 1902-32
Quinquennial.

Telephones—census of electrical industries, 1932: telephones and telegraphs. 49p. (Selected U.S. Government Publications) Washington: Government Printing Office, 1934

United States. Congress. House. Committee on Interstate and Foreign Commerce
Report on communication companies. 6v. maps, tables, diagrs., forms (73rd Congress, 2nd session, House Report n.1273) Washington, Government Printing Office, 1934-35
House calendar no.212.
Pt. II and III, submitted June 4, 1934, make up a complete report. Pt. I is a partial report.
Sections A, B and C: Summaries of the telephone, telegraph and cable, and radio industries. Section D, Div. 3: 73rd Congress, Aug. 2 session. House Report 1273, pt. II; No. 3: Telephones, etc. Section D, Div. 4: Telegraph and cable companies pursuant to H.R.59. H.J.R.572. 73rd Congress, 2nd session.
Results of a thorough investigation of American-owned and operated communication agencies by the new Federal Communications Commission.

United States. Congress. Senate. Committee on Interstate Commerce
Construction and operation of a radio broadcasting station designed to promote friendly relations among the nations of the western hemisphere. Hearings before a subcommittee of the Committee on interstate commerce, United States Senate, Seventy-fifth Congress, third session, on S. 3342, a bill to authorize the construction and operation of a radio broadcasting station designed to promote friendly relations among the nations of the western hemisphere, May 12, 18, 19, and 23, 1938. 162p. Washington: Government Printing Office, 1938

Federal control of systems of communication. Hearing before the Committee on interstate commerce, United States Senate, Sixty-fifth Congress, second session, on H.J. Res. 309, joint resolution to authorize the President, in time of war, to supervise or take possession and assume control of any telegraph, telephone, marine cable, or radio system or systems or any part thereof and to operate the same in such a manner as to provide just compensation therefor... 57p. Washington: Government Printing Office, 1918

Federal communications commission. Hearings before the Committee on interstate commerce, United States Senate, Seventy-third Congress, second session, on S. 2910, a bill to provide for the regulation of interstate and foreign communications by wire or radio, and for other purposes. March 9, 10, 13, 14, and 15, 1934... 219p. Washington: Government Printing Office, 1934
Hearings, under chairmanship of Senator Clarence Dill, leading up to the Federal Communications Act of 1934.

United States. Laws, Statutes, etc.
The Communications Act of 1934 with amendments and index thereto. Published by the Federal Communications Commission. Revised June 5, 1936. Washington: Government Printing Office, 1936
> From U.S. Statutes at Large, v.48, pt.1, p.1064.
> The Act was passed June 19, 1934, 73rd Congress, 2nd Session.

United States. President
A compilation of the messages and papers of the Presidents, 1789-1902. James D. Richardson. Washington: Bureau of National Literature and Art, 1897-1902
> What American Presidents had to say during the 19th century regarding official attitudes towards communications. Presidents Grant, Hayes and Theodore Roosevelt are particularly important in this connection.

United States. Signal Office
Annual report of the Chief Signal Officer, to the Secretary of War. 2v. Washington: 1919-20

West, A. G.
Rate rise protests continue in New York. Editor and Publisher. 66:xv. Jan. 27, 1934
> Bankers' and brokers' committees protest increase in cable and radio rates.

Willey, Malcolm M.
Communication agencies and the volume of propaganda. Annals of the American Academy. 179:194-200. May 1935
> The three main media of mass communication (the press, moving picture and radio) and conclusions regarding their effectiveness in the control of public opinion.

——and Rice, Stuart A.
Communication agencies and social life. 299p. (Recent Social Trends in the United States. Monographs) New York, London: McGraw-Hill, 1933

Worsley, Frank Arthur and Griffith, Capt. Glyn
The romance of Lloyd's. From coffee house to palace. 292p. London: Hutchinson, 1932
> The rise of Lloyd's of London to the distinction of being regarded as "the most important corporation in the world." Lloyd's relation to British shipping communications and the Royal Navy.

Wright, Charles and Fayle, C. Ernest
A history of Lloyd's. 475p. London: Macmillan, 1928
> A detailed, well-documented history of Lloyd's, covering two centuries of the commercial, naval and social history of England.

B. TELEGRAPH

Archambault, G. H.
Phone supplanting wire in Europe. Editor and Publisher. 67:viii. Apr. 13, 1935

Bright, Charles
Imperial telegraphy at a popular tariff. Fortnightly Review. 91:526-41. Mar. 1, 1909
> Costs of telegraph messages and cablegrams.

The story of telegraphy and a history of the great Atlantic cable. 255p. New York: Rudd and Carleton, 1858
> Commercial and technical history of land and submarine telegraphy.

Brown, Frank J.
The cable and wireless communications of the world. 153p. London, New York: Sir I. Pitman and Sons, 1930
> A survey of international communications by cable and wireless, containing chapters on cable and wireless finance. An authoritative source book.

Burleson dropping the wires. Literary Digest. 61:16-17. May 10, 1919
> Postmaster-General Burleson's allegedly autocratic control of cable and telegraph.

Gnaedinger, L. B. N.
Wire entanglements. World's Work. 60:23-9. Mar. 1931
> The struggle for business between Western Union and the International Telephone and Telegraph Corporation.

Godwin, George
A century of communications. Fortnightly. 147 (n.s.141): 732-6. June 1937
> Difficulties faced in establishing telegraph and cable communications.

MacDonagh, Michael
The wires and the newspapers. p.30-6. *In* Sell's Directory of the World's Press. London: H. Sell, 1906

Morse, Samuel Finley Breese
> About

The life of Samuel F. B. Morse. S. I. Prime. New York Telegraph and Telephone Age, 1875
Samuel Finley Breese Morse. John Trowbridge. 134p. Boston: Small, Maynard, 1901

Prime, S. I.
The life of Samuel F. B. Morse. New York Telegraph and Telephone Age, 1875

Schreiner, George Abel
Cables and wireless. 269p. Boston: Stratford, 1924
> A standard work on the subject, particularly the effect of the World War on communications.

Sellars, H. G.
Short history of the telegraph [British]. 13p. (The Post Office Green Papers, no. 5) London: Eyre and Spottiswoode, 1934

Telefunken, Gesellschaft für drahtlose Telegraphie m.b.H., Berlin
25 Jahre Telefunken. Festschrift der Telefunkengesellschaft, 1903-1928. 328p. Berlin: W. Simon, 1928
> A quarter-century of wireless development in Germany.

The **Telegraph** system of French West Africa. Scientific American. Suppl. 44: 18104. Sept. 18, 1897

Trowbridge, John
Samuel Finley Breese Morse. 134p. Boston: Small, Maynard, 1901

C. CABLE

Aligny, Henry Ferdinand Quarré d'
Outline of the history of the Atlantic cables. 13p. Washington: Government Printing Office, 1868

All-British Pacific cable. National Review. 32:132-4. Sept. 1898

All-British trans-Pacific cable. Blackwood's Magazine. 161:269-79. Feb. 1897; Engineering Magazine. 13:120. Apr. 1897

Allot German cables by U.S. plan. Editor and Publisher. 55:12. Dec. 23, 1922
Washington believes powers, on learning of Italian contract, are agreed on Rome-Azores link with New York.

Anniversary of the submarine cable. Scientific American. 83:278. Nov. 3, 1900

Atcheson, George, jr.
The cable situation in the Pacific ocean, with special reference to the Far East. Annals of the American Academy. 122: 70-7. Nov. 1925
Cable communications bear a significant relation to the political, military and commercial progress of the United States in its dealings with the Orient.

Atkins, John Black
The life of Sir William Howard Russell, C.V.O., LL.D. 2v. London; John Murray, 1911
The great British war correspondent's meeting with Lincoln, Seward and Davis, his experience in the Crimean War and an eye-witness account of the laying of the first transatlantic cable.

Baker, Ray Stannard
Woodrow Wilson and world settlement. v.2. Garden City, N.Y.: Doubleday, Page, 1922
Includes the story of the negotiations between the United States and Japan relative to disposition of the important Pacific cable station, the island of Yap, formerly owned by Germany. See p.418 ff.

Bell, Samuel W.
Cable monopoly to South America ended by new agreements. Editor and Publisher. 55:12. July 15, 1922
Four routes open after All America, Western Telegraph and Western Union abandon old rights.

Bent, Silas
Regarding a new Pacific cable. Asia. 19: 251-2. Mar. 1919
The inadequacy of our cable communications with the Far East, and the commercial need for expanded facilities.

Briggs, Charles Frederick and Maverick, Augustus
The story of telegraphy and a history of the great Atlantic cable. 255p. New York: Rudd and Carleton, 1858
Commercial and technical history of land and submarine telegraphy. The completion of the Atlantic telegraph may be regarded as the culmination of all past efforts and inventions in telegraphy.

Bright, Charles
All-British, or Anglo-American, Pacific cable. map Fortnightly Review. 70: 422-8. Sept. 1898
Abstract, *Public Opinion.* 25:426. Oct. 6, 1898.
The vulnerability of the submarine telegraph cable in time of war, and the threat of interrupted communication.

Imperial telegraphy at a popular tariff. Fortnightly Review. 91:526-41. Mar. 1, 1909
Costs of telegraph messages and cablegrams.

The story of the Atlantic cable. 222p. New York: D. Appleton, 1903
Includes technical detail.

Telegraphs in war time. Nineteenth Century. 77:861-78. Apr. 1915
Naval supremacy is paramount in the control of cables. Distribution of cable service in war time is mitigated if the number of cables between two points is increased and if the cables are laid at sufficiently great depth.

Burleson dropping the wires. Literary Digest. 61:16-17. May 10, 1919
Postmaster-General Burleson's allegedly autocratic control of cable and telegraph.

Cable between Newfoundland and the Azores. Science. n.s. 73:suppl. 12. Jan. 30, 1931

Cable communications with South America. Weekly Review. 4:455. May 14, 1921
Rivalry of the Western Union and the All-American Cables companies in establishing cable rates between the United States and Brazil.

The **Cable** in operation. Outlook. 60:420-3. Oct. 15, 1898

Cable peril in the Far East. Outlook (London) 1:360, 410, 423, 475, 521. Apr. 23, 30; May 7, 14, 28, 1898
The importance of cable control to empires like Great Britain. Unsatisfactory conditions prevail in China.

Cables and canals. Nation. 112:782. June 1, 1921

Los **Cables** submarinos de Cádiz á las Américas. 135p. Madrid: M. Tello, 1864
"Documentos": p.55-135.

Castle, William R., jr.
The President's control of cables. Congressional Digest. 9:106. Apr. 1930
The President has the power to deny foreign cable companies, engaged in monopolistic practices, licenses to operate cable lines in America.

Chambers, R. E.
How telegrams are sent in China. Scientific American. 109:367. Nov. 8, 1913

Collins, Henry Michael
From pigeon post to wireless. 312p. London: Hodder and Stoughton, 1925
Early difficulties with cable communication. See ch.10, p.257.

Danger to submarine cables in case of war. Scientific American. suppl. 43:17798. May 1, 1897
The Russian government laid plans, in case of war, to cut submarine cables.

DeWolf, F. C.
Cairo telecommunication conferences, 1938. American Journal of International Law. 32:562-8. July 1938

E.P.U. obtain new flat rate for Empire news. World's Press News. 21:3. Apr. 20, 1939
Cable press rate within British empire, excepting Canada, is set at 2¼d.

Field, Henry Martyn
The story of the Atlantic telegraph. 415p. New York: C. Scribner's Sons, 1898
A chronicle of the Atlantic telegraph, depicting particularly the career of Cyrus W. Field, whose efforts made it possible.

The **First** Atlantic cable station in America. Scientific American. 89:46. July 18, 1903
Lord Kelvin's contribution to submarine telegraphy, the siphon recorder.

Fricke, Alfred K., ed.
A half century of cable service to the three Americas. 128p. New York: All America Cables, Inc., 1928

Giuli, Italio de
Submarine telegraphy: a manual. 225p. London: Sir I. Pitman and Sons, 1932
Tr. from the Italian.

Gnaedinger, L. B. N.
Wire entanglements. World's Work. 60: 23-9. Mar. 1931
The struggle for business between Western Union and the International Telephone and Telegraph Corporation.

Godwin, George
A century of communications. Fortnightly. 147 (n.s. 141):732-6. June 1937
Difficulties faced in establishing telegraph and cable communications.

Hanson, Haldore
Communications are a vital element in China's plans for defense against Japan. map China Weekly Review. 80:7-8. Mar. 6, 1937

Haynie, Henry
Submarine telegraphy: a new French transatlantic cable. Scientific American. suppl. 44:18124-5. Sept. 25, 1897
Technical problems connected with laying the second submarine telegraph cable linking the United States and France.

Hearst associations protest wire rate. Editor and Publisher. 67:57. Apr. 20, 1935

Herrle, Gustave
The submarine cables of the world. National Geographic. 7:102-7. Jan. 1896
Steps in the development of the submarine telegraph cable.
Large folding map.

Higgins, A. Pearce
Submarine cables and international law. p.25. In British Yearbook of International Law, 1920-21. London: Oxford Univ. Press, 1920
Traders accused the British of tapping commercial news during the World War.

High tension submarine cable between Denmark and Sweden. Scientific American. 116:349. Apr. 7, 1917

I. T. & T. Fortune. 2:34-45, 124. Dec. 1930
The romance of the International Telephone and Telegraph Corporation. The company was launched in 1921 by the brothers Behn.

International Telecommunication Bureau, Bern
Nomenclature des câbles formant le réseaux sous-marin du globe. 56p. Berne: Bureau de l'Union International des Télécommunications. July 1934
An official listing of cables and cable companies throughout the world.

Proposals for the International Radio Conference of Cairo, 1938. vii,587p. diagr.
Berne: Bureau of the International Telecommunications Union, 1937.
Mimeographed.
International Radiotelegraph Conference, Cairo, 1938 (4th Revisional Conference).

International Telegraph Bureau, Bern
Conférence international pour la protection des câbles sous-marins, Paris, 1882-84. Procès verbaux. 192p. Paris: Imp. Nationale, 1882
Procès-verbal de signature. 22p. Paris: Imp. Nationale, 1884
Procès-verbaux. Paris: Imp. Nationale, 1882-83. 2v. Paris, 1886-87.
Procès-verbaux. Paris: Imp. Nationale, 1886.

I. International Telegraph Convention of St. Petersburg 1875. II. Service regulations. Translation of the text issued by the International Bureau of the Telegraph Union, Berne, May 1930. Washington: Government Printing Office, 1930

Protection of submarine cables. Preliminary conference in London on the further protection of submarine telegraph cables. Procès-verbaux et annexes... 37p. (Great Britain. Parliament. Cd. 7079) London: Darling, 1913

International Telegraph Conference, St. Petersburg, 1875
Conférence Télégraphique Internationale, St. Petersburg, 1875. International Telegraph Convention of Saint-Petersburg and Service regulations annexed. Revision of Paris, 1925. 156p. London: H.M. Stationery Office, 1926
French and English in parallel columns.

Japan's overseas electric communications. Far Eastern Review. 33:336-8. Sept. 1937
Development of overseas submarine cables, wireless telegraphy and wireless telephony carried on by the International Electric Communication Co., Ltd.

Kabel und Radio. Zeitungswissenschaft. 1:195. Dec. 15, 1926
The use of cables and radio in international news communications.

McDonald, Philip B.
A saga of the seas; the story of Cyrus W. Field and the laying of the first Atlantic cable. 288p. New York: Wilson-Erickson, 1937

McGrath, P. T.
Transatlantic cables and their control. Review of Reviews. 51:591-5. May, 1915

MacKay, Clarence H.
International cable communication. 24p. Washington: Government Printing Office, Jan. 10, 1921
Report of statement before U.S. Senate Committee on Interstate Commerce.

Maverick, Augustus. See Briggs, Charles Frederick, jt. auth.

Mills, J. Saxon
The press and communications of the Empire. 289p. (The British Empire, v.6) New York: Henry Holt, 1924

Montgomery, P.
Canada lays the first cable. map Canadian Magazine. 77:45-6. Mar. 1932

Morris, John
Lower cable rates. Editor and Publisher. 56:6. Nov. 3, 1923

Morse, A. P.
Neutral use of cables. Scientific American. suppl. 45:18489-90. Mar. 5, 1898

Mullaly, John
The laying of the cable, or the ocean telegraph. 329p. New York: D. Appleton, 1858

New Atlantic cable to be great aid to news services and papers. Editor and Publisher. 56:7. Sept. 1, 1923
The cable will speed transmission of dispatches from Central Europe.

New cable service from Europe. Editor and Publisher. 66:4. June 10, 1933

The **New** ocean cable. Harper's Weekly. 18:546. June 27, 1874
Structural changes made in the manufacture of the fifth cable connecting the United States and England.

Odell, George T.
The cable control controversy. Nation. 112:169-70. Feb. 2, 1921
Because of her control of the cables, London is a bottle-neck through which world news must pass. This gives Britain an unusual advantage in the commercial struggle between nations.

Oppenheim, Lassa F. L.
International law: a treatise. 2v. London, New York: Longmans, Green, 1920-21
Brief statement regarding international law and cables.

Pacific cable. Quarterly Review. 253:161-76. July 1929
The growth and development of international electric communication between Great Britain and her dominions.

Pacific cables. Canadian Magazine. 10:456-7. Mar. 1898
The future of commerce on the Pacific and the need for a cable linking Canada with Australia and the Orient as discussed in the London *Times*.

Pew, Marlen
Shop talk at thirty. Editor and Publisher. 66:44. Mar. 31, 1934
The cable as it existed in old days.

Rodgers, Admiral W. L.
The effect of cable and radio control on news and commerce. Annals of the American Academy. 112:240-51. Mar. 1924
It is essential in the interest of national policy that the United States hold and develop leadership in radio and international news.

Rogers, Walter S.
Electrical communications in the Pacific. Annals of the American Academy. 122:78-81. Nov. 1925
The cable activities in the Orient of the United States and various European nations.

Rorty, M. C.
Electrical communication services and international relations. Annals of the American Academy. 150:47-52. July 1930
"The uses and the purposes, the present position, and the probable future development of international communications."

Russell, Sir William Howard
The Atlantic telegraph. London: 1866

Scholz, Franz
Krieg und Seekabel. 161p. Berlin: F. Vahlen, 1904
Submarine cables in wartime.

Schreiner, George Abel
Cables and wireless. 269p. Boston: Stratford, 1924
A standard work on the subject, particularly the effect of the World War on communications.

Scott, James Brown
The Hague Peace Conference of 1899 and 1907. v.2, p.403-5. Baltimore: Johns Hopkins Press, 1909
Agreements regarding cables in war and peace. Documents.

Shoup, G. Stanley
The control of international cable and radio communications. Congressional Digest. 9:107-9. Apr. 1930
The dominant role Great Britain plays in the control of international cable and radio communications.

The **Strategic** value of cables. Scientific American. suppl. 45:18740. June 11, 1898
A discussion of the importance to combatants of maintaining cable communication in wartime.

Submarine cables that engirdle the globe. Pan American Magazine. 39:66-8. May 1926

A Transatlantic telephone cable. Science.
70: suppl. 10. Sept. 27, 1929
  Technical improvements in a proposed
  cable between London and New York.

Tribolet, Leslie Bennett
The international aspects of the electrical
communications in the Pacific area.
282p. Baltimore: Johns Hopkins Press,
1929
  An account of electrical communications
  in the Pacific area as found not only in international formal agreements, but also in
  the arrangements of private corporations
  and syndicates.

United States. Congress
S. 535, act relating to landing and opera-
tion of submarine cables in United
States. Approved May 27, 1921. 1p.
(Public 8, 67th Congress, 1st session)
Washington: Government Printing Of-
fice, 1921
  Statutes at Large, v.42, pt.1, p.8-9.
S. 3285, an act for the regulation of inter-
state and foreign communication by
wire or radio. (Approved June 19,
1934) 46p. (Public Laws 416, 73rd
Congress) Washington: Government
Printing Office, 1934
  S. 3285 creates the Federal Communica-
  tions Commission and abolishes the Federal Radio Commission, transferring its
  functions to the newly created commission.
  Statutes at Large, v.48, pt. I, p. 1064-
  1105.

United States. Congress. House. Commit-
tee on Interstate and Foreign Commerce
Cable-landing licenses; hearings before the
Committee on interstate and foreign
commerce, House of representatives,
Sixty-seventh Congress, first session, on
S. 535, a bill to prevent the unauthor-
ized landing of submarine cables in the
United States. May 10, 11, 12, and 13,
1921. 187p. Washington: Government
Printing Office, 1921
Unauthorized landing of submarine cables
in United States; report to accompany
S. 535 (relating to landing and opera-
tion of submarine cables in United
States); submitted by Mr. Webster.
May 16, 1921. 4p. (House Report 71,
67th Congress, first session) Washing-
ton: Government Printing Office, 1921

United States. Congress. Senate. Committee on Foreign Relations
International wireless telegraphy. Hearing before the Committee on foreign
relations, United States Senate ... February 21, 1912 ... 43p. Washington:
Government Printing Office, 1912
  Statements by representatives at an international wireless telegraph convention,
  with service regulations annexed, a supplementary agreement, and a final protocol, all signed at Berlin on November 3,
  1906, by delegates of the United States
  and several other powers.

United States. Congress. Senate. Committee on Interstate Commerce
Cable-landing licenses. Hearings before
a subcommittee of the Committee on
interstate commerce, United States Senate, Sixty-sixth Congress, third session,

on S. 4301, a bill to prevent the unauthorized landing of submarine cables in
the United States. 513p. Washington:
Government Printing Office, 1921
  Submitted by Senator Clarence Dill.
...Communications act of 1934... Report.
(to accompany S. 3285)... 11p. (73rd
Congress, 2d session, Senate. Report
781) Washington: Government Printing Office, 1934
  Submitted by Senator Clarence Dill.

Walsh, George E.
Cable cutting in war. North American.
167:498-502. Oct. 1898
  The strategic importance of cable cutting
  in war time, with specific reference to the
  isolation of Cuba from Spain during the
  Spanish-American War.
Girdling the globe with submarine cables.
New England Magazine. n.s. 16:584-97.
July 1897

West, A. G.
Increased cable and radio rates to be resisted in Congress. Editor and Publisher. 66:24. Dec. 30, 1933
Rate rise protests continue in New York.
Editor and Publisher. 66:xv. Jan. 27,
1934
  Bankers' and brokers' committees protest increase in cable and radio rates.
Storm of protest follows rise in "urgent"
rate on cables. Editor and Publisher.
66:38. Jan. 13, 1934

Western Union. Fortune. 12:90-6, 140, 142,
144, 149-50. Nov. 1935
  A good survey of the Western Union
  Telegraph Company and its extensive facilities.

Wilson, George Grafton
Submarine telegraphic cables in their in-
ternational relations, lectures delivered
Aug. 1901. Naval War College. 40p.
Washington: Government Printing Of-
fice, 1901
  Lectures delivered at the Naval War
  College, August 1901.

Wood, K. L.
British Empire telegraph communication.
Nature. 143:823-4. May 13, 1939

D. RADIO

  See also
  Washington Radio News, p.30; Propaganda—
  Radio, p.51.

1. GENERAL REFERENCES

Abbott, Mabel
U.S. reporters chat with London via
radio. Editor and Publisher. 58:9-10.
Mar. 13, 1926

Agencies seek to control radioed news.
Editor and Publisher. 57:26. Apr. 4,
1925
  Twenty-five European services combine
  in movement to ask that Bern resolutions be made agenda to Washington conference.

Anderson, Paul Y.
The Radio Corporation in the news. Nation. 130:9-10. Jan. 1, 1930
Remarks on a proposal to merge transoceanic cable and radio systems and the domestic telegraph lines in one gigantic communications monopoly.

Another Government lark? Control of radio, telephone, telegraph and our international communications. National Republic. 21:10. Dec. 1933

Archambault, G. H.
Phone supplanting wire in Europe. Editor and Publisher. 67:viii. Apr. 13, 1935

Archer, Gleason L.
Big business and radio. 503p. New York: American Historical Co., 1939
Formation and development of RCA, and the battle among big industries for control of the radio business.

Arrange radio pact; division of broadcasting channels between North American countries concluded at Havana. Business Week. p.33. Dec. 25, 1937

Bell, Samuel W.
Japanese again seek radio entry into Chinese communications. Editor and Publisher. 57:26. July 26, 1924

Bent, Silas
International broadcasting. Public Opinion Quarterly. 1:117-21. July 1937
The role of short-wave radio as a propaganda medium and as a means of spreading publicity and stimulating good will among nations.

Blankenhorn, Heber
Battle of radio armaments. Harper's. 164:83-91. Dec. 1931
Radio difficulties of foreign countries, and why many European governments have prohibited private ownership and control of radio.

Broadcasting abroad. 104p. Chicago: Univ. of Chicago Press, 1934

Cable and radio people protest control. Newsweek. 3:26. Mar. 24, 1934

Cable and wireless communication with Latin America. map Review of Reviews. 58:96. July 1918

Cable and wireless to purchase beam radio. Newspaper World. 41:4. Apr. 9, 1938

Chronology of the development of communication by wire and wireless. Congressional Digest. 9:98-100. Apr., 1930

Churchill, Winston Leonard Spencer
You get it in black and white. Collier's. 96:32, 36. Dec. 28, 1935

Communications in Manchuria. Far Eastern Review. 34:199. May 1938
Improvements and additions in telephone, radio and wireless communications.

Courtney, Rear Admiral C. E.
The development of navy radio. Army and Navy Journal. 75:61, 106. Sept. 3, 1938

Crowell, Chester T.
Dogfight on the air waves. Saturday Evening Post. 210:23, 38, 40-2. May 21, 1938
International propaganda directed at Latin America.

Dill, Clarence
Radio and the press: a contrary view. Annals of the American Academy. 177: 170-5. Jan. 1935
Freedom of speech as it is affected by the radio and the newspaper.

Dunlap, Orrin E., jr.
Marconi: the man and his wireless. 360p. New York: Macmillan, 1937
A lively, readable account of the life of Marconi, dealing with his inventions from a non-technical viewpoint.

Ensor, R. C. K.
Coronation milestones: news and communications. Spectator. 158:801-2. Apr. 30, 1937

FCC allots frequencies for spot news reports. Editor and Publisher. 71:4. Dec. 17, 1938
Frequencies set aside by the Federal Communications Commission for radioequipped reporters of "spot" news.

Federal Communications Commission. Fortune. 17:60-2, 124, 126, 128, 130, 135. May 1938
A study of the F.C.C. and the peculiar problems with which it is confronted in dealing with radio.

First land wireless newspaper. Scientific American. 88:298. Apr. 18, 1903
The first daily newspaper dispatches received by wireless at station established March 25, 1903 at Avalon, Santa Catalina Island.

Fleet, John
B.B.C. inquest: the news. Spectator. 155: 49-50. July 12, 1935

25 Jahre Telefunken. Zeitungswissenschaft. 2:110. July 15, 1928
Twenty-five years of radio.

Gelderland, Karl van, pseud.
War in the ether. Nation. 146:300-1. Mar. 12, 1938
The short-wave propaganda methods whereby the totalitarian states seek to influence the world politically.

Gower, Francis
Broadcasting in Germany. Spectator. 162: 294-5. Feb. 24, 1939

Hanighen, Frank C.
Propaganda on the air; the international problem of radio censorship. tables Current History. 44:45-51. June 1936
How European nations influence world opinion through government control of radio facilities.

Harbord, James G.
My visit to South America. Outlook. 141:351-2. Nov. 4, 1925
Radio links the two Americas, thereby helping to break the foreign monopoly of communication between the two continents.

Shall America lead in radio? Saturday Evening Post. 201:6-7, 171, 173-4. June 1, 1929

Harbord, James G.—*Continued*
World wireless. 57p. Princeton: Princeton Univ. Press, 1936

Harris, E. H.
Radio and the press. Annals of the American Academy. 177:163-9. Jan. 1935
Development of radio broadcasting compelled newspapers to safeguard their property rights in news.

Hits newspaper control of radio. Editor and Publisher. 69:9. Oct. 3, 1936
Boake Carter urges press-radio peace.

Hooper, Stanford C.
Keeping the stars and stripes in the ether. Radio Broadcast. 1:125-32. June 1922
The author, a Navy official, describes the formation of the R.C.A. and the subsequent purchase by that corporation of the important Alexanderson alternator or transmitter and other patents, which allowed the United States to keep these important devices out of British control.
Naval radiotelegraph in peace and war; with review of international law with respect to radio. Annals of the American Academy. 142:suppl. 90-4. Mar. 1929
A navy expert discusses the application of radio to the Navy, and reviews international law with respect to radio.

Howell, C. E.
The wireless daily achieved. Independent. 55:2436-40. Oct. 15, 1903

Hurd, V. D.
How an international daily gets the world news by radio; Christian Science Monitor. Radio News. 11:248-51. Sept. 1929

International Radiotelegraph Conference, London, 1912 (*1st Revisional Conference*)
Documents de la Conférence radiotélégraphique internationale de Londres. 650p. illus. map. Berne: Bureau international de l'Union télégraphique, 1913

International Radiotelegraph Conference, Washington, D.C., 1927 (*2nd Revisional Conference*)
International radiotelegraph convention, and general and supplementary regulations relating thereto. Message from the President of the United States transmitting International radiotelegraph convention and the general regulations, adopted by and signed at the International radiotelegraph conference, which closed its labors at Washington on Nov. 25, 1927. 293p. (70th Congress, 1st session, Senate. Executive Board) Washington: Government Printing Office, 1927

International Radiotelegraph Conference, Madrid, 1932
Telecommunication convention; general radio regulations and final radio protocol between the United States and other powers, signed at Madrid, Dec. 9, 1932, proclaimed June 27, 1934; and additional radio regulations. 324p. (United States. Department of State. Treaty Series, no.867) Washington: Government Printing Office, 1934

International technical consulting committee on radio communication. Science. n.s. 70:372. Oct. 18, 1929

International Telecommunication Bureau, Bern
Nomenclature des voies de radiocommunication entre points fixes. 48p. Berne: Bureau de l'Union Internationale des Télécommunications. Oct. 1934
A directory of international radio circuits released periodically by the International Telecommunication Union.

International Union of Radio Telegraphy, American section formed. Science. n.s. 53:253-4. Mar. 18, 1921
Brief outline of the duties of the American section of the International Union of Scientific Radio Telegraphy.

Japan's overseas electric communications. Far Eastern Review. 33:336-8. Sept. 1937

Kabel und Radio. Zeitungswissenschaft. 1: 195. Dec. 15, 1926
The use of cables and radio in international news communications.

Kaltenborn, Hans V.
Radio's place in distributing news. *In* Education on the air. Fifth yearbook of the Institute for Education by Radio. Columbus: Ohio State Univ., 1934
Discussion: p.205-16.

Kelsey, W. A.
What wireless is doing for Hawaii. Editor and Publisher. 47:1076. May 22, 1915

Labrousse, André
La radio française: points forts et points faibles. L'Europe Nouvelle. 22:791-3. July 22, 1939
Strong and weak points of French radio broadcasting.

McClatchy, Leo A.
President enters fight for amity on Pacific. Editor and Publisher. 54:5-6. Apr. 1, 1922
Congressional deadlock stirs world-wide protest against threatened monopoly of Radio Corporation.

McClatchy, V. S.
Communication between U.S. and Orient. Editor and Publisher. 54:8. Dec. 24, 1921
Only one cable and one private radio firm serve Pacific nations.
Trans-Pacific news communication essential. Editor and Publisher. 53:5-6. Mar. 12, 1921
Navy radio is necessary factor in upholding American interests in Far East.

Manning, George H.
Press wireless given permit for network. Editor and Publisher. 63:11. Jan. 24, 1931

Meyer, Luther
News broadcasts for schools. *In* Education on the air. Fifth yearbook of the Institute for Education by Radio. Columbus: Ohio State Univ., 1934
Discussion: p.86-96.

Morecroft, John Harold
How the propagandists work in radio. Radio Broadcast. 7:332-4. July 1925

Morris, John R.
Navy radio must be speeded to win Far-East business. Editor and Publisher. 55:6. July 1, 1922

Newspapers' use of the radio phone. Wireless Age. 8:10-11. Nov. 1920

No parliamentary interference with B.B.C. news. World's Press News. 18:5. Jan. 20, 1938

Pacific communications come to the fore. Editor and Publisher. 54:7. Dec. 17, 1921
Adjourned meeting of Pan-Pacific Press Conference re-assembles in Washington to advocate continuance of naval radio service and improved facilities.

Paley, W. S.
International broadcasting: now and in the future. Annals of the American Academy. 150:40-6. July 1930

Propinquity not friendship. World Tomorrow. 14:38. Feb. 1931

R.C.A.—blue chip. Fortune. 6:45-9, 102, 104-7. Sept. 1932

Radio Corporation of America. Fortune. 1:82-4, 128, 130, 140, 142. Feb. 1930
How the Radio Corporation of America was born, and the part played by President Wilson in establishing the United States radio industry.

Radio pick-up foils Nicaragua censors. Editor and Publisher. 59:18. Feb. 5, 1927

Radio: the fifth estate. Annals of the American Academy. v.177. Jan. 1935
The entire volume is given over to the subject of radio.

Reed, Clifton
Radio censors labor. Nation. 141:357. Sept. 25, 1935

Rodgers, Admiral W. L.
The effect of cable and radio control on news and commerce. Annals of the American Academy. 112:240-51. Mar. 1924
It is essential in the interest of national policy that the United States hold and develop leadership in radio and international news.

Saerchinger, César
Radio as a political instrument. Foreign Affairs. 16:244-59. Jan. 1938
The domestic and foreign political aspects of radio broadcasting. Radio control in Europe is contrasted with that of America.

Radio, censorship and neutrality. Foreign Affairs. 18:337-49. Jan. 1940
An illuminating discussion of the issues in the controversy between "free time" and "paid time" which confronts the broadcasting system.

Radio in Europe. Atlantic Monthly. 161: 509-18. Apr. 1938
A discussion of the place of radio in England, Germany, France, Russia and other European countries, in social, commercial and political life.

Shoup, G. Stanley
The control of international cable and radio communications. Congressional Digest. 9:107-9. Apr. 1930
The dominant role Great Britain plays in the control of international cable and radio communications.

Stewart, Irvin
International regulation of radio in time of peace. Annals of the American Academy. 142:suppl. 78-82. Mar. 1929

Street, James
World war has come—with radio. Radio Guide. 7:2-3, 17. Jan. 22, 1938

Telephoning our press photographs. Scientific American. 131:87, 139. Aug. 1924

20 transocean radio wave bands are allotted to newspapers. Editor and Publisher. 62:8. June 22, 1929
The need for a public utilities corporation.

United States. Congress. Senate. Committee on Interstate Commerce
Commission on communications. Extract from Hearings before the Committee on interstate commerce, United States Senate, Seventy-first Congress, second session, on S. 6, a bill to provide for the regulation of the transmission of intelligence by wire or wireless. Statements by officials of the Radio Corporation of America... Dec. 9, 10, 12, 13, 14, 16 and 17, 1929. 307p. Washington: Government Printing Office, 1930
Commission on communications. Hearings, 71st Congress, 1st session (and 2nd session), on S.6, for regulation of transmission of intelligence by wire or wireless, May 8 1929 (-Feb. 26, 1930). 2v. il. 2 pl. 2 maps. Washington: Government Printing Office, 1930
Details regarding formation of the Radio Corporation, v.2, p.1081-1456.

United States. Federal Trade Commission
Report of the Federal trade commission on the radio industry in response to House resolution 548, 67th Congress, fourth Session, Dec. 1, 1923. 347p. Washington: Government Printing Office, 1924
Deals especially with the development of the Radio Corporation of America.

United States Delegation to Madrid radio meet includes no press representatives. Editor and Publisher. 65:5-6. Aug. 13, 1932

Valot, Stephen
La presse radiophonique: a-t'elle besoin d'un statut? Cahiers de la Presse. (2): 129-36. Apr.-June 1939
The drafting of an equitable law to govern the radio broadcasting of news is not an insurmountable problem.

Wagenführ, Kurt
In the troubled Mediterranean; war in the air waves. Living Age. 353:299-301. Dec. 1937

Warren, C. H.
Freedom at the B.B.C. Bookman (London) 86:38. Apr. 1934

West, A. G.
Increased cable and radio rates to be resisted in Congress. Editor and Publisher. 66:24. Dec. 30, 1933
Rate rise protests continue in New York. Editor and Publisher. 66:xv. Jan. 27, 1934
Bankers' and brokers' committees protest increase in cable and radio rates.

Winterbottom, W. A.
Inter-American radio communication. il. Pan American Magazine. 43:404-6. Dec. 1930
Opening of radio circuits between the United States and other countries of the New World has brought about lower telegraph tariffs.

World affairs and the telephone. il. map diag. Scientific American. 145:182-3. Sept. 1931
The transatlantic telephone service, inaugurated in 1927, is handled by means of four radio channels.

Young, James C.
Is the radio newspaper next? Radio Broadcast. 7:575-80. Sept. 1925
Newspaper organizations have been quick to seize the opportunity of radio. The possibilities of the tabloid radio newspaper.

Young, Owen D.
Freedom of the air. Ed. by M. M. McBride. Saturday Evening Post. 202: 16, 193-4. Nov. 16, 1929

2. PRESS-RADIO CONFLICT

A.P. and radio. Newsweek. 11:28. May 9, 1938

A.P. curbs radio use of news. Printers' Ink. 163:65, 68. Apr. 27, 1933

Ask more news via radio in Britain. Editor and Publisher. 58:47. Dec. 19, 1925

Barton, Winfield
What broadcasting does for a newspaper. Radio Broadcast. 4:344-6. Feb. 1924

Bent, Silas
Radio takes over the news. American Mercury. 36:228-30. Oct. 1935

Bickel, Karl August
New empires; the newspaper and the radio. 112p. Philadelphia: J. B. Lippincott, 1930
Competition and cooperation between the newspaper and the radio.

Bjørnson, Hjalmar
Higher news standard is advocated and radio hit at N.E.A. meet. Inland Printer. 87:45-8. July 1931

Boucheron, Pierre
News and music from the air. Scientific American. 125:104-5. Dec. 1921

Brindze, Ruth
Next the radio newspaper. Nation. 146: 154-5. Feb. 5, 1938

Broun, Heywood
Tip to Uncle Sam; newspapers and radio suffering from insufficient rivalry. New Republic. 94:98. Mar. 2, 1938

Carskadon, T. R.
The press radio war. New Republic. 86: 132-5. Mar. 11, 1936

Compact between the broadcasters and the daily press. New Republic. 77:209. Jan. 3, 1934

Dailies drop radio. Business Week. p.28. June 18, 1938

Digges, I. W.
Battle of Bellingham. Printers' Ink. 170: 63-6. Jan 3, 1935
The Associated Press versus radio broadcasting station KVOS.

Dreher, Carl
Glaring faults in newspaper radio journalism. Radio Broadcast. 9:243-5. July 1926

Fortune survey: newspapers versus news broadcasts. Fortune. 17:104, 106, 109. Apr. 1938
Radio listeners are not so positive regarding foreign policy or reforms, are less belligerent, have fewer definite opinions on any subject than those who get their news from the newspapers alone. See also the January survey.

Home newspapers by radio. Scientific American. 158:334-5. June 1938

Hopper, Silas
Newspapers have new policy on radio programs. Printers' Ink. 137:33-4, 36. Dec. 23, 1926

Huston, McCready
How sick is the newspaper? Commonweal. 20:499-500. Sept. 28, 1934

Hutchinson, Paul
Freedom of the air. Christian Century. 48:340-3, 376-9, 407-9. Mar. 11-25, 1931
The menace of monopoly among the chief agencies of communications.

Kartman, Ben
Dailies fighting for freedom of the air to improve exchange of news. Editor and Publisher. 62:5, 46. Apr. 12, 1930

Keating, Isabelle
Pirates of the air. Harper's. 169:463-72. Sept. 1934
The battle between press and radio over the right to broadcast news; the rise of radio news agencies.
Radio invades journalism. Nation. 140: 677-8. June 12, 1935

Marconi views radio as an aid to press. Editor and Publisher. 60:86. Oct. 29, 1927

News and comment from the national capital. Literary Digest. 116:12. Nov. 11, 1933
  Application of the Columbia Broadcasting System for access to the Congressional press galleries revived press-air feud.

News on the air; is a press-wireless struggle coming? Review of Reviews (London) 86:14-15. Sept. 1935

Newspapers now big watt and airwave buyers. Newsweek. 3:28. June 16, 1934

The Press and the microphone. Christian Century. 50:1462. Nov. 22, 1933

Press associations decry radio as a competitor and demand commission regulation. Public Utilities. 8:47-8. July 9, 1931

Press gallery: Radio news men seek entrée to Congress. Newsweek. 2:26. Nov. 11, 1933

Press vs. radio. Business Week. no. 284: 10. Feb. 9, 1935
  Clark-Hooper announces first survey results, and radiomen object to broadcasting cost figures.

The Radio and the press. New Republic. 62:314. May 7, 1930

Radio keen competitor of French press. Newspaper World. 41:6. Apr. 9, 1938

Radio news competition with daily press projected. Public Utilities. 14:420-1. Sept. 27, 1934

Radio news services get Havas report. Editor and Publisher. 66:40. May 5, 1934

Raymond, Allen
  The coming fight over news. New Outlook. 161:13-18. June 1933
  Radio versus press. Excerpts. Review of Reviews (London) 85:35-6. Apr. 1934

Rose, Marc A.
  Radio or newspaper—can both survive? Nation. 119:699-700. Dec. 24, 1924

Stockbridge, F. Parker
  Radio vs. the press. Outlook and Independent. 156:692-4. Dec. 31, 1930

T.P.; transradio to be used exclusively by Rochester paper. Time. 32:20. Aug. 1, 1938

Whipple, Leon
  No news on the air. Survey. 59:53-4. Oct. 1, 1927

Whittemore, C. W.
  Radio's fight for news. New Republic. 81:354-5. Feb. 6, 1935

Willert, Arthur
  Opportunities for press-radio co-operation in international fields. World's Press News. 17:3. May 27, 1937
  The demand for foreign news will, in the future, increase. Functions of radio and the press, and their relationship.

Wireless inventions and the press. Scientific American. 113:462. Nov. 27, 1915

E. MISCELLANEOUS

Cheng Ming-Ju
  The influence of communications, internal and external, upon the economic future of China. 178p. London: G. Routledge, 1930

Chu Chia-Hua
  China's postal and other communication services. 259p. London: Kegan Paul, 1937

Communications in Korea. Far Eastern Review. 35:113-16, 119. Mar. 1939
  See descriptive summary, p.115.

Indian posts and telegraphs in 1932-33. Near East. 43:367. May 10, 1934

Indian posts and telegraphs in 1933-34. Near East. 44:444. Apr. 11, 1935

Japan speeds up sea-land communications with Manchukuo—for peace or war? map China Weekly Review. 76:149-50. Apr. 4, 1936

Land communications in Italian East Africa. il. map Great Britain and the East. 49: suppl. 15-17. July 15, 1937

Löwenthal, Rudolf
  Public communications in China before July, 1937. Chinese Social and Political Science Review. 22:42-58. Apr.-June 1938

Luke, P. V.
  How the electric telegraph saved India. Macmillan's Magazine. 76:401-6. Oct. 1897
  How the telegraph aided Britain in administering its affairs in India and how disorders were thereby suppressed.

Sams, H. A.
  India's improving communications. Great Britain and the East. 48:614-15. Apr. 29, 1937

Sullivan, Mark
  Our times: the turn of the century. v.1, p.318-21. New York, London: Scribner's, 1931
  Picture of the United States in 1900 and after. For growth of telephone communication in the United States see p.384-5.

Who hampers spread of British news abroad? World's Press News. 21:5. Feb. 23, 1939
  British U. P. finds it hard to expand in Far East because of high cable tolls and lack of radio facilities.

II. NEWS-GATHERING ORGANIZATIONS

A. HISTORY AND ANALYSIS

Bömer, Karl
Das internationale Zeitungswesen. 134p. Berlin, Leipzig: Walter de Gruyter, 1934
—— See Douglass, Paul F., jt. auth.

Capehart, Charles
A general history of American journalism. Editor and Publisher. 12:11-26. Apr. 26, 1913
This special issue contains an introduction giving a concise history of news chroniclers from Egyptian and Babylonian times to early European journalism. Illustrated.

Council on Foreign Relations, Inc.
Political handbook of the world. New York: Harper and Bros., for Council on Foreign Relations, Inc., 1928-39
Annual.
Information on parties, parliaments and the press. In the press section the emphasis is on those papers most likely to be quoted abroad.

Douglass, Paul F. and Bömer, Karl
The international combination of news agencies. Annals of the American Academy. 162 suppl.:265-8. July 1932
How the world news agencies were organized in 1932, explained graphically by means of charts.

Editor and Publisher
Editor and Publisher International yearbook. New York: Editor and Publisher, 1921-39
Annual.
Directory by states and cities of all daily newspapers in the United States, supplemented by lists of leading foreign newspapers, press associations and other facts concerning the newspaper press.

Fischer, Helmut
Geschichtliche Entwicklung des Nachrichtenwesens und der Nachrichtentechnik. Zeitungswissenschaft. 9:308-13. July 1, 1934
A chronological narrative of the development of the earliest newspapers and news bureaus and the mechanics of their services.

Groth, Otto
Die Zeitung; ein System der Zeitungskunde (Journalistik). 4v. Mannheim: J. Bensheimer, 1928-30
Includes a general history of journalism and press associations.
Bibliography.

Internationaler katholischer Nachrichtendienst. Zeitungswissenschaft. 3:110. July 15, 1928
Catholic news services.

Jarkowski, Stanislaw
Eine Statistik der Presse des Erdballs. Zeitungswissenschaft. 6:292-5. Sept. 16, 1931
A survey of statistics gathered by a Polish student on the extensiveness of newspapers in the world and the newspaper units published in various languages.

Leading news agencies of the world. Editor and Publisher. 53:160. Jan. 22, 1921

Pitkin, Walter B.
World news services and their bearing on international relations. p233-8. In Institute of International Relations, Proceedings, 1931. Los Angeles: Univ. of Southern California, 1932
Vast increase in news of foreign affairs is due to the expansion of cable and radio facilities. Millions of words "killed" because of lack of newspaper space.

Schwedler, Wilhelm
Das Nachrichtensystem der Weltpresse. Zeitungswissenschaft. 9:281-90. July 1, 1934
History of the great European news cartel or "ring combination" that stretched its tentacles over the entire world before the World War; its members today and agencies that have arisen subsequently.

Stuart, G. B.
Congress of the press at Lisbon. Athenæum. 2:531. Oct. 15, 1898

When telegraph companies collected and distributed news. Newspaper World. 41:7. Feb. 25, 1939
Press Association secretary discusses origin of P.A. and history of news-gathering.

B. UNITED STATES PRESS ASSOCIATIONS

1. HISTORY AND ANALYSIS

Bickel, Karl August
New empires: the newspaper and the radio. 112p. Philadelphia: J. B. Lippincott, 1930
Relationship and growing competition between two empire builders, the newspaper and the radio, which should be complements, not rivals. The author was general manager of the Limited Press.

Bleyer, Willard Grosvenor
Main currents in the history of American journalism. 464p. Boston, New York: Houghton Mifflin, 1927

Broun, Heywood
Loose construction. Nation. 142:157-8. Feb. 5, 1936

Capehart, Charles
A general history of American journalism. Editor and Publisher. 12:11-26. Apr. 26, 1913

Cornering Washington news. New Republic. 74:34. Feb. 22, 1933

Desmond, Robert William
News around the clock; 90th anniversary. Christian Science Monitor. Weekly Magazine Section. p.8-9. Sept. 14, 1938

Furay, James H.
America—news gatherer for the world. Quill. 19:10-11, 15. June 1931

Hudson, Frederic
Journalism in the United States. 789p.
New York: Harper, 1873

Lee, Alfred M.
The daily newspaper in America. 797p.
New York: Macmillan, 1937

Lee, James Melvin
History of American journalism. 462p.
Boston, New York: Houghton Mifflin,
1923

McCrae, Milton A.
Forty years in newspaperdom; the auto-
biography of a newspaperman. 496p.
New York: Brentano's, 1924

Pacific news volume is increasing. Editor
and Publisher. 55:24. Oct. 14, 1922

Pew, Marlen E., jr.
China war costs services more than any
event since 1917. Editor and Publisher.
70:5-6. Sept. 4, 1937

European crisis piled up costs on U.S.
services. Editor and Publisher. 71:7.
Oct. 8, 1938
Cable traffic increased 30 per cent. News
associations reported the biggest file from
abroad since World War.

Rings, Joachim
Amerikanische Nachrichtenagenturen. 101p.
(Zeitung und Zeit. Schriftenreihe des
Instituts für Zeitungswissenchaft an
der Universität Berlin, Neue Folge,
Reihe A, B, und II) Frankfurt a. M.:
M. Diesterweg, 1937
A résumé of the history of the three
great American news agencies.

Rosewater, Victor
History of coöperative news-gathering in
the United States. 430p. New York,
London: D. Appleton, 1930
Evolution of news-gathering agencies
from the coffeehouse news rooms to the
modern complex organizations of the Associated Press, United Press and others.
Newsboats.

Seitz, Don Carlos
The James Gordon Bennetts, father and
son. 405p. Indianapolis: Bobbs-
Merrill, 1928
Proprietors of the *New York Herald*.

Shun, J. C.
World-wide activities of America's leading
news agencies. China Weekly Review.
65:70-2. June 10, 1933

Sinclair, Upton
The brass check. 446p. Long Beach,
California: The Author, 1919. 1928
A study of American journalism.

Stone, Melville E.
Fifty years a journalist. 371p. Garden
City, N.Y., Toronto: Doubleday, Page,
1921

News gathering. Editor and Publisher.
48:1418-21. Apr. 22, 1916

Times, Associated Press, and New York
Times. Nation. 111:148. Aug. 7, 1920

Topliff, Samuel
Topliff's Travels: letters from abroad in
the years 1828 and 1829. 245p. Ed. by
E. S. Bolton. Boston: Boston
Athenæum, 1906
Letters and memoirs of Samuel Topliff,
an employee of the first commercial news-
room in this country. The commercial
newsroom was installed in the Exchange
Coffee House in Boston.

Villard, Oswald Garrison
The press today. I.-II. The Associated
Press. III. The United Press. IV.
The chain daily. V. Standardizing the
daily. VI. The Philadelphia cabbage
patch. VII. What's wrong with the
'World'? VIII. Montana and 'the
company.' IX. The opportunity in the
small city. X. Hugenberg and the
German dailies. Nation. 130:443-5; 486-
9; 539-42; 595-7; 646-7; 671-3; 724-7;
131:39-41; 120-2; 197-8. Apr. 16, 23;
May 7, 21; June 4, 11, 25; July 9, 30;
Aug. 20, 1930

World news gathered wholesale. Literary
Digest. 52:921. Apr. 1, 1916

2. ASSOCIATED PRESS

A.P. codifies its general news orders. Editor
and Publisher. 60:5. Mar. 3, 1928

A.P. elects McLean president; rejects news
sale to radio. Editor and Publisher.
71:9-10, 90. Apr. 30, 1938

A.P. rounding off new chapter in its epic
with retirement of President Noyes.
Newsweek. 11:23-4. Jan. 24, 1938

Associated Press
Law of the Associated Press. 2v. New
York: Associated Press, 1914-17
Vol. I. Decisions, statutes, arguments.
Vol. II. Property in news. Associated
Press vs. International News Service, in
the U.S. District court, Southern district
of New York, and the U.S. Circuit Court
of Appeals for the Second Circuit.

Special report of Committee of Conferences of Western A.P. 1891. (Annual
Reports of the Board of Directors, Associated Press) Chicago, 1891

The **Associated Press.** Outlook. 107:631-2.
July 18, 1914

The **Associated Press** and its news sources.
Nation. 110:504-5. Apr. 17, 1920

The **Associated Press** as a trust. Literary
Digest. 48:364. Feb. 21, 1914
The New York *Sun* petitions the Federal
Government to prosecute the Associated
Press for monopoly under the Sherman
Anti-trust Law.

The **Attacks** on the Associated Press. Editor and Publisher. 12:10. May 3, 1913
An answer to attacks in Congress charg-
ing that the A.P. colors the news, is a
monopoly and menaces the freedom of the
press. See also "How the A.P. Works."
Editor and Publisher. 12:15. May 3, 1913.

Cooper, Kent
Address given at hotel Commodore, describing the complexity of getting the news for the A.P. 8p. New York: Associated Press, Apr. 21, 1930

Cooper tells progress of A.P. in past year. Editor and Publisher. 67:8, 36. Apr. 20, 1935

Costs reduced, but service was expanded, Cooper reports. Editor and Publisher. 65:40, 42. Apr. 29, 1933
Annual report of the general manager of the Associated Press.

Defends Associated Press. Editor and Publisher. 14:78. July 11, 1914
General manager explains organization of the news service and justifies its method of handling the world's news.

Editor and Publisher
Editor and Publisher annual Associated Press number. v.50. 54p. Apr. 20, 1918
Information on the activities, personnel, organizations and problems of the Associated Press during the World War.

Grenzow, D. B.
Old man of the A.P. World Review. 8: 262. June 3, 1929

Harrison, Richard Edes
Associated Press. Fortune. 15:1, 89-93, 148ff. Feb. 1937

In justice to the 'A.P.' Collier's. 53:16. June 6, 1914

Irwin, Will
What's wrong with the Associated Press? Harper's Weekly. 58:10-12. Mar. 28, 1914

Is there a news monopoly? Collier's. 53:16. June 6, 1914
Editorial.
Suggests that the Associated Press is monopolistic; also, that newspapers should be regarded as public utilities and therefore should be supervised by public authority.

Kennan, George
The Associated Press. II. A defense. Outlook. 107:240, 249-50. May 30, 1914
See also Gregory Mason, "The Associated Press."

Mason, Gregory
The Associated Press. I. A. criticism. Outlook. 107:237-40. May 30, 1914
See also George Kennan, "The Associated Press."

Noyes, Frank B.
The Associated Press. 8p. Boston: Associated Press, Dec. 19, 1929

The Associated Press, Article relating to methods, operation, organization, and collection and distribution of news matter by Associated Press. 9p. (S. Doc. 27, 63rd Congress, first session) Washington: Government Printing Office, 1913

Owens, Dewey M.
The Associated Press. American Mercury. 10:385-93. Apr. 1927

The **Problem** of the Associated Press. Atlantic. 114:132-7. July 1914
See also "In justice to the 'A.P.' "

Robb, Arthur, T.
F. B. Noyes, retiring, proud of 38 reelections as A.P. chief. Editor and Publisher. 71:7-8. Apr. 23, 1938

Shanks, W. F. G.
How we get our news. Harper's. 34: 511-22. Mar. 1867
The development of communication by the New York Associated Press. How newsboats, the railroad and the telegraph facilitated news-gathering.

Smith, Charles Stephenson
How the United States gets its news of Europe. Address of Charles Stephenson Smith, chief of foreign service of the Associated Press, delivered at the Institute of European Affairs, William and Mary College, Williamsburg, Va. Oct. 14, 1931. New York: Associated Press, 1931
Mimeographed.

News exchange brings American nations closer together; South and Central America depend on services of United States news agencies. Pan American Magazine. 43:309-15. Nov. 1930
As chief of the foreign service of the Associated Press the writer had travelled throughout Latin America and had found more international news published in Latin America than in the United States.

Stone, Melville E.
The Associated Press. Collier's. 53:28-9. July 11, 1914
The general manager of the Associated Press answers the charge that the organization is a monopoly.

The Associated Press: I. Its general foreign service. Century. 69:888-95. Apr. 1905
Experiences of the general manager of the Associated Press in establishing European contacts in the interests of his organization. News-gathering system in peace and war.

The Associated Press: II. The removal of the Russian censorship on foreign news. Century. 70:143-51. May 1905

The Associated Press: III. Newsgathering as a business. Century. 70:299-310. June 1905

The Associated Press: IV. The method of operation. Century. 70:379-86. July 1905

The Associated Press: V. Its work in war. Century. 70:504-10. Aug. 1905

A story of the Associated Press. Editor and Publisher. 12:56, 58. Apr. 26, 1913
The story of news-gathering technical advances in communications; phenomenal growth of world-wide news reporting.

United States. Congress. Senate. Committee on Finance
Statement of Melville E. Stone, manager and secretary of the Associated Press, at hearing before the Committee on Finance, (62d Congress, 1st Session, Sen. Doc. 56. v.2, p.1350-65), of Reciprocity with Canada, on H.R.4412, an act to promote reciprocal trade relations with the Dominion of Canada and for other purposes. Washington: Government Printing Office, 1911
Testimony regarding the organization and functions of the Associated Press, by the General Manager.

3. UNITED PRESS

Benét, Stephen Vincent
The United Press. Fortune. 7:67-72, 94 97-8, 100, 102, 104. May 1933
Inception and growth of the United Press, with detailed information regarding news and business ramifications.

Foreign bureaus added. Editor and Publisher. 66:90. Apr. 21, 1934
United Press opens new offices in Istanbul and Copenhagen.

Furay, James H.
Papers in 37 foreign countries now receive news from United Press. Editor and Publisher. 59:136. Apr. 30, 1927
United Press: a giant of news distribution. World's Press News. 2:10-11. Sept. 5, 1929

Hornblow, Arthur, jr.
The amazing armistice. Century Magazine. 103:90-9. Nov. 1921
The story of the premature peace report of November 7, 1918. How the United Press dispatch originated.

Howard, Roy W.
The United Press. Publishers' Guide. 21:31-3. June 1913
The United Press Association. Editor and Publisher. 12:98. Apr. 26, 1913
A short history by the chairman of the Board of Directors.

Irwin, Will
The United Press. Harper's Weekly. 58: 6-8. Apr. 25, 1914

Jones, Joseph L.
Press services tell Americas about each other; Latin America now rivals Europe as an important news source. Pan American Magazine. 43:302-8. Nov. 1930
The Foreign Editor of the United Press tells how that organization distributes in Latin America.
Map shows cable lines and location of principal bureaus and correspondents in the western hemisphere.

4. MISCELLANEOUS

Catholic Press Association; meeting (28th) 1938, New Orleans. Catholic World. 147:492-3. July 1938

International News Service. v.66. Editor and Publisher. Anniversary Supplement. Apr. 21, 1934

New press agency. Editor and Publisher. 10:4. Mar. 25, 1911
The International Press, with offices in New York, London and Paris.

Two wire services spliced in retrenchment move. Newsweek. 10:25-6. Aug. 28, 1937
Hearst's Universal Service absorbed by International News Service.

Welch, M. H.
History of New England Woman's Press Association. Harper's Bazaar. 31:887. Oct. 15, 1898

C. FOREIGN PRESS ASSOCIATIONS

See also
The Foreign Press, p.105.

1. HISTORY AND ANALYSIS

Bullard, Arthur
The breakdown of Europe's news services. Our World. 5:15-21. May 1924

The **Foreign** press. Journalism Quarterly. See department notes in each issue.

Leeper, Janet
European news services. Spectator. 163: 471. Oct. 6, 1939

2. CHINA

The **China** yearbook. Shanghai: Commercial Press; Chicago: Univ. of Chicago Press; London: Simpkin, Marshall, Ltd., 1919-39
Annual.

Green, O. M.
The organization of news from the Far East. 12p. London: Royal Institute of International Affairs, 1933

Kuo Wei-hung
China's need of a national and independent news service. China Weekly Review. 71:196-8. Jan. 5, 1935
China depends on foreign news services even for internal news. The Kuo Min News Agency is the first Chinese news agency of any consequence.

Legislative Yuan adopts revised press law. China Weekly Review. 73:263. July 20, 1935
Main features of the revised press law, consisting of 49 articles; adopted July 12, 1935.

Löwenthal, Rudolph
Western literature on Chinese journalism: a bibliography. 69p. Tientsin: Nankai Institute of Economics, 1937
One of the few bibliographies in English on the press of China, by a diligent observer of the press in Yenching University.

Mayer, Norbert
Die Presse in China. Zeitungswissenschaft.
10:589-606. Dec. 1935
    The development and contemporary
status of the press in China.

Nanking's ban on the Rengo News Service.
China Weekly Review. 56:221-2. Apr.
18, 1931
    As a result of the circulation of allegedly
inaccurate reports, the Nanking authorities
withdrew telegraphic, telephonic and mail
privileges enjoyed by the Japanese Rengo
service.

Patterson, Don D.
The journalism of China. 89p. (Univ. of
Missouri Bulletin. v.23. Journalism
Series, no. 26) Columbia, Mo.: Univ. of
Missouri, Dec. 1922
    The field of journalism and the press in
China, its history, background, characteris-
tics, foreign publications in China, legal
aspects, journalistic education in China,
technical equipment, press associations and
agencies.
    List of Chinese newspapers.

Shanghai subjected to anti-Comintern culture. China Weekly Review. 87:323-4.
Feb. 11, 1939
    Editorial.
    Concerning a recent news exchange
agreement under which Japan's Domei
agency disseminates news received from
the Stefani agency of Italy.

Vom chinesischen Nachrichtenwesen. Zeitungswissenschaft. 11:467. Oct. 1, 1936
    News-gathering facilities in China.

3. FRANCE

Agence Havas. Editor and Publisher. 67:32.
May 19, 1934

Die **Agence** Havas vom wirtschaftlichen
Standpunkt. Zeitungswissenschaft. 7:
361-2. Nov. 15, 1932
    The Havas news agency as a business
enterprise.

Annuaire de la presse française et étrangère
et du monde politique. Annuaire international de la presse, 1939. 57. ed. 1607,
60p. Paris: Maurice Roux-Bluysen, 1939
    This annual directory of the press in-
cludes brief notes on the press associations.
It continues E. Mermet's *La Publicité en
France* (1878-80).

Boyer, Jacques
Le centre française des informations jour-
nalistiques mondiales: l'Agence Havas.
La Nature. 63(2):312-15. Oct. 1, 1935

Chesnier du Chesne, A.
L'Agence Havas. Cahiers de la Presse.
1:105-8. Jan.-Mar. 1938

Dailies take Havas service. Editor and
Publisher. 67:16. Aug. 11, 1934

Fontenay, Alfred
The power of the news agency. Magazine Digest. 14:74-5. Feb. 1937
    From *Die Neue Weltbühne.* (Prague) Nov.
26, 1936.

The **Havas** agency. Mimeograph. New
York: United Press, 1933

Havas in the U.S. Time. 23:40-1. Mar.
19, 1934

Der **Jahresbericht** der Agentur Havas.
Zeitungswissenschaft. 12:654-6. Sept.
1, 1937
    A financial report of the Executive Com-
mittee of Havas for the year 1936.

Ein **Jahrhundert** Nachrichtenagentur Havas.
Zeitungswissenschaft. 11:348-52. July
1, 1936
    An item concerning the mother of news
agencies, Havas, purporting to give some
new details not found in previous articles
in *Zeitungswissenschaft.*

Laney, Albert G.
Havas world power in news and adver-
tising. Editor and Publisher. 59:
French Section F8, F10. June 19, 1926

Legigan, E.
L'agence Havas. Paris: 1929

Die **Messageries** Hachette, das französische
Grossunternehmen für Zeitungsvertrieb.
Zeitungswissenschaft. 13:20-3. Jan. 1,
1938
    The powerful newspaper and periodical
distributing agency of France.

Perry, John W.
France plans propaganda drive in U.S.
Editor and Publisher. 65:7, 34. Apr.
15, 1933

Premier forces out Havas director. Editor
and Publisher. 69:45. Nov. 7, 1936

Radio news services get Havas report. Editor and Publisher. 66:40. May 5, 1934

Schulté-Strathaus, Ludwig
Die Agence Havas. Zeitungswissenschaft.
9:301-2. July 1, 1934
    A concise account of the growth, work-
ings and strength of the Havas agency.

Über die Geschichte der "Agence Havas."
Zeitungswissenschaft. 14:346-7. May
1, 1939
    A brief survey of the work and history
of the Havas agency.

Über die wirtschaftliche Entwicklung der
Agentur Havas. Zeitungswissenschaft.
5:55. Jan. 15, 1930
    The status of Havas as a business enter-
prise during the year 1929.

Die **Wirtschaftliche** Entwicklung der Agentur Havas. Zeitungswissenschaft. 4:
187-8. May 15, 1929
    The economic development of the Havas
agency. Comparative figures on capitaliza-
tion, dividends and profits.

4. GERMANY

Bömer, Karl
Handbuch der Weltpresse. 340p. Berlin:
Carl Duncker, 1934

Bullard, Arthur
The breakdown of Europe's news service.
Our World. 5:15-21. May 1924

Die **Deutsche** Wirtschaft und ihre Führer.
v.3. I. Die Zeitungen. Emil Dovifat.
II. Das Nachrichtenwesen. Wilhelm
Schwedler. 220p. Gotha: Flamberg,
1925

Galtier-Boissière, Jean and **Zimmer, Bernard**
Germany inside out. Living Age. 340:
46-61. Mar. 1931
French and Austrian views.

German agencies merged. Editor and Publisher. 66:35. Dec. 2, 1933
Wolff and Telegraphen-Union now under Nazi control.

Groth, Otto
Die Zeitung. v.1, p.482-542. Mannheim,
Leipzig, Berlin: J. Bensheimer, 1928
The world's press associations.

Heerdegen, Ernst
Nachrichtendienst der Presse. v.1. 128p.
(Abhandlungen aus dem Institut für
Zeitungskunde an der Universität Leipzig) Leipzig: Emmanuel Reinicke, 1920
The news-gathering agencies.

Jaryc, Marc
Les gazettes des Fugger. Cahiers de la
Presse. 1:143-8. Jan.-Mar. 1938
Review of *Die Entstehung der sogenannten Fuggerzeiten in der Wiener National-Bibliothek.* 81p. Vienna: R. M. Rohrer, 1937.

Kleinpaul, Johannes
Der bayerische Hofnachrichtendienst im
16. und 17. Jahrhundert. Zeitungswissenschaft. 2:97-9; 115-17. July 15,
Aug. 15, 1927
The news service of the Bavarian court in the 16th and 17th centuries.
Der Nachrichtendienst der Herzöge von
Braunschweig im 16. und 17. Jahrhundert. Zeitungswissenschaft. 5:82-94. Mar. 15, 1930
A historical study of the news services developed in the 16th and 17th centuries by the dukes of Brunswick.

Mejer, Otto
Ein aktueller Beitrag zum Kapitel der
internationalen Nachrichtenverträge.
Zeitungswissenschaft. 9:291-7. July 1,
1934
The president of the Board of Directors of the German News Bureau tells how Wolff was forced out of the news cartel in Europe by the political isolation of Germany and then by the World War, and how she was shut off from the use of the cable. The Telegraph Union of Germany, by using wireless and working with strong independent agencies like the United Press of the United States, attracted the attention of Havas and Reuter. The eventual union of W.T.B. and T.U. forced Reuter and Havas into a new world agreement on July 1, 1934.
Die Nachrichtenverbreitung des DNB.
Zeitungswissenschaft. 13:671-2. Oct. 1,
1938
How and with what equipment DNB disseminates and receives its domestic and foreign news.

News service of long ago: Fugger newsletters. Mentor. 15:63. Dec. 1927

Salomon, Ludwig
Geschichte des deutschen Zeitungswesens
von den ersten Anfängen bis zur
Wiederaufrichtung des Deutschen
Reiches. 3v. Oldenburg, Leipzig: A.
Schwartz, 1906
A notable work on the history of the German press up to the early years of the twentieth century.

Schwedler, Wilhelm
Die Nachrichtenversorgung der Presse.
Zeitungswissenschaft. 1:165-9. Nov.
15, 1926
The story of the German news-gathering agencies.

Schöne, Walter
Die Zeitung und ihre Wissenschaft. 235p.
Leipzig: Heinrich, F. A. Timm, 1928
A discussion of the press associations.

Zimmer, Bernard. See Galtier-Boissière,
Jean, jt. auth.

20 Jahre Depeschenbureau Europapress.
Zeitungswissenschaft. 12:124-7. Feb. 1,
1937

5. GREAT BRITAIN

a. HISTORY AND ANALYSIS

Bailey, Herbert
About
Herbert Bailey dies at 44. World's Press
News. 21:2. Mar. 23, 1939
Herbert Bailey: he simplified foreign
news. World's Press News. 20:499.
Sept. 22, 1938

Collins, Henry Michael
From pigeon post to wireless. 312p. London. Hodder and Stoughton, 1925

Dibblee, G. B.
The newspaper. 256p. (Home University Library of Modern Knowledge)
New York: H. Holt, 1913

Grant, James
The newspaper press. 3v. London:
Tinsley Bros., 1872
Its origin, progress and present position.

Groth, Otto
Die Zeitung; ein System der Zeitungskunde (Journalistik). v. 1, p.482-548.
Mannheim: J. Bensheimer, 1928-30

Imperial press conference and its limitations.
Blackwood's Magazine. 186:123-30.
July 1909
The changing character of the press and its relation to the defense of the British Empire.

Jones, Sir Roderick
Transmission of news. Address at the
Second Annual Conference of the Empire Press Union in London, May 26,
1937. 13p. London: Waterlow and Sons,
1937

Martin, Frederick R.
Lloyd's News, and the rise of Lloyd's coffee-house. p.65-85. *In his* The history of Lloyd's and of marine insurance in Great Britain. London: Macmillan, 1876
    The meager news communications of the day led Edward Lloyd in 1696 to establish *Lloyd's News*. This chapter describes the paper and also the news exchange in the coffeehouse.

Mills, J. Saxon
The press and communications of the Empire. 289p. (The British Empire, v.6) New York: Henry Holt, 1924
    See especially ch.6, p.103-31, "Newspapers of the Empire." Surveys the press, its extent and influence; accomplishments of the Imperial Press Conferences and the Empire Press Union; Reuter's News Agency.

Press combinations in England. Literary Digest. 79:21-2. Nov. 24, 1923

Simonis, H.
The street of ink. 372p. New York: Funk and Wagnalls Co., 1917

Smith, Norman
Cooperative Empire news services. p.43-51. *In* The Fifth Imperial Press Conference in South Africa. London: Empire Press Union, 1935

When telegraph companies collected and distributed news. Newspaper World. 41:7. Feb. 25, 1939

Who hampers spread of British news abroad? World's Press News. 21:5. Feb. 23, 1939
    British U.P. finds it hard to expand in Far East because of high cable tolls and lack of radio facilities. House of Commons debaters ask government support for effective presentation of British news abroad; Reuter's denies monopoly in Far East news.

Williams, Valentine
Getting the news in 1860. Saturday Review of Literature. 18:11-12. Aug. 6, 1938

Wynter, Andrew
Our social bees. 532p. London: R. Hardwicke, 1869
    Town and country life recorded in newspapers.

b. PRESS ASSOCIATION

How the Press Association gets the news. World's Press News. 1:7. June 13, 1929

M.P. tells Commons of P.A.'s war preparations. World's Press News. 21:3. June 22, 1939
    Post Office cooperating with press associations to assure proper communications.

Robbins, H. C.
The Press Association and its work. Nineteenth Century. 97:99-109. Jan. 1925

When telegraph companies collected and distributed news. Newspaper World. 41:7. Feb. 25, 1939
    Press Association secretary discusses origin of P.A. and history of news-gathering.

c. REUTER'S

Bailey, Herbert
Reuters' monopoly in foreign news. Nation and Athenæum. 34:370-1. Dec. 8, 1923
    Reuter's has working arrangements with news agencies of the countries in which it operates. This great agency is charged with being an instrument for the spreading of propaganda.

Bone, F. D.
Reuter's are always right. World Press News. 1:3, 10. July 4, 1929
    Reuter's revolutionized the foreign intelligence of the London newspapers. Brief history of the great news agency, describing its world-wide ramifications.

Collins, Henry Michael
From pigeon post to wireless. 312p. London: Hodder and Stoughton, 1925
    Contains much material on Reuter's, particularly its development in the Near East and Far East.

De Reuter condemned. Editor and Publisher. 13:385. Nov. 1, 1913
    London newspapers protest against mingling of news and advertising.

Fräntel, Ludwig
Reuter. 53:319-21. *In* Allgemeine deutsche Biographie, Duncker und Humblot, 1907

Government grants Reuters £6,000 for extra news. World's Press News. 22:3. Mar. 2, 1939
    Supplementary civil estimates included items for expenses for "news to foreign countries since September, 1938, at the request of His Majesty's Government."

Government request to Reuters in crisis. Newspaper World. 41:2. Nov. 26, 1938
    Government agreed to pay Reuter's cost of sending out 2,000 additional words a day to foreign countries during crisis leading up to Munich conference.

Grünbeck, Max
Organisation und Persönlichkeiten des Reuter-Büros. Zeitungswissenschaft. 9:304-8. July 1, 1934
    A brief account of the organization, personnel, and clients of the British Reuter's agency.

Japan in news service pact. Editor and Publisher. 13:634. Jan. 31, 1914
    Reuter's agency said to have contract with Japanese government.

The **Japanese** threat to "kill" Reuters news service. China Weekly Review. 74:365-6. Nov. 16, 1935

Jones, Sir Roderick
News and modern conditions. Address at a meeting of the Tomorrow club, London, March 1936. 9p. London: Waterlow and Sons, 1936
    This and succeeding citations of addresses by the Reuters chief, constitute an official story of the great British press association.

Reuters. Address at Cardiff, April 1932.
12p. London: Waterlow and Sons, 1932

Reuters. Address at the School of Military Engineering, Chatham, Oct. 25, 1928. 13p. Chatham: Mackays, 1928

The romance of Reuters. Journal of the British Institute of Journalists. 18:223-4. Dec. 1930

New Reuter development will aid Indian commerce. World's Press News. 18: suppl. III. Sept. 30, 1937
Service being greatly expanded in India.

New Reuter-P.A. building has beds and bathrooms for staff. World's Press News. 22:3. July 13, 1939
Brief sketch of Reuter's facilities during past century.

Perry, A. P.
"Semi-official" incorrect. Editor and Publisher. 63:43. Mar. 14, 1931
New York correspondent of Reuter's protests against use of phrase.
See also *Editor and Publisher.* 63:12. Mar. 7, 1931.

Reuter's. Nation and Athenæum. 17:108. Apr. 24, 1915

Reuters director's plea for government subsidy. Newspaper World. 41:2. Feb. 18, 1939
Wants to be independent, but asks some government aid.

Schuyler, Philip
Reuters' deeds seen as romance by Sir Roderick Jones. Editor and Publisher. 56:7. Oct. 13, 1923

Simonis, H.
The street of ink. 372p. New York: Funk and Wagnalls Co., 1917
Includes discussion of Reuter's.

Uncontaminated news. Editor and Publisher. 13:412. Nov. 8, 1913
Editorial.
Protest against Reuter's mingling of news and advertising.

Who hampers spread of British news abroad? World's Press News. 21:5. Feb. 23, 1939

William, Douglas F.
The romance of Reuter's of Great Britain. Editor and Publisher. 54:5, 27. Aug. 27, 1921
History of this privately owned British news agency.

Williams, Valentine
The world of action: autobiography. 479p. London: H. Hamilton, 1938
Contains chapter on historical background of the Reuter agency.

d. BRITISH UNITED PRESS

Herbert Bailey dies at 44. World's Press News. 21:2. Mar. 23, 1939
Managing editor of British United Press had formerly been foreign correspondent.

Herbert Bailey: he simplified foreign news. World's Press News. 20:499, p.11. Sept. 22, 1938
Biographical sketch of the managing editor of the British United Press.

Who hampers spread of British news abroad? World's Press News. 21:5. Feb. 23, 1939

e. MISCELLANEOUS

Bone, F. D.
The history of the "Central News". World's Press News. 1:7. June 6, 1929
The romantic history of the "Topical." World's Press News. 1:7. June 20, 1929

The **British** Associated Press. Living Age. 215:215-16. Oct. 16, 1897

British news abroad swamped by subsidized foreign services. Newspaper World. 40:1-2. Aug. 7, 1937

Empire press chiefs discuss news, radio and legal problems. World's Press News. 22:3. July 6, 1939
British government asked to increase dissemination of news of British origin to meet competition of foreign agencies.

M.P.'s discuss subsidies for British agencies. World's Press News. 18:3. Feb. 24, 1938

Press and agencies must join to fight tendencious news. World's Press News. 18:5. Nov. 11, 1937
Sir Roderick Jones, Reuter's chairman, on rival agencies and misleading world news.

The **Printed** word in propaganda. Newspaper World. 42:3. July 8, 1939
Sir Roderick Jones, Reuter's chairman, urges help for increasing volume of news of British origin to counteract menace of powerful rivals among news agencies.

Staggering rise in news agency operating costs. World's Press News. 17:15. July 8, 1937

6. ITALY

Annuario della stampa italiana. 971p. Bologna: N. Zanichelli, 1916-38
The annual official directory of Italian newspapers and press organizations, edited by Nicola Zanichelli.

Dresler, Adolf
Cavour und die Presse. 72p. Würzburg-Aumühle: Konrad Triltch, 1939
Cavour and the press.

Geschichte der italienischen Presse. 2v. Berlin, Munich: R. Oldenbourg, 1933-34
History of the Italian press, including the newspaper career of Mussolini.

Morgagni, Manlio
L'agenzia Stefani. 64p. Milan: Alfieri e LaCroix, 1930
Origins and development of the Italian news agency by its official historian.

Orth, Paul
Die "Agenzia Stefani" in Rome. Zeitungs-wissenschaft. 10:318-22. July 1, 1935
History of Stefani agency; its founder; expansion.

Piccioni, Luigi
Il giornalismo. 66p. Rome: Istituto per la Propaganda della Cultura Italiana, 1920
Bibliography.

Zur Geschichte der Agenzia Stefani. Zeit-ungswissenschaft. 5:251. July 15, 1930
Newly discovered facts on the relation of Cavour to the beginning of the Stefani news agency.

7. JAPAN

Hanazono, Kanesada
The development of Japanese journalism. 100p. Tokyo: Tokyo Nichi-Nichi, 1934
Historical treatise by the foreign editor of the *Nichi-Nichi* and lectures in journal-ism at Waseda University.

Inside details of the proposed Japanese news agency amalgamation. China Weekly Review. 73:217. July 13, 1935

Iwamoto, Kiyoshi
Denies control by "Domei." Editor and Publisher. 69:37. July 25, 1936

Japan agency's new home. Editor and Pub-lisher. 66:10. July 8, 1933

Japan will have new national news agency soon. World's Press News. 14:15. Oct. 3, 1935

Japanese national news agency plan opposed by provincial press. China Weekly Re-view. 74:351. Nov. 9, 1935

Japanese news agency chief dead. News-paper World. 42:9. Sept. 9, 1939
Domei agency said to have 500 war cor-respondents in European capitals and in United States.

Kennedy, Malcolm Duncan
The changing fabric of Japan. p.180-203. New York: R. R. Smith, 1931
Japanese press and its influence.

More evidence on objectives of Japanese news monopoly. China Weekly Review. 78:2-3. Sept. 5, 1936

National news body chartered in Japan. Editor and Publisher. 68:13. Nov. 23, 1935
Government privileges are granted to new press association in Japan, the Domei agency.

Rengo-Nippon Dempo merger marked end of independent journalism in Japan. China Weekly Review. 77:410-12. Aug. 22, 1936

Saito denies Japan wants censorship. Edi-tor and Publisher. 68:11. May 18, 1935

Takaishi, S.
The Domei press agency makes its bow. Contemporary Japan. 5:245-53. Sept. 1936
Rising from the merger of smaller news agencies, the Domei is modeled on the Associated Press of America.

Wildes, Harry Emerson
Japan in crisis. 300p. New York: Mac-millan, 1934
Includes a discussion of the relations of government and press.

Social currents in Japan. 390p. Chicago: Univ. of Chicago Press, 1927
The Japanese press and its relation to various classes of citizens; influence of the press on political, economic, and social thought.

8. RUSSIA

Doletzky, J. G.
Die Nachrichtenversorgung der Presse: die Telegraphenagentur der Sowjetun-ion. Zeitungswissenschaft. 2:49. Apr. 15, 1927
Sketch of the Russian news-gathering agency, Tass, by a former director.

Durant, Kenneth
Soviet news in the American press. Jour-nalism Quarterly. 13:148-56. June 1936
By a correspondent in the United Press of Tass, official Soviet news agency.

Groth, Otto
Die Zeitung. v.1, p.482-548. Mannheim: J. Bensheimer, 1928

Just, Arthur W.
Ausbau der Sowjetpresse. Zeitungswis-senschaft. 11:385-93. Sept. 1936

Romm, Vladimir
The press in the U.S.S.R. Journalism Quarterly. 12:20-6. Mar. 1935
By a former Washington correspondent of *Izvestia*.

Russia using radio to transmit news. Editor and Publisher. 57:27. Nov. 22, 1924
Rosta, Russian telegraph agency, send-ing daily report to 20 papers.

Tass director honored. Editor and Pub-lisher. 67:11. Nov. 10, 1934

Tass director sails for Moscow; has ex-change hook-up with U.P. Editor and Publisher. 67:12. Dec. 1, 1934

9. SCANDINAVIA

Arstad, Sverre
Das norwegische Nachrichtenbüro. Norsk Telegram Byraa. Zeitungs-wissenschaft. 10:635-6. Dec. 1935
The leading Norwegian press association.

Ritzaus Bureau. Zeitungswissenschaft. 11:143-4. Mar. 1936
A brief history of the Danish news agency, its growth, organization and activ-ity.

Das schwedische Telegrammbüro. Zeitungswissenschaft. 11:144-5. Mar. 1936
A brief account of the organization and history of the Tidningarnas Telegrambyrran (T.T.), the Swedish news agency.

Eliassen, Peter
Ritzau's Bureau, 1866-1916. Copenhagen: Nielson och Lydiche, 1916
The story of the Danish news-gathering agency.

Fleck, Rudolf
Entwicklung und Bedeutung des danischen Nachrichtenbüros Ritzau. Zeitungswissenschaft. 14:479-81. July 1, 1939
An account of the Ritzau news agency in Denmark.

Groth, Otto
Die Zeitung. v.1. p.482-548. Mannheim: J. Bensheimer, 1928

Oiseth, Howard
News agency practices in Scandinavia. Journalism Quarterly. 15:12-18. Mar. 1938

10. MISCELLANEOUS

Canadian Newspaper Directory. 2v. Montreal: McKim, 1901

Canadian press limited. Editor and Publisher. 10:1. Nov. 26, 1910
New news service for daily papers of the Dominion.

Die **Geschichtliche** Entwicklung des tschoslowakischen Pressebüros. Zeitungswissenschaft. 11:99-101. Feb. 1936
A short survey of the history of the CTK or Czechoslovakian news bureau, with a little of the politics involved in its development.

Government subsidy hotly denied by Canadian press chief. Editor and Publisher. 66:24. June 10, 1933

Die **Nachrichtenagenturen** in Belgien. Zeitungswissenschaft. 12:786. Nov. 1, 1937
A list of the news agencies in Belgium.

Neues Nachrichtenbüro in Finnland. Zeitungswissenschaft. 14:40. Jan. 1, 1939
Founding and activities planned for a new news-gathering bureau in Finland.

Press combinations. Spectator. 131:44. Oct. 20, 1923

Smith, Charles Stephenson
News exchange brings American nations closer together. il. Pan American Magazine. 43:309-15. Nov. 1930

Um die politische Beeinflussung der Nachrichtenagenturen. Zeitungswissenschaft. 14:618. Sept. 1939
Accusations that Swiss agencies are in the service of Italy and Germany are proved false.

III. WASHINGTON CORRESPONDENCE

See also
Freedom of the Press, p.40; Propaganda, p.45; National Public Opinion—United States, p.56; World War, 1914—Press Regulation, p.91.

A. GENERAL DISCUSSION

Chambers, Julius
The press and the public official. Forum. 44:14-25. July 1910

Donovan, William J.
News alone an incomplete newspaper. Editor and Publisher. 63:31, 138. Apr. 25, 1931
Increasing demands on government intensify interpretative function of press.

Lawrence, David
Government by impression. Century. 96:117-23. May 1918
Washington correspondents have grave responsibility of creating correct impressions of government in public opinion.

Ludlow, Louis
From cornfield to press gallery; adventures and reminiscences of a veteran Washington correspondent. Washington: W. F. Roberts Co., 1924

Pew, Marlen
Shop talk at thirty. Editor and Publisher. 66:92. Apr. 21, 1934
Retrospect, including many incidents concerning reporting in Washington.

Pollard, James E.
The presidents and the press. Quill. 26: 12-14, 22. Apr. 1938
From George Washington to Franklin Delano Roosevelt; a survey of relations between presidents and the press down through the years.

Poore, Benjamin Perley
Reminiscences of sixty years in the national metropolis. 2v. Philadelphia: Hubbard Bros., 1886
By a veteran journalist, clerk of the Senate Printing Records, editor of the Congressional Directory. Ch.3, p.50-62, "Journalism of 1828," discusses Washington correspondents and other prominent newspapermen.

Rice, Stuart A. See Willey, Malcolm M., jt. auth.

This is a writers' administration. Editor and Publisher. 13:86. July 19, 1913

Washington correspondents were once stormy petrels in the national capital. Publishers Auxiliary. 69:1. Oct. 6, 1934
Anecdotes from the history of Washington correspondents.

What is hostility to government? Outlook. 104:351. June 21, 1913

Willey, Malcolm M. and Rice, Stuart A.
Communication agencies and social life. p.168-70. New York, London: Mc-Graw–Hill, 1933
Washington as a center of news dissemination.

B. PRESIDENTS AND THE PRESS

1. To 1928

At the White House. Public. 21:1283. Oct. 12, 1918

Barry, David S.
News-getting at the capital. Chautauquan. 26:282-6. Dec. 1897
Relations existing between the press and Washington officialdom during the early 90's. Statesmen were generally secretive.

Brown, Henry S. and Williams, Samuel M.
Theodore Roosevelt originated idea of newspaper cabinet. Editor and Publisher. 51:20, 22. Jan. 11, 1919
Two Washington correspondents, contemporary with Theodore Roosevelt, relate from the inside the relations between Colonel Roosevelt and the newspapers.

Corey, Herbert
The presidents and the press. Saturday Evening Post. 204:25, 96, 100-1, 104. Jan. 9, 1932

Dickinson, J. J.
Theodore Roosevelt: press agent. Harper's Weekly. 51:1410, 1428. Sept. 28, 1907
The publicity machinery by which Theodore Roosevelt impressed his views upon the nation.

Dunn, Arthur
From Harrison to Harding. 2v. New York: G. P. Putnam's Sons, 1922

Essary, J. Frederick
President, Congress, and the press correspondents. American Political Science Review. 22:902-9. Nov. 1928
Tendencies toward centralization of the government make Washington the world's leading news center. Washington correspondents are largely self-disciplined.

How editors view Coolidge press attack. Editor and Publisher. 60:5-6, 22. Feb. 11, 1928
Contains full text of President Coolidge's National Press Club address.

How the White House became a glass house. il. Literary Digest. 88:38-45. Feb. 20, 1926

Lawrence, David
The President and the press. Saturday Evening Post. 200:27, 117-18, 120, 125-6, 129-30. Aug. 27, 1927

McCoy, Samuel
Trials of the White House spokesman. Independent. 115:317-19, 336. Sept. 19, 1925

Peck, H. T.
Newspaper criticism of the President. Bookman. 14:413-14. Dec. 1901

Pew, Marlen
Shop talk at thirty. Editor and Publisher. 67:40. May 26, 1934
Editor M. Hood, A.P., advised President Theodore Roosevelt on how to be brief and explicit.

President takes World Court fight to press. Editor and Publisher. 55:5, 38. Apr. 21, 1923
United States has no place in League of Nations.

Shepherd, William Gunn
The White House says. Collier's. 83:19. Feb. 2, 1929

Stoddard, Henry Luther
As I knew them. 571p. New York, London: Harper, 1927
Presidents and politics from Grant to Coolidge.

Suydam, Henry
Secrecy veils nation's public business, menacing free press principle. Editor and Publisher. 58:3. Apr. 3, 1926
Correspondents confused and hampered by disavowals of interviews and "official spokesman" system.

Villard, Oswald Garrison
Press and presidents. Century. 111:193-200. Dec. 1925

Williams, Samuel M. See Brown, Henry S., jt. auth.

2. HOOVER ADMINISTRATION

Anderson, Paul Y.
Hoover and the press. Nation. 132:93-4; 133:382-4. Jan. 28, Oct. 14, 1931
Washington news. Nation. 128:645-6. May 29, 1929

Back stage in Washington: the White House press relations. Outlook. 153:578. Dec. 11, 1929

Feeding the press: newspapermen at the White House. Collier's. 83:34. Aug. 16, 1930

Manning, George H.
Hoover's press system best instituted by any president. Editor and Publisher. 61:5. Mar. 16, 1929
Joslin suggests news "consultations." Editor and Publisher. 64:7. Sept. 19, 1931
Government officials develop tendencies "subversive" of the ideals of a free press.
President Hoover and White House corps at odds over news "leaks." Editor and Publisher. 64:15. July 11, 1931
Strained air pervades press circle as White House "leak" is sought. Editor and Publisher. 64:10. July 18, 1931

White House news ban on bank parley upset by correspondents. Editor and Publisher. 64:5. Oct. 10, 1931
Newspapermen free to write what they will, but declarations are accompanied by "suggestions" that they write only what is handed out officially.

Mr. Hoover's refusal to be humanized. Literary Digest. 110:8. July 25, 1931

Reporters who travel with presidents. Literary Digest. 102:74-6. Sept. 14, 1929

Tucker, Raymond T.
Mr. Hoover lays a ghost. White House press relations. North American Review. 227:661-9. June 1929

3. F. D. ROOSEVELT ADMINISTRATION

Broun, Heywood
Roosevelt shows up the press. Nation. 143:522. Oct. 31, 1936

Butler, James J.
News and editorials digested for F.D.R. Editor and Publisher. 68:28. Nov. 23, 1935
100-page mimeographed report presented daily by Department of Commerce group to the President and his aides.
Newsmen fight back in breach with FDR in "Rhine Frontier." Editor and Publisher. 72:3. Feb. 11, 1939
Correspondents resent President's charge of deliberate lying in news stories, organize senatorial backing for showdown.
Roosevelt releases show his confidence in press. Editor and Publisher. 71:7. Mar. 19, 1938
Trust not violated in "off the record" conferences.

Carroll, Gordon
Propaganda from the White House. American Mercury. 42:319-36. Nov. 1937

Clapper, Raymond
Why reporters like the President. Review of Reviews. 89:14-17. June 1934

Clemow, Bice
F.D.R. retains "open" conferences. Editor and Publisher. 67:9. Mar. 2, 1935
The old written-in-advance question formula will not change the present open conference policy despite rift with writers over "misinterpretation" of news.

Early, Stephen T.
Below the belt. Saturday Evening Post. 211:7, 111-13. June 10, 1939
President's secretary charges unfair blows against the President and his policies.

Essary, J. Frederick
New Deal for nearly four months. Literary Digest. 116:3-4, 35. July 1, 1933
The presidency and the press. Scribner's. 97:305-7. May 1935
The presidency and the press. Journalism Quarterly. 13:177-8. June 1936
Any good reporter should be able to sift news from propaganda.

"F.D." nose for news. Editor and Publisher. 66:26. Jan. 13, 1934
Editorial.
Roosevelt's friendliness and candor with press lauded.

F.D.R. evasiveness irks press men. Editor and Publisher. 70:16. July 24, 1937
James L. Wright of the *Buffalo Evening News* calls President Roosevelt's semi-weekly conferences with the press "hotbeds of mutual irritation."

Free press needed by people and government—Roosevelt. Editor and Publisher. 71:3, 67. Dec. 17, 1938
Freedom not curtailed, President asserts in message to *St. Louis Post-Dispatch.*

Herrick, John
With the reporters at the summer White House. Literary Digest. 116:5, 29. Aug. 12, 1933

Hurd, Charles W. B.
President and press: a unique forum. New York Times Magazine. p.3, 19. June 9, 1935
Mr. Roosevelt develops his news conference on striking lines.

Krock, Arthur
Press and government. Annals of the American Academy of Political and Social Science. 180:162-7. July 1935
Mr. Krock, of *The New York Times*, discusses White House press conferences and the rise of government propaganda under Wilson, Hoover and the New Deal.

Laski, Harold J.
President Roosevelt and foreign opinion. Yale Review. n.s. 22:707-13. June 1933
President Roosevelt must carry public opinion with him to achieve his domestic objectives; and that opinion is best gained by brilliant achievements in the international arena.

Manning, George H.
Capital corps hopes for "New Deal." Editor and Publisher. 65:5. Mar. 4, 1933
New president popular with press acquaintances—likes mental battle with reporters.
New Deal for press begins at once as nation faces bank crisis. Editor and Publisher. 65:3-4. Mar. 11, 1933
President and Cabinet welcome newspaper cooperation in allaying public fear.
President candidly consults reporters in advance of budget announcement. Editor and Publisher. 66:3-4. Jan. 6, 1934
Roosevelt gives reporters candid "preview" of budget.

Martel, James K.
Washington press conference. American Mercury. 43:197-205. Feb. 1938

Mr. Roosevelt ungags the press. Literary Digest. 115:10. Mar. 25, 1933

Pew, Marlen
Shop talk at thirty. Editor and Publisher. 65:36. Apr. 8, 1933
The President's affability and his initiation into the National Press Club.
Shop talk at thirty. Editor and Publisher. 67:36. Nov. 10, 1934
The actual happenings at a press conference with President Roosevelt.

Poll of U.S. press shows 38% supporting FDR now. Editor and Publisher. 71:6. Aug. 20, 1938

President gives Krock exclusive interview, but takes parity vow. Editor and Publisher. 70:42. Mar. 6, 1937
President Roosevelt breaks rule of impartiality among all accredited correspondents.

President greets American press. Editor and Publisher. 66:3. Apr. 21, 1934
Contains information on the different news services and conditions of press employment.

President Roosevelt makes history by dealings in press conferences. Newsdom. 6:5. Aug. 24, 1935
Roosevelt displays knowledge of reporters' professional difficulties and obligations throughout press conferences.

President voices faith in the nation's press. Editor and Publisher. 71:6. Sept. 10, 1938

Press conferences. American Press. 52:3. Dec. 1933
Arthur Krock, *New York Times* correspondent, explains why press conferences are useful.

Roosevelt angered by PWA stories. Editor and Publisher. 68:12. Nov. 23, 1935
A "certain newspaper" charged with deliberate misrepresentation of the truth.

Rosten, Leo Calvin
President Roosevelt and the Washington correspondents. Public Opinion Quarterly. 1:36-47. Jan. 1937
A "slant" on the nature of the journalistic process, inter-personal relationship of the press conference and the psychology of newspapermen.

White House attacks W. R. Hearst for hostility to New Deal. Editor and Publisher. 69:11. Sept. 26, 1936

Wile hits press "seances" held by Roosevelt. Editor and Publisher. 71:4. Oct. 1, 1938
Columnist says many newsmen "crave less irrelevancy, ribaldry."

Williams, Michael
Views and reviews; newspapers and the President. Commonweal. 27:721-2. Apr. 22, 1938

C. OFFICIAL PRESS BUREAUS

See also
Committee on Public Information, p.94.

1. To 1933

Essary, J. Frederick
Uncle Sam's ballyhoo men. American Mercury. 23:419-28. Aug. 1931
On government publicity offices.

Kaltenborn, Hans V.
Propaganda land where playing on the mass mind is the chief business of Government. Century. 114:678-87. Oct. 1927

Press agents in Washington. Boston Transcript. June 3, 1913
Editorial.
Assails tendency in government departments.

Robb, Arthur
Keen criticism of press at Princeton. Editor and Publisher. 63:7, 46-8, 50. May 2, 1931
Certain Washington departments have press agentry barrier to news.

2. 1933-1939

Atwood, A. W.
The great propaganda machine. Saturday Evening Post. 207:23, 94-6, 98. June 15, 1935

Bargeron, Carlisle
Invisibly supported. Nation's Business. 25:27-8, 119, 121. Oct. 1937
Washington, the propaganda factory for the nation.

Berchtold, William E.
Press agents of the New Deal. New Outlook. 164:23-30, 61, 63-4. July 1934

Branch, Zelda
Women writers in government public relations. Matrix. 21:7-10. Apr.-May, 1936
Interesting article on women in the public eye and the press.

Butler, James J.
F.C.C. official restricts news to department handouts. Editor and Publisher. 68:14. Sept. 28, 1935
The formal "handouts" contain only essential details.

Carroll, Gordon
Dr. Roosevelt's propaganda trust. American Mercury. 42:1-31. Sept. 1937

A Censorship issue? Editor and Publisher. 70:36. June 5, 1937
Editorial.

Central U.S. press office aim denied by Mellett. Editor and Publisher. 71:21. Aug. 6, 1938

Copeland bill held up in house, stymied by holding company measure. Editor and Publisher. 68:3. June 8, 1935
Measure introduced by Copeland authorizes consolidated staff to distribute government news.

Early, Stephen T.
Hobgoblins—1935 model. Redbook. 64: 24-5, 100-3. Apr. 1935
Stephen Early, secretary to President Roosevelt, replies to the article in *Redbook*, Feb. 1935, by Theodore G. Joslin, cited below.

Government propaganda issue aired. Editor and Publisher. 67:11, 42. Jan. 19, 1935

Hanson, Elisha
Official propaganda under the New Deal. Annals of the American Academy. 179: 176-86. Philadelphia, May 1935

Herring, E. Pendleton
Official publicity under the New Deal.
Annals of the American Academy. 179:
167-75. May 1935

Joslin, Theodore G.
Freedom of the press—1935 model. Redbook. 64:26-9, 78, 80. Feb. 1935
    A list of the most prominent newspaper-
    men hired by the New Deal, by a former
    secretary of President Hoover.

Kent, Frank R.
Washington's ballyhoo brigade. American
Magazine. 124:61-2, 64, 66. Sept. 1937

Kirchhofer, Alfred H.
Bureaucratic silence and secrecy hamper-
ing Washington news men. Editor and
Publisher. 58:14. Dec. 5, 1925
    Correspondents protest "air-tight" con-
    trol of Department of Justice and general
    attempt to censor even unimportant news.

Krock, Arthur
Press vs. government—a warning. Public
Opinion Quarterly. 1:45-9. Apr. 1937
    Washington correspondent for *The New
    York Times* looks with distrust on plans
    for a centralized federal government press
    bureau.

McCamy, James L.
Government publicity: its practice in fed-
eral administration. 275p. Chicago:
Univ. of Chicago Press, 1939

Variety in the growth of federal publicity.
Public Opinion Quarterly. 3:285-92.
Apr. 1939

Mallon, Paul
Has the New Deal colored the news?
New York Times Magazine. p.6, 22.
Feb. 17, 1935
    An observer in Washington holds that the
    truth ultimately reaches the public.

Mann, Robert S.
Capital corps no propaganda victim,
writers tell journalism teachers. Editor
and Publisher. 69:3-4, 12. Jan. 4, 1936

Manning, George H.
Huge N.I.R.A. publicity campaign directed
by Michelson. Editor and Publisher.
66:16. Aug. 5, 1933

Vast publicity drive mobilizing U.S. behind Recovery Act. Editor and Publisher. 66:8. July 29, 1933
    Countrywide campaign starts on war-
    time scale, using all publicity channels.

Michael, George
Handout. p.3-242. New York: G. P.
Putnam's Sons, 1935

News regulation in Washington seen as
step to coordination. Editor and Publisher. 66:10. Apr. 7, 1934
    Arthur Krock, of *The New York Times*,
    believes there is justification for new press
    policy; government has unprecedented effi-
    ciency as a press agent.

One hundred press agents. Editor and Publisher. 66:10. Apr. 7, 1934
    Representative Hamilton Fish, jr., of
    New York says U.S. payrolls carry that
    number in Washington.

$1,200,222 for publicity. Editor and Pub-
lisher. 70:40. Jan. 23, 1937
    United States approximate expenditure
    for employees directly or indirectly working
    in the publicity set-ups.

Robinson, Arthur R.
Freedom of speech and of the press.
Congressional Record. (Seventy-third
Congress, Second Session) 78:1:862-5.
Jan. 18, 1934
    Indiana senator, in Senate speech, cites
    evidences of dangerous encroachment by
    the Administration upon freedom of press
    and speech.

Rogers, Charles E.
The newspaper in government. Journalism
Quarterly. 12:1-8. Mar. 1935
    Government press services under the New
    Deal.

Secret government in Washington; government propaganda and censorship. New
Republic. 83:62-3. May 29, 1935

Sullivan, Lawrence
Government by mimeograph. Atlantic
Monthly. 161:306-15. Mar. 1938

United States. Congress. Senate. Select
Committee to Investigate the Executive Agencies of the Government
Investigation of executive agencies of the
government. Senate report no. 1275,
76th Congress, 1st session. 16v. in 1
Washington: Government Printing Office, 1937
    Ch. x, p.523-53, discusses the govern-
    ment library, information, and statistical
    services. Specifically, it describes the ex-
    tensive use which the Roosevelt admin-
    istration has made of these services as
    well as controls of government publicity
    activities which have been suggested with
    a view to co-ordination.

Washington news system. Editor and Publisher. 67:20. Nov. 3, 1934
    Editorial.
    Relationship between President and press.
    Handout system has become a vice.

Wood, Kingsley
Publicity. Spectator. 159:889. Nov. 19,
1937

D.   THE PRESS AND THE
ADMINISTRATION

Bell, Samuel W.
State Department useless as source of
international affairs news. Editor and
Publisher. 55:6. Dec. 30, 1922
    Washington corps forced to get informa-
    tion elsewhere.

Bell, Ulric
The Democratic diplomacy of Secretary
Hull. Public Opinion Quarterly. 2:36-
47. Jan. 1938
    Secretary Hull recognizes the need of
    correctly informed public opinion as a safe-
    guard to American institutions.

Butler, James J.
Treasury is pleased by franc story. Editor and Publisher. 69:10. Oct. 3, 1936
   Wealth of background required for coverage of epochal move toward currency entente.
United States officials "called" for blaming press. Editor and Publisher. 67:14. Dec. 1, 1934
   Secretary Ickes and Housing Administrator James A. Moffett attempt to shift responsibility of wrangle to newspapermen's shoulders.

Cooperation of Navy unusual at Portsmouth. Editor and Publisher. 72:26. June 3, 1939
   Department officials aided in every way, newsmen report.

Francis, Warren B.
Secrecy policy of Shipping Board attacked by Washington writer. Editor and Publisher. 64:16. Sept. 19, 1931

Hulen, Bertram D.
Inside the State Department. 328p. New York: McGraw–Hill, 1939
   By a New York Times correspondent. Ch.8 and 9 deal with the press conference system and communications.

Hull asks restored foreign trade. Editor and Publisher. 66:7. Apr. 28, 1934
   Secretary of State Hull praises A.P., hails free press.

Hull rebukes delegation before eyes of State Department corps. Editor and Publisher. 69:3. Sept. 26, 1936

Hull scores Havas for "inside" story. Editor and Publisher. 68:12. Nov. 2, 1935
   Washington correspondent's dispatch contradicted expressed public attitude of U.S. on neutrality.

Ickes asks "sportsmanship" in editing. Editor and Publisher. 67:4, 66, 68. Apr. 27, 1935
   Urges fair treatment of political opponents and vigilance in defending free speech and free press in address at A.P. luncheon.

Ickes broadens attack on press in new speech. Editor and Publisher. 72:14. Feb. 18, 1939

"Kept newspapers" blast draws Levands' fire. Editor and Publisher. 71:7. Jan. 8, 1938
   Publishers of Wichita Beacon challenge Secretary Ickes to name them.

NRA press gag eased but is not lifted. Editor and Publisher. 67:16. May 26, 1934
   General Hugh S. Johnson says divisional administrators may talk freely to reporters, but deputies are still gagged.

No press "gag" meant, Johnson declares. Editor and Publisher. 66:6. Apr. 7, 1934
   NRA chief holds first conference with reporters in several weeks.

Press slow to fight for others—Ickes. Editor and Publisher. 67:12. Jan. 5, 1935
   Quick to defend its own freedom, but often condones abuses of free speech privilege, secretary tells college men.

Roper establishes a strict censorship. Editor and Publisher. 69:10. Mar. 14, 1936
   Employees must get written permission to give out any information at the Department of Commerce.

Westbrook, Lawrence
Error and remedy in WPA publicity. Public Opinion Quarterly. 1:94-8. July 1937

E. THE PRESS AND CONGRESS

Butler, James J.
Journalists had stellar roles in current Congress session. Editor and Publisher. 70:5-6. Aug. 7, 1937

Congress helps reporters. Editor and Publisher. 11:5. Dec. 30, 1911
   Facilities for gathering and handling news provided for Washington correspondents.

Crowell, E. M.
Congress and the power of the press. New Republic 89:321-2. Jan. 13, 1937

Manning, George H.
Bennett fight opened Senate to press. Editor and Publisher. 67:116, 118. July 21, 1934

Press forces Senate to alter rules. Editor and Publisher. 62:9, 56. June 1, 1929
   Washington expects open Senate sessions.

Senators ridicule customs censor, but law is still on books. Editor and Publisher. 62:24. Oct. 19, 1929
   Books admissible in original French and English are barred if published in Spanish.

Solons now censor speeches first. Editor and Publisher. 67:9. June 9, 1934
   Reporters barred by a ruling of Speaker Henry T. Rainey from obtaining official transcript of speeches made on floor of House of Representatives until members "revise" them.

Pew, Marlen
Shop talk at thirty. Editor and Publisher. 65:36. July 9, 1932
   Paul Y. Anderson, Washington correspondent of St. Louis Post-Dispatch, discusses Congress and the press in Pew's column.

Shop talk at thirty. Editor and Publisher. 66:48. June 24, 1933
   Editorial writers severely criticized by Paul Y. Anderson for ignorance in articles on Congress.

Rainey's gag order is modified. Editor and Publisher. 67:6. June 16, 1934
   Remarks of House members will be given to reporters except where members specifically object.

United States. Congress. Senate
Use of reporters' galleries in Senate. Senate report no.317, to accompany S. Res.117. 1st session, 76th Congress. 6p. Washington: Government Printing Office, 1939
   Gallery rules, supplemented by a brief history of the press gallery written by Paul J. McGahan of the Philadelphia Inquirer.

Wants United States body to hear complaints against press. Editor and Publisher. 67:22. Feb. 23, 1935
  Representative Theodore L. Moritz of Pittsburgh in a speech on the floor of the House assails newspapers of his home city for alleged political activity.

F. THE PRESS AND THE SUPREME COURT

Butler, James J.
High Court rulings prepared for press. Editor and Publisher. 69:38. Apr. 4, 1936
  United States Supreme Court now furnishing copies of decisions as justice begins reading; chance for error still exists.

Handling of verdict goes smoothly. Editor and Publisher. 69:11. Jan. 11, 1936
  Rapid coverage on Supreme Court's A.A.A. decision.

"Press contact man" to aid Supreme Court reporters. Newsdom. 7:10. Jan. 4, 1936
  Appointment follows request by news writers seeking data on New Deal legislation.

G. CORRESPONDENTS IN WASHINGTON

1. FIELD AND TECHNIQUE

Anderson, Paul Y.
A Washington honor roll. Nation. 132: 93-4. Jan. 28, 1931

Back stage in Washington. Independent. 120:256-7. Mar. 17, 1928

Barry, Robert T.
Eager to eliminate lobbyists from correspondents' ranks. Editor and Publisher. 51:10, 35. Feb. 1, 1919

Black, Ruby A.
"New deal" for news women in capital. Editor and Publisher. 66:11, 31. Feb. 10, 1934
  Women journalists attend Mrs. Roosevelt's conferences.

Brandt, Raymond P.
The Washington correspondent. Journalism Quarterly. 13:173-6. June 1936

Bunking trustful readers. Independent. 116: 598-600. May 22, 1926
  Washington correspondents and political news.

Butcher, Harold
Coverage of the New Deal is big job for foreign writers in U.S. Editor and Publisher. 66:16. Apr. 7, 1934

Butler, James J.
Press wires jammed with capital news. Editor and Publisher. 69:11. Jan. 11, 1936
  A.A.A. "upset" and Roosevelt budget message provides capital with one of greatest "news days" since World War.

Clapper, Raymond
All eyes are turned on Washington. Editor and Publisher. 66:9. Jan. 13, 1934
  500 writers in Washington are eyes and ears of public.

Cornering Washington news. New Republic 74:34. Feb. 22, 1933

Curb on press passes hits lobbyists. Editor and Publisher. 70:7. Mar. 13, 1937
  Only working newspapermen are entitled to floor privileges of California assembly.

Erhardt, Leslie
Day book of a Washington correspondent. Quill. 22:3-4. July 1934
  A series of articles telling something of what goes on behind the capital date line.

Essary, J. Frederick
Covering Washington. 280p. Boston: Houghton Mifflin, 1927
——See Lawrence, David, jt. auth.

Exclusive set gathers capital news. Literary Digest. 123:28-30. Mar. 6, 1937

Kent, Frank R.
Pulling the covers off politicians. Editor and Publisher. 63:30, 144. Apr. 25, 1931
  True pictures of public men as they are and the interests they represent.

Krock, Arthur
Washington, D.C. p. 3-28. *In* We saw it happen. Ed. by Hanson W. Baldwin and Shepard Stone. New York: Simon and Schuster, 1938

Lawrence, David and Essary, J. Frederick
Reporting the political news at Washington. American Political Science Review. 22:893-909. Nov. 1928

Ludlow, Louis
How Washington news is gathered. p. 181-90. *In his* From cornfield to press gallery. Washington: W. F. Roberts Co., 1924
  Adventures and reminiscences of a Washington correspondent.

News and comment from the national capital. Literary Digest. 116:12. Nov. 11, 1933

Oulahan, Richard V.
Capital corps praised for diligence. Editor and Publisher. 63:32, 138. Apr. 25, 1931

Perry, John W.
Leaders in professions view the press, point way to greater public service. Editor and Publisher. 63:5, 50, 52. May 16, 1931
  Senator Hiram Bingham and Congressman John Q. Tilson speak well of press representatives in Washington.

Rosten, Leo C.
The professional composition of the Washington press corps. Journalism Quarterly. 14:221-5. Sept. 1937
  Data on the professional equipment of 127 Washington press correspondents.

Rosten, Leo C.—*Continued*
The social composition of Washington correspondents. Journalism Quarterly. 14:125-32. June 1937
    Analysis of the social data on 127. Washington press correspondents.
The Washington correspondents. 436p. New York: Harcourt, Brace, 1937
    A picture, an analysis and an interpretation of Washington newspaper correspondents. The appendices contain numerous references and a bibliography.
Washington scribes' salaries. Digest. 1:28. Oct. 2, 1937

Sheperd, William Gunn
Our ears in Washington. Everybody's. 43:68-73. Oct. 1920
Why I am in Washington. Everybody's. 39:24. Dec. 1918

Tucker, Raymond T.
The political reporter finds his job exciting. American Press. 51:4. Feb. 1933

Ward, P. W.
Think pieces; thumb-sucking season in Washington journalism. Nation. 143:594-5. Nov. 21, 1936

Washington correspondent is a moulder of public opinion. Editor and Publisher. 50:10. Feb. 2, 1918
    David Lawrence, of the New York *Evening Post*, discusses need for clear interpretation of daily happenings in nation's capital.

2. BIOGRAPHY AND MEMOIRS

Anderson, Paul Y.
About
Anderson of the *Post-Dispatch.* Quill. 23:8-10. Apr. 1935
    Highlights on the life of Paul Y. Anderson, Washington correspondent whose flair for something to uncover has made him an outstanding newsman.

Butler, James J.
C. A. Hamilton, "Capitol Dean," is press corps' chronicler. Editor and Publisher. 72:9, 34. Apr. 1, 1939
    "Old timers" honor 83-year-old correspondent commissioned by Roosevelt to write observations on Washington newsmen since 1883.

Erhardt, Leslie
He covers the capital for Collier's. Quill. 23:6-7, 10. Jan. 1935
    An entertaining portrayal of Ray Turker, Washington correspondent for *Collier's.*

Hamilton, C. A.
About
C. A. Hamilton, "Capitol Dean," is press corps' chronicler. James J. Butler. Editor and Publisher. 72:9, 34. Apr. 1, 1939

Ludlow, Louis
From cornfield to press gallery. Washington: W. F. Roberts Co., 1924
    Adventures and reminiscences of a Washington correspondent.

Sullivan, Mark
The education of an American. Autobiography. 320p. Garden City, N. Y.: Doubleday, Doran, 1938
    The memoirs of a veteran among Washington correspondents.

Turker, Ray
About
He covers the capital for Collier's. Leslie Erhardt. Quill. 23:6-7, 10. Jan. 1935

H. WASHINGTON RADIO NEWS

See also
Radio, p.8; News Transmission, p.88.

Correspondents bar conference bid. Editor and Publisher. 66:16. Dec. 9, 1933
    Press gallery rights denied for reporters of Columbia News Service pending conference between executives of radio and press in New York.

Radio reporters get rights at White House. Editor and Publisher. 72:12. May 6, 1939
    Radio news reporters granted equal rights with the press in attending and covering presidential press conferences.

Would amend rules of press gallery. Editor and Publisher. 66:4. Nov. 19, 1933
    Radio reporters desire place in press galleries.

I. MISCELLANEOUS

Barclay, Thomas S.
Publicity division of Democratic party. American Political Science Review. 25:68-72. Feb. 1931

Barlow, Reuel R.
What the big dailies did. Editor and Publisher. 69:42. Dec. 5, 1936
    A computation of the amount of publicity matter and space that was given over to 1936 national election news.

Basset, Warren
Why the United States is rapidly becoming the news capital of the world. Editor and Publisher. 57:3, 27. Mar. 14, 1925

Butler, James J.
United States would keep tab on press agents. Editor and Publisher. 68:8. June 29, 1935
    Correspondents hired by foreign countries or individuals must register with State Department under new bill.

Chandler, Julia
"Guilty of friendship." Christian Science Monitor. Weekly Magazine Section. p. 5, 13. Aug. 28, 1935
    "Jim" Preston, counselor to two generations of Washington correspondents, is serving the press again in the new Archives Building after an interlude as Senate librarian.

City news service in Washington. Editor
and Publisher. 66:34. Apr. 14, 1934
United Press now operating teletype service from strategic points in Washington.

Cornering Washington news. New Republic. 74:34. Feb. 22, 1933
A.P. provides regional service from
Washington to meet demands of local com-
munities.

Gallup, George
Government and the sampling referendum.
American Statistical Association Jour-
nal. 33:131-42. Mar. 1938

Manning, George H.
Mussolini is barred from National Press
Club as enemy of free press. Editor
and Publisher. 61:16. June 9, 1928
Press Club (Washington) had previously
approved Premier's application.

Mobley, Radford, jr.
A.P. regional service grows. American
Press. 51:5. Feb. 1933
A new and more specialized service out
of Washington.

President's Supreme Court bombshell rocked
nation, surprised press. Editor and
Publisher. 70:3-4, 5. Feb. 13, 1937
Newspaper repercussions in news, editorials, cartoons continue after crescendo of
first coverage. Cartoons on p.5.

Price, Jack
Capital cameramen need a dozen "pass-
ports" to do their work. Editor and
Publisher. 69:18. Jan. 11, 1936

Probing press courtesies. Editor and Publisher. 66:8. May 12, 1934
Washington press corps gathering data
on treatment of American reporters abroad.

Proposed army bill would gag press. Editor and Publisher. 67:38. Dec. 22, 1934
Legislation planned by War Policies Commission would lead to strict censorship of
the press in wartime.

Publicity on income taxes under fire. Editor and Publisher. 67:10. Mar. 2, 1935
Publicizing names of tax payers provides
opportunities for extortionists, kidnappers,
and "sucker" lists.

37 present or former news men are members of 75th Congress. Editor and Publisher. 70:38. Mar. 6, 1937

U.S. registering agents for alien propaganda.
Editor and Publisher. 71:29. Sept. 10,
1938
Test is whether pay comes from abroad
and product is read in United States.

Young, Marguerite
Ignoble journalism in the nation's capital.
American Mercury. 34:239-43. Feb.
1935
Opportunity in capital city completely
missed by local papers.

IV. FOREIGN CORRESPONDENCE

A. HISTORY AND ANALYSIS

Brown, Robert U.
Frazier Hunt praises foreign correspond-
ents. Editor and Publisher. 71:14.
Apr. 2, 1938

Carter, John
American correspondents and British delegates. Independent. 119:150-2 Aug.
13, 1927

Crucy, François
U.S. press through the eyes of a French-
man. Editor and Publisher. 55:5, 31.
Apr. 7, 1923
Journalist impressed by the weight of
American newspapers, but notes failure to
distinguish between curiosity and indiscre-
tion.

Davis, Elmer H.
History of The New York Times. 434p.
New York: The New York Times, 1921

Desmond, Robert W.
The press and world affairs. 421p. New
York, London: D. Appleton-Century,
1937
Includes a survey of news-gathering
abroad and of the foreign press.

Dithmar, Edward A.
The American newspaper. III. The
European correspondent. Bookman.
19:244-57. May 1904

Drexel, Constance
The foreign correspondent. New Republic. 37:252-4. Jan. 30, 1924

Furay, James H.
America—news gatherer for the world.
Quill. 19:10-11, 15. June 1931

Gunther, John
Inside Europe. 470p. New York, London: Harper, 1936

Huddleston, Sisley
A correspondent in Paris. Blackwood's.
216:321-31. Sept. 1924

Kihss, Peter F.
Headline hunting in South America.
Quill. 23:6-7. May 1935

Loomis, Charles B.
Our correspondents in the East. Critic.
27:297-8. May 1, 1897

Lyons, Eugene, ed.
We cover the world. 441p. New York:
Harcourt, Brace, 1937
A symposium of experiences by various
foreign correspondents.

McEvoy, J. P.
Honorable revolution. Saturday Evening
Post. 208:6-7, 115-16. Apr. 25, 1936
With the foreign correspondents during
the Japanese rebellion.

Ogden, Rollo
The press and foreign news. Atlantic
Monthly. 86:390-3. Sept. 1900

Paine, Ralph D.
Roads of adventure. 402p. Boston, New York: Houghton Mifflin, 1925

Salmon, Lucy M.
The newspaper and the historian. 566p. New York: Oxford Univ. Press, 1923
Much material on the activities of foreign correspondents.

Scooping the world. World's Work. 61: 55-6. Feb. 1932
Some historic American news beats.

Seitz, Don Carlos
Joseph Pulitzer. p.239-40. Garden City, N.Y.: Simon and Schuster, 1924

Stuart, G. B.
Foreign journalists in London. Athenæum (London) no.3777:336. Mar. 17, 1900

Visit of foreign journalists to London. Athenæum (London) no.3775:275. Mar. 3, 1900

Study of international news urged. Editor and Publisher. 67:9. Sept. 29, 1934

Whitaker, John T.
And fear came. 273p. New York: Macmillan, 1936

William's world tour. Editor and Publisher. 13:722. Feb. 28, 1914
Editor and journalism teacher from Columbia, Missouri, gives his impressions of journalism in England, Ireland, France, Germany, Russia, Holland, Greece, and Australia.

Young, Eugene J.
Looking behind the censorships. 350p. Philadelphia, New York: J. B. Lippincott, 1938

B. NEWS VALUES, SOURCES AND TECHNIQUES

Arm of press penetrates Arctic solitudes to picture Nobile rescue heroism. Editor and Publisher. 61:3. July 21, 1928
Newspaper services make history for human communications.

Cummings, Arthur J.
Political journalism—a British view. Journalism Quarterly. 15:1-11. Mar. 1938
Personal experiences establish the fact that a successful political journalist must be not only a reporter but also a judicious commentator.

Fahey, John H.
Faking by foreign correspondents and unreliable news sources scored. Editor and Publisher. 58:82. Apr. 17, 1926

Gilbert, Morris
From usually reliable sources. Harper's. 179:385-96. Sept. 1939
How we get our foreign news.

Gunther, John
Dateline Vienna. Harper's. 171:198-208. July 1935
How a correspondent reports from a foreign capital.

Funneling the European news. Harper's. 160:635-47. Apr. 1930
Concise and useful sketch of the foreign correspondent's problems.

Harris, John P.
Exchange reporterships for publishers proposed. Editor and Publisher. 72: 3-41. Aug. 26, 1939
Difficulties confronting the foreign correspondent.

Heavy cost of foreign news service. Newspaper World. 42:1. Aug. 19, 1939

Hubbell, Horace J.
Think stuff unwanted. American Mercury. 10:263-7. Mar. 1927
The cable editor's "log" reflects the taste-level for news.

Jeans, Herbert
Traps for the foreign correspondent. Editor and Publisher. 59:33, 66. Oct. 9, 1926
By the chief editor of Reuter's.

Kielpinski, Tadeusz
Le sens de la responsabilité, qualité maîtresse du correspondent étranger. Presse Publicité. no. 32, p. 11. Feb. 21, 1938
The foreign correspondent should adapt himself to the French mentality in giving out his views on events of which he is a spectator.

Lack literary tone. Editor and Publisher. 13:768. Mar. 14, 1914
Editor of Le Journal finds New York newspapers inferior to those of Paris.

Linton Wells explains woes of foreign correspondents. Newsdom. 8:10. Dec. 11, 1937

Lists guideposts for foreign writers. Editor and Publisher. 64:12. Dec. 12, 1931
Sir Willmott Lewis of London Times says that the press is correcting some of the mistakes of diplomacy. Ten maxims for foreign correspondents.

Lochner, Louis P.
Die auszenpolitische Wirkung der Nachricht. Zeitungswissenschaft. 9:298-301. July 1, 1934
Effect of foreign news; how much can be used by the papers and the foreign reporter's responsibility for it; by the Associated Press correspondent in Berlin.

Merckx, Fernand J. J.
How a European correspondent "covers" news in this country. American Press. 48:34. Sept. 1930

Perry, John W.
Foreign news captures the front page. Editor and Publisher. 64:7. July 11, 1931

Polyzoides, Adamantios Th.
Isolation of U.S. newsmen abroad reflected in stories they send. Editor and Publisher. 58:80. Apr. 24, 1926
　　Editor of Greek language daily says inability of many writers to speak language of country hurts quality of news.

Sack suit and spy; Rome correspondents. Time. 26:19-20. Nov. 11, 1935

Sandford, Jack
Comment j'ai quitté la peinture pour devenir journaliste. Presse Publicité. no. 28, p. 5, 29. Dec. 21, 1937
　　First of a series of articles on foreign correspondents in Paris. In this article the author makes interesting comments on journalism in France.

Sensational foreign news. Nation. 79:494-5. Dec. 22, 1904
　　The increasing use of the cable has multiplied the quantity of foreign news while at the same time it has lowered its quality. Scrupulous news editors are needed to combat yellow journalism.

Short-lived Greek revolution taxed ingenuity of reporters. Editor and Publisher. 67:34. Mar. 16, 1935

Swift, Otis Peabody
Americans find 439 ways to buck censor. Editor and Publisher. 56:5-6. June 23, 1923
　　Ban on free news dispatches is curse of Europe.

Combing Europe for today's news today. Editor and Publisher. 55:5, 36. Mar. 17, 1923
　　Part of a series which explains the methods and techniques of the foreign correspondent.

Correspondents bluff way by frontiers. Editor and Publisher. 55:5, 29. Apr. 14, 1923

Crisis-chasing with the wagonlit knights. Editor and Publisher. 55:5, 32. Mar. 31, 1923
　　Experiences of a newspaperman in Europe.

Tabouis, Geneviève
Scooping the world. Living Age. 355:480. Aug. 1938
　　Disclosure of terms of the Hoare-Laval pact in the Paris *Oeuvre* and other experiences of a noted French newspaper woman.

Tucker, Raymond T.
Take it from us. Collier's. 94:16, 47. Dec. 1, 1934
　　Foreign correspondents in Washington must first find out for themselves, and then translate their findings.

U.P. news director finds skill needed to cover events abroad. Editor and Publisher. 67:14. Aug. 18, 1934
　　Reporters in Europe rarely have chance to interview government heads.

Van Loon, Hendrik Willem
Tricks of newspaper correspondents. Nation. 100:77-8 Jan. 21, 1915

Woodward, Julian L.
Foreign news in American morning newspapers. 122p. London: P. S. King and Son; New York: Columbia Univ. Press, 1930
　　A statistical study of the extent and nature of foreign news in a selected list of American newspapers.

Your mirrors of Europe. Saturday Evening Post. 195:5, 145-6, 149-50. Dec. 9, 1922
　　Press censorship in Europe lingers years after the Armistice. The author draws a distinction between facts and "news."

C. FIELD AND REQUIREMENTS

A.P. editors discuss news problems. Editor and Publisher. 67:15, 39. Oct. 20, 1934

Beals, Carleton
Color in our foreign news. Outlook and Independent. 157:300-2. Feb. 25, 1931
　　The foreign correspondent faces many obstacles in his attempts to gather legitimate news. News from three-fourths of the civilized world is controlled by governmental censorships.

Blowitz, Henri Stephan de
Journalism as a profession. Contemporary Review. 63:37-46. Jan. 1893
　　A noted war correspondent asks whether journalistic methods can be taught and suggests the qualifications which the profession should demand of aspirants.

Brandenburg, George A.
Local room training is essential to men on overseas assignments. Editor and Publisher. 64:20. Nov. 21, 1931

Chambers, Julius
News hunting on three continents. 405p. New York: M. Kennerley, 1921

Cummings, Arthur J.
The press and a changing civilization. 139p. London: John Lane, 1936

Denoyer, Pierre
Plus que dans la choix des faits, l'art du correspondant à l'étranger réside dans leur interprétation. Presse Publicité. no. 23, p.7. Oct. 24, 1937
　　Qualities that make a good foreign correspondent, by the New York correspondent of the *Petit-Parisien.*

France orders United States correspondent expelled. Editor and Publisher. 61:5, 52. Oct. 13, 1928
　　Harold J. T. Horan, Universal Service, who reported Anglo-French "secret treaty."

Lyons, Eugene
Why foreign correspondents go home. Saturday Review of Literature. 16:3-4, 14. Aug. 28, 1937

Oestreicher, J. C.
But the news came through! Quill. 22:16-17, 36. Oct. 1934
　　Foreign correspondents braved many dangers and censor's wrath to report recent events.

Fitting men for foreign fields. Quill. 23:8-9. May 1935

Seldes, George
Our journalistic noblesse. Nation. 142: 375-7. Mar. 25, 1936

Smith, Charles Stephenson
Training for foreign service. Quill. 18: 3-4, 16. Dec. 1930

Spain drafts new gag for alien reporters. Newsdom. 5:8. Nov. 17, 1934

Sudre, René
La morale professionale des journalistes. Cahiers de la Presse. 1:396-404. July-Sept. 1938
    Moral responsibilities of the professional journalist; the matter of codification and adoption of more definite rules of honor and professional conduct.

Swift, Otis Peabody
Jails, duels, bombs, fate of Europe's editors. Editor and Publisher. 56:5. July 14, 1923

D. BIOGRAPHY AND MEMOIRS

Abbe, James E.
Men of cablese. New Outlook. 162:27-32. Dec. 1933
    Thumb-nail sketches of America's foreign press corps—the men who help to form American opinion of foreign countries.

Abbot, Willis J.
Watching the world go by. 358p. Boston: Little, Brown, 1933

Atkins, John Black
The life of Sir William Howard Russell. 2v. London: John Murray, 1911
    Standard work on the life of the British war correspondent, noted particularly for his reports of the Crimean War.

Bartlett, Vernon
Intermission in Europe; the life of a journalist and broadcaster. 296p. London: Oxford Univ. Press, 1938
This is my life. 331p. London: Chatto and Windus, 1937
    Life of the political correspondent of News-Chronicle, now foreign news commentator over BBC.

Bell, C. F. Moberly
About
The life and letters of C. F. Moberly Bell. Introduction by Sir V. Chirol. E. H. C. Moberly Bell. 326p. London: Richards Press, 1927

Bok, Edward
An autobiography. 318p. Introduction by Viscount Northcliffe. 1921

Bonsal, Stephen
Heyday in a vanished world. 445p. New York: W. W. Norton, 1937
    A correspondent's experiences in the late nineteenth century.

Catling, Thomas
My life's pilgrimage. 402p. With introduction by Rt. Hon. Lord Burnham. London: John Murray, 1911

Cortesi, Salvatore
My thirty years of friendships. 296p. New York: Harper's, 1927
    An Italian journalist who served American papers from Rome.

Creelman, James
On the great highway. 418p. Boston: Lothrop, 1901
    The wanderings and adventures of a special correspondent.

Dafoe, J. W.
Press, politics and people: The life and letters of Sir John Willison, journalist and correspondent of the Times, by A. H. U. Colquhoun. Canadian Historical Review. 17:59-64. Mar. 1936
    Review.

Dasent, Arthur Irwin
John Thadeus Delane, editor of the Times. His life and correspondence. 2v. New York: C. Scribner's Sons, 1908

Davis, Charles B., ed.
Adventures and letters of Richard Harding Davis. 417p. New York: C. Scribner's Sons, 1917-21

Davis, Richard Harding
About
Adventures and letters of Richard Harding Davis. Ed. by Charles B. Davis. 417p. New York: C. Scribner's Sons, 1917-21
Richard Harding Davis: his day. Fairfax D. Downey. 322p. New York, London: C. Scribner's Sons, 1933

Delane, John Thadeus
About
John Thadeus Delane, editor of the Times. His life and correspondence. Arthur Irwin Dasent. 2v. New York: C. Scribner's Sons, 1908

Dent, J. M.
The memoirs of J. M. Dent, 1849-1926. 272p. With some additions by H. R. Dent. London: J. M. Dent and Sons, 1928

Dewey, Stoddard
About
Dewey dies in Paris; dean of U.S. writers. Editor and Publisher. 66:37. Aug. 5, 1933

Dilnot, Frank
Adventures of a newspaper man. New York: E. P. Dutton, 1913

Downey, Fairfax D.
Richard Harding Davis: his day. 322p. New York, London: C. Scribner's Sons, 1933

Dresler, Adolf
Die Frau im Journalismus. 136p. Munich: Knorr und Hirth, 1936
    A collection of biographical notices of women journalists in all times and in all countries.

Duranty, Walter
I write as I please. 349p. New York: Simon and Schuster, 1935
New York Times correspondent, noted for his reports from Moscow.

Durland, Kellogg and others
The red reign: the true story of an adventurous year in Russia. 533p. New York: Century, 1907

Falk, Bernard
He laughed in Fleet Street. 351p. London: Hutchinson, 1933
Autobiography.

Floyd Gibbons dies at 52; noted war correspondent. Editor and Publisher. 72: 14. Sept. 30, 1939

Forbes, Archibald
Memories and studies of war and peace. 368p. London: Cassell, 1895
Noted correspondent of the last three decades of the 19th century.

Forrest, Wilbur
Behind the front page. 350p. New York, London: D. Appleton-Century, 1934
New York newspaperman who served in England during the World War.

French, Joseph Lewis
Our London correspondents. Editor and Publisher. 12:12. Mar. 29, 1913

Gibbons, Floyd
About
Floyd Gibbons dies at 52; noted war correspondent. Editor and Publisher. 72: 14. Sept. 30, 1939

Gibbs, Sir Philip Hamilton
Adventures of an international reporter. World's Work. 45:478-86, 619-26; 46: 39-45, 202-6, 301-5. Mar.-July 1923

Grant, Bernard
To the four corners. 287p. London: Hutchinson, 1933
The memoirs of a news photographer.

Gunther, John
Inside England; diary of a foreign correspondent. Atlantic Monthly. 159: 266-78, 385-96. Mar.-Apr. 1937

Harrison, Marguerite
There's always tomorrow. 664p. New York: Farrar and Rinehart, 1935

Huddleston, Sisley
In my time; an observer's record of war and peace. 412p. New York: E. P. Dutton, 1938

Hunt, Frazier
One American. 400p. New York: Simon and Schuster, 1938
This bewildered world. 371p. New York: Frederick A. Stokes, 1934

James, Lionel
High pressure. 314p. London: J. Murray, 1929
Activities in the service of the *Times*; the record of a war correspondent.

Kammet, Laurence
Red-headed reporter from Texas. American Press. 52:3. May 1934
The story of H. R. Knickerbocker.

Knickerbocker, H. R.
About
Red-headed reporter from Texas. Laurence Kammet. American Press. 52: 3. May 1934

LeSage, Sir John M.
About
Grand old man of Fleet Street. Valentine Wallace. Editor and Publisher. 51: 5-6, 34; 51:13-14. July 20-27, 1918

Marcosson, Isaac F.
Adventures in interviewing. 314p. New York: John Lane, 1920
Interviews with many of the commanding figures of the day: statesmen, journalists, literary men, business men and actors.

Miller, Webb
I found no peace. 332p. New York: Simon and Schuster, 1936
By the foreign editor of the United Press.

Owen, Russell
South of the sun. 288p. New York: John Day, 1935
A *New York Times* reporter in the Antarctic.

Pew, Marlen
Shop talk at thirty. Editor and Publisher. 67:44. Nov. 24, 1934
Marlen Pew talks of Karl von Wiegand, who covers a great part of the world for the Hearst papers.

Powell, E. Alexander
Twenty years of travel and adventure. New York: Harcourt, Brace, 1937
Free-lancing since the World War.

Que pensez-vous, Madame, de l'état de journaliste? Presse Publicité. no. 39, p. 6; no. 40, p. 13; no. 41, p. 9. June 7, 21, July 15, 1938
The wives of many famous contemporary journalists and foreign correspondents tell what they think of their husbands' profession, and how they have collaborated.

Reed, William P.
He wants to be bombed. Quill. 23:6. Oct. 1935
Karl von Wiegand's busy life as a foreign correspondent.

The Reporters who travel with presidents and princes. Literary Digest. 102:74-6. Sept. 14, 1929

Robinson, Sir John R.
Fifty years of Fleet Street. Comp. and ed. by Frederick Moy Thomas. 418p. London: Macmillan, 1904

Rue, Larry
I fly for news. 307p. New York: A. and C. Boni, 1932

Russell, Sir William Howard

About

The life of Sir William Howard Russell. John B. Atkins. 2v. London, John Murray, 1911
    Standard work on the life of the British war correspondent, noted particularly for his reports of the Crimean War.

Schierbrand, Wolf von
Confessions of a foreign correspondent. World's Work. 5:3355-8. Apr. 1903
    Foreign correspondent gives side-lights on German political and social methods in pre-World War days. Social gatherings are important news sources.

Sheean, Vincent
Personal history. 403p. New York: Doubleday, Doran, 1935
    Reporting in France, the Riff, China, Palestine, Russia.

Smalley, George Washburn
Anglo-American memories. 2v. New York: G. P. Putnam's Sons, 1912
    Correspondent for American newspaper tells his story.

Spender, John Alfred
Life, journalism and politics. 2v. New York: F. A. Stokes, 1927
    Editor of the *Westminster Gazette* discusses the press and foreign affairs, particularly the sequence of events leading up to the World War.

Steed, Henry Wickham
Through thirty years, 1892-1922. 2v. 418p. Garden City, N.Y.: Doubleday, Page, 1925
    A personal narrative of journalistic reminiscences through 30 years of contacts with politics and policies of various European nations and their newspapers.

Steffens, Lincoln
Autobiography of Lincoln Steffens. 884p. New York: Harcourt, Brace, 1931

Stillman, William James
The autobiography of a journalist. 2v. New York: Houghton Mifflin, 1901
    Ch.xi, v.i, deals with the subject of journalism. The author relates his experience as an employee of the *Evening Post* under the leadership of William Bryant.

Thompson, Alex M.
Here I lie: the memorial of an old journalist. 324p. London: Routledge, 1937

Vaughn, Miles W.
Covering the Far East. 408p. New York: Covici-Friede, 1936
    A veteran reporter's experiences in the Far East.

Wallace, Valentine
Grand old man of Fleet Street. Editor and Publisher. 51:5-6, 34; 51:13-14. July 20, 27, 1918
    Sir John M. LeSage, editorial director of *London Daily Telegraph*, relates some of his adventures in reporting world's big events.

Washburne, E. B.
Recollections of a minister to France, 1869-1877. 2v. New York: Charles Scribner's Sons, 1887

Whitman, Sidney
Things I remember. 267p. London, New York: Cassell, 1916
    The recollections of a political writer in the capitals of Europe.

Wiegand, Karl von

About

He wants to be bombed. William P. Reed. Quill. 23:6. Oct. 1935

Shop talk at thirty. Marlen Pew. Editor and Publisher. 67:44. Nov. 24, 1934

Wile, Frederic W.
News is where you find it. 505p. Indianapolis: Bobbs-Merrill, 1939
    Includes dramatic accounts of the correspondent's experiences in Germany and elsewhere, preceding and during the World War.

Williams, Valentine
The world of action: autobiography. 479p. London: H. Hamilton, 1938

Williams, Wythe
Dusk of empire. 325p. New York: Scribner's, 1937
    The decline of Europe and the rise of the United States as observed by a foreign correspondent in a quarter century of service.

Willison, Sir John

About

Press, politics and people: the life and letters of Sir John Willison, journalist and correspondent of the Times, by A. H. U. Colquhoun. Review by J. W. Dafoe. Canadian Historical Review. 17: 59-64. Mar. 1936

E.   FOREIGN CORRESPONDENTS IN THE UNITED STATES

Butcher, Harold
Foreign writers celebrate 21st year of U.S. "coverage" from abroad. Editor and Publisher. 58:40. Mar. 27, 1926

Editor urges more Pan-American news. Editor and Publisher. 62:34. July 13, 1929
    Dr. Hall of *La Prensa* urges establishment of Pan American section in dailies.

Foreign correspondents in the U.S. Editor and Publisher. 53:160. Jan. 22, 1921

Foreign journalists end two-month tour of U.S.—praise press freedom. Editor and Publisher. 62:20. July 20, 1929

Schuyler, Philip
London writers decry "sensational" play of Vestris inquiry in U.S. Editor and Publisher. 61:3. Dec. 1, 1928
    Cables sent to home papers charge "yellow journalism."

V. CENSORSHIP

See also
Censorship and Propaganda, (Germany) p.132, (Italy) p.149, (Russia) p.154, (China) p.167, (Japan), p.172.

A. GENERAL ANALYSES

Bachman, Albert
Censorship in France from 1715-1750; Voltaire's opposition. 206p. New York: Columbia Univ. Press, 1934

Beals, Carleton
Color in our foreign news. Outlook. 157: 300-2. Feb. 25, 1931
Obstacles which tax the resources of the correspondent who attempts to gather legitimate news.

Beating the news censor at his own game. Editor and Publisher. 59:5. May 29, 1926
American reporters abroad get the story out somehow; seven European nations now under strict censorship.

Beman, Lamar T.
Selected articles on censorship of speech and the press. 507p. (Handbook Series, ser. 3, v.5) New York: H. W. Wilson, 1930
The difficulties of censorship and how the problem has been dealt with in the United States.
Bibliography.

Boyd, Ernest
Readers and writers. Outlook and Independent. 151:233, 235. Feb. 6, 1929

British censorship of the U.S. Independent. 82:230. May 10, 1915

Brown, Constantine
Censors grip most of world's press. Editor and Publisher. 66:15, 66. Apr. 21, 1934
Seventy-four per cent of Europe's inhabitants were living under press censorship in 1934. Only one-ninth of the world's population live in nations where formal press censorship does not prevail.

Buchanan, N. B.
Some thoughts on censorship. Library World. 37:208-9. Mar. 1935

Burton, Wilbur
Ways of the Oriental censor. Fortnightly. 147:724-31. June 1937
Regimented opinion in nazi-fascist states is not original methodology. It stems from Confucius and the Middle Kingdom.

Callwell, Sir Charles Edward
The press censorship. Nineteenth Century. 85:1132-45. June 1919

Causton, Bernard and Young, G. Gordon
Keeping it dark; or, The censor's handbook. 8p. London: Mandrake Press, 1930

Censor of yesterday. Bookman. 42:9-10. Sept. 1915

The Censorship abroad. Nation. 99:513-14. Oct. 29, 1914

Censorship terror. Editor and Publisher. 65:24. Apr. 1, 1933

Censorship under three flags: Great Britain, Japan, Italy. Living Age. 355:310-21. Dec. 1938

Cheyney, Edward Potts
Present importance of the First Amendment. Annals of the American Academy. 195:331-8. Jan. 1938
This historian discusses the line of cleavage between the authoritarian and the democratic state; the First Amendment states the most distinctive principle of the latter.

Craig, Alec
Wider censorship. Discussion. New Statesman and Nation. 14:641, 680, 716. Oct. 23-Nov. 6, 1937

Cummings, Arthur J.
Censorship making foreign correspondent's work hazardous. Newspaper World. 40:4. Dec. 11, 1937

Czecho-Slovakia censorship. Editor and Publisher. 67:38. July 14, 1934

Ferguson, Fred S.
Honor-bound censorship is greatest menace. Editor and Publisher. 56:3. Nov. 24, 1923
Peace by publicity has not yet been tried. Press must free itself from manacles of diplomatic confidences before truth in international affairs can be reached.

Foster, J. E.
Censorship as a medium of propaganda. Sociology and Social Research. 22:57-66. Sept. 1937
An analytical study of censorship showing that it may originate from political, social or economic motives.
Bibliographical footnotes.

Goebbels gives Nazi views on foreign press. Newsdom. 5:2. Mar. 24, 1934
Philosophy for foreign newspapermen working in Berlin.

Houben, Heinrich H.
Hier Zensur—wer dort? 207p. Leipzig: Brockhaus, 1918
Yesterday's answers to the questions of censorship today."
Verbotene Literatur von der klassischen Zeit bis zur Gegenwart. 2v. Dessau: Karl Rauch, 1925-28
Historical survey of censorship.

James, Lionel
High pressure. 314p. London: J. Murray, 1929
Activities in the service of the *Times*; the record of a war correspondent.
Times of stress. 320p. London: J. Murray, 1932

Johnson, Albin E.
League Council to study press censorship. Editor and Publisher. 60:9. Sept. 17, 1927
Adopts resolution opposing peacetime control of news.

Johnson, Albin E.—*Continued*
Moral disarmament treaty seen as new aid to censorship. Editor and Publisher. 65:19. July 2, 1932
150 million "mental robots" are pawns of dictators in European war scare. Editor and Publisher. 68:5. Sept. 7, 1935
  It is difficult for the foreign correspondent to get reliable news because most of the world is censor-ridden.
300 million citizens of Europe living under iron rule of censorship. Editor and Publisher. 67:3. June 30, 1934
  Seventy-four per cent of Europe's population living under press censorship.

Koenigsberg tells of foreign censors. Editor and Publisher. 60:22. Jan. 7, 1928
  Foreign governments hinder gathering and publication of news which they consider critical or impolitic.

Lawrence, Raymond D. See Young, Kimball, jt. auth.

MacPherson, Harriet Dorothea
Censorship under Louis XIV, 1661-1715: some aspects of its influence. 176p. New York: Institute of French Studies, 1929

Nafziger, Ralph O.
World war correspondents and censorship of the belligerents. Journalism Quarterly. 14:226-43. Sept. 1937

News freedom is lost abroad. Newsdom. 5:8. Nov. 3, 1934

Paris censors foreign news. Newsdom. 6:2. May 11, 1935

Peignot, Gabriel
Dictionnaire critique, littéraire et bibliographique des principaux livres condamnés au feu, suprimés ou censurés. 2v. Paris: A. A. Renouard, 1806
  A critical, literary and bibliographic dictionary of the principal books burned, suppressed or censored.

Restrictions on free publication of news. World's Press News. 13:25. Apr. 11, 1935
  Court of morals worst form of censorship.

Salmon, Lucy Maynard
The newspaper and authority. 505p. London, New York: Oxford Univ. Press, 1923
  Particularly useful as a guide book for studies in censorship.

Schroeder, Theodore Albert, comp.
Free speech bibliography. New York: H. W. Wilson Co., 1922
  Attitudes toward the problem; methods of transmitting ideas; methods of censorship.

Seldes, George
The poisoned springs of world news. Harper's. 169:719-31. Nov. 1934

Senator would ban war censorship. Editor and Publisher. 67:12. Apr. 13, 1935

Sharp, Eugene
The censorship and press laws of sixty countries. (Univ. of Missouri Bulletin. Journalism Series, no. 77) Columbia, Mo.: 1936
  A convenient digest of press laws throughout the world.

Slavic darkness. Editor and Publisher. 65:18. Sept. 10, 1932
  King Alexander's dictatorship over the press in Jugoslavia.

Spain crushes final hope of freedom. Editor and Publisher. 67:33. Feb. 16, 1935

Struve, Gustav
Actenstücke der Mannheimer Censur und Polizei. 160p. Mannheim: Im Verlage des Herausgebers, 1846

Taylor, William Sentman
Why not censureship? Sewanee Review. 43:311-26. July 1935

La Vie de la presse étrangère: Japon. Presse Publicité. no.22, p.10. Oct. 17, 1937
  Note on the work of the censors in Japan.

Warns against indirect curb on newspapers. Newsdom. 5:1, 3. June 9, 1934
  Arthur Hays Sulzberger, president of *The New York Times*, declares that freedom of the press might be abridged in other ways than by direct censorship.

Where the censor might halt. Literary Digest. 55:20. Dec. 15, 1917

Whipple, Leon
Freedom of communication in America; growth and development of free speech in the Colonial period. Congressional Digest. 9:38-41. Feb. 1930
  Steps in the struggle for free speech and press in America described by citing examples such as the famous Zenger trial and the Sedition Act of 1798.

Wilford, John T.
Deported editor attacks censorship. Editor and Publisher. 63:7, 46. Feb. 14, 1931
  Cuban President Machado's suppression of Havana newspapers in direct violation of Constitution.

Young, G. Gordon. See Causton, Bernard, jt. auth.

Young, Kimball and Lawrence, Raymond D.
Bibliography on censorship and propaganda. 133p. (University of Oregon Publications. Journalism Series, v.1, no.1) Eugene, Ore.: Univ. of Oregon Press, 1928

B. SPECIFIC CASES OF PRESS CENSORSHIP

Berkson, Seymour
Facing the foreign censor. Journalism Quarterly. 13:7-16. Mar. 1936
  Journalism in Italy is not a vocation but a "push-button" mechanism which responds instantly to the touch of Il Duce. Rigid press censorship is practiced by France whenever the need arises. The author is an experienced Hearst foreign editor.

Censor's instructions; text of circular from the Department of Press and Tourism. Spectator. 161:293. Aug. 19, 1938

Censorship beaten by U. P. correspondent. Editor and Publisher. 59:42. July 10, 1926
    Webb Miller, member of London staff, wires Primo de Rivera direct in order to get news through Spanish censors.

Chamberlain, William Henry
According to the press. Christian Science Monitor. Weekly Magazine Section. p.6, 12. July 15, 1936
    The fourth estate in Russia and in Japan show marked differences in public temperament and news emphasis, but both serve as object lessons on muzzled journalism.

Irwin, Will
The news that passes the war censor. Guild Reporter. 2:5. Nov. 1, 1935

Johnson, Albin E.
Fight on censorship will continue. Editor and Publisher. 65:10. Mar. 4, 1933
    A Geneva correspondent expresses dissatisfaction with the results of the debate on peacetime censorship at the International Telegraphic and Radio-Telegraphic Conference in Madrid, September to mid-December, 1932.

Manchester Guardian Shanghai correspondent "invited" to Japanese censor's office. World's Press News. 18:11. Jan. 20, 1938

Manning, George H.
Press gag averted in "secrets" bill. Editor and Publisher. 65:7. Apr. 8, 1933

Nakano, Suyeo
Press censorship. Trans-Pacific. 16:5. June 30, 1928

National Guard given authority to censor Louisiana newspapers. Editor and Publisher. 67:8. Feb. 2, 1935

Perry, John W.
Dictator's fist crushes Cuban press as opposition to Machado grows. Editor and Publisher. 65:3-4. Feb. 11, 1933

Indirect intimidation is new technique in foreign news censorship. Editor and Publisher. 64:5. June 27, 1931

Prelate hits Sun article. Newsdom. 5:2. July 7, 1934

Reference to Loyola aroused Catholics. Editor and Publisher. 67:9. July 21, 1934
    Baltimore Sun allows no censorship.

Russian lèse majesté. Editor and Publisher. 10:21. Dec. 24, 1910
    St. Petersburg editors imprisoned for printing a speech made in Douma.

Seldes, George
Can these things be! 433p. New York: Brewer, Warren and Putnam, 1931
    Pt. II. "The Truth Behind Censorship," p.195-287. Discusses corruption of press by fascism; bunkum in American press; church censorship.

The poisoned springs of world news. Harper's. 169:719-31. Nov. 1934

You can't print that! 465p. Garden City, N.Y.: Payson and Clarke, 1929
    The news behind the news, 1918-1928, by a foreign correspondent who ran afoul of censorships and propaganda.

Sinclair, Upton
How censorship actually works. Everybody's. 26:135-6. Jan. 1912

Stone, Melville E.
The Associated Press: the removal of the Russian censorship on foreign news. Century. 70:143-51. May 1905

Streit of Times exiled from Rumania; protest rigid censorship rules. Editor and Publisher. 59:5. May 29, 1926
    Correspondent declines to recant series of articles which aroused wrath of government officials.

Yun, Arthur
The American revolt against Chinese censorship. China Weekly Review. 57: 421-2. Aug. 15, 1931

C. MISCELLANEOUS DISCUSSION

Auerbach, Joseph Smith
Authorship and liberty. Argument before the Appellate Division of the Supreme Court (first department), in the suppression of The Genius by Theodore Dreiser. North American Review. 207: 902-17. June 1918

Beman, Lamar T.
Selected articles on censorship of the theatre and moving pictures. 385p. New York: H. W. Wilson, 1931

Cable censorship causes stir here. Trans-Pacific. 13:13. Jan. 16, 1926

Great Britain, United States protest Japanese cable censorship. China Weekly Review. 83:261. Feb. 5, 1938

Japanese impose cable censorship. World's Press News. 18:18. Dec. 9, 1937
    Japanese install censors in Shanghai offices during Sino-Japanese War.

Manning, George H.
Law passed in 1921 permits U.S. bureau to censor advertising. Editor and Publisher. 66:12. Dec. 23, 1933

Neilson, William Allan
The theory of censorship. Atlantic Monthly. 145:13-16. Jan. 1930
    A discussion of censorship as it applies in the fields of literature and art.

Poynter, J. W.
Papal Index. Saturday Review. 153:270. Mar. 12, 1932
    Without arguing as to the merits of the institution Mr. Poynter names an interesting list of books forbidden in Indice dei Libri Prohibiti. Rome: Vatican Press, 1929.

Putnam, George H.
The censorship of the Church of Rome and its influence upon the production and distribution of literature. 2v. New York: G. P. Putnam's Sons, 1906-07
"A study of the prohibitory and expurgatory indexes, together with some consideration of the effects of Protestant censorship and of censorship by the State."
Bibliography: v.1, p. xvii-xxv.

Shillito, Edward
Alfred Noyes defies Church; refuses to alter book on Voltaire. Christian Century. 55:1102. Sept. 14, 1938

Williams, Michael
Views and reviews; Mr. Noyes's study of Voltaire. Commonweal. 28:555-6. Sept. 23, 1938

VI. PRESS LAW

See also
Press Regulation (United States) p.91; Press Laws (France) p.120, (Germany) p.131, (Great Britain) p.140, (Italy) p.149, (Russia) p.155, (China) p.167, (Japan) p.173.

A. FREEDOM OF THE PRESS

Ackerman, Carl William
Shall we control the press and radio; is it essential to world peace? German treaty proposals. Vital Speeches. 4: 382-4. Apr. 1, 1938
Shop talk at thirty. Editor and Publisher. 66:60. Mar. 3, 1934
Carl Ackerman discusses freedom of press as Hitler, Mussolini and Stalin interpret it.

Adam, Kenneth
Freemen of the press? Fortnightly. 150 (ns 144):34-41. July 1938

Adams, Franklin Pierce
Freedom of the press. New Republic. 94:15. Feb. 9, 1938

Adams, John
Ostracised frankness in America. Bookman (London) 64:224-5. Aug. 1923

Alengry, F.
"La liberté de la presse vue par Condorcet (1771-1776). Cahiers de la Presse. 1: 10-26. Jan.-Mar. 1939
The ideas of Condorcet on liberty of the press, as enunciated in his correspondence with Voltaire, the Encyclopœdists, and Turgot.

American press liberties limited in practice. New Republic. 68:138. Sept. 23, 1931

Anderson, Maxwell
Blue pencil. New Republic. 17:192-4. Dec. 14, 1918

Are we to have a reptile press? North American Review. 209:9-12. Jan. 1919

Attention Roy Howard. Nation. 146:548. May 14, 1938

Beard, Charles A.
On the advantages of censorship and espionage. New Republic. 27:350-1. Aug. 24, 1921

Belloc, Hilaire
The free press. 102p. London: G. Allen and Unwin, 1918
Mr. Belloc criticizes the "capitalist press" for misinforming the public.

Bliven, Bruce
Little liberty left. American Press. 52: 17. May 1934

Bliven sees losing fight against forces of press repression. Editor and Publisher. 67:14. Mar. 23, 1935

Block gives journalism status in five European countries. Editor and Publisher. 67:16. Sept. 29, 1934
Free press is a fact in England and France, publisher says, but in Italy, Austria and Germany it is non-existent.

Blue-penciled news: I. What Germans read; II. Secret orders to Italian editors. Living Age. 352:434-9. July 1937
News is indistinguishable from propaganda in Germany, Italy, Russia and many other countries. Examples show how the Nazi and Fascist regimes control their press.

Bolitho, William
Eyes and ears of democracy. Survey. 57: 731-3. Mar. 1, 1927

Brindze, Ruth
Freedom of the press again. Nation. 145: 98-9. July 24, 1937
Newspaper publishers declare that radio is unacceptable as medium for news transmission because it is licensed, therefore not free. Publishers at the same time have entered the radio field by acquiring more than 200 stations.

Brooks, George
Freedom of the press and collective bargaining. American Federationist. 44: 282-93. Mar. 1937
Bibliographical footnotes.

Broun, Heywood
Advertising and the free press. New Republic. 93:195. Dec. 22, 1937
Divine diversity. New Republic. 97:15. Nov. 9, 1938

Burton, Wilbur
Ways of the Oriental censor. Fortnightly. 147(n.s. 141) 724-31. June 1937

Chafee, Zechariah, jr.
Milwaukee Leader case. Nation. 112: 428-9. Mar. 23, 1921
The Supreme Court extended the power of the Postmaster-General to control the press in peacetime.

Clark, Grenville
Limits of free expression. United States Law Review. 73:392-404. July 1939

Dale, George R.
Fight for freedom of the press. Literary Digest. 90:9. Aug. 14, 1926

Dawson, Samuel Arthur
Freedom of the press. 120p. New York: Columbia Univ. Press, 1924
The legal doctrine of "qualified privilege": the right of citizens of a liberal government to publish, without malice, fair and true reports of judicial, legislative or other public and official proceedings.

Document on liberty; open letter from William Allen White to Governor Allen. Literary Digest. 74:32. Aug. 19, 1922

Dominique, Pierre
La liberté de la presse. L'Europe Nouvelle. 21:179. Feb. 19, 1938

Durham, Mary Edith
Very free press. New Statesman and Nation. 1:352-3. May 2, 1931

Eccentricities of Nippon's post office censors. China Weekly Review. 68:403-4. May 12, 1934

Engelbrecht, H. C.
Singeing the beard of the Spanish censor. World Tomorrow. 9:222-3. Nov. 1926

Europe's declining freedom of the press. Literary Digest. 117:15. Apr. 14, 1934

Fagan, John E.
Liberty of the press. American Catholic Quarterly. 48:68-71. Jan. 1923

Ford, Douglas M.
The growth of freedom of the press. English Historical Review. 4:1-12. Jan. 1889
The author traces various legislative steps leading to greater press freedom. The right to report debates of Parliament was granted in 1731.

Fortune survey: the press, its fairness and freedom. Fortune. 16:170, 173. Oct. 1937
A short statistical survey.

Frank, Glenn
Critical function in democracy. Vital Speeches. 1:550-2. May 20, 1935
The corrective voice of criticism is imperative in the modern world. Democracy broadens the base of judgment, dictatorships narrows it.

Free religious press. Commonweal. 27:393-4. Feb. 4, 1938

Freedom of the press. New Statesman (London) 27:4-5; 116-17. Apr. 17, May 15, 1926

Freedom of the press. Outlook. 102:831. Dec. 21, 1912

Freedom of the press. Survey. 24:365-8. June 4, 1910

The **Freedom** of the press. Vital Speeches. 5:238-42. Feb. 1, 1939
A discussion of English viewpoints by Dingle Foot, Nicholas Macaskie, Sir Stanley Reed, Lord Meston.

Freedom of the press in France. Nation. 108:305-6. Feb. 22, 1919

Freund, Ernst
Burning heretics. New Republic. 21:266-7. Jan. 28, 1920
Debs case and freedom of speech. New Republic. 19:13-15. May 3, 1919
Freedom of speech and press. New Republic. 25:344-6. Feb. 16, 1921

Garr, Max
Parlament und Presse. 75p. (Wiener Staatswissenschaftliche Studien, Bd. 8) Vienna, Leipzig: Franz Deuticke, 1908
Explains rights of press relative to parliamentary (government) procedure; traces their development in various constitutional countries.

Good, E. T.
Labour and the capitalist press. Spectator. 125:808-9. Dec. 18, 1920

Gotwald, William Kurtz
Ecclesiastical censure at the end of the fifteenth century. p.1-87. (Johns Hopkins Univ. Studies, v.45). Baltimore: Johns Hopkins Press, 1927

Greenwood, Frederick
The press and government. Nineteenth Century. 28:108-18. July 1890

Guardian corroborates illegality of Japanese censorship. China Weekly Review. 83:228-9. Jan. 29, 1938

Hall, Robert
An apology for the freedom of the press and for general liberty. 108p. London: 1793

Hanson, Elisha
Liberty's debt to the press, freedom's greatest safeguard. Vital Speeches. 4:752-6. Oct. 1, 1938
Publishers' legal counsel presents his views on encroachments by government.
Life, liberty and property; need for a free press. Vital Speeches. 4:254-6. Feb. 1, 1938

Headlam, Cecil
Censorship of the press. Quarterly Review. 234:123-46. July 1920

Hilaire Belloc's hope for the free press in England. Current Opinion. 65:250-1. Oct. 1918

Janmart de Brouillant, Léonce
La liberté de la presse en France aux XVIIe et XVIIIe siècles. 324p. Paris: Maison Quantin, 1888

Johnson, Albin E.
Fight for free speech and press fiercely fought in Saar, Danzig. Editor and Publisher. 66:31. Mar. 17, 1934
Both areas, under Council of League of Nations, have papers stoutly resisting suppression aims of Fascists and Nazis.

Johnson, Gerald White
Freedom of the newspaper press. Annals of the American Academy. 200:60-75. Nov. 1938
Mr. Johnson adduces evidence that the final arbiter of freedom of the press is not statute law, the Constitution, courts, or the army, but public opinion.

Johnson, Gerald White—*Continued*
Unfortunate necessity; freedom of the press and the public confidence. Century. 112:41-7. May 1926

Johnston, Sir Harry Hamilton
The press and the government of today. English Review. 21:166-77. Sept. 1915

Julien, Jules
Les sévères mesures de censure qui sont en usage dans certains pays sont bannies de l'administration française. Presse Publicité. no. 50, p.3. Dec. 21, 1938
The severe measures of censorship used by certain countries are banned by the French government.

Kane, Francis Fisher
Civil liberty in France. Survey. 45:509-10. Jan. 1, 1921

Kennedy, Malcolm Duncan
Freedom of the press; the great illusion. Nineteenth Century. 122:166-78. Aug. 1937

Kerr, Charles
Shall we have a free press? Outlook. 121:18-19. Jan. 1, 1919

Lang, George
Free press and religious freedom. Vital Speeches. 5:693-9. Sept. 1, 1939

The **Liberty** of the press. Dublin Review. 7:518-40. Nov. 1839

Liberty of the press. Edinburgh Review. 18:98-123. May 1811
Review of *Mémoires de Candide sur la liberté de la presse, la paix générale, les fondemens de l'ordre social, et d'autres bagatelles.* By Emmanuel Ralph.
This review is followed by observations on freedom of the press in Great Britain. The book itself, a satire in which the author professes to continue the adventures of Voltaire's celebrated hero, was first published in Altona, Germany, in 1808. It satirizes the difference between professions of press freedom in Paris and the experiences of the hero who sets out to take advantage of the liberty of the press. The French translation, based on the 3rd German edition, was said to have been "circulated by stealth."

Lord Campbell and Mr. Charles A. Huxley. New Statesman and Nation. 10:673. Nov. 9, 1935

Lytton, Edward Robert Bulwer-Lytton, 1st earl of
Liberty of the press: an old fable. (Poem). Fortnightly Review. 24:178-88. Aug. 1, 1875

McCormick, Robert R.
Freedom fight saved press. Editor and Publisher. 66:32, 34. Apr. 28, 1934
Chicago Tribune publisher presents his viewpoint on the fight against threats by government to freedom of the press.

McMaster, John Balch
A free press in the middle colonies. New Princeton Review. 1:78-90. Jan. 1886

McNaughton, John G.
Politics, not commerce, threatens free press, says English reporter. Editor and Publisher. 68:16. July 27, 1935

Madrolle, Antoine
Des crimes de la presse. 224p. Paris: Potey, 1825

Meyer, Mrs. Eugene
Freedom of the press, freedom of speech and religious tolerance. Academy of Political Science, Proceedings. 18:301-10. May 1939

Milton, John
Areopagitica. 159p. Oxford: Clarendon Press, 1878
First published in 1644.

Mr. Wells and the Daily Mail. New Statesman (London) 18:250-1. Dec. 3, 1921

Modern ideals and the liberty of the press. Dublin Review. 81:193-222. July 1877

Myth of a free press. Nation. 128:576. May 15, 1929

Nash, Vernon
Freedom within the press. China Weekly Review. 77:312. Aug. 1, 1936

Naudeau, Ludovic
La liberté de la presse et le fascisme. L'Illustration. 168:460-2. Oct. 30, 1926

New varieties of censorship. Survey. 43:222-4. Dec. 13, 1919

On news suppression; speakers at Socialist Press Club dinner attack Collier's Weekly and the A.P. Editor and Publisher. 13:453. Nov. 22, 1913

Paper suspended for criticism. Newsweek. 3:15. May 12, 1934

Peignot, Gabriel
Dictionnaire critique, littéraire et bibliographique des principaux livres condamnés au feu, suprimés ou censurés. 2v. Paris: A. A. Renouard, 1806

Press censorship by judicial construction. New Republic. 26:123-5. Mar. 30, 1921

Press freedom is safeguard against violent revolution. World's Press News. 22:2. Aug. 17, 1939

Press freedom war sponsored by publishers. Newsdom. 5:1-2. Apr. 28, 1934

Die **Pressefreiheit** in England. Zeitungswissenschaft. 12:694-6. Oct. 1, 1937

Publishers protest Leipzig Congress; freedom of the press called basic need of publishing. Publisher's Weekly. 133:194, 211-13. Jan. 15, 1938

Robson, Norman
The Official Secrets Act and the British press. Journalism Quarterly. 15:253-8. Sept. 1938
Act construed against lobby journalists to prevent publication of confidential information. Author cites cases of its use against journalists and is very critical of it as being prejudicial to freedom of the press.

Rogers, Lindsay
Freedom of the press in the United States. Contemporary Review. 114:177-83. Aug. 1918
The postal power of Congress as it affects freedom of the press. p.245-71 (Johns Hopkins Univ. Studies, v.34) Baltimore: Johns Hopkins Press, 1916

Ross, Edward Alsworth
Suppression of important news. Atlantic Monthly. 105:303-11. Mar. 1910

Rowell, Chester H.
Freedom of the press. Annals of the American Academy. 185:182-9. May 1936

Rudd, Martin
Democracy and the press; world's freeest press and the forces that affect what it prints. Scholastic. 32:255-85. Mar. 26, 1938

Sakanishi, Shio
Prohibition of import of certain Chinese books and the policy of the Edo Government. American Oriental Society Journal. 57:290-303. Sept. 1937
Bibliographical footnotes.

Schroeder, Theodore Albert, ed.
Free press anthology. 267p. New York City: Free Speech League, Truth Seeker Publishing Co., 1909
Free speech bibliography. New York: H.W. Wilson; London: Grafton and Co., 1922
Attitudes toward the problem; methods of transmitting ideas; methods of censorship.

Schuyler, L. R.
Liberty of the press in the American colonies before the Revolutionary War. Nation. 83:267-8. Sept. 27, 1906

Seldes, George
Freedom of the press. 380p. Indianapolis, New York: Bobbs-Merrill, 1935
The business-dominated press suppresses the news. An emotional exposition of the subject.

Smith, C. E.
Press: its liberty and license. Independent. 55:1371-5. June 11, 1903

Society pledges free press defense. Editor and Publisher. 66:22. Apr. 28, 1934
Editors' Society convention adopts resolutions to oppose potential censor.

Spender, John Alfred
Liberty of the press. Spectator. 155:857-8. Nov. 22, 1935

Stephen, Leslie
The suppression of poisonous opinions. Nineteenth Century. 13:493-508, 653-66. Mar.-Apr. 1883

Stevens, Orin Alva
Freedom of the press and the scientist. Science. n.s. 86:491-2. Nov. 26, 1937

The **Sun** rises in Baltimore. Survey. 46:491. July 16, 1921

Suppression of malicious, scandalous and defamatory newspapers and periodicals by injunction on the suit of the state held to violate the constitutional guarantee of freedom of the press. Law and Labor. 13:153-8. July 1931

Supreme Court strikes at the press. Nation. 112:422. Mar. 23, 1921
Impugns Supreme Court decision upholding right of Postmaster-General to bar from the mails, in this case, the *Milwaukee Leader* edited by Victor Berger.

They snoop to conquer. Saturday Review. 147:309-10. Mar. 9, 1929

Tributes to the ideal of freedom of expression. Annals of the American Academy. 200:292-306. Nov. 1938
Quotations from Socrates, Milton, John Locke, and other thinkers on freedom of inquiry and expression of opinions.

Unmuzzling the press. Literary Digest. 69:11. June 11, 1921

Valot, Stephen
L'Organisation Internationale des Journalistes et la liberté de la Presse. Cahiers de la Presse. 1:369-76. July-Sept. 1938
The International Federation of Journalists seeks to extend its membership to all countries but refuses to yield to or affiliate itself with organizations which uphold totalitarian principles.

Villard, Oswald Garrison
The freedom of the press. The American Scholar. 3:28-39. Jan. 1934
American press has been negligent in defending American liberties but "has demanded freedom to debase the public taste." Mr. Villard considers the N.R.A. and its relation to the press.
On telling truths in the presence of admirals. Christian Century. 41:1211-12. Sept. 18, 1924

Vingtain, Jean Thomas Léon
De la liberté de la presse. 432p. Paris: M. Levy Frères, 1860
Concerning the freedom of the press, with an appendix containing the warnings, suspensions and suppressions incurred by the daily and periodical press from 1848 to 1860.

White, William Allen
How free is our press? Nation. 146:693-5. June 18, 1938
Elaborate mechanical devices involving heavy investment have changed the character of American journalism.

Whose freedom of the press? New Republic. 91:266. July 14, 1937
The closed-shop proposal of the American Newspaper Guild stimulates publishers to charge that the plan menaces freedom of the press.

Why Japan banned Blakeslee's book on censorship. China Weekly Review. 71:345-6. Feb. 9, 1935

Wickwar, William H.
The struggle for the freedom of the press, 1819-1832. 326p. New York, London: Allen and Unwin, 1928

Wright, Herbert
Henry Brooke's Gustavus Vasa. Modern Language Review. 14:173-82. Apr. 1919
Bibliographical footnotes.

B. LAWS

Ackermann, W.
Pressefreiheit? Zeitungswissenschaft. 6:
340-3. 1931

Action against newspaper for misleading advice. U.S. Law Review. 71:248-52. May 1937

Ancel, Marc
La diffamation et la réform du régime de la presse. Cahiers de la Presse. 1:349-56. July-Sept. 1938
How the French attitude toward libel and slander and means of redressment at law differs from the Anglo-American.

Austerlitz, Fritz
Pressefreiheit und Presserecht. 126p. Vienna: J. Brand, 1902

Brown, Rome G.
Some points on the law of the press. American Law Review. 56:514-51. July, 1922
Restraints on the freedom of the press, with many illustrative cases and extensive documentation.

California court ruling bars right of press to comment on pending cases. Newsweek. 12:29. Aug. 29, 1938

Chaudet, Gustave
La règlementation administrative de la presse dans les principaux pays. 158p. Vevey: Marchino, 1938

Dickinson, Edwin D.
Defamation of foreign governments. American Journal of International Law. 22: 840-4. Oct. 1928
Defamation by publishers of persons in authority in foreign countries may be construed as libel. Hearst's Mexican forgeries are considered.

Edge, Norman Charles Worthington
Libel and peace of Europe. World's Press News. 20:499, p.17. Sept. 22, 1938
Story of libels against foreign potentates.

Goodhart, A. L.
Newspapers and contempt of court in English law. Harvard Law Review. 48:885-910. Apr. 1935
Bibliographical footnotes.

Guardian corroborates illegality of Japanese censorship. China Weekly Review. 83: 228-9. Jan. 29, 1938

Gusti, Demetrius
Die Grundbegriffe des Presserechts. 131p. Berlin: J. Guttentag, 1908
A study of the fundamental problems in the law of the press.

Harley, Hugh J.
Strange contrasts in press laws of various nations. Editor and Publisher. 58:16. Mar. 27, 1926
British Foreign Office compiles large volume of foreign statutes as result of recent British agitation for drastic regulation.

Hudson, Manley O.
International protection of property in news. American Journal of International Law. 22:385-9. Apr. 1928
Publishers of news in the United States are protected only to a limited extent by the copyright law.

Hungarian press law causes riot. Editor and Publisher. 13:649. Feb. 7, 1914
Press reform bill designed to protect government against attacks by the press.

Johnson, Albin E.
Professional honor of news writers protected by contracts abroad. Editor and Publisher. 62:22. Sept. 21, 1929

Kenealy, Alex
Conscience of the English editor. Editor and Publisher. 13:178. Aug. 16, 1913
He is carefully hedged about by libel laws, contempt of court rules, and conservative public sentiment. See reply by George A. Schreiner, "Mr. Kenealy and American Editors." Editor and Publisher. 13:194. Aug. 23, 1913.

Levi, K. E.
Press and the Constitution. Wisconsin Magazine of History. 16:383-403. June 1933
Bibliographical footnotes.

Manchukuo invokes crushing press law. China Weekly Review. 65:460. Aug. 12, 1933

Manton, Martin T.
"Popularizing" the law and "legalizing" the news. U.S. Law Review. 65:419-25. Aug. 1931

Nisot, Marie-Thérèse
The protection of professional titles. I-II. International Labour Review. 41:30-5, 124-5. Jan.-Feb. 1940
By the general secretary of the Belgian Confederation of Professional Workers. Pt. I includes introduction and general regulations; pt. II, section on "Journalists," p.124-5, in Belgium, France, Germany, Great Britain, Greece and Hungary.

No property in news, says Koenigsberg. Editor and Publisher. 61:30. Apr. 27, 1929
Neither Supreme Court of United States nor Geneva Conference recognized right to monopoly.

Police and the Press. Spectator. 160:666. Apr. 15, 1938

Press and the bar. U.S. Law Review. 68: 457-9. Sept. 1934
Discussion, 68:557-60. Oct. 1934.
Sensational treatment of court trials by the press is subjected to analysis and criticism by members of the bar.

Property in news heads Geneva program. Editor and Publisher. 59:5. Aug. 28, 1926
Press Association chiefs will address League on public character of official news.

Qu' est-ce qu' une fausse nouvelle? Presse Publicité. no.41, p.5-6. July 1938
Translation of a Swiss editorial on what constitutes false news; the manner in which it must be combatted.

Rayner, O. T. See Sherman, Montague, jt. auth.

Recueil universel de lois et décrets. v.I. 738p. Geneva: Center of International Legislative Information, 1938
A monthly publication of legislative activity in the world. The matter is culled from some 100 official journals, arranged under several principal branches of law.
The section devoted to texts and analyses of laws and decrees affecting the press is a useful compilation.
French and English.

Right of reply law vexes French press. Editor and Publisher. 53:29. Mar. 12, 1921
Anyone mentioned in French press may reply at equal length.

Ross, Edward Alsworth
Social control. II—Law and public opinion. American Journal of Sociology. 1:753-70. May 1896

Saunders, E. Paul
Human element of the fourth estate; based on conditions of work and life of journalists. Study made by the International Labor Office. American Federationist. 37:429-36, 577-80, 708-12, 846-50. Apr.-July 1930

Schreiner, George Abel
Mr. Kenealy and American editors. Editor and Publisher. 13:194. Aug. 23, 1913
Libel laws and contempt of court rulings not the unmixed blessings they seem. Reply to Alex Kenealy's criticism. See Alex Kenealy, "Conscience of the English Editor." Editor and Publisher. 13:178. Aug. 16, 1913.

Sherman, Montague and Rayner, O. T.
The press laws of foreign countries. London: H.M. Stationery Office, 1926

Suppression of malicious, scandalous and defamatory newspapers and periodicals by injunction on the suit of the State held to violate the constitutional guarantee of freedom of the press. Law and Labor. 13:153-8. July 1931

Supreme Court recognizes property rights in news by gathering associations. Editor and Publisher. 51:5-6, 27-32. Dec. 28, 1918
Court, by a 5 to 3 decision, upholds Associated Press in its suit against International News Service and continues injunction preventing the latter from pirating dispatches or bulletins and from bribing employees to give tips on news matters.

Thompson, Slason
Newspapers; their rights and duties. Open Court. 3:2058-60. Jan. 23, 1890

Werth, Alexander
Poor France! New Statesman and Nation. 12:971-3. Dec. 12, 1936

Wettstein, Otto
Über das Verhältnis zwischen Staat und Presse. 94p. Zürich: A. Müller. 1904
A discussion of freedom of the press, with special reference to Switzerland.

Working conditions of journalists in various countries. Monthly Labor Review. 28: 45-8. Jan. 1929

VII. PROPAGANDA

See also
World War, 1914—Official Press Bureaus, p.84; Second World War, 1939—Propaganda, p.102; France—Propaganda and Public Opinion, p.122; Censorship and Propaganda (Germany) p.132, (Russia) p.154, (China) p.167, (Japan) p.172.

A. HISTORY AND THEORY

Abel, Theodore Fred
Pattern of a successful political movement. American Sociological Review. 2:347-52. June 1937
Bibliographical footnotes.

Baudrillart, Alfred
Notre propagande. La Revue Hebdomadaire. 4:141-84. Apr. 1916

Bell, Edward Price
The press and social safety. Academy of Political Science, Proceedings. 12:460-70. July 1926
Emphasizes the dependence of democracy upon the press, asserting that democracy throughout the world is on trial.

Berchtold, William E.
The world propaganda war. North American Review. 238:421-30. Nov. 1934

Bernays, Edward L.
Propaganda. 159p. New York: H. Liveright, 1928
The propagandist forms public opinion, changing the habits of the people. An apologia for the public relations counsel.
Public education for democracy. Annals of the American Academy. 198:124-7. July 1938
——and Lundberg, Ferdinand
Does propaganda menace democracy? Forum. 99:341-5. June 1938
——See Martin, E. D. jt. auth.

Biddle, William W.
Psychological definition of propaganda. Journal of Abnormal Psychology. 26: 283-95. Oct. 1931
Bibliography.

Blumenstock, Dorothy. See Lasswell, Harold D. jt. auth.

Brown, Ralph Adams
New Hampshire editors win the war; a study in revolutionary press propaganda. New England Quarterly. 12: 35-51. Mar. 1939
Showing the wide use of Whig and Tory press propaganda during the American Revolution.

Buck, Pearl S. (Mrs. Richard John Walsh)
Friends and enemies of China. Asia. 36: 279-80. Apr. 1936

Busch, Moritz
Bismarck; some secret pages of his history. 2v. London, New York: Macmillan, 1898
A private diary kept by Dr. Busch during 25 years of official and private contacts with Chancellor Bismarck.

Casey, Ralph D. See Lasswell, Harold D. jt. auth.

Childs, Harwood L.
Public opinion—first line of defense. Annals of the American Academy. 198: 109-15. July 1938
The types and functions of propaganda. The author suggests methods for the relieving of "psychological tensions."

Chinese children get Japanese propaganda. Asia. 38:661. Nov. 1938

Communist plottings in the Far East. map, tables Far Eastern Review. 34:129-34. Apr. 1938

Complete impartiality. New Statesman and Nation. 9:64-5. Jan. 19, 1935
Discussion, 9:102, 138, 171. Jan. 26-Feb. 9, 1935.

Copeland, Fayette
Civil War editors called it propaganda. Journalism Quarterly. 14:144-5. June 1937
A discussion of the meaning acquired by the word "propaganda"; its history.

Curse of propaganda. Independent. 110: 4-5. Jan. 6, 1923

Davidson, Philip G.
Whig propagandists of the American revolution. American Historical Review. 39: 422-53. Apr. 1934
Bibliographical footnotes.

Dennis, Lawrence
Propaganda for war: model 1938. American Mercury. 44:1-10. May 1938

Doob, Leonard W.
Propaganda; its psychology and technique. 424p. New York: Henry Holt, 1935

Elvin, René
Purpose of propaganda. Spectator. 163: 20. July 7, 1939

Engelbrecht, H. C.
How war propaganda won. World Tomorrow. 10:159-62. Apr. 1927

Erdmann, Carl
Die Anfänge der staatlichen Propaganda im Investiturstreit. Bibliog. für Historische Zeitschrift. 154:491-512. 1936
The beginning state of propaganda in the litigation over investitures during the quarrel between Pope Gregory VII and Emperor Henry IV (1076).

Fairsworth, John
How anti-American sentiment is fostered in Japan. China Weekly Review. 63: 475. Feb. 18, 1933

First aid to propaganda-hunters. Scholastic. 31:11-12. Oct. 9, 1937

Fisher, Herbert W.
Propaganda in Russia. New Republic. 15:319. July 13, 1918

Fletcher, Richard
The trail of the serpent. Saturday Review. 161:780. June 20, 1936

Flynn, John Thomas
Recovery through war scares. New Republic. 96:360-1. Nov. 2, 1938

Garrett, Garet
A primer of propaganda. Saturday Evening Post. 199:3-5, 158, 161-2, 165-6, 169. Jan. 15, 1927
Analysis of propaganda, how it was used in early history, its modern agents and their subtle methods.

Gavit, John Palmer
By their fruits ye shall know them. Survey Graphic. 25:434. July 1936

Glasgow, George
Propaganda. Contemporary Review. 153: 229-33. Feb. 1938

Grady, Eve Garrette
Russian propaganda. Saturday Evening Post. 204:23, 80, 82. Aug. 15, 1931

Grande, Julian
Propagandist warfare. Spectator. 123: 365-6. Sept. 7, 1919

Grattan, Clinton Hartley
Red opinion in the United States. Scribner's. 96:299-305. Nov. 1934

Gruening, Ernest H.
The public pays. 273p. New York: Vanguard Press, 1931
A study of power propaganda.

Hearnshaw, Fossey J. C.
History as a means of propaganda. Fortnightly. 120:321-31. Aug. 1, 1923

Hollis, Ernest V.
Antidote for propaganda. School and Society. 50:449-53. Oct. 7, 1939

Howard, Sidney Coe
Our professional patriots. New Republic. 39:346-52; 40:12-16, 37-41, 71-5, 93-5, 119-23, 143-5, 171-3. Aug. 20, Sept. 3, Oct. 15, 1924

Huxley, Aldous
Dictators' propaganda. Spectator (London) 157:888-9. Nov. 20, 1936
Notes on propaganda. Harper's. 174:32-41. Dec. 1936
Commercial advertising contrasted with political propaganda. The latter is effective only when circumstances have proved the worth of the propagandist's thesis.

Institute for Propaganda Analysis
Propaganda analysis. v.1-2. New York: Institute for Propaganda Analysis, 1937-39
A monthly letter designed to help the American citizen detect and analyze propaganda.
First issued in Oct. 1937.

Langenhove, Fernand van
The growth of a legend. A study based
upon the German accounts of francs-
tireurs and "atrocities" in Belgium. Tr.
by E. B. Sherlock, with a preface by
J. Mark Baldwin. 321p. London, New
York: G.P. Putnam's Sons, 1916

Lasswell, Harold D.
Function of the propagandist. International Journal of Ethics. 38:257-68. Apr.
1928

The propagandist bids for power. American Scholar. 8:350-7. July 1939
If propaganda succeeds in removing the
basic causes of social insecurity it may
well become a servant of business; otherwise political propaganda may become master here as elsewhere.

——and Blumenstock, Dorothy
The volume of communist propaganda in
Chicago. Public Opinion Quarterly. 3:
63-78. Jan. 1939

——Casey, Ralph D.; and Smith, Bruce L.
Propaganda and promotional activities.
450p. Minneapolis: Univ. of Minnesota
Press, 1935
A comprehensive and annotated bibliog-
raphy dealing with various phases of prop-
aganda and censorship.
Bibliography.

Lumley, Frederick E.
The essential aspects of propaganda. So-
ciology and Social Research. 16:517-26.
July-Aug. 1932

Nature of propaganda. Sociology and
Social Research. 13:315-24. Mar. 1929

The propaganda menace. 454p. New
York, London: Century, 1933

Lundberg, Ferdinand. See Bernays, Edward
L. jt. auth.

Machray, Robert
Nazi plots in Tanganyika; anti-British
propaganda that must be stamped out.
Saturday Review. 156:488. Nov. 11,
1933

MacLeish, Archibald
Munich and the Americans. Nation. 147:
370-1. Oct. 15, 1938

Marcosson, Isaac F.
Red poison. Saturday Evening Post. 197:
25, 89-90, 93, 96, 99. Jan. 24, 1925

Martin, E. D. and Bernays, Edward L.
Are we victims of propaganda? Forum.
81:142-9. Mar. 1929
Discussion, 81: suppl. 49-52. Apr. 1929.

Merz, Charles
Propaganda against Mexico. World Tomorrow. 10:152-5. Apr. 1927

Meyers, Gustavus
Bolshevist propaganda ninety years ago.
Review. 1:369-70. Sept. 6, 1919

Miller, John C.
Sam Adams. 437p. Boston: Little, Brown,
1936
The propagandist of the 18th century.

Nathan, George Jean
Press agents of royalty. Harper's Weekly.
53:27. Dec. 11, 1909

Nazis and Rumania. New Statesman and
Nation. 11:957-8. June 20, 1936

Nicholson, Ivor
An aspect of British official wartime
propaganda. Cornhill. 70 n.s.:593-606.
May 1931

Nock, Albert J.
New dose of British propaganda. American Mercury. 42:482-6. Dec. 1937

North, Anthony
Unbelieveable! New Outlook. 163:17-21.
May 1934

Panton, Selkirk
Tuning in on the Nazis: loudest voice
on earth. Living Age. 352:316-18. June
1937

Pearson, Lionel
Propaganda in the Archidamian war.
Classical Philology. 31:33-52. Jan. 1936
Bibliographical footnotes.

Prévost, Jean
Psychology of propaganda. Atlantic Monthly. 161:674-7. May 1938

Propaganda can not cause war, minds must
be ready. Science News Letter. 33:299.
May 7, 1938

Propaganda is futile unless listeners are
ready. Science News Letter. 32:278.
Oct. 30, 1937

Redman, H. Vere
Anglophobia in Japan. Quarterly Review.
261:254-65. Oct. 1933

Riegel, Oscar W.
Nationalism in press, radio and cinema.
American Sociological Review. 3:510-
15. Aug. 1938

Will we stay out of the next war? New
Republic. 84:11-13. Aug. 14, 1935

Rogerson, Sidney
Propaganda and truth. Spectator. 162:
535. Mar. 31, 1939

Scott-Montagu, Elizabeth
Some thoughts on propaganda. Nineteenth
Century. 126:264-9. Sept. 1939

Seldes, George
Can these things be! 433p. New York:
Brewer, Warren and Putnam, 1931
"The truth about terrorism. —The truth
behind the censorship. —The truth about
dictators and others."

Seligman, Herbert Jacob
New barbarian invasion; Fascist propaganda. New Republic. 95:175-7. June
22, 1938

Siebert, Fred Seaton
Freedom of propaganda. Journalism Quarterly. 12:27-36. Mar. 1935
This article brings together a considerable number of conflicting viewpoints in
regard to the meaning of "propaganda"
and the "freedom of the press."

Smith, Bruce L. See Lasswell, Harold D.
jt. auth.

Soviet hand in India. Saturday Review. 162:
725. Dec. 5, 1936

Stowe, Leland
Propaganda over Europe. Scribner's. 96:
99-101. Aug. 1934

Strong, Edward K., jr.
Control of propaganda as a psychological
problem. Scientific Monthly. 14:234-
52. Mar. 1922

Ten commandments offered for propaganda
protection. Science News Letter. 36:
250. Oct. 14, 1939

Thompson, Basil
Does international propaganda pay? Current Opinion. 73:36-9. July 1922

Thompson, Dorothy (Mrs. Sinclair Lewis)
Propaganda in the modern world. Vital
Speeches. 2:66-8. Nov. 4, 1935

Townsend, Ralph
Soviet propaganda in America. Far Eastern Review. 34:295-6. Aug. 1938

Truth and propaganda. Spectator. 159:
1167. Dec. 31, 1937

United States profitless, Americans pessi-
mistic, lose interest in China—Frederick
Moore. China Weekly Review. 77:
374-7. Aug. 15, 1936

Van Loon, Hendrik Willem
Napoleon as propagandist. Nation. 108:
501. Apr. 5, 1919

War propaganda. Saturday Evening Post.
201:3-5, 141-2; 201:12-13, 158, 161-2, 165-
6; 201:20-1, 169-70, 173-4; 202:26, 28,
134, 137-8; 202:41, 43-4, 114, 117. June
15, 22, 29; July 27; Aug. 17, 1929
A series of articles dealing with war
propaganda, its history, psychology and
methods.

Wright, Quincy
Public opinion and world-politics. 237p.
(Lectures on the Harris Foundation)
Chicago: Univ. of Chicago Press, 1933
A series of lectures by well-known jour-
nalists on public opinion as a factor in
government; molders of public opinion;
methods of political propaganda; World
War propaganda; the strategy of revolu-
tionary and war propaganda.

B.   SOURCES OF PROPAGANDA

1.   Official Bureaus

Allais, Claude
Riviera irredenta; Il Duce's unceasing
campaign to recover the French Riviera.
Living Age. 354:520-4. Aug. 1938

Axis falsehoods on Arabia. Great Britain
and the East. 52:687. June 22, 1939

Baldwin and journalists head world public
relations body. World's Press News.
21:3. Apr. 6, 1939
New organization, the British Association for International Understanding, will
publish **Fortnightly Review, British Survey**, as a part of its activities.

Beals, Carleton
Swastika over the Andes; German pene-
tration in Latin America. Harper's.
177:176-86. July 1938
Totalitarian inroads in Latin America.
Foreign Affairs. 17:78-89. Oct. 1938

Belina-Podgaetski, N.
Soviet propaganda in foreign ports. Tr.
by M. Burr. English Review. 58:701-6.
June 1934

Bentwich, Norman de Mattos
Britain, Scandinavia and the Nazis. Spectator. 156:165-6. Jan. 31, 1936

Bland, John Otway Percy
A study of Kuomintang propaganda. English Review. 49:582-90. Nov. 1929

Buchanan, Meriel
Moscow intrigues. Saturday Review. 161:
712-13. June 6, 1936
Red terror stalks Europe. Saturday Re-
view. 162:166-7. Aug. 8, 1936
This is the work of Russia. Saturday
Review. 162:744-5. Dec. 12, 1936

Burton, Wilbur
Swastika and sigma in Brazil. Spectator.
159:419. Sept. 10, 1937

Cabinet plans attack on anti-British propaganda. World's Press News. 18:1.
Dec. 30, 1937

Canham, Erwin D.
Government by propaganda. Christian
Science Monitor. Weekly Magazine Sec.
p.3, 12. Oct. 6, 1937
The New Deal has tried to "sell" itself
to the American taxpayers through elaborate and costly publicity, but outside
forces and skeptics in the press curb its
success.

Cole, Taylor
The Italian Ministry of Popular Culture.
Public Opinion Quarterly. 2:425-34.
July 1938

Developments in the international battle of
propaganda. China Weekly Review.
88:3. Mar. 4, 1939

Dudley, Owen
Red hate. Saturday Review. 162:590-1.
Nov. 7, 1936

Eccard, Frédéric
Le bolshévisme paralyse la France. Revue
des Deux Mondes. s.8, 45:56-89. May
1, 1938

Efron, David
Latin America and the fascist "Holy Al-
liance." Annals of the American Academy. 204:17-25. July 1939
Evidence of Fascist and Nazi penetration
in Latin America, by the executive secretary of the Committee for Pan American
Democracy.

Ehrenbourg, I. and Lütly, H. F.
Shadow of Hitler; some results of Nazi propaganda in Alsace and in Switzerland. Living Age. 355:355-61. Dec. 1938

First details of Britain's Ministry of Information. World's Press News. 20: 25. Oct. 6, 1938
Plans call for a program which shall be ready to go into action immediately in an emergency.

Governments, spying and propaganda. Nation. 124:626. June 8, 1927

Huxley, Aldous
The collapse of propaganda. Magazine Digest. 14:6-10. Jan. 1937
"Even a despot cannot govern for any length of time without the consent of his subjects. Dictatorial propaganda, therefore, aims first of all at the legitimizing in popular estimation of the dictator's government."

Japan's official propaganda. Literary Digest. 71:16. Nov. 5, 1921

K.K. Kawakami's new book and Japanese intrigue in China; Manchukuo—child of conflict. China Weekly Review. 64: 488-90. May 27, 1933

Kaltenborn, Hans V.
Propaganda land where playing on the mass mind is the chief business of government. Century. 114:678-87. Oct. 1927

Lasker, Bruno
Propaganda as an instrument of national policy. Pacific Affairs. 10:152-60. June 1937
General propaganda must rely upon appeal to sentiment and specialized propaganda upon reason in order to achieve effectiveness.

Lütly, H. F. See Ehrenbourg, I. jt. auth.

Merk, Frederick
British government propaganda and the Oregon Treaty. American Historical Review. 40:38-62. Oct. 1934

Mutual Soviet American pledge against propaganda; text of the Roosevelt-Litvinov exchange of letters. China Weekly Review. 67:138-9. Dec. 23, 1933

No special press and propaganda dept. Newspaper World. 41:3. Dec. 3, 1938
Foreign Office organizing British publicity abroad more extensively.

Politische Propaganda in der Weltgeschichte. Salzburg: Bergland, 1938
Historical survey of political propaganda.

Propaganda by German Nazis in the United States. New Republic. 76:264. Oct. 18, 1933

La **Propagande** à l'ordre du jour. L'Europe Nouvelle. 22:731-3. July 8, 1939

Rogerson, Sidney
Britain needs national propaganda council. World's Press News. 20:19. Oct. 6, 1938

Propaganda in the next war. 196p. London: Geoffrey Bles, 1938

Schmulowitz, Nat
Thou shalt not read the rights of man. United States Law Review. 73:271-86. May 1939
Futility of a government imposing a "thou shalt not read" commandment on its subjects.

Should Congress pass the Dickstein Bill to terminate the stay of alien propagandists? Congressional Digest. 14:284-5. Nov. 1935

Soviet propaganda fails to 'click,' says writer back from Russia. Editor and Publisher. 60:20. Nov. 26, 1927

Stating the British case to the world. Great Britain and the East. 52:685. June 22, 1939

Steed, Henry Wickham
Propaganda and policy. Spectator. 162: 1079-80. June 23, 1939

Swan, Alfred Wilson
Lies that feed the war fires. Christian Century. 46:836-8. June 26, 1929

Teeling, William
Totalitarian propaganda. Spectator. 159: 895-6. Nov. 19, 1937

The Third International and colonial propaganda. Slavonic Review. 10:509-24. Apr. 1932
Erroneously ascribed to Alexander Guchkov.

Thompson, Dorothy (Mrs. Sinclair Lewis)
German propaganda in the United States and the world. Vital Speeches. 3:712-14. Sept. 15, 1937

Viereck, George S.
Spreading germs of hate. 327p. New York: H. Liveright, 1930
Foreword by Colonel E. M. House.
By an American poet and journalist connected during the World War with German propaganda agencies.

Wile, Frederic W.
Government by propaganda. Outlook. 150: 1387-9. Dec. 26, 1928

Willert, Sir Arthur
National advertisement. Fortnightly. 151 (ns 145):1-7. Jan. 1939
The author, formerly head of the British Foreign Office News Department, cites the generosity of the totalitarian states in comparison with the niggardly allotments of the British government for disseminating news and culture abroad. He believes the existing freedom of the press should not and need not be endangered by the adoption of any totalitarian methods.

2. NON-OFFICIAL GROUPS

Buchanan, Meriel
The peril of Red propaganda. Saturday Review. 161:584-5. May 9, 1936

Childs, Harwood Lawrence, ed.
Pressure groups and propaganda. Annals of the American Academy. 179:1-239. May, 1935
A description of pressure methods customarily employed in the competitive struggle for the control of public opinion.

Foster, J. E.
Group in terms of propaganda. American Sociological Review. 2:247-52. Apr. 1937
Bibliographical footnotes.

Geneva correspondents recall Shearer's propaganda at Naval Conference. Editor and Publisher. 62:5. Sept. 21, 1929

Manning, George H.
Merchant marine propaganda told. Editor and Publisher. 66:9. Oct. 14, 1933

Wright, Chester M.
How the propagandists work for war with Mexico. American Federationist. 27:550-6. June 1920

C. TECHNIQUE AND APPEALS

Athearn, Clarence Royalty
How an anti-Red committee works; United States Chamber of Commerce's Committee on Combating Subversive Activities. New Republic. 87:8-10. May 13, 1936

Beaverbrook, William Maxwell Aitkin, baron
The truth about war-time propaganda. World's Press News. 21:3. June 29, 1939
Propaganda is a stimulant, not a food.

Brown, H. C.
Advertising and propaganda: a study in the ethics of social control. International Journal of Ethics. 40:39-55. Oct. 1929
Men must be treated as persons and not as things. High-powered sales methods will eventually defeat their own purpose.

Crowther, Samuel
Radical propaganda; how it works. World's Work. 39:618-24. Apr. 1920

Hitler, Adolf
Mein Kampf. 669p. New York: Stackpole Sons, 1939
See p. 177-86, 560-76.
Profiting by what he felt to be the superior propaganda methods of the Allies during the World War, Hitler expounds his ideas on that subject giving both his aims and his methods. This is a new and unexpurgated English translation.

How to counter Japanese propaganda in Mongolia. China Weekly Review. 70: 333. Nov. 3, 1934

Insidious propaganda. Spectator. 125:103-5. July 24, 1920

Irwin, Will
Age of lies; how the propagandist attacks the foundation of public opinion. Sunset. 43:23-5. Dec. 1919
Art of muddlement. il. Scribner's. 86:363-71. Oct. 1929

Lasswell, Harold D.
Research on the distribution of symbol specialists. Journalism Quarterly. 12: 146-56. June 1935

Lutz, Ralph Haswell
Propaganda and the development of the chauvinistic spirit. Institute of World Affairs, Proceedings. 16:91-4. 1938
Chauvinism moves more swiftly than propaganda in arousing a people to act.

McKenzie, Vernon
Propaganda in Germany and Czechoslovakia—pro- and anti-Nazi. Journalism Quarterly. 12:37-42. Mar. 1935

Millis, Walter
Propaganda for war. Southern Review. 5(2):201-10. 1939

Myths of anti-Semitism. New Republic. 96:145-6. Sept. 14, 1938

Patrick, Ted
Advertising the next war. Scribner's. 103:15-20. June 1938

Polish and Hungarian governments are best censor-propagandists. World's Press News. 18:13. Dec. 9, 1937

Raushenbush, Hilmar S.
High power propaganda. 89p. New York: New Republic Press, 1928

Rogerson, Sidney
Propaganda in the next war. 188p. London: Bles, 1938
How England should conduct war propaganda, particularly in neutral countries.

Sarolea, Charles
Strategy and tactics of bolshevism. Saturday Review. 162:488-9, 526-7. Oct. 17-24, 1936

Street, J. W.
Hitler's strategy in the international crisis. Nineteenth Century. 124:525-37. Nov. 1938

Working up a war. Nation. 85:26. July 11, 1907

D. CHANNELS

1. PRESS

Abbot, Willis J.
Dragon's teeth. Virginia Quarterly Review. 4:367-78. July 1928
International ill-will is fostered by newspapers which act as agents provocateurs, stressing sensational aspects of foreign correspondence.

Angell, Sir Norman
Press and propaganda. Spectator. 159: 890-1. Nov. 19, 1937

Attwater, Donald
People, press and propaganda. Commonweal. 24:317-18, 337-8. July 24-31, 1936

Broun, Heywood
What is news and what is propaganda? Nation. 143:75. July 18, 1936

Carleton, Edward
Power of the press. Outlook. 58:471-2. Feb. 19, 1898

Dix-huit millions de francs pour la propagande allemande en Belgique. Presse Publicité. no. 35, p.10. Apr. 7, 1938
Belgian deputy reveals to his Parliament that German industrialists wish to found a Belgian daily.

Ellis, William T.
Urges press to back abolition of international propaganda. Editor and Publisher. 62:26. Nov. 16, 1929

Hillson, Norman
Print factual news about Europe. World's Press News. 17:15. June 24, 1937

Houser, Ernest O.
News of the Far East in U.S. dailies. Public Opinion Quarterly. 2:651-8. Oct. 1938

Howard, Harry Paxton
Japanese propaganda, journalism, and history. China Weekly Review. 62: 338-41. Oct. 22, 1932
A review of half a dozen books, one of which is H. W. Wilde's *Social Currents in Japan.*

Irwin, Will
If you see it in the paper, it's —? The menace of propaganda. Collier's. 72: 11-12. Aug. 18, 1923
Propaganda and the news. 325p. New York, London: McGraw-Hill, 1936
Mr. Irwin's book is "interesting propaganda against propaganda." The use of propaganda in war and peace.

News versus propaganda. National Education Association Journal. 19:73. Mar. 1930

Pendergast, L. O.
Press-war on Mexico. Nation. 147:222-5. Sept. 3, 1938

Pew, Marlen
Shop talk at thirty. Editor and Publisher. 67:36, 34. Jan. 12, 1935
Propaganda and hoaxes in newspapers.

Pratt, Fletcher
Propaganda captures the newspapers. American Mercury. 44:450-8. Aug. 1938
Regular news channels have been tapped and used by Leftists, particularly to disseminate viewpoints on the Spanish Civil War.

Propaganda from the Manchukuo news agency. Time. 24:26. Dec. 17, 1934

Rea, George Bronson
Curb on propaganda: advocating a Congressional investigation into the conduct of American owned and edited newspapers, published in foreign countries. Far East Review. 31:328-30. Sept. 1935

Scott-James, R. A.
The influence of the press. 320p. London: S. W. Partridge, 1913
Undertakes to discover the function of the press as revealed by history.

Seldes, George
You can't print that. 465p. New York: Payson and Clark; Garden City, N.Y.: Garden City Publishing Co., 1929

Tainted news in peace. New Republic. 51: 293-4. Aug. 10, 1927

What France spends on propaganda. Newspaper World. 41:1-2. Jan. 1, 1938
Of 195,447,000 francs in a special fund, much goes for foreign propaganda. L'Agence Havas subsidized to carry news to North and South America. Propaganda directed from Press Services Department of the Foreign Office under Pierre Comert.

2. RADIO

See also

Communication—Radio, p.8; Washington Radio News, p.30.

B.B.C. plans all-day news bulletins in event of war. World's Press News. 20:499, p.3. Sept. 22, 1938

Blankenhorn, Heber
Battle of radio armaments. Harper's. 164:83-91. Dec. 1931

Broadcasts in Arabic. Great Britain and the East. 50:4. Jan. 6, 1938

Crowell, Chester T.
Dogfight on the air waves. Saturday Evening Post. 210:23, 38, 40-2. May 21, 1938
International propaganda directed at Latin America.

Flynn, John Thomas
Open letter to the FCC; radio as an instrument of propaganda for money groups. New Republic. 94:395. May 4, 1938

Gelderland, Karl van, pseud.
War in the ether. Nation. 146:300-1. Mar. 12, 1938

Hanighen, Frank Cleary
Propaganda on the air; the international problem of radio censorship. tables Current History. 44:45-51. June 1936
A brief survey of propaganda methods in European nations and a description of the part radio plays in its propagation.

Morecroft, John Harold
How the propagandists work in radio. Radio Broadcast. 7:332-4. July 1925

Sharp, Roland Hall
Propaganda on the air waves. Christian Science Monitor. Weekly Magazine Section. p.5, 14. Oct. 27, 1937
Governments and radio listeners long have been annoyed by subtle distortion of facts in news and other international broadcasts, but now there is some promise of relief.

Wagenführ, Kurt
In the troubled Mediterranean; war in the air waves. Living Age. 353:299-301. Dec. 1937

Propaganda in the news; teacher's responsibility for training students to recognize and analyze propaganda. Scholastic. 33:1T. Oct. 8, 1938

Randall, R. G.
Education in the war. Nation (London) 44:316-17. Dec. 1, 1928

Red peril in the schools; Empire Day propaganda. Saturday Review. 157: 597. May 26, 1934

Spender, John Alfred
History perverted into propaganda. Hibbert Journal. 35:341-8. Apr. 1937

Tyson, Levering
Education vs. propaganda; are they incompatible? Vital Speeches. 4:431-4. May 1, 1938

Uenoda, Setsuo
Examples of the anti-Japanese propaganda in Chinese schools. Trans–Pacific. 19: 4, 18. Dec. 10, 1931
The use of songs, questions and exercises designed to inspire hatred of Japan among China's youth.

3. Schools

Biddle, William W.
Propaganda and education. 84p. New York: Teachers College, Columbia Univ., 1932

Broome, Edwin C.
Report of the Committee on Propaganda —Abstract. p.204-17. (National Education Association, Proceedings, 1929, v.67) Washington: National Education Association, 1929

Carr, William George
The school child and propaganda; the conundrum of the educator. p.597-605. In National conference of social work, Boston, 1930. Proceedings. Chicago, Univ. of Chicago Press, 1931

Dell, Robert
Nazi propaganda in English preparatory schools. New Statesman and Nation. 12:849-50. Nov. 28, 1936
Discussion, 12:889-975. Dec. 5-12, 1936

Ginsbourg, Mark J.
Hupeh's propaganda schools. China Weekly Review. 71:94. Dec. 15, 1934

Martin, Kingsley
Public opinion and the wireless. Political Quarterly. 10:280-6. Apr. 1939

Miller, Charles G.
The poisoned loving cup. 208p. Chicago: National Historical Society, 1928
United States school histories falsified through pro-British propaganda in name of amity.

Problem of revising text-books to suit Japanese. China Weekly Review. 74: 110. Sept. 28, 1935

Propaganda bibliography for students and teachers. Scholastic. 33:3T-4T. Oct. 8, 1938

4. Miscellaneous

Are newsreels news? Nation. 141:369-70. Oct. 2, 1935

Carter, John
Propaganda as seen in recent books. Outlook. 155:471. July 23, 1930

Cousins, E. G.
Cinema and propaganda. Bookman (London) 85:480-1. Mar. 1934

Huxley, Aldous
Propaganda, religious and secular (I—II) Spectator (London) 157:800-1, 844-5, 985-6. Nov. 6-13, Dec. 4, 1936
Propaganda. IV. The influence of authors. Spectator (London) 157:939-40. Nov. 27, 1936

Miller, Clyde Raymond
Propaganda or interpretation? Education. 58:600-2. June 1938

Mitchell, Peter C.
Report on the Propaganda Library. 3v. London: H. M. Stationery Office, 1917

Steele, Walter S.
Radicals and film propaganda. National Republic. 19:40. Aug. 1931

Stern, Madeleine B.
Propaganda or art? Sewanee Review. 45:306-27, 453-68; 46:45-69. July 1937-Jan. 1938
Bibliographical footnotes.

Van Doren, Mark
Literature and propaganda. Virginia Quarterly Review. 14:no. 2, p.203-8. Apr. 1938

VIII. THE PRESS AND PUBLIC OPINION

See also
France—Propaganda and Public Opinion, p.122; Great Britain—The Press and Public Opinion, p.143.

A. HISTORY AND THEORY

A "La nouvelle école de la paix": M. Jacques Chastenet parle de "La presse et la formation de l'opinion publique." L'Europe Nouvelle. 16:103-4. Feb. 4, 1933
Some passages from a lecture in which M. Chastenet discusses the reciprocal influence of the press and public opinion.

Ackerman, Carl W.
Public opinion and the press in politics, economics and science. Vital Speeches. 3:521-4. June 15, 1937

Angell, Norman
Commercialization of demagogy. **Nation** (London) 34:113-15, 180-2. Oct. 20-7, 1923
A certain section of the press caters to human folly to insure circulation and continued existence.

Peace and the public mind. Spectator. 153:869-70. Dec. 7, 1934

The press and the organization of society. 123p. London: Labour Pub. Co., 1922
The importance to Labor of achieving control of the press as a means of obtaining and maintaining a favorable public opinion. Suggests the cooperative principle of newspaper publishing.

The public mind; its disorders: its exploitation. 232p. New York: E. P. Dutton, 1927

Bauer, Wilhelm
Die öffentliche Meinung in der Weltgeschichte. Wildpark-Potsdam: Akademische Verlagsgesellschaft Athenaion, 1930
Fully illustrated history of public opinion.

Bernays, Edward L.
Crystallizing public opinion. 218p. New York: Boni and Liveright, 1923
Discussion of propaganda and public opinion by an American public relations counsel.

Freedom of propaganda; constructive forming of public opinion. Vital Speeches. 2:744-6. Sept. 1, 1936

Blanshard, Paul
Manufacturing public opinion. table New Republic. 69:102. Dec. 9, 1931

Bobbitt, Joseph M.
Measurement of public opinion. Sociology and Social Research. 19:55-60. Sept. 1934

Brinkmann, Carl. See Kapp, Dr. jt. auth.

Brown, George R.
Lynching of public opinion. North American Review. 209:795, 802. June 1919

Buré, Émile
La crise du journalisme d'opinion n'est pas seulement liée à la crise économique. Presse Publicité. 24:1. Oct. 31, 1937
The problem of journalism and public opinion is not merely economic in nature but is bound up with the crisis of democracy.

Burke, Kenneth
Symbolic war. Review of Proletarian Literature in the United States; an Anthology, ed. by G. Hicks and others. Southern Review. 2:134-47. 1936

Bury, John B.
A history of freedom of thought. 256p. New York: Henry Holt, 1913
History of the freedom of thought and speech from the earliest days in Greece up to 1913.

Carr, Edward H.
Public opinion as a safeguard of peace. International Affairs. 15:846-62. Nov. 1936
Bibliographical footnotes.

Chafee, Zechariah, jr.
Freedom of speech. 431p. New York: Harcourt, Brace and Howe, 1920
An inquiry into the proper limitations upon the freedom of speech, supplemented by a bibliography and an index of cases.

Chase, Stuart
The tyranny of words. Harper's. 175: 516-19. Nov. 1937
A discussion of semantics.

Chauchat, A. M.
Le rôle intellectuel de la presse. Cahiers de la Presse. 1:580-6. Oct.-Dec. 1938
An excellent discussion of the part played by the press in the intellectual development of the public.

Cobb, Frank I.
The press and public opinion. New Republic. 21:144-7. Dec. 31, 1919
A broad discussion of the press, propaganda, press agents and public opinion, by the editor of the New York *World*.

Conant, James Bryant
Defenses against propaganda; history is a mirror. Vital Speeches. 4:542-4. June 15, 1938

Corruption of public opinion. Century. 73: 480-1. Jan. 1907

Dewey, John
New paternalism; molding public opinion. New Republic. 17:216-17. Dec. 21, 1918

Dovifat, Emil. See Kapp, Dr. jt. auth.

Eckardt, Hans von. See Kapp, Dr. jt. auth.

Eddy, William Alfred
Ridding public opinion of superstition the task of our editors. Vital Speeches. 4:471-4. May 15, 1938

Ferdinand Tönnies and his theory of public opinion. Public Opinion Quarterly. 2: 584-95. Oct. 1938
Tönnies distinguished three states of public opinion, the solid, fluid, and gaseous. The gaseous type is more readily influenced by the daily press, and influences it in turn.

Foreign opinion. Outlook. 87:285-6. Oct. 12, 1907

Giovanoli, Fritz
Zur Soziologie des modernen Zeitungswesen. Zeitschrift für Völkerpsychologie und Soziologie. 6:175-92, 267-81. June, Sept. 1930
A sociological study of the modern press.

Godkin, Edwin Lawrence
Growth and expression of public opinion. Atlantic Monthly. 81:1-15. Jan. 1898
How public opinion exercises its power over the conduct of public affairs. By the editor of The Nation.

Goose stuffing. Saturday Evening Post. 196:6-7, 62, 64, 66, 68. Mar. 15, 1924

Grane, W. Leighton
Public opinion and war. Contemporary Review. 104:360-7. Sept. 1913

Graves, W. Brooke, ed.
Readings in public opinion, its formation and control. With an introduction by Clyde L. King. 1281p. New York, London: D. Appleton, 1928

Hard, William
Radio and public opinion. Annals of the American Academy. 177:105-13. Jan. 1935
Competition between radio stations and between radio and the press results in greater freedom of speech.

Harding, Denys W.
General conceptions in the study of the press and public opinion. Sociological Review. 29:370-90. Oct. 1937
Principles of the relation between public opinion and press.

Hashagen, Justus
Ausdrucksmittel der öffentlichen Meinung. Zeitungswissenschaft. 1:53. Apr. 15, 1926
Media and appeals in the expression of public opinion.

Haskell, Henry J.
Public, the newspaper's problem. Outlook. 91:791-5. Apr. 3, 1909

Hertz, Fr. See Kapp, Dr. jt. auth.

Jebb, Sir Richard Claverhouse
Ancient organs of public opinion. Eclectic Magazine. 104:107-19. Jan. 1885

Jenks, Jeremiah W.
The guidance of public opinion. American Journal of Sociology. 1:158-69. July 1895
How public opinion is formed in the nations of the world.

Jerrold, Blanchard
On the manufacture of public opinion. Nineteenth Century. 13:1080-92. June 1883

Kapp, Dr.; Schmitt, Carl; Stampfer, Friedrich; Hertz, Fr.; Dovifat, Emil; Voegelin, E.; Tönnies, F.; Eckardt, Hans von; and Brinkmann, Carl
Diskussion über "Presse und öffentliche Meinung." Deutsche Gesellschaft für Soziologie. Schriften. 7:51-80. 1931
A discussion of the press and public opinion by a distinguished group of German social scientists.

Kittle, William
Making of public opinion. Arena. 41: 440-6. July 1909

Lang, André
Les journalistes et le public. Annales Politiques et Littéraires. 108:287-9. Sept. 25, 1936

LeBon, Gustave
The crowd: a study of the popular mind. 239p. London: T. F. Unwin, 1903

Lewis, Sir George C.
An essay on the influence of authority in matters of opinion. 296p. London: Longmans, Green, 1875

Likert, Rensis. See Murphy, Gardner, jt. auth.

Lippmann, Walter
Barriers of information; toward a critique of public opinion. Century. 103:121-31. Nov. 1921
Censorship and limitations on the circulation of ideas are barriers to information.

Public opinion. 427p. New York: Macmillan, 1930
The concept of stereotypes and other phenomena of public opinion.

Lowell, Abbott Lawrence
Public opinion in war and peace. 302p. Cambridge: Harvard Univ. Press, 1923
President Lowell's study of public opinion, its growth and development.

Lundberg, George A.
Newspaper and public opinion. table Social Forces. 4:709-15. June 1926
A case example of the influence of the press in political affairs. Political influence of the city newspaper is less than that of the small-town publication.

Manheim, Ernst
Die Träger der öffentlichen Meinung; Studien zur Soziologie der Öffentlichkeit. 145p. Brünn: Rudolph M. Rohrer, 1933
Sociological aspects of public opinion.

Mr. Henry W. Kinney's strictly-confidential document; with text. China Weekly Review. 60:391-3. May 21, 1932

Moran, Thomas F.
Fight for public opinion. Mississippi Valley Historical Review. suppl. 454-75. May 1919

Murphy, Gardner and Likert, Rensis
Public opinion and the individual. 324p. New York: Harper, 1938

Myer, Walter Evert
Studies in public opinion. National Education Association Journal. 26:48. Feb. 1937

Nevins, Allan
American press opinion—Washington to Coolidge. 598p. New York, Boston: D. C. Heath, 1928
A documentary record of editorial leadership and criticism, 1785-1927.

Ogden, Rollo
Journalism and public opinion. American Political Science Review. 7:suppl. 194-200. Feb. 1913
Politics is not the only testing ground for measuring the influence of the press. The public shares the responsibility for bad newspapers.

Orton, William
News and opinion. American Journal of Sociology. 33:80-93. July 1927
The need for a separation of the functions of news-gathering and news interpretation. Fact and opinion are not always sharply distinguishable.

Our rulers—public opinion. Cornhill Magazine. 21:288-98. Mar. 1870

Palmer, Paul A.
The concept of public opinion in political theory. In Essays in history and political theory, in honor of C. H. McIlwain. Cambridge: Harvard Univ. Press, 1936
Ferdinand Tönnies and his theory of public opinion. Public Opinion Quarterly. 2:584-95. Oct. 1938

Peters, Alfred
Die Zeitung und ihr Publikum. 174p. Dortmund: F. W. Ruhfus, 1930
A study of the sociology of the newspaper.

Pierce, D. T.
Does the press reflect public opinion? Gunton's. 19:418-25. Nov. 1900

Pringle, Henry F.
Mass psychologist. American Mercury. 19:155-62. Feb. 1930

Public opinion. Spectator. 124:577-8. May 1, 1920

Public opinion and propaganda. Science Progress. 17:283-92. Oct. 1922

Public opinion and the press. Commonweal. 25:85-6. Nov. 20, 1936

Quigg, Lemuel Ely
The court of public opinion. North American Review. 144:625-30. June 1887

Quincy, Josiah
Increasing power of public opinion. Public Opinion. 15:478-9. Aug. 26, 1893

Reid, T. Wemyss
Public opinion and its leaders. Fortnightly Review. 34:230-44. Aug. 1, 1880

Ridout, Herbert C.
Missionary instincts developed press to lead public opinion. Editor and Publisher. 53:42. Apr. 30, 1921
English cleric traces tendencies of modern journalism.

Russell, Bertrand Arthur William Russell, 3rd earl
Power over opinion, an inquiry into cause and effect. Saturday Review of Literature. 18:13-14. Aug. 13, 1938
Excerpt from his Power.

Schmitt, Carl. See Kapp, Dr. jt. auth.

Shepard, Walter J.
Public opinion. American Journal of Sociology. 15:32-60. July 1909

Social factors in world affairs. p.106-15. In Institute of World Affairs, Proceedings, 1938. Los Angeles: Univ. of Southern California, 1939
A summary of the Institute's round table discussions of public opinion and propaganda, vehicles of opinion, techniques, problems of racial conflicts in Europe.

Stampfer, Friedrich. See Kapp, Dr. jt. auth.

Strong, Ellery
Public opinion, if, as, and when; reply to B. Bliven, with rejoinder. New Republic. 74:21. Feb. 15, 1933

Tönnies, Ferdinand. See Kapp, Dr. jt. auth.

Trotter, William
The instincts of the herd in peace and war. 213p. New York: Macmillan; London: T. F. Unwin, 1916

Villard, Oswald Garrison
World opinion exists. Nation. 142:7. Jan. 1, 1936

Voegelin, E. See Kapp, Dr. jt. auth.

Waples, Douglas
People and print: social aspects of reading in the depression. 228p. Chicago: Univ. of Chicago Press, 1938

Williams, Talcott
The press and public opinion. American Political Science Review. 7:suppl. 201-3. Feb. 1913
The newspaper press represents the opinion of the public better than magazines, books, lectures or mass meetings.

Wilson, Francis G.
Concepts of public opinion. American Political Science Review. 27:371-91. June 1933

Woodward, Hugh McCurdy
Public opinion and world peace. p.262-5. In Institute of World Affairs, Proceedings, 1935. Los Angeles: Univ. of Southern California, 1936

Woodward, Julian Laurence
Foreign news in American morning newspapers; a study in public opinion. 122p. New York: Columbia Univ. Press, 1930
A statistical study.

Woodward, Julian Laurence—*Continued*
Quantitative newspaper analysis as a technique of opinion research. Social Forces. 12:526-37. May 1934
Bibliographical footnotes.

Wright, Quincy, ed.
Public opinion and world-politics. 237p. Chicago: Univ. of Chicago Press, 1933
Harris Foundation lectures by well-known journalists. Public opinion as a factor in government; molders of public opinion; methods of political propaganda; World War propaganda; the strategy of revolutionary and war propaganda.

Yarros, Victor S.
Press and public opinion. American Journal of Sociology. 5:372-82. Nov. 1899

Zahniser, Charles R.
Pulpit, press and public opinion. Christian Century. 47:1411-12. Nov. 19, 1930

B. PUBLIC OPINION AND GOVERNMENT

Bonaparte, Charles Joseph
Government by public opinion. Forum. 40:384-90. Oct. 1908

Borden, Sir Robert Laird
Collective public opinion. International Conciliation. 325:639. Dec. 1936

Brammer, Karl
Presse, Demokratie und öffentliche Meinung. p.551-7. *In* Zehn Jahre Deutscher Republik. Berlin: 1928

Butler, Nicholas Murray
American public opinion and international affairs; with discussion. International Affairs. 11:618-32. Sept. 1932
American constitutional limitations and their relation to public opinion.

Casey, Ralph D.
The menace of propaganda. American Press. 52:2. Mar. 1934

Hutchinson, Paul
Who makes public opinion? Survey Graphic. 28:373-6, 406. June 1939
Analysis of agencies of inquiry and expression with special reference to government publicity and newspapers; polls of public opinion; politicians. By the managing editor of *The Christian Century*.

Institute of World Affairs
Public opinion and propaganda; summary of round table discussions. p.106-15. *In* Institute of World Affairs. Proceedings, 1937. Los Angeles: Univ. of Southern California, 1938

King, Clyde L.
Public opinion in government. Introduction to W. B. Graves' Readings in Public Opinion. 24p. New York, London: D. Appleton, 1928

Lowell, Abbott Lawrence
Public opinion and popular government. 415p. New York: Longmans, Green, 1921
The president of Harvard University discusses freedom of expressing dissent as a condition beneficial to a public opinion. See p.36-40.

MacGregor, Hugh
Government, press and people. Spectator. 163:169. Aug. 4, 1939
Reply: 163:222. Aug. 11, 1939.

C. NATIONAL PUBLIC OPINION

1. UNITED STATES

See also
Washington Correspondence, p.23.

Kao, George
What America is reading about the Far East. China Weekly Review. 84:248. Apr. 30, 1938

Manufacturing public opinion. McClure's Magazine. 26:450-2. Feb. 1906
Propaganda in the guise of news at the turn of the century. How the Standard Oil Company and other corporations influenced the press.

Measuring foreign news. The A.A.U.W. newspaper survey. Journal of the American Association of University Women. 26:93-5. Jan. 1933
The purpose of this survey was to ascertain the trends in public opinion on foreign affairs. The result gives evidence of superficiality in foreign news reports.

Nelson, Carl J. See Wright, Quincy, jt. auth.

A New technique in journalism. Fortune. 12:65-6. July 1935
Fortune applies to factual journalism the technique of the commercial survey: a sampling of public opinion by methods long familiar to the industrialist in the sampling of ore and cotton.

Odegard, Peter H.
The American public mind. 308p. New York: Columbia Univ. Press, 1930
A study of the forces which have shaped American character and opinion, including the family, the church, the school, the newspaper, the political party, propaganda, advertising, etc.

Spinks, C. N.
The formation of American public opinion toward Japan. Contemporary Japan. 6:616-22. Mar. 1938

White, Elizabeth B.
American opinion of France from Lafayette to Poincaré. 346p. New York: A. A. Knopf, 1927
Cis-Atlantic views of French morality as revealed by an examination of press literature, public addresses and political correspondence.

Woodward, Julian Laurence
Foreign news in American morning news-
papers. 122p. New York: Columbia
Univ. Press, 1930
A study in public opinion.

Wright, Quincy and Nelson, Carl J.
American attitudes toward Japan and
China, 1937-1938. Public Opinion Quar-
terly. 3:46-62. Jan. 1939
An interesting measurement of news-
paper attitudes, represented by the *New
York Times*, Chicago *Daily News* and Chi-
cago *Tribune*.

2. OTHER COUNTRIES

Anti-British news from foreign agencies.
Newspaper World. 40:1. June 26, 1937

Arabic broadcasts from London. Great
Britain and the East. 50:46-7. Jan. 13,
1938

Bromwell, James
Public opinion and peace. Spectator.
162:671. Apr. 21, 1939
The fatalistic attitude of the English
people in fighting for non-existent international law calls for a peace conference.

Carroll, E. Malcolm
French public opinion and foreign affairs,
1870-1914. 348p. New York, London:
Century, 1931
Relations between a democracy and the
conduct of foreign affairs.

Failure of newspapers to influence voters.
World's Press News. 1:3. June 6, 1929

Greenwood, Harry Powys
Public opinion in Germany. Spectator.
162:407. Mar. 10, 1939
Evidences of awakening public opinion
in Germany and in the Nazi party itself.

Hanighen, Frank C.
What France and England think about us.
Harper's. 179:376-85. Sept. 1939
An estimate of public opinion and press
reactions written on the eve of the War.

Making Britain understood. Spectator. 160:
213. Feb. 11, 1938

Matter of the Japanese secret documents;
excerpts from the address by Vice Admiral Imamura to the Japanese resi-
dents of Sydney, Australia. China
Weekly Review. 61:228. July 16, 1932

Pan-Germanism in the United States.
World's Work. 30:135-7 June 1915

Public opinion and foreign policy in Germany. Review of Reviews. 34:228-9.
Aug. 1906

Reinsch, Paul Samuel
Politics and public opinion in Japan. Outlook. 87:115-18. Sept. 21, 1907

Robison, Georgia
Molding public opinion under the French
directory. Public Opinion Quarterly.
2:281-6. Apr. 1938

Spending vast sums to influence world opinion. China Weekly Review. 60:383-5.
May 21, 1932

Steed, Henry Wickham
Making public opinion. Fortnightly. 139:
565-73. May 1, 1933
Mr. Steed attempts to analyze the forces
which changed Britain from pro-German
to pro-French. Opinion is based upon
knowledge, and "a good part of knowledge is remembering."

Stinnes power of the press. Literary Digest. 72:18. Feb. 11, 1922
Hugo Stinnes dreamed of a Central
European Empire and acquired numerous
newspapers as a means to making that
dream a reality.

Vast crowds that gather in lands of the dictators. New York Times Magazine.
p.12. Feb. 3, 1935

Washio, Shogoro
Japan's public opinion. Trans-Pacific. 13:
5. Apr. 24, 1926

Wedgewood, Josiah C.
History of Parliament and of public opinion. Political Quarterly. 5:506-16. Oct.
1934

Young, Arthur Morgan
The press and Japanese thought. Pacific
Affairs. 10:412-19. Dec. 1937
What Japan tells England. Asia. 38:411-
12. July 1938

D. CARICATURES AND CARTOONS

See also
World War, 1914—Caricatures and Cartoons,
p.97.

Beerbohm, Max
Tales of three nations; a series of histori-
cal cartoons of the relations of England,
France and Germany since the time of
Napoleon. Yale Review. n.s. 13:suppl.
11. Jan. 1924

Chen, Jack (Chen I-wan)
China's militant cartoons. Asia. 38:308-
12. May 1938

Chinese cartoons of the day. Asia. 36:507.
Aug. 1936

Chinese cartoons on the Brussels conference.
China Weekly Review. 83:suppl. 17.
Dec. 4, 1937

Dyson, William H.
Cartoons. London Mercury. 8:239-42,
355-8, 455-8, 574-7; 9:16-19, 126-9.
July-Dec. 1923

Fascism in the funnies: in Little orphan
Annie, H. Gray continues his attack
upon the New deal. New Republic. 84:
147. Sept. 18, 1935

Fuchs, Eduard
Die Karikatur der europäischen Völker vom Altertum bis zur Neuzeit. 479p. Berlin: Hofman, 1904
Fully illustrated description of political caricatures in Europe from ancient to modern times.

Der Weltkrieg in der Karikatur. 309p. Munich: A. Langen, 1916
Illustrated discussion of caricatures in modern times leading up to and including the early part of the World War.

Hindle, Wilfrid H.
Soviet cartoonist; Boris Yefimoff. Review of Reviews (London) 83:69-72. Feb. 1933

Hines, Edna
Caricatures as a means of social control. Sociology and Social Research. 17:454-64. May 1933
History of the American cartoon, and its close relationship with the press.

Hornaday, Mary
He who wields the pencil. Christian Science Weekly. Magazine Section. p.3. Oct. 14, 1936
Cartoonist exercises an influence greater than the writer's.

Low, David
A cartoon history of our times. 174p. New York: Simon and Schuster, 1939

Maurice, Arthur B.
War cartoons of 1870. Bookman. 40:47-54. Sept. 1914

Murrell, William
Nast, gladiator of the political pencil. American Scholar. 5:472-85. Sept. 1936

Riddle of Hitler Germany; two years in cartoons. Review of Reviews (London) 86:51-66. Feb. 1935

Signor Mussolini; a brief history in cartoons. Review of Reviews (London) 86:35-48. Oct. 1935

Where West laughs with East; Japanese humour; cartoons. Review of Reviews (London) 86:55-7. Jan. 1935

Working up patriotism and the Nicaraguan imbroglio. Nation. 89:590. Dec. 16, 1909

IX. THE PRESS AND WORLD AFFAIRS

A. INTERNATIONAL AFFAIRS

America, fuddled by propaganda, gropes way in world, says Irwin. Editor and Publisher. 59:11. Nov. 13, 1926
Interested parties tint news from foreign lands; war publicity methods described.

Angell, Sir Norman
Peace and the plain man. 334p. New York, London: Harper, 1935

Bent, Silas
International window-smashing; role of our newspapers in foreign affairs. Harper's. 157:421-8. Sept. 1928

Bömer, Karl. See Douglass, Paul F. jt. auth.

British public opinion and foreign affairs. The Journal of the Institute of Journalists. 25:84-5. May 1937
Harold Nicolson suggests cures for a "nervous illness" of the British public.

Bryce, James Bryce, viscount
International relations. 275p. New York: Macmillan, 1922

Bullard, Arthur
Our relations with Great Britain. Atlantic Monthly. 118:451-61. Oct. 1916

Bush, Chilton R.
The press as a factor in international relations. p. 95-9. *In* Institute of World Affairs, Proceedings, 1938. Los Angeles: Univ. of Southern California, 1939
Blame for the increasing difficulty of the press in differentiating positively between stage play and authenticity rests on government officials, not with the press.

Butler, Nicholas Murray
American public opinion and international affairs; with discussion. International Affairs. 11:618-32. Sept. 1932
Public opinion and its relation to government in the United States. Influences affecting American opinion in regard to international affairs.

La Campagne italienne contre la Suisse. L'Europe Nouvelle. 22:211. Feb. 25, 1939

Campbell, J. Bart
Diplomat's propaganda attempt exposed. Editor and Publisher. 59:5. Dec. 5, 1926
State Department officer tried to make press associations carry "spokesman" story of Mexican bolshevism.

Cary, Edward
Journalism and international affairs. 12p. (International Conciliation Documents, no.21) New York: American Association for International Conciliation, 1909

Corwin, Edward S.
President's control of foreign relations. 216p. Princeton: Princeton Univ. Press, 1917

Cummings, Arthur J.
The press and a changing civilization. 139p. London: John Lane, 1936
Contemporary conditions in the press of Europe and America, with emphasis on the dangers besetting the concept of a free press. By a distinguished British journalist.

Deming, William C.
The opportunity and duty of the press in relation to world peace. 14p. (International Conciliation Documents, no.66) New York: American Association for International Conciliation, 1913

Dodd, William E.
Woodrow Wilson and his work. 369p. Garden City, N.Y.: Doubleday, Page, 1920

Dominique, Pierre
La presse anglaise et l'Italy. L'Europe Nouvelle. 20:475. May 15, 1937

Douglass, Paul F. and Bömer, Karl
The press as a factor in international relations. Annals of the American Academy. 162:245-72. July 1932
> The organization of the press at the Disarmament Conference; a study of the relationship between journalism and diplomacy. The international combination of news agencies, and the organization of the foreign press in a capital European city.

Ellis, William T.
Feeding the world's press at Lausanne. Editor and Publisher. 55:5. Feb. 10, 1923
> News handout system at conference came perilously near to journalistic mendicancy.

Propagandists feed new fires of world hate. Editor and Publisher. 55:5, 37. Sept. 23, 1922
> Onward march of Turks in Near East brings new responsibility to American editors.

Foreign policy and a free press. Nation (London) 33:108-9. Apr. 28, 1923

Frantz, Harry W.
Havana international news center as Pan-American conference opens. Editor and Publisher. 60:35. Jan. 21, 1928
> 150 correspondents from papers all over the world present.

G. Ward Price sums up Europe's year of "bloodless war." World's Press News. 22:2. July 27, 1939
> Daily Mail correspondent criticizes tendency of press to intensify international strain.

Hale, Oren James
Nationalism in press, films, and radio. Annals of the American Academy. 175: 110-16. Sept. 1934

Hodges, Charles
The background of international relations, our world horizons: national and international. 743p. New York: John Wiley, 1931
> Chapters on the press and communications.

Houser, Ernest O.
News of the Far East in U.S. dailies. Public Opinion Quarterly. 2:651-8. Oct. 1938

Il faut s'organiser professionellement contre la propagation des fausses nouvelles. Presse Publicité. 45:3-4, 31. Oct. 7, 1938
> Succession of crises in 1938 showed the necessity of prompt and concerted action on part of journalists to suppress false news lest the government take a hand.

International hatred and the press. Nation. 86:276. Mar. 26, 1908

Is freedom to be sacrificed to Hitler? World's Press News. 21:3. Apr. 27, 1939
> The menace of a doctrine of international press control.

J. A. Spender urges government should take press more into its confidence. Newspaper World. 42:7. July 1, 1939

Journalistic ethics and world affairs. Address delivered at the Fifteenth Annual Journalism Week, May 12-17, 1924. 31p. (Univ. of Missouri Bulletin, v.25. Journalism Series, no.32) Columbia, Mo.: Univ. of Missouri, 1924

Kurth, Karl
Bundespräsident Baumann und Bundesrat Motta über die Propaganda gegen Deutschland in der Schweiz. Zeitungswissenschaft. 14:42-3. Jan. 1, 1939
> Officials of the Swiss Federation disclose propaganda of the Third Internationale intended to create trouble between Germany and Switzerland.

League of newspapers is world need. Editor and Publisher. 54:10. July 2, 1921
> Japanese journalist says world peace is possible only by closer cooperation from press of all nations.

McKenzie, Vernon
The press and international friction. p. 213-24. In Institute of World Affairs, Proceedings, 1938. Los Angeles: Univ. of Southern California, 1939
> Greater understanding among nations does not necessarily lead to sympathy with their objectives and an intense desire for peace.

Die Mobilmachung der Gewissen gegen die Presslüge. Zeitungswissenschaft. 13: 635-8. Oct. 1, 1938
> The political question concerning false news in the world's press, as discussed by the German press chief, Dr. Otto Dietrich, and the problems which the situation offers in counter defence and journalistic research.

Moon, Parker T.
Syllabus on international relations. 280p. New York: Macmillan, 1925-29

Newspapers return to normal as crisis fever abates. World's Press News. 20:3, 19. Oct. 6, 1938
> Aftermath of the Czechoslovakia and Munich crisis.

Open the Disarmament Conference doors. Editor and Publisher. 54:5. Aug. 13, 1921
> Foreign editors and journalists join with Americans in urging sessions open to press.

Paris writers deferred interpretive treatment of foreign news. Editor and Publisher. 59:16. May 21, 1927

Pew, Marlen
Shop talk at thirty. Editor and Publisher. 65:52, 51. June 25, 1932
The importance of international news.
Shop talk at thirty. Review of Libby's book The causes of war. Editor and Publisher. 67:48. May 11, 1935

Poole, DeWitt C.
The conduct of foreign relations under modern democratic conditions. 208p. New Haven: Yale Univ. Press, 1924

Press and peace. Editor and Publisher. 10:3. Mar. 11, 1911
Newspapers vitally concerned in the peace question, says Count Apponyi of Hungary.

Preuss, Lawrence
International responsibility for hostile propaganda against foreign states. American Journal of International Law. 28:649-68. Oct. 1934
No state is obliged to punish private individuals who promote hostile propaganda against foreign nations, according to a survey of international practice.
Extensively documented.
Bibliographical footnotes.

Rowell, Chester H.
The press in international affairs. p. 243-4. In Institute of World Affairs, Proceedings, 1932. Los Angeles: Univ. of Southern California, 1933

Russell, Bertrand Arthur William Russell, 3rd earl
Why men fight; a method of abolishing the international duel. 272p. New York: Century, 1917

Le Scandale de radio-Sarrebrück. L'Europe Nouvelle. 22:508. May 13, 1939

Scelle, Georges
À propos des "accords de presse." Pt. 1-2. Cahiers de la Presse. 1:43-54; 202-10. Jan.-Mar., Apr.-June 1938
Intergovernmental press agreements and freedom of the press with special reference to recent Polish-German and Austro-German accords.

Schlesinger, Arthur M.
Colonial newspapers and the Stamp Act. New England Quarterly. 8:63-83. Mar. 1935
Bibliographical footnotes.

Schuyler, Philip
What an American editor saw in Europe. Editor and Publisher. 59:29. Oct. 9, 1926
Fundamental foreign editorial issues and problems of United States newsmen abroad analyzed by H. V. Kaltenborn.

Scott, Jonathan F.
The press and foreign policy. Journal of Modern History. 3:627-38. Dec. 1931
The relationship of the European press to foreign policy from 1870 to 1914, by an American historian.

Siebert, Frederick S.
International protection of rights in news. Journalism Quarterly. 9:290-304. Sept. 1932
Reprinted from Press Congress of the World. Regional Convention, Mexico City, 1931. Fourth Regional Convention of the World Press Congress. Mexico City, 1931. p.100-7.
The need for a recognition of property in news increased by technological changes in publishing and communications. Rights in news a complex juridical problem.

Some international press courtesies. Athenæum (London) no. 3639:130. July 24, 1897

Spender, John Alfred
The press and international affairs. Yale Review. ns 17:485-98. Apr. 1928
By the former editor of the Westminster Gazette.

Stowe, Leland
The press and international friction. Journalism Quarterly. 13:1-6. Mar. 1936

Stratton, George Malcolm
Social psychology of international conduct. 387p. New York, London: D. Appleton, 1929

Villard, Oswald Garrison
Bunkum and bunting; attitude of our press toward the coronation. Nation. 144:592. May 22, 1937
The press and the international situation. Nation. 106:314-15. Mar. 21, 1918

West, V. Royce
American neutrality on Europe's front pages. Journalism Quarterly. 14:158-66. June 1937
A survey of German, British and French newspapers.

Who inspired Reuters and The Times comments on Premier's pledge? Newspaper World. 42:3. Apr. 8, 1939
Reports of British pledge to Poland offer case example of the close relations between the press and foreign politics.

Wright, Quincy
Public opinion and world politics. Lectures, Harris foundation, 1933, by J. W. Dafoe, J. A. Sauerwein, and others. 236p. Chicago: Univ. of Chicago Press, 1933

B. DIPLOMACY AND THE PRESS

Abbot, Willis J.; Koenigsberg, Moses; and Bent, Silas
The press; its responsibility in international relations. 24p. (Foreign Policy Association. Pamphlet no. 49) New York: 1928

Angell, Sir Norman
Public opinion in foreign policies. Annals of the American Academy. 66:136-9. July 1916
In a democracy negotiations with foreign nations should be arrived at openly. Informed public opinion is needed for the right settlement of public questions.

Barry, Robert T.
British the only source of news at Genoa. Editor and Publisher. 54:5. May 20, 1922
  Press of all nations, failing to get news from own chancellories, turn to Anglo-American meetings for uncolored news.

Bower, Norman
Need for a ministry of propaganda. Newspaper World. 40:1-2. Mar. 13, 1937

Brodie, Edward E.
Just another assignment. Christian Science Monitor, v.27, no. 272. Weekly Magazine Section. p.6. Oct. 16, 1935
  Many newspapermen have served the United States as ambassadors, ministers and consuls.

Butcher, Harold
News men wield great power for peace, French ambassador says. Editor and Publisher. 58:22. Apr. 3, 1926

Child, Richard W.
Popgun opinion and our foreign policy. Saturday Evening Post. 199:35, 165-6, 168. Mar. 26, 1927

Clark, J. Reuben
News gathering and news giving. p.117-26. In Press Congress of the World in Mexico, Aug. 1931. Columbia, Mo.: E. W. Stephens, 1934

Coggeshall, Reginald
Diplomatic implications in international news. Journalism Quarterly. 11:141-59. June 1934
  Relations between diplomats and the press, the cumulative effect of dispatches from abroad, and the responsibility of foreign correspondents.

Colcord, Lincoln
Making diplomatic correspondence public. New Republic. 3:124-5. June 5, 1915

Crockett, Albert S.
When James Gordon Bennett was caliph of Bagdad. 414p. New York, London: Funk and Wagnalls, 1926

Crucy, François
The diplomat and the journalist. Nation (London) 37:288-90. June 6, 1925

Debuchi, Katsuji and Tellez, Manuel C.
Journalism and diplomacy. 10p. (Univ. of Missouri Bulletin, v.30. Journalism Series, no.56) Columbia, Mo.: Univ. of Missouri, 1929

Dickinson, G. Lowes
The international anarchy, 1904-14. 516p. London: G. Allen and Unwin, 1926

Diplomacy and journalism. Spectator. 81:513. Oct. 15, 1898

Diplomacy and the press. Spectator. 101:435-6. Sept. 26, 1908

Dovifat, Emil
The press as a factor in international relations. Introduction. Annals of the American Academy. 162:243-4. July 1932

Draper, Arthur
Public opinion and disarmament. p. 21-7. In Institute of Politics. Williams College. Report of the round tables and general conferences at the eleventh session. Ed. A. H. Buffington. Williamstown, Mass.: Institute of Politics, 1931

Engle, Edward T.
Journalism had done its work. Quill. 18:3-5, 18. Feb. 1930
  How Bell of the *Daily News* set the stage for the London Peace Conference.

Essary, J. Frederick
Covering Washington. p. 146-51, 152-71. Boston, New York: Houghton Mifflin, 1927
  Washington correspondent of the Baltimore *Sun* describes his relations with government officials, contacts with Woodrow Wilson and reporting in Europe during the World War.

Fate of democracy rests with press. Editor and Publisher. 67:6. July 7, 1934

Fay, Sidney Bradshaw
The influence of the pre-war press in Europe. Boston: Massachusetts Historical Society, 1932
  Press politics before the World War.

Pre-war diplomacy and the European press. Current History. 33:212-17. Nov. 1930

Ferguson, Fred S.
Honor bound censorship is greatest menace. Editor and Publisher. 56:3. Nov. 24, 1923

Foreign Office and the newspapers. Spectator. 80:189. Feb. 5, 1897

Gosnell, Cullen Bryant and Nixon, Raymond Blalock, eds.
Public opinion and the press. 177p. Atlanta, Georgia: Institute of Citizenship, Emory Univ., 1933

Hanna, Paul
The State Department and the news. Nation. 111:398-9. Oct. 13, 1920
  Mr. Hanna challenges the State Department to defend its conducting of press interviews. Certain of its rules, he feels, are "inimical to public welfare and hostile to democracy."

Heindel, Richard H.
British diplomats and the press. Public Opinion Quarterly. 2:435-41. July 1938
  The distinction which the pre-war British diplomatic mind made between press opinion and public opinion and the extent of influence of each on foreign policy.

Hough, Henry B. See Lewinson, Minna, jt. auth.

Johnson, Albin E.
Geneva looming as world capital. Editor and Publisher. 58:9. June 20, 1925
  103 correspondents at last session.

Journalists and diplomatists. Living Age. 236:123-5. Jan. 10, 1903

Journalists and peace. New Republic. 60:311-12. Nov. 6, 1929

Lewinson, Minna and Hough, Henry B.
A history of the services rendered to the public by the American press during the year 1917. 31p. New York: Columbia Univ. Press, 1918

Lippmann, Walter
The stakes of diplomacy. 235p. New York: H. Holt, 1915

Lloyd-George, David
War memoirs of David Lloyd-George. 6v. Boston: Little, Brown, 1933-36

Milton, George Fort
Responsibility of the press in a democracy. American Political Science Review. 30:681-91. Aug. 1936
The president and editor of the *Chattanooga News* treats the newspaper as embracing in a single institution a factory, a business, and a profession, which involves a high degree of public trusteeship.

Morelock, T. C., ed.
Visit of the German ambassador and the gift from the press of his country. 31p. (Univ. of Missouri Bulletin, v.31. Journalism. Series, no.61) Columbia, Mo.: Univ. of Missouri, 1930

Nicolson, Hugh
Modern diplomacy and British public opinion; with discussion. International Affairs. 14:599-618. Sept. 1935

Nixon, Raymond Blalock. See Gosnell, Cullen Bryant, jt. ed.

Noble, George Bernard
Policies and opinions at Paris, 1919; Wilsonian diplomacy, the Versailles peace, and French public opinion. 465p. New York: Macmillan, 1935

Norton, Henry Kittredge
Foreign Office organization: publicity. Annals of the American Academy. 143: suppl. 64-9. May 1929

Odegard, Peter H.
The American public mind. 308p. New York: Columbia Univ. Press, 1930

O'Malley, Frank W.
Slowing down through Fleet Street. Saturday Evening Post. 195:9, 156-8. Apr. 21, 1923

Pome, Louis
Le journalisme? une "singulière profession." Presse Publicité. 40:5. June 21, 1938
Paris representative of *Giornale d'Italia* tells why he thinks a foreign correspondent has a unique responsibility.

Poole, DeWitt C.
The conduct of foreign relations under modern democratic conditions. 208p. New Haven: Yale Univ. Press, 1924

Press is diplomatic force, says Ackerman, citing Matsuoka visit. Editor and Publisher. 65:33. May 6, 1933

Salmon, Lucy Maynard
The newspaper and authority. 505p. London, New York: Oxford Univ. Press, 1923
Important as a reference book for students of the press, censorship, and relations of press and government.

Schreiner, George Abel
The craft sinister. 422p. New York City: G. A. Geyer, 1920
World War correspondent in Central Europe describes his vain attempts to funnel the news to America.

Seldes, George
The poisoned springs of world news. Harper's. 169:719-31. Nov. 1934

You can't print that. 465p. New York: Payson and Clark, 1929
"The truth behind the news, 1918-28." Sensational in tone.

Spender, John Alfred
Life, journalism and politics. 2v. London, New York: Cassell, 1927
Valuable for its discussions of press relations with the British government and conflicts between the British and German press prior to the World War.

Sprout, Harold H.
Pressure groups and foreign policies. Annals of the American Academy. 179: 114-23. May 1935

Statesmen and the press. Spectator. 98: 822. May 25, 1907

Stead, W. T.
Government by journalism. Contemporary Review. 49:653-74. May 1886

Stimson, Frederick J.
My United States. 478p. New York, London: C. Scribner's Sons, 1931
An autobiography dealing especially with the author's diplomatic experiences in Argentina during the World War.

Teweles, Heinrich
Presse und Staat. 37p. Prague: D. Kuh, 1886

Thompson, Elbert N. S.
War journalism three hundred years ago. Modern Language Association of America. Publications. 35:93-115. 1920
A description of the news-books of the 17th century showing the manner and style in which the news was presented. The period between the outbreak of the Civil War in England in 1642 and 1647 taught editors much about influencing public opinion.

Wilkerson, Marcus M.
Public opinion and the Spanish-American war; a study in war propaganda. 141p. (University Studies, no. 8) Baton Rouge, La.: Louisiana State Univ. Press, 1932
An authoritative and important study on this subject.

Wolseley, Roland E.
Our foreign policy and the public. American Scholar. 3:361-3. May 1934

C. THE LEAGUE OF NATIONS AND THE PRESS

See also
Conference of Press Experts, p.66.

Angell, Sir Norman
The press and the organization of society. 123p. London: Labour Pub. Co., 1922

Ask open sessions of the League. Editor and Publisher. 58:37. Apr. 17, 1926
Working correspondents give views on convention of press experts.

Bömer, Karl. See Douglass, Paul F. jt. auth.

Breycha-Vauthier, A. C. de
La documentation par la presse à la Bibliothèque de la Société des nations. Cahiers de la Presse. 1:131-5. Jan.-Mar. 1938
An efficient system of filing and indexing of the vast number of articles having international import received by the League daily attests the importance of the press as a source for research in the League's library.

Douglass, Paul F. and Bömer, Karl
The organization of the press at the Disarmament Conference. Annals of the American Academy. 162. suppl:243-64. July 1932

European press approves League plan for world press meet. Editor and Publisher. 58:12. Jan. 16, 1926

Graves, W. Brooke
International public opinion. p. 1219-65. *In* Readings in public opinion: its formation and control. New York, London: D. Appleton-Century, 1928

Hickok, Guy
Wild days at Geneva told from inside. Editor and Publisher. 58:13. Apr. 3, 1926
How more than 300 newspaper correspondents sought to unravel diplomatic snarl at recent League meeting.

International Institute of Intellectual Co-operation
Recueil des Accords Intellectuels. 232p. Paris: 1938

International Labor Office, Geneva
Conditions of work and life of journalists. (International Labor Office, Studies and Reports. Series L, Professional workers, no. 2) Geneva: 1928

Johnson, Albin E.
Fascist journalists omit Geneva group. Editor and Publisher. 60:50. Oct. 1, 1927
Six resign when unable to unseat anti-Fascist.

Geneva group ironing out wire transmission difficulties abroad. Editor and Publisher. 60:37. Mar. 17, 1928
Direct wire now connects League capital and London.

Geneva now world's propaganda center. Editor and Publisher. 60:94. Apr. 21, 1928
Representatives of all causes flock there to gain attention of world press.

Geneva ready for minorities battle. Editor and Publisher. 61:13. Mar. 2, 1929
Rights of oppressed peoples to be debated at League council and in press.

Geneva writers protest "official" reports sent out by League. Editor and Publisher. 64:16. Oct. 24, 1931

Inside story of Geneva Press Gallery's jolting of old-world diplomacy. Editor and Publisher. 58:3. May 1, 1926
Correspondents refuse to be hoodwinked into placing blame for "reconciliation" failure upon Germans.

Pack-reporting threatens Geneva press. Editor and Publisher. 61:7. Aug. 11, 1928
Tendency toward docile and stereotyped reporting; "scoops" frowned upon.

Publicity in press sustains League's power in international affairs. Editor and Publisher. 61:8. Aug. 4, 1928

League of Nations
Collaboration of the press in the organization of peace. Proposal from the Chilean delegation for the convening of a committee of press experts. (A.114. VII) 2p. Geneva: 1925

Conference for the reduction and limitation of armaments. Co-operation of the press in the organisation of peace. (IX. Disarmament. 56) 40p. Geneva: 1932

Co-operation of the press in the organization of peace. (Geneva Sec. L.o.N.P., 1932 G.Q.7) 26p. Boston: World Peace Foundation, 1932
Replies from press organizations to the enquiry into the "spread of false information which may threaten to disturb the peace or the good understanding between nations."

Documents relating to further studies concerning the establishment of a wireless station for the purpose of ensuring independent communications for the League in times of emergency. (Sec. L.o.N.P., 1929. VIII.9) 16p. Boston: World Peace Foundation, 1929

Government press services. 45p. Geneva: Information Section, 1935
A practical handbook of information on the organization of the official press bureaus of some 28 countries.

The League and public opinion. 19p. Geneva: Information Section, 1931
Excerpt from *Ten Years of World Co-operation.* (ch. XIV, p.398-414) Geneva: League of Nations Secretariat; Boston: World Peace Foundation, 1930.

Organisation for communications and transit. Systematic survey of the régime of communications of importance to the working of the League of Nations at times of emergency. Measures foreseen in accordance with the resolutions of the Assembly and the Council. (VIII.6) 101p. Geneva: 1934

League of Nations—*Continued*
——**Assembly. Third Committee**
Establishment of a wireless station destined to ensure independent communications to the League of Nations in times of emergency. Report of the Third Committee to the Assembly. (A.85. 1929. IX) 3p. Geneva: J. de G., 1929

League of Nations Press Gallery. Editor and Publisher. 53:49-50. Jan. 22, 1921
Nations and newspapers represented in the League of Nations Press Gallery.

League of Nations' press meeting call interests American editors. Editor and Publisher. 58:3-4. Dec. 12, 1925

La Liberté de la presse menacée a Genève. L'Europe Nouvelle. 20:34. Jan. 2, 1937
A protest against the arrest and expulsion of a responsible journalist at Geneva for having criticised the League.

Move for world press meet at Geneva to plan moral disarmament. Editor and Publisher. 58:3. Dec. 5, 1925

No idleness for "specials" covering League of Nations at Geneva. Editor and Publisher. 58:57. Mar. 13, 1926
Must keep in close touch with politics of virtually every country.

Potter, Pitman B.
League publicity: cause or effect of League failure? Public Opinion Quarterly. 2:399-412. July 1938
A careful consideration of the League of Nations' theory of publicity and some inconsistencies in its application.

Propaganda by fake; methods used by the League of Nations Union. Nation (London) 26:596-8. Jan. 31, 1920

Recouly, Raymond
Journalism and international politics. Harper's. 146:99-106. Dec. 1922

Source of attack on U.S. writers sought. Editor and Publisher. 60:14. July 23, 1927
Swing of New York Post credits British Foreign Office with saying steel trust dominates Geneva correspondents.

Star writers cover London conference. Editor and Publisher. 66:18. June 3, 1933

Wood, Henry
Ripping off the diplomatic lid at Lausanne. Editor and Publisher. 55:5. Mar. 3, 1923
All nations except the United States get their case before the peoples of the world.

World Peace Foundation
League of Nations and the press. 65p. Boston: 1928

Wireless station for the, purpose of ensuring independent communications for the League in times of emergency. 4p. Brief general Report. (A.18. 1929. VIII. 10) Boston: World Peace Foundation, 1929

D. INTERNATIONAL CONFERENCES OF JOURNALISTS

1. GENERAL WORKS

League of Nations
League of Nations handbook of international organizations. (Sec. VIII, Press) p. 255-63. Geneva: 1938
This section of the handbook summarizes the structure, activities and object of the following international press organizations:
International Federation of the Agricultural Press
International Bureau of Catholic Journalists
International Catholic University Press Secretariat
International Federation of the Cinematographic Press
Permanent International Commission of Editors of Catholic Newspapers
International Federation of Journalists
International Association of Journalists Accredited to the League of Nations
International Newsreel Union
International Federation of Associations of Newspaper Managers and Publishers
International Federation of the Periodical and Trade and Technical Press
International Union of Press Associations
The Press Congress of the World

2. MISCELLANEOUS CONFERENCES

International Chamber of Commerce. Congress, Vienna, 1933
Amended resolution passed in Vienna. Editor and Publisher. 66:9. June 3, 1933
At the International Chamber of Commerce Congress in Vienna, a clause was inserted in the International Convention for Protection of Industrial Property, declaring for indiscriminate issuance of government news.

International press conference meets with approval. Editor and Publisher. 54:7. July 30, 1921
Leading journalists advocate a press conference in Washington to precede the proposed Disarmament Conference.

Johnson, Albin E.
Freer circulation of newspapers in Europe is conference topic. Editor and Publisher. 62:20. Nov. 23, 1929
The Geneva correspondent of *Editor and Publisher* discusses the approaching European Conference on the Transport of Newspapers (Nov. 25, 1929) which sought to eliminate legal and tariff barriers hindering newspaper circulation in Europe.

Langelaan, G.
European news men want special tribunals to settle craft problems. Editor and Publisher. 59:56. Feb. 12, 1927
Comment on a meeting of the Executive Committee of the International Federation of Journalists which considered notices of dismissal, payment in lieu of notice, and "conscience indemnity" for journalists who felt bound to withdraw from newspapers whose policy had changed through transfer of ownership or other reasons.

Morris, John R.
International writers' association reorganized at Tokyo. Editor and Publisher. 55:74. May 19, 1923
Comments and opinions on the reorganization of the International Journalists Association of Tokyo as expressed at dinner celebration of the event at Tokyo. Mr. Zumoto, editor of the *Herald of Asia*, was elected first president.

Poole, DeWitt C., ed.
Conference on the press, held at Princeton University, April 23-25, 1931, under the auspices of the School of Public and International Affairs, with the financial assistance of Chester D. Pugsley. 145p. Washington, D.C.: The Printing Corporation of America, 1931

Valot, Stephen
Le Congrès de la Fédération Internationale des Journalistes. Cahiers de la Presse. p. 316-20. July-Sept. 1939
Summary of the Seventh International Press Congress held at Bordeaux, France, June 27 to 30, 1939.

Wack, H. W.
The International League of Press Clubs. Overland Monthly. 29:619-36. June 1897
The International League of Press Clubs, embracing the membership of over 40 of the largest press clubs in the United States, was founded on January 27, 1891 in Pittsburgh by Thomas J. Keenan, Jr., then editor and proprietor of *The Pittsburgh Press*. The second convention was held in San Francisco in January 1892; the third in St. Paul, Minnesota, May, 1893; fourth, Atlanta, Georgia, May 1894; fifth, Philadelphia, 1895; sixth, Buffalo, June 1896 and the seventh annual convention, New York City, 1897.

3. CONGRESO DE LA PRENSA LATINA

Chauvelot, Robert
La Presse Latine à Athènes. L'Illustration. 178:68. Jan. 10, 1931
Ninth Congress held in Athens.
La Presse Latine au Caire. Mercure de France. 233:686-96. Feb. 1, 1932
The writer prefaces his description of the Tenth Congress of the Latin Press (Cairo) with observations on Anglo-Egyptian relationships.
Le tricentenaire des Antilles et le XIII° Congrès de la Presse Latine en Haïti. Mercure de France. 265:649-54. Feb. 1, 1936
The Thirteenth Congress of the Latin Press was held at Port au Prince, Haiti, concurrently with the 300th Anniversary celebration in the Antilles.

Clair-Guyot, Jean
Le Congrès de la Presse Latine en Touraine. L'Illustration. 174:445-6. Oct. 19, 1929
Brief account of annual Congress of the Latin Press, at which fraternizing, rather than serious discussion, was emphasized. Sessions had been held in Bucharest, October 22, 1927, and in Havana, April 14, 1928.

Congreso de la Prensa Latina
La prensa latina y sus congresos. Con caricaturas originales de Armando Maribona. 59p. Havana: Diario de la Marina, 1928

Congreso de la Prensa Latina. 1st, Lyons, 1923
Congreso de la Prensa Latina. Compte rendu in extenso des débats. Congrès de la Presse Latine. 166p. Lyons: Noirclerc and Fénétrier, 1923

Congreso de la Prensa Latina. 7th, Havana, 1928
Cuba en 1928; reminiscencias, documentos, informaciones, gráficos, articulos y opiniones. 127p. Paris: Battemberg, 1928

Langelaan, G.
Latin Press Congress at Lyons, France. Editor and Publisher. 55:7. Mar. 10, 1923
Romance nations of Europe and South America represented at meeting.

Monmarché, Marcel
Le Congrès de la Presse Latine à Athènes. Annales Politiques et Littéraires. 96:191. Feb. 15, 1931
The Ninth Congress desired to include Greece among Latin Press confrères.

Press of all Latin nations unite. Editor and Publisher. 55:33. Apr. 14, 1923
The Congress of the Latin Press held at Lyons, March 4-8, 1923, brought together 80 representatives of newspapers from 13 different countries in which a Latin language is spoken.

4. INTERNATIONAL PRESS CONGRESS

International Press Congress, 1st, Antwerp, 1894
Renseignements, procès-verbaux des séances et discours communiqués. Congrès International de la Presse. Antwerp, 1894. Account, minutes of the meetings, and addresses delivered, at the International Press Congress held at Antwerp, 1894. 104p. Antwerp: Buschmann, 1894

About

The Press Congress at Antwerp. Athenæum (London) no. 3482:96-7. July 21, 1894
Review of the proceedings of the First International Congress of the Press held at Antwerp, July 9-11, 1894.

International Press Congress, 3rd, Budapest, 1896
Compte rendu des travaux du 3me Congrès International de la Presse. Budapest, 1896. 64p. Bordeaux: G. Gounouilhou, 1897

International Press Congress, 5th, Lisbon, 1898
Compte rendu des travaux du 5me Congrès International de la Presse, Lisbonne, 1898. Report of the 5th International Press Congress at Lisbon, 1898. 146p. Bordeaux: Gounouilhou, 1899

International Press Congress, 9th, Vienna, 1904
IXe Congrès International de la Presse, Vienne, 1904. Rapports. Vienna. Steyrermühl, 1904
Report of addresses and proceedings pertaining to problems of communications, professional dignity and ethics, rate reductions for telegraph and postal service.
Rapports. IX Congrès International de la Presse. Vienne, 1904. Report of the 9th International Press Congress, Vienna, 1904. 104p. Vienna: Steyrermühl, 1904
Addresses and proceedings pertaining to problems of communications, professional dignity and ethics, rate reductions for telegraph and postal service.

World's Press Congress. Editor and Publisher. 10:6. May 6, 1911
International Press Congress opening in Rome with 500 delegates attending.

5. CONFERENCE OF PRESS EXPERTS

a. PRELIMINARY PLANS

Geneva meeting of press experts assured as 25 nations approve. Editor and Publisher. 58:12. Apr. 3, 1926
Announcement of preparatory meetings which were to have been held in order to assist the Secretary-General of the League of Nations in preparing agenda for the approaching World's Press Congress (Geneva and Lausanne, Switzerland, April 7-13, 1926).

League of Nations
Collaboration of the press in the organization of peace. Resolution adopted by the Assembly on Sept. 25, 1925. (A.138. VII) Geneva: 1925
Documents relating to the preparation of the press experts committee. Resolution of the Sixth Assembly, 1925. (Sec. L.o.N.P. 1926. General. 15) 15p. Geneva: 1926

b. CONFERENCE AT GENEVA, AUGUST 1927

Conference of Press Experts
Conference of Press Experts, Aug. 24, 1927. Preparatory Documents. (General. 1) 31p. Geneva: Sec. L.o.N.P., 1927
Conference of Press Experts, Aug. 24, 1927. Protection of press information. (General. 5) 28p. Geneva: Sec. L.o.N.P., 1927
Pt. I. A draft model law establishing the protection of press information. Pt. II. A collection of laws in force in various countries and draft laws relating to the protection of press information.
Conference of Press Experts. Final Report, Aug. 1927. (General. 15) 32p. Geneva: Sec. L.o.N.P., 1927
Conference of Press Experts, Geneva, Aug. 24-29, 1927. Final resolutions and various other documents. (General. 8) 24p. Geneva: Sec. L.o.N.P., 1927

Conference of Press Experts. Report presented to the Assembly by the Sixth Committee. (General. 9) 2p. Geneva: Sec. L.o.N.P., 1927
Conference of Press Experts. Resolution adopted by the Assembly on Sept. 22, 1927. (General. 10) 1p. Geneva: Sec. L.o.N.P., 1927
Vote of thanks by the Assembly for the work of the Conference of Press Experts.

Geneva press parley attracts 60 delegates. Editor and Publisher. 60:7. Aug. 13, 1927
Announcement giving provisional agenda of the International Press Conference which opened Aug. 24, 1927 at Geneva under the auspices of the League of Nations.

Johnson, Albin E.
Absolute freedom and no favors asked by overseas writers. Editor and Publisher. 59:28. Feb. 19, 1927
Ask better transit and transmission facilities in memorandum to Council of League of Nations which met to fix a date for the approaching International Press Conference.

Geneva conference denounces censorship. Editor and Publisher. 60:5. Sept. 3, 1927
Resolutions regarding press rates, equality in government news, and property rights in news as dealt with at the International Conference of Journalists, Geneva, 1927.

Government news the property of all, opinion of League press delegates. Editor and Publisher. 60:3, 18. Aug. 27, 1927
International Press Conference, August 24, 1927, held under auspices of the League of Nations. See also the author's article of previous week in *Editor and Publisher*, p.8, dealing with same subject. This Conference stated the principle of property rights in news, and discussed the indiscriminate issuance of government announcements and news.

Invitations issued for Geneva meet of press experts Aug. 24. Editor and Publisher. 60:64. June 25, 1927
Meeting to consider press rates, censorship, communications and facilities for journalists.

World-wide protection of news as property sought at Geneva. Editor and Publisher. 60:8. Aug. 20, 1927
International Press Conference, Geneva.

c. CONFERENCE AT MADRID, NOVEMBER 1933

American delegates active at Madrid. Editor and Publisher. 66:10. Nov. 11, 1933
The fight waged against attempts to restrict the activities of correspondents in foreign countries at the Press Conference in Madrid.

League of Nations. Assembly. Second Committee
Co-operation of the press in the organization of peace. Report submitted by the Second Committee to the Assembly. (A.44. 1934) 3p. Geneva: 1934
Results of the conference of government press bureaus and press representatives held at Madrid, November 7 to 11, 1933.

Madrid parley peril to press, U.P. aide says. Newsdom. 4:1-2. Oct. 28, 1933

Perry, John W.
Curb on false news asked at Madrid. Editor and Publisher. 66:5, 39. Nov. 18, 1933
A fact-finding body of experts to study the problem of false news was recommended by representatives at the Second International Press Conference which met at Madrid, November, 1933, under the auspices of the League of Nations.

True news. Editor and Publisher. 66:22. Nov. 18, 1933
Editorial praising the action of the International Press Conference held at Madrid, November, 1933, under the auspices of the League of Nations, in which the Conference voted to maintain a fact-finding body to investigate sources of false news.

Urges U.S. call world press meeting. Editor and Publisher. 65:7. Feb. 11, 1933
Article quotes at length from address by Dean Carl W. Ackerman of the Columbia University School of Journalism.

World press "Tribunal of Honor" shunned by U.S. representatives. Editor and Publisher. 64:26. Feb. 27, 1932
The Copenhagen press conference, held in January, 1932 at the request of Danish government to discuss the "problem of false and tendentious news regarding international affairs of a nature likely to disturb international peace," preceded the session at Madrid.

6. PAN-AMERICAN CONGRESS OF JOURNALISTS, 1926

Campbell, J. Bart
Permanent Pan-American press body urged. Editor and Publisher. 58:18, 18. Apr. 17, 1926
The text of the 29 resolutions adopted at the First Pan-American Press Congress of Journalists, Washington, April 7-13, 1926. Author believes the resolutions reflect the sentiment, opinion and matured ideas of foremost journalists.

U.S. welcomes Latin-American editors. Editor and Publisher. 58:25. Apr. 10, 1926
First Pan-American Congress of Journalists, Washington, D.C. Account of the first few sessions.

The First Pan American Congress of Journalists. Washington, D.C., April 7-13, 1926. Bulletin of the Pan American Union. 60:128-30. Feb. 1926
Announcement giving purposes and program of the first Pan-American Congress of Journalists was provided for by resolution of the Fifth Pan-American Conference at Santiago, Chile, in 1923.

News service binds people of Americas, Coolidge tells press congress. Editor and Publisher. 58:23, 66. Apr. 10, 1926
Text of President Coolidge's address to the members of the first Pan-American Congress of Journalists at Washington, April 7-13, 1926.

One hundred Latin-American editors to attend Washington conference. Editor and Publisher. 58:18. Mar. 20, 1926
List of delegates to the first Pan-American Congress of Journalists at Washington.

Pan American Congress of Journalists. 1st, Washington, 1926
Proceedings. 229p. Washington: Pan American Union, 1926

7. PRESS CONGRESS. OF THE WORLD

a. GENERAL SESSIONS

(1) HONOLULU, 1921

Ethics and understanding press congress aim. Editor and Publisher. 54:5. Dec. 3, 1921
Success of international organization of journalists assured at this session in Honolulu. The first drive will be for better news communications between nations. The Pan-Pacific Press Conference was organized at these sessions.

Pan-Pacific unity and Committee's high accomplishments—Williams. Editor and Publisher. 54:7-9. Dec. 3, 1921
Understanding will be fostered throughout world by the Press Congress. Address by Walter Williams, president of Press Congress, summarizes results of the Hawaiian meeting and lists officers of the Press Congress elected at Honolulu.

The Press Congress of the World. Bulletin of the Pan American Union. 53:485-9. Nov. 1921
Program and highlights of the Conference in 1921, Honolulu.

Rodriguez, Virgilio B.
World peace ideal of Press Congress. Editor and Publisher. 54:5-6, 40. Sept. 24, 1921
Plan of Honolulu convention is to form permanent organization of journalists for better international understanding, with welfare of all peoples as sole object.

Williams, Walter, ed.
Press Congress of the World in Hawaii. (Honolulu, 1921) New York: J. W. Brown, 1921

(2) GENEVA AND LAUSANNE, 1926

Press Congress of the World. 2d, Geneva and Lausanne, 1926
The Press Congress of the World in Switzerland, with foreword by William E. Rappard . . . ed. by Walter Williams. 249p. Columbia, Mo.: E. W. Stephens, 1928

Williams makes plea for crusading press. Editor and Publisher. 59:7, 47. Sept. 18, 1926
Full text of Dean Walter Williams' address, opening sessions of the Press Congress of the World at Geneva, September 14, 1926, in which he discussed the origin of the Congress, its purpose and its objectives.

World wide free press to serve all men. Editor and Publisher. 59:33. Oct. 9, 1926
Proceedings of Press Congress at Geneva and Lausanne, Switzerland. Article quotes set of resolutions and summarizes remarks of delegates on important phases of journalism.

b. REGIONAL SESSIONS

(1) PAN-PACIFIC PRESS CONFERENCE, 1921

Pan-Pacific Press Conference. 1st, Honolulu, 1921

About

Pan-Pacific Press Conference. p.419-505. *In* Press Congress of the World, 2d Honolulu, Hawaii, 1921. Ed. by Walter Williams. 605p. Columbia, Mo.: E. W. Stephens, 1922

Program and proceedings; first Pan-Pacific Press Conference, a regional section of the Press Congress of the World. Honolulu, Oct. 21, 1921. Held under the auspices of the Pan-Pacific Union and called by Dr. Walter Williams, president of the Press Congress of the World. 95p. Honolulu: Honolulu Star-Bulletin, 1921

Thurston, Lorrin A.
Problems of the Pan-Pacific press. Editor and Publisher. 54:8-12, 41. Dec. 17, 1921
Presented in reports and addresses of the resolutions committee at the first Conference meeting in Honolulu.

(2) REGIONAL CONVENTION, MEXICO CITY, 1931

Press Congress of the World. Regional Convention, Mexico, 1931
The Press Congress of the World. Regional meeting in Mexico City. With a foreword by Dr. Walter Williams. Ed. by Frank L. Martin. 174p. Columbia, Mo.: E. W. Stephens, 1934
A summary of the proceedings. The Press Federation of America was organized at this convention. Cf. p.68-89.

Starr-Hunt, Jack
Press Congress meets in Mexico City. Editor and Publisher. 64:9. Aug. 15, 1931
President Rubio and other high Mexican officials addressed the Regional Conference of editors.

World Press Congress. Bulletin of the Pan American Union. 65:1281-2. Dec. 1931
American Press Federation, organized August 17, 1931, approved at this Regional Meeting of the World Press Congress in Mexico City, August 10-14, 1931.

E. NEWS WRITERS' ORGANIZA-TIONS—ENGLISH SPEAKING COUNTRIES

Brandenburg, George A.
Newspaper guild adopts ethics code. Editor and Publisher. 67:7, 41-2. June 16, 1934
Text of Constitution, p. 41-2.

British Journalists' Union urges thirty dollar weekly minimum. Editor and Publisher. 70:37. Mar. 6, 1937

Brown, Lawrence
The press faces a union. New Republic. 81:297-9. Jan. 23, 1935

Butcher, Harold
Bullen tells how Institute works. Editor and Publisher. 66:7, 35. Dec. 30, 1933
Brief survey of the British Institute of Journalists.
Writers' Union powerful in Britain. Editor and Publisher. 66:7, 33. Jan. 6, 1934

Cole, Percy T.
Guild idea praised by Blumenfeld. Editor and Publisher. 66:5. Dec. 16, 1933

Delafons, Allan
British group formed to aid writers. Editor and Publisher. 62:11, 56. June 15, 1929
To elevate professional status of newspapermen.

Frederick, David
Union idea a success in Australia. Editor and Publisher. 67:9, 37. June 2, 1934

Grigg, Joseph
London proprietors' pact with unions hailed as charter of press freedom. Editor and Publisher. 58:3. May 22, 1926
Employers win right to "employ, promote and discharge" without strike danger.

Institute of Journalists
Fifty years of Institute leadership. Institute of Journalists' Journal. 27:73. Apr. 1939
Survey of the organization's record of services.

Murasken, Estelle
Newswriters' unions in English speaking countries. 144p. New York: U.S. Works Progress Administration, 1938
A helpful survey of newspaper employees' organizations in Australia, Great Britain and Canada.

Williams, Walter
Organization of journalists in Great Britain. 39p. (Univ. of Missouri Bulletin. v.30. Journalism Series, no. 58) Columbia, Mo.: Univ. of Missouri, Dec. 14, 1929
The six most important organizations. Particularly, however, the Institute of Journalists.

World Federation salutes the Guild. Guild Reporter. 1:2. June 15, 1934
Roger Dapoigny, representing the International Federation of Journalists with headquarters in Paris, brought greetings from his organization to the American Newspaper Guild, meeting in St. Paul, Minnesota, June, 1934. He explained that the Federation consisted of 23 national associations and 8 foreign press agencies, with a total membership of 25,000 professional members.

X. WAR AND THE PRESS

A. HISTORY AND THEORY

Another Ems message. World's Work. 33: 9-11. Nov. 1916

Bleyer, Willard Grosvenor
Main currents in the history of American journalism. 464p. New York, Boston: Houghton Mifflin, 1927

Briggs, Herbert W. and Buell, Raymond Leslie
American neutrality in a future war. Foreign Policy Reports. 11:26-36. Apr. 10, 1935

Bruntz, George C.
Propaganda as an instrument of war. Current History. 32:743-7. July 1930

Buell, Raymond Leslie. See Briggs, Herbert W. jt. auth.

Bullard, F. Lauriston
Famous war correspondents. 437p. Boston: Little, Brown, 1914
    Biographical sketches of war correspondents, mainly in the 19th century.

Claes, Major E. and others
Die Führungstruppe der Wehrmacht. Die Nachrichtentruppen in Krieg und Frieden. Hrsg. von Hellmut Blume. 3. Aufl. 199p. Stuttgart, Berlin, Leipzig: Union Deutsche Verlagsgesellschaft, 1937
    Military treatise on the press and intelligence sections of the German army.

Coverage of general war "previewed" by Driscoll. Editor and Publisher. 72:8. Apr. 8, 1939
    New York Herald Tribune correspondent predicts complete censorship and little opportunity for war reporters if conflict should break out.

Davis, Elmer H.
History of The New York Times. 434p. New York: New York Times, 1921

Douie, Charles O. G.
Some literature of the Great war. Nineteenth Century. 108:116-36. July 1930

Forbes, Archibald
War correspondents and the authorities. Nineteenth Century. 7:185-96. Jan. 1880
    Arguments favoring special privileges for war correspondents. Rules laid down for governing the conduct of war reporters analyzed.

Graves, W. Brooke, ed.
Readings in public opinion; its formation and control. 1281p. New York, London: D. Appleton, 1928

Hamlin, Charles Hunter
The war myth in United States history. 102p. New York: Vanguard Press, 1927

Hughes, L. M.
Results of last war indicate advertising need fear nothing. Editor and Publisher. 72:5. July 1, 1939

Kittel, Erick K.
Das Nachrichtwesen der Wehrmacht. Zeitungswissenschaft. 12:782-6. Nov. 1, 1937
    News, official army news divisions, and the defense forces.

Lees, Frederic
Some writers on war. Fortnightly. 74: 472-85. Sept. 1, 1900

Leiter, Friedrich
Die Zeitung im Kriege und nach dem Kriege. 89p. Vienna: Moritz Perles, 1915
    War and the newspapers.

Lingelbach, William E.
The press as a preventive of war. Annals of the American Academy. 114:150-2. July 1924
    The responsibility of the newspaper as an agency of peace in promoting international understanding and education.

Lowell, Abbott Lawrence
Public opinion in war and peace. 302p. Cambridge: Harvard Univ. Press, 1923

McClatchy, V. S.
News communication—the great peace promoter. p. 100-8. In Institute of International Relations, Proceedings, 1930. Los Angeles: Univ. of Southern California, 1931

Mac Orlan, Pierre
Correspondents de guerre et grands reporters. Annales Politiques et Littéraires. 90:465. May 15, 1928

Mansfield, F. J.
Stories of eminent war correspondents. World's Press News. 20:210. Dec. 1937
    Chiefly men of the 19th century.

Matthews, Herbert L.
War's fog. Guild Reporter. 5:8. Jan. 10, 1938

Maude, Frederic Natusch
Pessimism in the press and its causes. Contemporary Review. 113:495-8. May 1918
    Reprinted in Living Age. 297:769-72. June 29, 1918.

Millis, Walter
Propaganda for war. Southern Review. 5(2):201-10. 1939

—Riegel, Oscar W.; Stone, William T.; and Soule, George
Will we stay out of the next war? New Republic. 83:323-7, 351-4; 84:11-13, 38-41. July 31, Aug. 7, 14, 21, 1935

Nevins, Allan
American press opinion, Washington to Coolidge. 598p. New York, Boston: D. C. Heath, 1928

The Evening Post; a century of journalism. 590p. New York: Boni and Liveright, 1922

Newspaper correspondence. Army and Navy Journal. 76:113. Oct. 1, 1938
Major General W. C. Sweeney, chief of the A.E.F. Censorship Division, believes that war correspondents are an important part of an army, and can do much to assist in a military effort.

O'Brien, Frank M.
The story of the Sun, New York: 1833-1928. 305p. New York: D. Appleton, 1928

Odegard, Peter H.
The American public mind. 308p. New York: Columbia Univ. Press, 1930

Ralph, Julian
The war correspondent of today. Harpers' Weekly. 44:854. Sept. 8, 1900
Suggestions of a British war correspondent during the Boer War for improving war reporting.

Rieben, Charles
Les journaux et la guerre. Bibliothèque Universelle et Revue Suisse. 96:241-58, 408-28. Nov.-Dec. 1919

Riegel, Oscar W. See Millis, Walter, jt. auth.

Rogerson, Sidney
Propaganda in the next war. 188p. London: Bles, 1938
How England should conduct war propaganda, particularly in neutral countries.

Salmon, Lucy Maynard
The newspaper and authority. 505p. New York: Oxford Univ. Press, 1923
The newspaper and the historian. 566p. New York: Oxford Univ. Press, 1923

Scott, Jonathan F.
The press and foreign policy. Journal of Modern History. 3:627-38. Dec. 1931

Seitz, Don Carlos
The James Gordon Bennetts, father and son. 405p. Indianapolis: Bobbs-Merrill, 1928
Joseph Pulitzer, his life and letters. 478p. New York: Simon and Schuster, 1924

Soule, George. See Millis, Walter, jt. auth.

Stone, Melville E.
Fifty years a journalist. 371p. Garden City, N.Y., Toronto: Doubleday, Page, 1921
How the Associated Press built up a system of foreign correspondence and means of reporting wars during the early 20th century.

Stone, William T. See Millis, Walter, jt. auth.

Unger, Frederic W.
The war correspondent's future. Booklover's Magazine. 4:767-70. Dec. 1904

Watterson, Henry
Marse Henry; an autobiography. 2v. New York: Geo. H. Doran, 1919

What shall be done with the press in war time? Review of Reviews. 34:236-7. Aug. 1906

Working up a war. Nation. 85:26. July 11, 1907

World journalism termed peace help. Trans-Pacific. 22:15. May 24, 1934
James J. Furay, speaking to Pan-Pacific Club, holds up truth as an ideal in news work.

B. ARMAMENTS AND THE PRESS

Angell, Sir Norman
The unseen assassins. 283p. New York, London: Harper, 1932

Arms and the men. Fortune. 9:52, 113-14, 116, 118, 120, 125-6. Mar. 1934

The **Arms** investigation. Living Age. 346:303-8. June 1934

Commends press for squareness. American Press. 51:4. Feb. 1933
Under Secretary Castle says papers in America try to print the truth.

Davenport, Guiles
Zaharoff, high priest of war. 319p. Boston: Lothrop, Lee and Shepard, 1934

Engelbrecht, H. C. and Hanighen, F. C.
Merchants of death; a study of the international armament industry. 308p. New York: Dodd, Mead, 1934

Gunther, John
Slaughter for sale. Harper's. 168:649-59. May 1934

Hanighen, F. C. See Engelbrecht, H. C. jt. auth.

The **Inside** story of the Vickers meeting. Living Age. 346:326-8. June 1934

Japanese press on disarmament. Current Opinion. 71:158-60. Aug. 1921

Johnson, Albin E.
Arms parley ignores public opinion. Editor and Publisher. 64:66. Apr. 23, 1932

Knecht, Marcel
Public opinion and disarmament. Annals of the American Academy. 144:148-50. July 1929

Lehmann-Russbüldt, Otto
War for profits. 175p. New York: 1934
Introduction by Pierre Loving.
First pub. in German under title Die Blutige Internationale der Rüstungindustrie. Berlin: Fackelreiter, 1929.

Let there be peace propaganda. Newsdom. 5:4. Mar. 31, 1934
Editorial.

McConnell, Burt Monroe
Our Fourth Estate looks at the Navy. Current History. 48:31-4. Apr. 1938

MacDonald bars inquiry into British arms firms. New York Times. 83:1. Apr. 24, 1934

Madariaga, Salvador de
Disarmament. 379p. New York: Coward-McCann, 1929

Seldes, George
Iron, blood and profits: an exposure of the world-wide munitions racket. 397p. New York, London: Harper, 1934

Selfish publishers block peace move. Editor and Publisher. 66:11. Mar. 17, 1934

Stone, William T.
The munitions industry; an analysis of the Senate investigation, September 4-21, 1934. Foreign Policy Reports. 10:250-68. Dec. 5, 1934
Revised edition, *Foreign Policy Reports,* Jan. 21, 1935.

C. PRE-19th CENTURY

Brown, Ralph Adams
New Hampshire editors win the war; a study in revolutionary press propaganda. New England Quarterly. 12:35-51. Mar. 1939
New Hampshire's "trumpeters of sedition," printers and newspaper editors of Civil War days, adept in the use of propaganda.

Dewey, Davis R.
The news of the French Revolution in America. New England Magazine. 1(ns):84-9. Sept. 1889
News of the fall of the Bastille, July 14, 1789, reached the United States two months after the event.

Diary of the American revolution. Comp. by Frank Moore. 2v. New York: C. Scribner, 1860
American newspaper reports of the Revolutionary War, drawn "from Whig and Tory newspapers" and other contemporaneous writings.

Gallinger, Herbert P.
Die Haltung der deutschen Publizistik zu dem amerikanischen Unabhängigkeitskriege, 1775-1783. 77p. Leipzig: O. Schmidt, 1900
Dissertation.
The American Revolutionary War and publicly expressed viewpoints in Germany.

Grossbart, Julien
La presse polonaise et la Révolution Française. Annales Historiques de la Révolution Française. 15:234-66. May-June 1938
Polish opinion on the French Revolution to the Kosciusko insurrection (Sept. 1792-Mar. 1794).

Ogg, Frederic Austin
Newspaper satire during the American Revolution. New England Magazine. 30:366-76. May 1904

Thomas, Charles M.
The publication of newspapers during the American Revolution. Journalism Quarterly. 9:358-73. Dec. 1932
The experiences of colonial newspapers, including those which remained loyal to England, others which were adherents of the revolutionary cause, and a third group which changed loyalties whenever necessary.

Thompson, Elbert N. S.
War journalism three hundred years ago. Baltimore: Modern Language Association of America, 1920

Tyler, Moses Coit
The literary history of the American Revolution, 1763-1783. 2v. New York, London: G. P. Putnam's Sons, 1897

Waitt, Ernest L.
How the news of the battle of Lexington reached England. New England Magazine. 40:92-7. Mar. 1909

D. EARLY 19th CENTURY

Atkins, John Black
The life of Sir William Howard Russell. 2v. London: John Murray, 1911
Standard work on the life of the British war correspondent, noted particularly for his reports of the Crimean War.

Bullard, F. Lauriston
Famous war correspondents. 437p. Boston: Little, Brown, 1914

Ester, Karl d'
Ein Propagandablatt Napoleons I. Zeitungswissenschaft. 13:726-7. Nov. 1, 1938
A brief account of French propaganda methods employed in the newspaper *Argus,* printed in English in London.

Fischaleck, Lorenz
Napoleon und die Press. Zeitungswissenschaft. 13:100-6. Feb. 1, 1938
Napoleon's use of the press as a means of influencing the public in his favor.

Forbes, Archibald
The Afghan wars, 1839-42 and 1878-80. 337p. New York: Charles Scribner's Sons, 1892

——See Russell, Sir William Howard, jt. auth.

Hamburger, Ernest
Épisodes de la lutte entre Napoléon I. et la presse anglaise. Cahiers de la Presse. 1:617-23. Oct.-Dec. 1938
Some details of the vicissitudes of a dictator-controlled press in conflict with the free press of a foreign power.

Heroes of the camera. Outing. 46:728-33. Sept. 1905

Kendall, George Wilkins
Narrative of the Texan Santa Fé expedition. Historical introduction by Milo Milton Quaife. 585p. Chicago: R. R. Donnelley and Sons, 1929
Kendall, who founded the *New Orleans Picayune* in January, 1837, describes a tour through Texas, with an account of the sufferings, losses and capture of the Texans and their long march as prisoners to the City of Mexico.
Only v.I and v.II, ch.1 are reprinted in this edition.

About
First of his kind. Tom Mahoney. Quill. 19:5-6. Nov. 1931

Pioneer Louisiana editor's dispatches to his paper in 1815 give him a claim to title of "first war correspondent." Publishers' Auxiliary. 73:1, 5. May 21, 1938

Mahoney, Tom
First of his kind. Quill. 19:5-6. Nov. 1931.
George Wilkins Kendall, an American, became a war correspondent 85 years ago.

Pioneer Louisiana editor's dispatches to his paper in 1815 give him a claim to title of "first war correspondent." Publishers' Auxiliary. 73:1, 5. May 21, 1938

Prebble, John E.
When Napoleon sued a London paper for libel. World's Press News. 19:4. Apr. 14, 1938
In 1802 Napoleon asked the British government to "crack down" on *L'Ambigu*, Royalist paper published in London in French by M. Peltier. Receiving no satisfaction, he sued and won.

Rein, Adolf
Die Teilnahme Sardiniens am Krimkrieg und die öffentliche Meinung in Italien. 175p. Leipzig: R. Voigtländer, 1910
Dissertation.
Sardinia in the Crimean War and public opinion in Italy.

The **Rise** and fall of the war correspondent. Macmillan's. 90:301-10. Aug. 1904

Robinson, Henry Crabb
About
Diary, reminiscences and correspondence of Henry Crabb Robinson. Ed. by Thomas Sadler. 2v. New York: Macmillan, 1872

Russell, Sir William Howard
The British expedition to the Crimea. 629p. London, New York: G. Routledge, 1858

The war: from the landing at Gallipoli to the death of Lord Raglan. 507p. London: G. Routledge, 1856
——and Forbes, Archibald
War correspondents. Edinburgh Review. 183:129-42. Jan. 1896
About
The life of Sir William Howard Russell. John Black Atkins. 2v. London: John Murray, 1911
Standard work on the life of the British war correspondent, noted particularly for his reports of the Crimean War.

Sadler, Thomas, ed.
Diary, reminiscences and correspondence of Henry Crabb Robinson. 2v. New York: Macmillan, 1872

Urquhart, David
The Edinburgh Review and the Afghan War. 61p. London: J. Maynard, 1843

E. CIVIL WAR PERIOD

Abrams, Ray H.
The Jeffersonian, Copperhead newspaper. Pennsylvania Magazine. 57:260-83. July 1933
The story of a colorful and influential Democratic paper during the Civil War.

Adams, Ephraim D.
Great Britain and the American Civil War. 2v. London, New York: Longmans, Green, 1925

Atkins, John Black
The life of Sir William Howard Russell. 2v. London: John Murray, 1911

Babcock, H. B.
The press and the Civil War. Journalism Quarterly. 6:1-5. Mar. 1929

Bennett, James Gordon
Federal generals and a good press; selections from the confidential correspondence of J. G. Bennett. American Historical Review. 39:284-97. Jan. 1934
About
When James Gordon Bennett was caliph of Bagdad. Albert S. Crockett. 414p. New York, London: Funk and Wagnalls, 1926

Brady, Mathew B.
About
Mathew B. Brady, the first man to "cover" a war with a camera. Elmo Scott Watson. Quill. 25:10-11, 21. Sept. 1937
The photographer of the Civil War.

Brantley, Rabun Lee
Georgia journalism of the Civil War period. 134p. Nashville: Peabody College, 1929

A Southern paper and the Civil War. Journalism Bulletin. 2:23-8. June 1925

Coffin, Charles Carleton
The boys of '61'. 558p. Boston: Estes and Lauriat, 1882
The war correspondent of the *Boston Journal* includes his experiences with the Union armies.
About
Charles Carleton Coffin, war correspondent, traveler, and statesman. William E. Griffis. 357p. Boston: Estes and Lauriat, 1898

Copeland, Fayette
Civil War editors called it propaganda. Journalism Quarterly. 14:144-5. June 1937
A discussion of the meaning acquired by the word "propaganda"; its history.

Cortissoz, Royal
The life of Whitelaw Reid. 2v. New York: C. Scribner's Sons, 1921

Crockett, Albert S.
When James Gordon Bennett was caliph of Bagdad. 414p. New York, London: Funk and Wagnalls, 1926

Crounse, L. L.
The army correspondent. Harper's. 27:627-33. Oct. 1863
Intimate glimpses of the day-to-day activities of a correspondent with the army during the Civil War.

Dana, Charles A.
Recollections of the Civil War. 296p. New York: D. Appleton, 1898

Daniel, John M.
The Richmond Examiner during the War. 232p. New York: Dauber and Pine, Printed for the Author, 1868

Day, S. P.
Down South; or, An Englishman's experience at the seat of the American war. 2v. London: Hurst and Blackett, 1862

Fahrney, Ralph Ray
Horace Greeley and the Tribune in the Civil War. 229p. Cedar Rapids, Iowa: Torch Press, 1936

Greeley, Horace
About
Horace Greeley and the Tribune in the Civil War. Ralph Ray Fahrney. 222p. Cedar Rapids, Iowa: Torch Press, 1936

Griffis, William E.
Charles Carleton Coffin, war correspondent, traveler, and statesman. 357p. Boston: Estes and Lauriat, 1898

Halley, R. A.
A rebel newspaper's war story. American Historical Magazine. 8:124-53. Apr. 1903
    A narrative of the history of the *Memphis Commercial Appeal* during the Civil War.

How we get our news. Harper's. 34:511-22. Mar. 1867

Jones, John Beauchamp
A Rebel war clerk's diary at the Confederate States capitol. Ed. with an introduction and historical notes by Howard Swiggett. 2v. New York: Barnes and Noble, 1935

Jordan, Donaldson and Pratt, E. J.
Europe and the American Civil War. 299p. Boston, New York: Houghton Mifflin, 1931

McDonald, Helen G.
Canadian public opinion on the American Civil War. 239p. New York: Columbia Univ. Press, 1926

Page, Charles A.
Letters of a war correspondent. 397p. Boston: L. C. Page, 1898
    Edited with notes by James R. Gilmore.

Poore, Benjamin Perley
Perley's reminiscences of sixty years in the national metropolis. 2v. Philadelphia: Hubbard Bros., 1886

Pratt, E. J. See Jordan, Donaldson, jt. auth.

The Press in war-time. Fortnightly Review. 85:528-36. Mar. 1906

Randall, James G.
The newspaper problem in its bearing upon military secrecy during the Civil War. American Historical Review. 23:303-23. Jan. 1918
    Discusses laxity of newspaper control in the North during Civil War. This was a period of keen journalistic enterprise.

Reid, Whitelaw
About
The life of Whitelaw Reid. Royal Cortissoz. 2v. New York: C. Scribner's Sons, 1921

Richardson, Albert D.
The secret service, the field, the dungeon and the escape. 512p. Hartford, Conn.: American Publishing Co., 1865
    Experiences of a *New York Tribune* Civil War correspondent.

Russell, Sir William Howard
My diary North and South. 225p. New York: Harper, 1863
    The British correspondent's tribulations in the North during the Civil War.
About
The life of Sir William Howard Russell. John Black Atkins. 2v. London: John Murray, 1911

Sala, George Augustus
My diary in America in the midst of war. 2v. London: Tinsley Bros., 1865
    Correspondent for *London Daily Telegraph*, 1863-4.

Sanger, Donald Bridgman
The Chicago Times and the Civil War. Mississippi Valley Historical Review. 17:557-80. Mar. 1931

Shand, Alexander Innes
Some literary recollections of a golden age. Living Age. 250:100-2. July 14, 1906

Sherman, William Tecumseh
About
The Sherman letters. Ed. by G. R. S. Thorndike. 398p. New York: C. Scribner's Sons, 1894
    General Sherman's comments on his conflicts with press representatives are included in these letters.

Skidmore, Joe
The Copperhead press and the Civil War. Journalism Quarterly. 16:345-55. Dec. 1939

Smalley, George Washburn
Anglo-American memories. 2v. New York, London: Putnam's, 1911

Smith, Henry B.
British sympathy with America. 64p. New York: W. H. Bidwell, 1862
    "A review of the course of the leading periodicals of Great Britain on the rebellion in America."

Thorndike, G. R. S., ed.
The Sherman letters. 398p. New York: C. Scribner's Sons, 1894
    General Sherman's comments on his conflicts with press representatives are included in these letters.

Villard, Henry
Memoirs of Henry Villard, journalist and financier. 2v. Boston, New York: Houghton Mifflin, 1904
    v.1. 1835-62. v.2. 1863-1900.

Watson, Elmo Scott
Mathew B. Brady, the first man to "cover" a war with a camera. Quill. 25:10-11, 21. Sept. 1937
    The photographer of the Civil War.

West, Warren R.
Contemporary French opinion on the American Civil War. (Johns Hopkins University Studies, ser. 42, no. 1) Baltimore: Johns Hopkins Univ., 1924

F. FRANCO-PRUSSIAN WAR PERIOD

Abel, Karl
Letters on international relations before and during the War of 1870. 2v. London: Tinsley Bros., 1871

The **Adventures** of a war correspondent. Blackwood's Edinburgh Magazine. 130: 724-44. Dec. 1881
The reminiscences of a British correspondent at the front with the German Army during the Franco-Prussian War.

Atkins, John Black
The life of Sir William Howard Russell. 2v. London: John Murray, 1911

Bauer, Wilhelm
Die französische Presse im Kriege 1870-71. Österreichische Rundschau. 48:114-21. Aug. 1, 1916

Benjamin, Hazel C.
Official propaganda and the French press during the Franco-Prussian War. Journal of Modern History. 4:214-30. June 1932

Bismarck und die englische Kriegsberichterstattung des Deutsch-Französischen Krieges, 1870-1871. Zeitungswissenschaft. 11:616. Dec. 1, 1936
Bismarck's evaluation of the influence of the English press in the building-up of public opinion during the Franco-Prussian War and his high estimate of the English war correspondent, Forbes.

Blowitz, Henri Stephan de
Memoirs of M. de Blowitz. 321p. New York: Doubleday, Page, 1903

Busch, Dr. Moritz
Bismarck in the Franco-German War. 2v. New York: Charles Scribner's Sons, 1884

Carroll, Eber Malcolm
French public opinion and foreign affairs, 1870-1914. 348p. New York, London: Century, 1931

Corvin, Otto
In France with the Germans. 2v. Vienna: Correspondence New Free Press; London: Richard Bentley and Son, 1872

Filon, Augustin
Recollections of the Empress Eugénie. 335p. London: Cassell, 1920

Forbes, Archibald
Memories and studies of war and peace. 368p. London, Paris: Cassell, 1895
Includes an account of experiences in the Franco-Prussian War.

A war correspondent's reminiscences. Nineteenth Century. 30:185-96, 414-29. Aug.-Sept. 1891
The correspondent's life at the front and his efforts to get "the latest intelligence from the seat of war" during the Franco-Prussian and the Russo-Turkish wars.

Halstead, Murat
War correspondence in 1870. Cosmopolitan. June, 1894

Labouchere, Henry
About
Labby: life and character of Henry Labouchere. Hesketh Pearson. 318p. New York: Harper, 1937

The life of Henry Labouchere. Algar Labouchere Thorold. 513p. London: Constable, 1913

Letters on international relations before and during the War of 1870. By the Times correspondent at Berlin. 2v. London: Tinsley Bros, 1871

Maillard, Firmin
Histoire des journaux publiés à Paris pendant le Siége et sous la Commune, 4 septembre 1870 au 28 mai 1871. 267. Paris: E. Dentu, 1871
History of newspapers published in Paris during the Siege and under the Commune, Sept. 4, 1870 to May 28, 1871.

Maurice, Arthur Bartlett
War cartoons of 1870. Bookman. 40:47-54. Sept. 1914

Pearson, Hesketh
Labby: life and character of Henry Labouchere. 318p. New York: Harper, 1937
Labouchere's account of a correspondent's life during the siege of Paris is largely comic relief.

Robinson, Sir John R.
Fifty years of Fleet Street. Comp. and ed. by Frederick Moy Thomas. 418p. London: Macmillan, 1904

Ryan, Charles E.
With an ambulance during the Franco-German War, 1870-71. 368p. New York: C. Scribner's Sons, 1896

Sheridan, Philip H.
From Gravelotte to Sedan. Scribner's. 4:515-35. Nov. 1888

Smalley, George Washburn
Anglo-American memories. 2v. New York, London: Putnam, 1911

Some narrow escapes during the Franco-German War. Littell's Living Age. 172:437-43. Feb. 12, 1887
The problem of the press correspondent in the Franco-German War was to get his reports to his newspaper.

Thorold, Algar Labouchere
The life of Henry Labouchere. 513p. London: Constable, 1913

Villiers, Frederic
The story of a war correspondent's life. Cosmopolitan. 10:595-613, 702-21. Mar.-Apr. 1891

Twenty years on the war path. Canadian Magazine. 15:122-7, 247-51, 357-61. June-Aug. 1900

Villiers: his five decades of adventure. 2v. New York: Harper, 1920
Includes the story of news correspondence during the Franco-Prussian War.

The War correspondence of the Daily News, 1870, edited, with notes and comments, forming a continuous narrative of the war between Germany and France. 2v. London: Macmillan, 1871
Contains 5 maps.
Vol. 2 entitled: *The War Correspondence of The Daily News, Continued from the Recapture of Orleans by the Germans, to the Peace.*

G. LATE 19th CENTURY AND THE BOER WAR

Barnes, James
The great war trek with the British army on the veldt. 372p. New York: D. Appleton, 1901
Correspondent with the British army in the Boer War.

Blowitz, Henri Stephan de
Memoirs of M. de Blowitz. 321p. New York: Doubleday, Page, 1903

Brex, Twells, comp.
Scaremongerings from the Daily Mail, 1896-1914. 176p. London: 1914

Brisbane, Arthur
Great problems in organization: the modern newspaper in war time. Cosmopolitan. 25:541-57. Sept. 1898

Churchill, Winston Leonard Spencer
From London to Ladysmith via Pretoria. 496p. New York, London: Longmans, Green, 1900

The **Daily News** and events in the East in 1876. 53p. London: Bradbury, Agnew, 1876
Extracts from the Daily *News* for August, September and October, 1876, including an account of the Bulgarian massacres, 1876-1877.

Davis, Charles B., ed.
Adventures and letters of Richard Harding Davis. 417p. New York: C. Scribner's Sons, 1917

Davis, Richard Harding
Notes of a war correspondent. 263p. New York: C. Scribner's Sons, 1912

About
Adventures and letters of Richard Harding Davis. Ed. by Charles B. Davis. 417p. New York: C. Scribner's Sons, 1917

Richard Harding Davis: his day. Fairfax D. Downey. 322p. London, New York: C. Scribner's Sons, 1933

Downey, Fairfax D.
Richard Harding Davis: his day. 322p. London, New York: C. Scribner's Sons, 1933

Dunn, James
Charlie Hands—reporter. Newspaper World. 40:4. Nov. 6, 1937
Death of Hands recalls his work as war correspondent in 19th century and Boer War.

Forbes, Archibald
The Afghan wars 1839-42 and 1878-80. 337p. New York: C. Scribner's Sons, 1892

Czar and sultan. 381p. New York: C. Scribner's Sons, 1895

Memories and studies of war and peace. 368p. London, Paris: Cassell, 1895

War correspondence as a fine art. Century. 45:290-303. Dec. 1892

——See Russell, Sir William Howard, jt. auth.

Greene, F. V.
Sketches of army life in Russia. New York: Scribner's, 1885
Chapter VII: War correspondents. p. 152-67.

Gribayêdoff, Valerian
The modern war correspondent. Munsey's. 13:34-41. Apr. 1895
American war correspondent's reports of Turkish atrocities changed British public opinion, thus averting threat of Russo-British conflict. Brief sketches of eminent 19th century war correspondents.

Hales, A. G.
The life of a war correspondent. Pall Mall. 23:204-11. Feb. 1901

Hands, Charles
About
Charlie Hands—reporter. James Dunn. Newspaper World. 40:4. Nov. 6, 1937
Death of Hands recalls his work as war correspondent in 19th century and Boer War.

Hastings, E. B.
War correspondents. National. 8:358. July 1898

How the Daily Mail would work in the event of war. Academy. 55:206-7. Nov. 5, 1897

James, Lionel
High pressure. 314p. London: J. Murray, 1929
The exciting account of thirteen years in the service of the London *Times* in nearly every quarter of the globe.

The **Literature** of the African war. American Historical Review. 12:299-321. Jan. 1907

MacDonagh, Michael
Can we rely on our war news? Fortnightly Review. 69:612-25. Apr. 1, 1898

MacGahan, J. A.
Campaigning on the Oxus, and the fall of Khiva. 438p. New York: Harper, 1874

The war correspondence of the Daily Mail, 1877. London: Macmillan, 1878

McKenzie, Fred A.
English war-correspondents in South Africa. Harper's. 101:209-16. July 1900

Mansfield, F. J.
Stories of eminent war correspondents. World's Press News. 20:210. Dec. 1937
Chiefly men of the 19th century.

Melgund, Viscount
Newspaper correspondents in the field. Nineteenth Century. 7:434-42. Mar. 1880
A reply to Archibald Forbes' article in the January number of this review; Mr. Melgund tells why he thinks "that every word of the new press regulations is necessary."

Musings without method; camp-followers of falsehood; the war correspondent. Blackwood's. 168:915-22. Dec. 1900
A scorching criticism of alleged slanders of war correspondents who reported the Boer War.

Musings without method; journalism and the war; the exaggeration of correspondents. Blackwood's. 167:283-6. Feb. 1900

Ralph, Julian
Toward Pretoria; a record of. the war between Briton and Boer, to the relief of Kimberley. 328p. New York: F. A. Stokes, 1900
War's brighter side. 471p. New York: D. Appleton, 1901
A Yankee correspondent in South Africa. Century. 61:67-73. Nov. 1900

Russell, Sir William Howard
About
War correspondents, past and present. Spectator. 98:244-5. Feb. 16, 1907
——and Forbes, Archibald
War correspondents. Edinburgh Review. 183:129-42. Jan. 1896

Shand, Alexander Innes
Some literary recollections of a golden age. Living Age. 250:92-102. July 14, 1906

Smalley, George Washburn
Anglo-American memories. 2v. New York: G. P. Putnam's, 1912
Reminiscences of an American journalist and foreign correspondent who knew American and European notables of the last century.
Vol. I, ch.xxv cites great examples of war correspondence.

Speed, J. G.
Notes and comments: war correspondents. North American Review. 168:381-4. Mar. 1899
War correspondents should be picked men, intelligent, and closely regulated to minimize the danger of disseminating damaging news.

Steevens, G. W.
From Capetown to Ladysmith. 198p. New York: Dodd, Mead, 1900
With Kitchener to Khartum. 326p. New York: Dodd, Mead, 1899

Stillman, William James
The autobiography of a journalist. 2v. New York: Houghton Mifflin, 1901

Unger, Frederick William
With "Bobs" and Krüger. 412p. Philadelphia: Coates, 1901

Villiers, Frederic
The story of a war correspondent's life. Cosmopolitan. 10:595-613, 702-21. Mar.-Apr. 1891

Twenty years on the war path. Canadian Magazine. 15:122-7, 247-51, 357-61. June-Aug. 1900

Villiers: his five decades of adventure. 2v. New York: Harper, 1920

Wallace, Valentine
Defied Sultan, dared awful Turkish death to gather Armenian news for his paper. Editor and Publisher. 51:13-14. Aug. 3, 1918
The experiences of Dr. E. J. Dillon of the London Daily Telegraph who reported to the world in 1895 that the Turks were guilty in the Armenian massacres.

The **War** correspondence of the Daily News, 1877-8, continued from the fall of Kars to the signature of the preliminaries of peace, with a connecting narrative forming a continuous history of the war between Russia and Turkey. 599p. London: Macmillan, 1878

The **War** correspondence of the Daily News, with a connecting narrative forming a continuous history of the war between Russia and Turkey, including the letters of Mr. Archibald Forbes, Mr. J. A. MacGahan .... containing a full description of the taking of Kars. 643p. London: Macmillan, 1878

War correspondents and the Sirdar. Academy. 54:331-2. Oct. 1, 1898

War correspondents, past and present. Spectator. 98:244-5. Feb. 16, 1907
A note on the passing of the British war correspondent, Sir William Howard Russell. His career and character sketched briefly.

War news and the markets. Leslie's Weekly. 84:292. May 6, 1897

Williams, George Forrester
Bullet and shell. 454p. New York: Fords, Howard and Hulbert, 1883

H. SPANISH-AMERICAN WAR

Anderson, H. M.
The American newspaper: I. The war correspondent. Bookman. 19:24-41. Mar. 1904

Archibald, J. F. J.
The war correspondents of today. Overland Monthly. 37:791-803. Mar. 1901

Auxier, George W.
Propaganda activities of the Cuban Junta in precipitating the Spanish American war, 1895-1898. Hispanic American Historical Review. 19:286-305. Aug. 1939

Baker, Ray Stannard
How the news of the war is reported. McClure's. 11:491-5. Sept. 1898
Dispatch-boats were used by American newspapers in Spanish-American War to evade censor's restrictions. New York correspondents filed 5,000 words a day.

Bartholomew, C. L.
Cartoons of the Spanish-American War. Minneapolis: Mineapolis Journal Printing Co., 1899

Brandt, M. von
The German press and foreign politics. Living Age. 226:114-16. July 14, 1900
Difficulties in foreign affairs encountered by the German government during the Spanish-American War were caused by the contrary attitude of the German press.

Brisbane, Arthur
The modern newspaper in war time. Cosmopolitan. 25:541-58. Sept. 1898

Creelman, James
On the great highway. 418p. Boston: Lothrop, 1901
"The wanderings and adventures of a special correspondent."

Davis, Charles B., ed.
Adventures and letters of Richard Harding Davis. 417p. New York: C. Scribner's Sons, 1917

Davis, Elmer H.
History of the New York Times. 434p. New York: New York Times, 1921

Davis, Richard Harding
Notes of a war correspondent. 263p. New York: C. Scribner's Sons, 1910
Our war correspondents in Cuba and Puerto Rico. Harper's. 98:938-48. May 1899
About
Adventures and letters of Richard Harding Davis. Ed. by Charles B. Davis. 417p. New York: C. Scribner's Sons, 1917

Richard Harding Davis: his day. Fairfax D. Downey. 322p. London, New York: C. Scribner's Sons, 1933

Downey, Fairfax D.
Richard Harding Davis: his day. 322p. London, New York: C. Scribner's Sons, 1933

Flint, Grover
Marching with Gomez. 290p. Boston, New York: Lamson, Wolffe, 1898
"A war correspondent's field note-book, kept during four months with the Cuban army."

Godkin, Edwin Lawrence
The "new diplomacy" and war. Nation. 69:421-2. Dec. 7, 1899

About
Life and letters of Edwin Lawrence Godkin. Ed. by Rollo Ogden. 2v. London, New York: Macmillan, 1907

Harrington, Fred H.
Literary aspects of American anti-imperialism, 1898-1902. New England Quarterly. 10:650-67. Dec. 1937
nightly Review. 69:612-25. Apr. 1, 1898
Bibliographical footnotes.

Hearst, William Randolph
About
W. R. Hearst, an American phenomenon. John K. Winkler. 354p. New York: Simon and Schuster, 1928
"List of publications owned by William Randolph Hearst": p.319.

Journalists of the Spanish-American War; pictures. Illustrated American. 24:139. Aug. 1898

Kennan, George
How war news is collected. Outlook. 59:369-73. June 11, 1898
The use and perils of news dispatch-boats employed by American newspapers in the Spanish-American war.

MacDonagh, Michael
Can we rely on our war news? Fortnightly Review. 69:612-25. Apr. 1, 1898

Martin, Harold
The Manila censorship. Forum. 31:462-71. June 1901

Millis, Walter
The martial spirit. 427p. Boston, New York: Houghton Mifflin, 1931
"A study of our war with Spain."

The **Newspaper** correspondents in the war. Review of Reviews. 18:538-41. Nov. 1898
The huge cost of getting war news from Cuba.

Ogden, Rollo, ed.
Life and letters of Edwin Lawrence Godkin. 2v. London, New York: Macmillan, 1907

Paine, Ralph D.
Roads of adventure. 402p. New York: Houghton Mifflin, 1925
Autobiography of an adventurer and war correspondent during the Spanish-American War, Boxer Rebellion and the World War.

Spears, John R.
Afloat for news in war time. Scribner's. 24:501-4. Oct. 1898

Squires, Grant
Experiences of a war censor. Atlantic Monthly. 83:425-32. Mar. 1899
Censor in Spanish-American War explains how news was kept from the press, and how lines of communications between Spain and Cuba were severed.

Sullivan, Mark
The turn of the century, 1900-1904. (His. Our times, the United States, 1900-1925, v.1) New York, London: Scribner's, 1926-35

Wilkerson, Marcus M.
Public opinion and the Spanish-American War: a study in war propaganda. 141p. Baton Rouge: Louisiana State Univ. Press, 1932
    A careful study of the war-mongering press prior to and during the Spanish-American War.
    Bibliography.

Williams, George Forrester
Important services rendered by war correspondents. Independent. 54:210-12. Jan. 23, 1902

Winkler, John K.
W. R. Hearst, an American phenomenon. 354p. New York: Simon and Schuster, 1928
    "List of publications owned by William Randolph Hearst": p.319.

Wisan, Joseph E.
The Cuban crisis as reflected in the New York press (1895-1898). 477p. New York: Columbia Univ. Press, 1934

Yellow journalism and the Maine disaster. Public Opinion. 24:263. Mar. 3, 1898

Yellow newspaper correspondents at Santiago. Public Opinion. 25:136-7. Aug. 4, 1898

I. EARLY 20th CENTURY

The **Anglo-German** paper war. Contemporary Review. 87:11-21. Jan. 1905

Ashmead-Bartlett, Ellis
With the Turks in Thrace. 335p. New York: Geo. H. Doran, 1913
    A British war correspondent's experiences.

Atkins, John Black
The work and future of war correspondents. Monthly Review. 4:81-9. Sept. 1901

Bennett, Ernest Nathaniel
Personal observations during the Balkan war. Nineteenth Century. 73:28-40. Jan. 1913

Brex, Twells
"Scaremongerings" from the Daily Mail, 1896-1914. 176p. London: 1914

Brooks, Sydney
The press in war time. Harper's Weekly. 56:21. Dec. 21, 1912

Campbell, Cyril
A correspondent at Adrianople. Atlantic. 111:846-53. June 1913

Davis, Charles B., ed.
Adventures and letters of Richard Harding Davis. 417p. New York: C. Scribner's Sons, 1917

Davis, Oscar King
Reporting a cosmopolitan war. Harper's Weekly. 45:748-9, 772, 796. July 27, Aug. 3-10, 1901
    Primitive methods followed in reporting the Boxer uprising in China.

Davis, Richard Harding
Notes of a war correspondent. 263p. New York: C. Scribner's Sons, 1910
The war correspondent. Collier's. 48: 21-2, 30. Oct. 7, 1911
    About
Adventures and letters of Richard Harding Davis. Ed. by Charles B. Davis. 417p. New York: C. Scribner's Sons, 1917
Richard Harding Davis: his day. Fairfax D. Downey. 322p. London, New York: C. Scribner's Sons, 1933
With Davis in Vera Cruz, Brussels and Salonika. John T. McCutcheon. Scribner's. 60:91-7. July 1916

Dillon, E. J.
Foreign complications and the German press campaign. Contemporary Review. 85:592-5. Apr. 1904

Dinwiddie, William
Experiences of a war correspondent. Harper's Weekly. 48:862-4. June 4, 1904
    A war correspondent relates the difficulties encountered in reporting the Russo-Japanese War.
Trials of the war correspondent. Harper's Weekly. 48:971-3, 989. June 25, 1904

Downey, Fairfax D.
Richard Harding Davis: his day. 322p. London, New York: C. Scribner's Sons, 1933

Emerson, Edward, jr.
The making of a war correspondent. Reader. 4:162-9. July 1904

The **End** of the war correspondent. Review of Reviews. 30:607-8. Nov. 1904
    The Japanese closed the door to reporters during the Russo-Japanese War.

Fuller, Hector
Getting into Port Arthur. Reader. 4:607-16; 5:38-47. Nov.-Dec. 1904

The **Future** of the war correspondent. Review of Reviews. 31:94-5. Jan. 1905

Gallagher, Patrick
War correspondents of to-day. Editor and Publisher. 13:986. May 9, 1914
    Conflict with Mexico afforded opportunity to develop news sense, literary skill, self confidence.

Giving out war news. Editor and Publisher. 13:1043. May 30, 1914
    System developed in press room of State, War and Navy departments.

Hamilton, Angus
A captured war correspondent. Fortnightly Review. 99:58-67. Jan. 1, 1913

James, Lionel
High pressure. 314p. London: J. Murray, 1929
With the conquered Turk; the story of a latter-day adventurer. 315p. Boston: Small, Maynard, 1913

Landon, Perceval
War correspondents and the censorship. Nineteenth Century. 52:327-37. Aug. 1902
> Conditions under which the war correspondent works in active service, with suggestions for reaching the objectives of the censor and the censored, based on experiences during the Boer War.

McCullagh, Francis
The question of the war correspondent. Contemporary Review. 103:203-13. Feb. 1913
> See reply: Has the War Correspondent Seen His Last Fight? *Review of Reviews.* 47:486-8. Apr. 1913

McCutcheon, John T.
With Davis in Vera Cruz, Brussels and Salonika. Scribner's. 60:91-7. July 1916

Marvin, George
Chroniclers of the Balkan War. Independent. 74:1390-6. June 19, 1913

Maxwell, William
The war correspondent in sunshine and eclipse. Nineteenth Century. 73:608-23. Mar. 1913

Mellard, Thomas F.
The war correspondent and his future. Scribner's. 37:242-8. Feb. 1905
> A criticism of the effect of military censorship of the press during war. It is futile as a means of preventing information from reaching the enemy.

Mels, Edgar
War news: its collection and cost. Saturday Evening Post. 177:16-17. July 2, 1904
> "It is a losing game for the newspapers, but they have to play it."

Nevinson, Henry W.
The end of the war correspondent? Living Age. 268:625-8. Mar. 11, 1911

Newman, Henry
A roving commission. 328p. London: Bell, 1937
> Observations during Boxer Rebellion, Lhasa Mission of 1903, and Afghan War of 1919.

Palmer, Frederick
With Kuroki in Manchuria. New York: C. Scribner's Sons, 1904

Phillips, Phillip Lee
Out in the cold. Saturday Evening Post. 185:14-15, 26-8. Feb. 1, 15, 1913

Pilcher, George
In the Chatalja lines during the November battle. Nineteenth Century. 73:624-43. Mar. 1913

Plans press corps. Editor and Publisher. 14:93. July 18, 1914
> Secretary Garrison would put war correspondents under American flag.

The **Press** in war time. Fortnightly Review. 99:741-52. Apr. 1, 1913

Prior, Melton
Campaigns of a war correspondent. 340p. London: E. Arnold, 1912

The **Rise** and fall of the war correspondent. Macmillan's. 90:301-10. Aug. 1904
> The part played by the development of the telegraph as an aid to war reporting. War reporting really began during the Crimean War.

Ruhl, Arthur
The gallery at San Antonio. Collier's. 47:13, 25. Apr. 29, 1911

Spender, John Alfred
Life, journalism and politics. 2v. New York: Stokes, 1927

Stone, Melville E.
The Associated Press: its work in war. Century. 70:504-10. Aug. 1905
> The Associated Press was responsible for the first prompt report of a naval engagement on the high seas in connection with the Spanish-American War. How the Associated Press at Port Arthur beat the special correspondents.

To censor war news. Editor and Publisher. 13:962. May 2, 1914
> Government prepares strict regulations for newspaper correspondents covering conflict with Mexico.

Villari, Luigi
The effect of the war on Russian public opinion. p.96-7, 296-325. *In his* Russia under the great shadow. London: T. F. Unwin, 1905
> The author's impressions of public opinion in Russia, especially during the Russo-Japanese War.

Villiers, Frederic
Villiers: his five decades of adventure. 2v. New York: Harper, 1920

Wagner of the Reichspost. Literary Digest. 45:1193-5. Dec. 21, 1912
> Journalistic and military aptitudes enabled Wagner, Vienna correspondent, to outstrip his rivals in reporting the Turco-Balkan conflict.

War correspondents, past and present. Spectator. 98:224-5. Feb. 16, 1907

War correspondents: their future. Gunton's. 27:579-89. Dec. 1904

Washburn, Stanley
The cable game. 236p. Boston: Sherman, French; London: Andrew Melrose, 1913
> The adventures of an American pressboat in Turkish waters during the Russian Revolution. Illustrated.

Washington topics. Editor and Publisher. 13:1035. May 23, 1914
> Drastic orders concerning war correspondents in Mexico. Contrary to rules some correspondents had left commands to go into interior of Mexico.

Washington topics: Secretary Daniels denounces newspapers that print war scare news. Editor and Publisher. 12:1-2. May 24, 1913

What shall be done with the press in war time? Review of Reviews. 34:236-7. Aug. 1906

Wilber, Harry Lee
A fake that rocked the world. North American Review. 247, no. 1:21-6. Mar. 1939
> How faked news is said to have started the Boxer Rebellion in China.

Will the newspapers bring on a European war? Review of Reviews. 40:238-9. Aug. 1909

The Work of a war correspondent. Outlook. 103:716-18. Mar. 29, 1913

J. WORLD WAR, 1914

1. GENERAL REFERENCES

Baker, Ray Stannard
Woodrow Wilson and world settlement. 3v. Garden City, N.Y.: Doubleday, Page, 1922
"The first two volumes contain the narrative of what happened at Paris; the third is devoted wholly to the text of letters, memoranda, minutes and other crucial documents referred to or quoted in the narrative."

Barnes, Harry Elmer
The genesis of the World War. 750p. New York: A. A. Knopf, 1927
"An introduction to the problem of war guilt."

Clarkson, G. B.
Industrial America in the World War. 573p. Boston, New York: Houghton Mifflin, 1923
"The strategy behind the line, 1917-19."

Dahlin, Ebba
French and German public opinion on declared war aims, 1914-1918. 168p. (Stanford Univ. Series in History, Economics and Political Science. v.4, no. 2) Stanford Univ., Cal.: Stanford Univ. Press, 1933
An excellent source book.

Fay, Sidney Bradshaw
The origins of the World War. 2v. in 1. New York: Macmillan, 1934

Gooch, George Peabody
The lesson of 1914-1934. Current History. 40:513-20. Aug. 1934

Grattan, Clinton Hartley
The Walter Hines Page legend. American Mercury. 6:39-51. Sept. 1925
Why we fought. 453p. New York: Vanguard Press, 1929

Grey, Sir Edward
Twenty-five years, 1892-1916. 2v. New York: Frederick A. Stokes, 1925
Includes sections on press relations.

Grunberg, Ilias
La Suisse neutre et vigilante. Lausanne: 1920. 588p. Genève: Argus Suisse de la Presse, 1917

Hale, Oron James
Germany and the diplomatic revolution. 233p. Philadelphia: Univ. of Pennsylvania Press, 1931
"A study in diplomacy and the press, 1904-1906."

Hall, James Norman and Nordhoff, Charles Bernard, eds.
The Lafayette Flying Corps. 2v. Boston, New York: Houghton Mifflin, 1920

Hard to obtain news. Editor and Publisher. 14:169. Aug. 15, 1914
Rigid censorship demoralizes cable and wireless press service.

Koch, Theodore Wesley
War libraries and allied studies. 287p. New York: G. E. Stechert, 1918

Lansing, Robert
The difficulties of neutrality. Saturday Evening Post. 203:6-7, 102, 104-6. Apr. 18, 1931

Leland, Waldo G. and Mereness, Newton D. comps.
American official sources for the economic and social history of the World War. 532p. New Haven: Yale Univ. Press, 1926

McAdoo, William G.
Crowded years. 542p. Boston: Houghton Mifflin, 1931
Reminiscences, including references to the press.

McClure, Samuel Sidney
Obstacles to peace. 486p. Boston, New York: Houghton Mifflin, 1917

Mereness, Newton D. See Leland, Waldo G., jt. comp.

Morgenthau, Henry and Strother, Henry
All in a lifetime. 454p. Garden City, N.Y.: Doubleday, Page, 1922
Memoirs of the United States Ambassador to Turkey.

Neilson, Francis
How diplomats make war. 2nd ed. 382p. New York: B. W. Huebsch, 1916
Diplomatic maneuvers by Great Britain and other European powers, 1815-1914. The press is taken to task for warmongering and jingoism.

Nordhoff, Charles Bernard. See Hall, James Norman, jt. ed.

Noyes, Alexander D.
The war period of American finance. 459p. New York, London: G. P. Putnam's Sons, 1926

Piper, Edgar B.
The press and preparedness. p.42-7. In National Education Association, Addresses and Proceedings, 1917. Washington: N.E.A., 1917

Pollard, Albert Frederick
Rumour and historical science in time of war. Contemporary Review. 107:321-30. Mar. 1915

Redfield, William C.
With Congress and Cabinet. 307p. Garden City, N.Y.: Doubleday, Page, 1924

Riddell, George A.
Lord Riddell's war diary, 1914-18. 387p. London: I. Nicholson and Watson, 1934

Rintelen, Franz von
The dark invader. 287p. New York: Macmillan, 1933
Wartime reminiscences of a German naval intelligence officer.

Schieber, Clara Eve
The transformation of American sentiment toward Germany, 1870-1914. 294p. New York: Cornhill Pub. Co., 1923
An important book on public opinion prior to the World War.

Schmitt, Bernadotte E.
The coming of the War, 1914. 2v. New York, London: C. Scribner's Sons. 1930

Schönemann, Friedrich
Die Kunst der Massenbeeinflussung in den Vereinigten Staaten von Amerika. 212p. Stuttgart: Deutsche Verlagsanstalt, 1924
A German estimate of propaganda influence in the United States, particularly during the World War.

Schreiner, George Abel
The iron ration. 259p. London: J. Murray, 1918
The economic and social effects of the Allied blockade on Germany and the German people.
Entente diplomacy and the world. 762p. New York, London: Knickerbocker Press, 1921

Scott, Jonathan F.
Five weeks; the surge of public opinion on the eve of the Great War. 305p. New York: John Day, 1927

Seymour, Charles
The alleged isolation of Germany. Yale Review. 6:521-35. Apr. 1917
American diplomacy during the World War. 417p. Baltimore: Johns Hopkins Press, 1934
The intimate papers of Colonel House. 4v. Boston, New York: Houghton Mifflin, 1926-28

Slosson, Preston W.
The great crusade and after, 1914-1928. 486p. New York: Macmillan, 1931

Spender, John Alfred
Life, journalism and politics. 2v. New York: Stokes, 1927
By the wartime editor of the *Westminster Gazette*.
The public life. 2v. London, New York: Cassell, 1925

Stieve, Friedrich
Isvolsky and the World War. 254p. New York, London: G. Allen and Unwin, 1926
Translated by E. W. Dicks.
Based on the documents published by the German Foreign Office.

Strother, Henry. See Morgenthau, Henry, jt. auth.

United States. Library of Congress. Division of Bibliography
A check list of the literature and other material in the Library of Congress on the European War, comp. under the direction of Herman H. B. Meyer, chief bibliographer, with the cooperation of members of the Library staff. 293p. Washington: Government Printing Office, 1918
Contents: Books and pamphlets. Periodicals and newspapers. French and camp papers. Broadsides and poster broadsides. Prints, posters, cartoons, photographs. Music.

Villard, Oswald Garrison
The nakedness of Colonel House. Nation. 122:388-90. Apr. 14, 1926

Williams, Wythe
Dusk of empire. 325p. New York: Scribner's, 1937
"The decline of Europe and the rise of the United States as observed by a foreign correspondent in a quarter century of service."

2. THE PRESS BEFORE APRIL 1917

a. PRESS OF BELLIGERENTS

(1) FRANCE

Bainville, Jacques
La presse et la guerre. 158p. L'Action Française. 158p. Paris: Bloud et Gay, 1915

The **Big** German drive was no surprise to "The '9' Times." Literary Digest. 57: 74-8. Apr. 13, 1918

Chambure, A. de
Quelques guides de l'opinion en France pendant la Grande Guerre, 1914-1918. 223p. Paris: Celin, Mary, Elen, 1918
An attempt at a sincere and impartial study of the principal organs of public opinion in France during the World War.

Dodge, Henry G.
How Paris gets the news. Harper's Weekly. 62:209-10. Feb. 26, 1916

Drouilly, Georges
French newspapers hard hit by War. Editor and Publisher. 47:1052, 1064. May 15, 1915

Grundy, F. B.
Rheims daily paper lives through three years of constant bombardment. Editor and Publisher. 50:5, 30. Oct. 20, 1917

Indomitable gaiety of the French newspapers of the trenches. Current Opinion. 60:432. June 1916

Partridge, Edward Bellamy
La Guerre est finie! Sunset. 42:30-2. Mar. 1919

Rozet, Georges
Avec la presse française sur le front français. Revue de Paris. 25(1):625-40; 846-68. Feb. 1-15, 1918

Stanton, Theodore
Literary affairs in France. Dial. 60:526-8. June 8, 1916
The effect of the War on periodicals in Europe.

Stanton, Theodore—*Continued*
Recent losses in French journalism. Dial. 60:263-6. Mar. 16, 1916

Thebault, Eugène
La gazette infâme. Revue des Deux Mondes. 6. période. 47:514-48. Oct. 1, 1918
Describes a publication, *Gazette des Ardennes*, established November 1, 1914 by the Germans in occupied territories in France.

War news in France. Editor and Publisher. 14:283. Sept. 26, 1914
Paris editors produce two-page daily.

What the French are not allowed to learn. Independent. 92:499-500. Dec. 15, 1917

(2) GERMANY

Beaufort, J. M. de
Behind the German veil. 367p. London, New York: Dodd, Mead, 1917

Elimination of Vorwärts. Literary Digest. 53:1650. Dec. 23, 1916

The **German** press. New Europe. 6:370-2; 409-16. Apr. 4, 11, 1918

Germans publish French paper. Editor and Publisher. 48:147. July 17, 1915

Germany's muzzled press. Literary Digest. 55:29-30. Aug. 4, 1917

Gowans, Adam L.
A month's German newspapers. 275p. London, Glasgow: Gowans and Gray, 1915
Representative extracts from newspapers of December 1914.

Harris, G. W.
S. S. McClure on the truth about the war. Editor and Publisher. 48:1581, 1592. May 20, 1916
Magazine publisher comments on conditions in Germany.

Lawrence, David
International freedom of the press essential to a durable peace. Annals of the American Academy. 72:139-41. July 1917
German press was "timidly subservient to the autocratic interests of the Imperial Government." Freedom of press is essential for the development of public opinion.

Misjudging the German press. Nation. 107:448. Oct. 19, 1918

Nicolai, Walter
Nachrichtendienst, Presse und Volksstimmung im Weltkrieg. 226p. Berlin: E. S. Mitter und Sohn, 1920

Propper, Stanislaus M.
Was nicht in die Zeitung kam. 285p. Frankfurt a.M.: Frankfurter Societäts-Druckerei, 1929

Reinartz, Hans Armin
Südamerikanische Zeitungen zur Aufklärung über Deutschland im Weltkrieg. Zeitungswissenschaft. 13:32-3. Jan. 1, 1938
The attempt on the part of South American newspapers to make clear Germany's position in the World War.

Rotheit, Rudolf
Die Friedensbedingungen und die deutsche Presse. 58p. Berlin: Puttkammer und Mühlbrecht, 1915

Suppressed edition of Vorwärts. Survey. 34:458. Aug. 21, 1915

Villard, Oswald Garrison
Germany embattled. 181p. New York: C. Scribner's Sons, 1915

Westerkamp, Alix
A newspaper published from the German trenches. Survey. 33:688-9. Mar. 27, 1915

(3) GREAT BRITAIN

Angell, Sir Norman
The problem of Northcliffe. New Republic. 9:344-7. Jan. 27, 1917
Tremendous power of Northcliffe is made possible by his newspaper and periodical "trust."

Bertie of Thame, Francis Leveson Bertie, 1st viscount
The diary of Lord Bertie of Thame, 1914-1918. 2v. New York: George H. Doran, 1924

Brooks, Sydney
Lord Northcliffe and the War. North American Review. 202:185-96. Aug. 1915

Carson, William E.
Northcliffe, Britain's man of power. 456p. New York: Dodge, 1918

Criticism in war. English Review. 23:538-42. Dec. 1916

England's blindfold eyes. Literary Digest. 50:100-1. Jan. 16, 1915

Front page scoops from the war front. World's Press News. 13:5. May 30, 1935
Jeffries of the *Mail* tells his story; scoops from the War and other personal experiences.

Fyfe, Henry H.
Northcliffe: an intimate biography. 349p. London: Allen and Unwin, 1930

Harrison, Austin
The lion in blinkers. English Review. 19:204-15. Jan. 1915
The place of the press in a nation at war under a single military control. The author calls the press "the tool box of our English civilization."

The responsibility of the press. English Review. 21:113-23. Aug. 1915

Horwill, Herbert W.
The English newspaper in war time. Nation. 105:712-13. Dec. 27, 1917

MacDonagh, Michael
In London during the Great War. 336p.
London: Eyre and Spottiswoode, 1935

Marcosson, Isaac F.
Northcliffe—England's unofficial war
steward. Everybody's. 36:385-98. Apr.
1917

Mr. Lloyd George and press dictation.
Spectator. 117:761-2. Dec. 16, 1916

National discipline. English Review. 23:
159-62. Aug. 1916

The Neurasthenic press. Spectator. 116:
278. Feb. 26, 1916

Newspapers and war. By a member of the
British Foreign Office. Harper's Weekly. 60:184. Feb. 20, 1915

Northcliffe, Alfred Charles William Harmsworth, 1st viscount

About

The problem of Northcliffe. Norman
Angell. New Republic. 9:344-7. Jan.
27, 1917

Lord Northcliffe and the War. Sydney
Brooks. North American Review. 202:
185-96. Aug. 1915

Northcliffe, Britain's man of power. William E. Carson. 456p. New York:
Dodge, 1918

Northcliffe: an intimate biography. Henry
H. Fyfe. 349p. London: Allen and
Unwin, 1930

Northcliffe—England's unofficial war
steward. Isaac F. Marcosson. Everybody's. 36:385-98. Apr. 1917

Vagaries of Northcliffe. Literary Digest.
55:61. Oct. 13, 1917

Northcliffe; how he planned to avert war
with Germany by starting a newspaper
in Berlin. Frederic W. Wile. Saturday Evening Post. 195:6-7, 161-2. Oct.
7, 1922

The Partiality of the press. Independent.
84:44-5. Oct. 11, 1915

Playne, Caroline E.
Society at war, 1914-1916. 380p. Boston:
Houghton Mifflin, 1931
    "A narrative of the ways and actions of
British society during the first half of the
War."

A Plea for contented ignorance. Independent. 90:193-4. Apr. 28, 1917

The Policy of mystification. Spectator.
113:788-90. Dec. 5, 1914

Recruiting and the censorship. Quarterly
Review. 223:130-58. Jan. 1915
    Failure of British press to emphasize
the magnitude of the War is a hindrance
to recruiting.

Samuel, Herbert
Liberty of speech and of the press. New
Statesman (London) 9:223-5. June 9,
1917

Vagaries of Northcliffe. Literary Digest.
55:61. Oct. 13, 1917

Wile, Frederic W.
Northcliffe; how he planned to avert
war with Germany by starting a newspaper in Berlin. Saturday Evening
Post. 195:6-7, 161-2. Oct. 7, 1922

Willis, Irene Cooper
England's holy war; a study of English
Liberal idealism during the Great War.
New York: A. A. Knopf, 1928

Zimmermann, Walter
Die englische Presse zum Ausbruch des
Weltkrieges. 269p. Charlottenburg:
"Hochschule und Ausland," 1928
    The status of the English press at the
beginning of the World War.

(4) MISCELLANEOUS

Accidental literature of the war. Spectator.
117:764-5. Dec. 16, 1916

Barnouw, Adriaan J.
Holland's neutrality; the battle of the
Dutch newspapers. Nation. 102:431.
Apr. 20, 1916

Boyer, Jacques
Newspapers that are printed within gun
range of the enemy. Scientific American. 114:665, 672. June 24, 1916

Burgess, Gelett
The magazines of the trenches. Century.
92:641-58. Sept. 1916

Byers, Charles Alma
Sob sisters and the War. Open Court.
30:733-5. Dec. 1916

Corey, Herbert
Humor lurks beneath surface of Europe's
grim-visaged war. Editor and Publisher. 48:822. Jan. 1, 1916

Ferrari, Robert
. The Italian censorship. Journal of Crim-
inal Law. 6:921-2. Mar. 1916
    The case of an editor violating the
censorship law was held not to come under
provision of the Italian penal code.

A [Japanese] dream book. Outlook. 111:
535-6. Nov. 3, 1915

Journalism in the trenches. Literary Digest.
50:879. Apr. 17, 1915

Journalism in the trenches. Nation. 102:
214. Feb. 24, 1916

Jux, Anton
Der Kriegsschrecken des Frühjahrs 1914
in der europäischen Presse. 248p. Berlin, Charlottenburg: H. W. Hendriock,
1929
    The war scare in the European press
during the spring of 1914.

Lancellotti, Arturo
Riccordi di guerra: piccoli giornali italiani
da campo pubblicati fuori Italia. Nuova
Antologia. 237:85-95. Sept. 1, 1924
    Development of small newspapers among
Italian soldiers stationed outside of Italy
during the World War.

Lightbourn, Donald
L'Indepéndence Belge. Inland Printer.
56:485-6. Jan. 1916
    Fearing lest it fall into the hands of the
German invaders, this foremost Belgian
newspaper moved successively to Brussels,
Ghent, Ostende and finally to London.

Lying for the sake of war. Nation. 98:561.
May 14, 1914

McCormick, Robert R.
With the Russian army. 306p. London,
New York: Macmillan, 1915
    The experiences of the *Chicago Tribune*
publisher during a visit to Russia. As the
son of a former ambassador to Russia, he
was granted special privileges. Illustrated.

Massart, Jean
The secret press in Belgium. 96p. New
York: E. P. Dutton, 1918
    Tr. from the French by Bernard Mial.

Press may help or hurt in time of war.
Editor and Publisher. 48:1345, 1348.
Apr. 6, 1916
    Experiences of various nations cited.

Rohrback, Paul, ed.
Massenverhetzung und Volkskrieg in Belgium. 139p. Berlin: C. Curtius, 1916
    Stirring up popular hatreds in Belgium;
illustrated with numerous excerpts from
Belgian papers.

Sailors' and soldiers' journals. Spectator.
117:182. Aug. 12, 1916

Soldiers publish paper. Editor and Publisher. 14:721. Feb. 20, 1915

The **Trench Journal.** Living Age. 292:298-
301. Feb. 3, 1917

b. OFFICIAL PRESS BUREAUS

See also
Propaganda—Official Bureaus, p.48; Italy—
Official Press Bureau, p.149.

(1) GENERAL HISTORY

Bennett, Arnold
Public and the censor. Harper's Weekly.
59:508-10. Nov. 28, 1914

Broye, Eugène
La censure politique et militaire en Suisse
pendant la guerre de 1914-1918. 194p.
Paris: V. Attinger, 1934
    Political and military censorship in
Switzerland during the World War.

Censored to death. Editor and Publisher.
47:1019, 1037. May 8, 1915

Censorship and suppression. Nation. 104:
424-5. Apr. 12, 1917

The **Censorship** muddle. Nation. 104:648-9.
May 31, 1917

The **Conditions** of war correspondence.
Spectator. 113:257-8. Aug. 22, 1914

Covering war zone. Editor and Publisher.
14:133, 150. Aug. 1, 1914
    Strict censorship in Europe makes
trouble for news organizations.

Demartial, George
La guerre de 1914; comment on mobilise
les consciences. 325p. Paris: Éditions
des Cahiers Internationaux, 1922
    How public sentiment and opinion was
mobilized during the World War.

Hapgood, Norman
How fighting governments suppress opinion. Harper's Weekly. 61:76-8. July
24, 1915

Hardships imposed by the censor. Literary
Digest. 49:308. Aug. 22, 1914

Lasswell, Harold D.
Propaganda technique in the World War.
233p. New York: A. A. Knopf, 1927
    An important discussion of the subject.

The **Lies** of the Allies. Open Court. 30:
508-10. Aug. 1916
    Review and comment on a war periodi-
cal, *Lies of the Allies*, by Frank Koester,
which first appeared in 1914-15.

News censorship. Editor and Publisher.
14:297. Oct. 3, 1914
    Difficulties encountered trying to get
dispatches through to the United States.

Official correspondence relating to the censorship of telegrams transmitted by
cable and wireless. American Journal
of International Law. 9:spec. suppl.
270-313. July 1915
    Diplomatic correspondence dealing with
censorship of cables during the World War.

On the frontier of war; difficulties of correspondents. Nation. 99:341. Sept. 17,
1914

Peterson, Horace Cornelius
Propaganda for war: the campaign
against American neutrality, 1914-1917.
357p. Norman, Okla.: Univ. of Okla-
homa Press, 1939

Street, Major C. J. C.
Propaganda behind the lines. Cornhill.
47:488-99. Nov. 1919

Wanderscheck, Hermann
Weltkrieg und Propaganda. 260p. Berlin:
E. S. Mittler und Sohn, 1936
    Propaganda during the World War.

(2) FRANCE

Allard, Paul. See Berger, Marcel, jt. auth.

Baudrillart, Alfred
Notre propagande. La Revue Hebdomadaire. 4:141-84. Apr. 1916

Berger, Marcel and Allard, Paul
Les secrets de la censure pendant la
guerre. 382p. Paris: Éditions des
Portiques, 1932
    A graphic description of scenes in the
censor's office in France during the World
War. The authors discuss the maze of
orders and instructions, and quote verbatim
many deleted passages to demonstrate the
nature of the censorship.

Busy Paris censors. Editor and Publisher. 14:447. Nov. 21, 1914
They are obliged to read and pass 800 columns of news matter every day.

Dewey, Stoddard
The press in France; censorship and propaganda. Nation. 102:158-9. Feb. 10, 1916
By an American war correspondent.

Ferguson, Fred S.
Covering the "war beat" in France. Editor and Publisher. Sec. 2. Golden Jubilee number. 67:150, 154. July 21, 1934
An American correspondent discusses the limitations under which reporters operated during the World War.

Mansfield, Francis Miltoun
La Maison de la Presse: a service bureau. Editor and Publisher. 49:5-6. Jan. 13, 1917
An American correspondent describes the technique of the French Press Bureau during the World War.

Pierrefeu, Jean de
The sword and the pen. p.189-98. *In his* French headquarters, 1915-1918. Tr. by Major C. J. C. Street. London: G. Bles, 1924
The scene at French General Headquarters, Information Section, revealing the relations of the army to the war correspondents.

(3) GERMANY

The **German** censor at work. Literary Digest. 53:552. Sept. 2, 1916

German news scheme. Editor and Publisher. 14:221. Sept. 5, 1914
London *White Paper* tells of secret plan to influence foreign press.

German press bureau. Editor and Publisher. 14:675. Feb. 6, 1915
How press agents sought to create favorable sentiment for Germany in the United States.

Germany would sway press. Editor and Publisher. 13:1078. June 13, 1914
Commercial news agency started by government to boom the Fatherland abroad.

Getting war news from German fronts. Editor and Publisher. 49:24. Dec. 30, 1916
Karl von Wiegand, Berlin correspondent of the *New York World*, tells how dispatches are censored and the manner in which news reaches America.

Muzzling the German press. Literary Digest. 51:1344. Dec. 11, 1915

Randall, James G.
Germany's censorship and news control. North American Review. 208:51-62. July 1918
German censorship was extended far beyond military matters into civil and political life; not destined to give Germany any ultimate advantage.

Rathert, Helmut
Die deutsche Kriegsberichtstattung und Presse als Kampfmittel im Weltkrieg. Grossenheim-Plosnick: 1934

Reithdorf, F. V.
Censor in Germany. Canadian Magazine. 47:238-40. July 1916

Rouquette, Louis
Allemagne et Amérique; la propagande germanique aux États-Unis. 154p. Paris: Chapelot, 1916
German propaganda in the United States during the World War.

Von Wiegand tells of his experiences as war correspondent in Germany. Editor and Publisher. 48:852, 874. Jan. 8, 1916
Says military censorship in that country has been liberal.

Zensurbuch für die deutsche Presse. Kriegspresseamt. Berlin: Reichsdruckerei, 1917

(4) GREAT BRITAIN

Addison, Christopher
Politics from within, 1911-1918. 2v. London: Herbert Jenkins, 1924
Vol. 2, ch. XI, p.145-59: The use of the press during the war.
Press used for propaganda and to promote personal ambitions.

Bell, Edward Price
The British censorship. 21p. An address. London: T. Fisher Unwin, 1916

The **Blue** pencil. Living Age. 287:756-9. Dec. 18, 1915
Excess of the censor's zeal inspired this criticism of British censors during the World War.

British censorship of the United States. Independent. 82:230. May 10, 1915

Brownrigg, Sir Douglass
Indiscretions of the naval censor. 279p. London, New York: Cassell, 1920
The chief censor of the British Admiralty describes the naval censorships during the War and the problems of publicity and propaganda.

Bruntz, George G.
Allied propaganda and the collapse of the German Empire in 1918. 246p. (Hoover War Library Publications, no. 13) Stanford University: Stanford Univ. Press, 1938
Analysis of propaganda methods and appeals, with foreword by Harold D. Lasswell. A valuable reference work.

Campbell, Alexander
A censorship of the censor. English Review. 22:58-63. Jan. 1916

Censor all war news. Editor and Publisher. 14:153. Aug. 8, 1914
Strict regulations in England will confine dispatches to official bulletins.

The **Censor** as Britain's deadly peril. Literary Digest. 50:1238-40. May 22, 1915

Cook, Edward T.
The press in war time. 200p. London: Macmillan, 1920
A notable essay including an account of the official British Press Bureau.

Elton, Oliver
C. E. Montague: a memoir. 335p. Garden City, N.Y.: Doubleday, Doran, 1929
Includes the story of Montague's relations with the British war propagandists.

Fairlie, John A.
Censorship. British War Administration. p.133-7. New York: Oxford University Press, 1919

Gibbs, Sir Philip Hamilton
Now it can be told. 558p New York, London: Harper, 1920
A British war correspondent's afterthoughts, including his experiences with military authorities.

Keen, Edward L.
Good words for the British censorship. Editor and Publisher. 48:1256. Mar. 18, 1916
Never intentionally discriminated against any correspondent, writes United Press representative.

Koch, Theodore Wesley
British censorship and enemy publications. Library Journal. 42:697-705. Sept. 1917

Lytton, Neville S.
The press and the general staff. 231p. London: W. Collins Sons, 1921
How the British army in the field viewed and handled the newspaper correspondents. An important source book.

MacDonald, William
The press and the censorship in England and France. Nation. 105:287-9. Sept. 13, 1917

Montague, Charles Edward
Disenchantment. 228p. (Phoenix Library) London: Chatto and Windus, 1928

About

C. E. Montague: a memoir. Oliver Elton. 335p. Garden City, N.Y.: Doubleday, Doran, 1929
Includes the story of Montague's relations with the British war propagandists.

Parker, Sir Gilbert
The United States and the War. Harper's. 136:521-31. Mar. 1918
A British war propagandist describes the manner in which America was bombarded with information about the War.

Peterson, Horace Cornelius
British influence on the American press, 1914-17. American Political Science Review. 31:79-88. Feb. 1937
British manipulation of American public opinion during the World War.

Ponsonby, Arthur A. W. H.
Falsehood in war time. 192p. London, New York: G. Allen and Unwin, 1928
Noted description of the manner in which facts and photographs were perverted to serve the Allied cause during the War.

The Press censorship. English Review. 22:261-72. Mar. 1916

Squires, J. Duane
British propaganda at home and in the United States from 1914 to 1917. 113p. Cambridge: Harvard Univ. Press, 1935
A carefully drawn sketch of the British propaganda agencies developed during the World War.

Strachey, John St. Loe
The adventure of living. 500p. New York, London: G. P. Putnam's Sons, 1922
The former editor of the *Spectator* relates how he helped to entertain and to influence American war correspondents in England.

Stuart, Sir Campbell
Secrets of Crewe House. 256p. London, New York, Toronto: Hodder and Stoughton, 1920
The story of a famous British propaganda organization during the World War.

Thimme, Hans
Weltkrieg ohne Waffen. 293p. Stuttgart, Berlin: Cotta, 1932
A German study of propaganda by the Allies during the World War, particularly that directed at German troops.

What the censor senses. Literary Digest. 53:967-9. Oct. 14, 1916

Wood, Eric Fisher
The British censorship. Saturday Evening Post. 189:5-7, 101-2, 18-19, 105-6. Apr. 28, May 5, 1917

(5) MISCELLANEOUS

Banks, William
The press censorship. Canadian Magazine. 46:152-5. Dec. 1915

Bauer, Wilhelm
Die öffentliche Meinung in der Weltgeschichte. 402p. Wildpark-Potsdam: Akademische Verlagsgesellschaft Athenaion, 1930
An interesting and fully illustrated discussion of public opinion from ancient times to the post-World War period.

Broye, Eugène
La censure politique et militaire en Suisse pendant la guerre de 1914-1918. 194p. Paris: V. Attinger, 1934
Political and military censorship in Switzerland during the World War.

Hapgood, Norman
How fighting governments suppress opinion. Harper's Weekly. 61:76-8. July 24, 1915

Harrison, Austin
Gott strafe all intellect! English Review. 24:470-3. May 1917

Lasswell, Harold D.
Propaganda technique in the World War. 233p. New York: A. A. Knopf, 1927
This work stimulated widespread interest and further studies regarding war propaganda methods.

Lutz, Ralph Haswell
Studies of World War propaganda, 1914-1933. Journal of Modern History. 5:496-516. Dec. 1933
A well-documented study of propaganda methods employed by the belligerents during the World War.

Parsons, Elsie Clews
Dragon's teeth. Harper's Weekly. 60:
449. May 8, 1915

Roosevelt, Theodore
America and the World War. 277p. New
York: C. Scribner's Sons, 1915

Shepherd, William Gunn
The forty-two centimeter blue pencil.
Everybody's. 36:470-82. Apr. 1917
Censorship during the World War, by an
American correspondent.

Turner, Edward Raymond
Censorship and false news. Nation. 99:
280. Sept. 3, 1914
Letter addressed to the editor.

Vagaries of the Russian censorship. Outlook. 111:692. Nov. 24, 1915
The editors received from the Russian
post office three censored copies of *The
Outlook.*

Viereck, George S.
Spreading germs of hate. With a foreword by Colonel E. M. House. 327p.
New York: H. Liveright, 1930
American author connected with German
propaganda agencies during the World War
tells his story.

Villard, Oswald Garrison
The censorship abroad. Nation. 99:513-
14. Oct. 29, 1914
Editorial.

Yarmolinsky, Avrahm
Censorship in Russia. Russian Review.
3:93-103. July 1917
A historical study of censorship from
1700 to 1917. Censorship laws depended on
the policies of successive monarchs, and
varied in tone from terroristic to ridiculous.

c. THE AMERICAN PRESS

Addams, Jane
Peace and the press. Independent. 84:
55-6. Oct. 11, 1915

The American press on the war. Literary
Digest. 51:528-9. Sept. 11, 1915

American sympathies in the war. Literary
Digest. 49:939-41, 974, 976-8. Nov. 14,
1914

Another menace to the press. Nation. 104:
205-6. Feb. 22, 1917

Bernstorff, J. H., Graf von
My three years in America. New York:
C. Scribner's Sons; London: Skeffing-
ton and Son, 1920
These memoirs of the German Ambassador at Washington during the World War
include his impressions of American newspaper attitudes toward Germany.

British idea of our newspapers. Literary
Digest. 53:1330-1. Nov. 18, 1916

Brooks, Sydney
The press in war time. North American
Review. 200:858-69. Dec. 1914
The harm resulting from an unrestricted
press; the advantages of a restricted press.

Costrell, Edwin
Newspaper attitudes toward war in
Maine, 1914-17. Journalism Quarterly.
16:334-44. Dec. 1939

Crane, Charles E.
Mobilizing news. Scientific American.
112:134-5. Feb. 6, 1915

Creel, George
Hearst-made war news. Harper's Weekly.
59:186. Aug. 22, 1914

Davis, Elmer H.
History of The New York Times. 434p.
New York: New York Times, 1921
Includes briefly the story of the *Times*
during the World War.

Doesn't print war news. Editor and Publisher. 47:1079. May 22, 1915
Kansas editor is afraid of offending German readers.

Elser, Frank B.
Reporting the war from deskside. Outlook. 112:693-9. Mar. 22, 1916
The war reporter's difficulty in selecting
the truth from the tangle of truth, half-
truth, fakes, hearsay and rumor is here
described by an "indoor" war correspondent of the World War.

Federal authorities increase censorship.
Editor and Publisher. 49:7, 31. Feb.
10, 1917
All eventualities covered following break
in diplomatic relations with Germany.

Fine, Barnett
A giant of the press. 108p. (Editor and
Publisher Library, v.1) New York: Edi-
tor and Publisher, 1933
Biography of Carr Van Anda, managing
director of *The New York Times* 1904-32.

Foster, H. Schuyler, jr.
Charting America's news of the World
War. Foreign Affairs. 15:311-19. Jan.
1937
A quantitative method of analyzing war
news in the American press.

How America became belligerent. American Journal of Sociology. 40:464-75.
Jan. 1935

Graves, John Temple
The value of a free press. Academy of
Political Science, Proceedings. 7:365-
8. July 1917

Hall, Howard
Hearst: war-maker. Harper's Weekly.
61:436-7. Nov. 6, 1915

Hough, Henry B. See Lewinson, Minna,
jt. auth.

Irwin, William Henry
The news that passes the war censor.
Guild Reporter. 2:5. Nov. 1, 1935

Is our "free press" free? Recent tests by
foreign agents. Everybody's. 33:512.
Oct. 1915

Jusserand, J. J.
Le sentiment américain pendant la
Guerre. 157p. Paris: Payot, 1931
The French Ambassador to the United
States during the World War discusses
American public opinion toward France
during that period.

Lewinson, Minna and Hough, Henry B.
A history of the services rendered to the public by the American press during the year 1917. 31p. New York: Columbia Univ. Press, 1918

Lichtenberger, Henri
L'opinion américaine et la Guerre. 63p. Paris: Bloud et Gay, 1915

Millis, Walter
Road to war. 466p. Boston, New York: Houghton Mifflin, 1935

Nation hits back. Literary Digest. 54:1502. May 19, 1917

A **Newspaper** in time of war. Living Age. 285:605-11. June 5, 1915

Olds, Frank Perry
Disloyalty of the German-American press. Atlantic. 120:136-40. July 1917

Park, C. W.
Strategic retreat of the German language press. North American. 207:706-19. May 1918

Post-office censors under fire. Literary Digest. 55:19. July 28, 1914

The **Psychology** of war-news. Literary Digest. 50:753. Apr. 3, 1915

Roosevelt, Theodore
Roosevelt in the Kansas City Star. 295p. New York, Boston: Houghton Mifflin, 1921
"War-time editorials by Theodore Roosevelt with an introduction by Ralph Stout."

Russell, Isaac
Hearst-made war news. Harper's Weekly. 59:76-8. July 25, 1914

Schönemann, Friedrich
Die Kunst der Massenbeeinflussung in den Vereinigten Staaten von Amerika. 212p. Stuttgart: Deutsche Verlagsanstalt, 1926
Influencing the American public, particularly during the World War, from a German point of view.

Seitz, Don Carlos
Newspapers and the war. Review of Reviews. 50:465-8. Oct. 1914

Sense and the censor. Literary Digest. 51:1076. Nov. 13, 1915

Skeletons in the newspaper closet. Literary Digest. 51:592-3. Sept. 18, 1915
Meager war news dressed up by the telegraph-editor is turned out as thrillers. Examples quoted.

Strunsky, Simeon
War notes from a newspaper desk. Atlantic. 116:401-10. Sept. 1915
The role of the telegraph editor in wartime.

A year of war's emotions. Atlantic. 116:560-7. Oct. 1915

Sullivan, Mark
Over here, 1914-1918. (*His* Our times, the United States, 1900-1925, v.5) New York, London: Scribner's, 1926-36

Thwing, Charles F.
Public opinion in the United States in the last three years. Hibbert Journal. 16:89-102. Oct. 1917

Tompkins, Raymond S.
News from the front; censorship. American Mercury. 14:161-9. June 1928

Unofficial news. Spectator. 114:395-6. Mar. 20, 1915

"Uses of publicity." Spectator. 114:288-90. Feb. 27, 1915

Van Anda, Carr
About
A giant of the press. Barnett Fine. 108p. (Editor and Publisher Library, v.1) New York: Editor and Publisher, 1933

The **Veil** of secrecy that has dropped over the war. Current Opinion. 61:160-1. Sept. 1916

Villard, Oswald Garrison
The press as affected by the War. Review of Reviews. 51:79-83. Jan. 1915

Wager-Smith, Curtis
Associated Press in war time. Editor and Publisher. 48:950. Jan. 22, 1916
Cost of getting news.

War and the magazines. Bookman. 40:357-9. Dec. 1914

War and the press. Spectator. 113:222-3. Aug. 15, 1914

The **War-game** by innings. Literary Digest. 50:966-72. Apr. 24, 1915

Wheeler, Howard Duryée
At the front with Willie Hearst. Harper's Weekly. 61:340-2. Oct. 9, 1915
How Hearst and the International News Service faked war news.

Wilson, Woodrow
The President on neutrality and news. Editor and Publisher. 47:959. Apr. 24, 1915
Address before the Associated Press.

d. NEWS TRANSMISSION

See also
Radio, p.8.

Bright, Charles
Telegraphs in war time. Nineteenth Century. 77:861-78. Apr. 1915
Cable-cutting as a mode of warfare was employed by the belligerents during the World War. Value of radio limited by its lack of secrecy.

Telegraphy, aeronautics and war. 407p. London: Constable, 1918
Communications as they influenced the course of events during the World War. The author deals with nearly every phase of the subject of war time communications, particularly from the British viewpoint.

Censorship of telegrams transmitted by cable and wireless. American Journal of International Law. spec. suppl. 9: 270-313. July 1915
> A collection of presidential and departmental orders bearing upon the transmission of messages by cable and wireless prior to America's participation in the World War.

Munro, Henry F. See Stowell, Ellery C. jt. auth.

Richards, Sir Erle
The British prize courts and the war. p.11-34. *In* British Year Book of International Law, 1920-21. London: Oxford Univ. Press, 1920

Stowell, Ellery C. and Munro, Henry F.
International cases. v.2, p.232-3, 389-90, 565-9. Boston, New York: Houghton Mifflin, 1916
> Censorship of war correspondents; British censorship of cablegrams (1915), interception by Great Britain and France of neutral mails (1916), during the World War.

Submarine telegraphy during war. Scientific American. suppl. 43:17880. June 12, 1897
> A technical account of the use of submarine telegraphy in war time.

United States. Department of State.
Censorship of the cables by belligerent governments; censorship of the mails by belligerent governments. p.503-31, 591-630, 697-743. *In its* Foreign relations of the United States. World War supplements for 1914, 1915, 1916. Washington: Government Printing Office, 1928-29
> Texts of letters exchanged between the United States government and the belligerent governments concerning the interception of cable messages and mails to and from the United States.

The **Wires** and the war. Scientific American. 117:186. Sept. 15, 1917
> Editorial stressing the importance of telegraphic communication in war time, between Washington and the army cantonments, naval bases, aviation fields and other government war projects.

e. WAR CORRESPONDENCE

(1) AMERICAN CORRESPONDENTS IN EUROPE

The **Blue** pencil. Living Age. 287:756-9. Dec. 18, 1915

Cobb, Irvin S.
Paths of glory. 414p. New York: Geo. H. Doran, 1915
The red glutton. 414p. London: Hodder and Stoughton, 1915
> An author and war correspondent's story of the early months of the World War.

Davis, Charles B., ed.
Adventures and letters of Richard Harding Davis. 417p. New York: C. Scribner's Sons, 1917
> Includes letters written by Richard Harding Davis during the World War showing his attitude toward the belligerents while he was serving as a correspondent for American newspapers.

Davis, Richard Harding
The last message of Richard Harding Davis. Collier's. 57:19. Aug. 5, 1916
> *About*

Adventures and letters of Richard Harding Davis. Ed. by Charles B. Davis. 417p. New York: C. Scribner's Sons, 1917
Richard Harding Davis: his day. Fairfax D. Downey. 322p. London, New York: C. Scribner's Sons, 1933

Dewey, Stoddard
The behavior of war; criticism among Allies. Nation. 102:614-15. June 8, 1916

Dosch-Fleurot, Arno W.
Through war to revolution. 242p. London: John Lane, 1931
> A war correspondent for the New York *World* describes his experiences on the Western Front and in revolutionary Russia.

Downey, Fairfax D.
Richard Harding Davis: his day. 322p. London, New York: C. Scribner's Sons, 1933

Dunn, Robert
Five fronts. 308p. New York: Dodd, Mead, 1915
> A war correspondent on the firing lines with English, French, Austrian, German and Russian troops.

Forrest, Wilbur
Behind the front page. Stories of newspaper stories in the making. 350p. New York, London: D. Appleton-Century, 1934
> Forrest reported the sinking of the "Lusitania."

Fortescue, Granville
Front line and dead line. 310p. New York: G. P. Putnam's Sons, 1937
> The experiences of a war correspondent.

Forty-six reporters accompany Mr. Ford. Editor and Publisher. 48:723-4. Dec. 11, 1915
> List of publicity and newspaper men on the famous Peace Ship.

Herrick, Myron T.
> *About*

Myron T. Herrick, friend of France. Thomas Bentley Mott. 399p. Garden City, N.Y.: Doubleday, Doran, 1929

Herrick, Robert
> *About*

Robert Herrick's indictment of American war correspondents. Current Opinion. 59:265. Oct. 1915

War correspondents not fakes says Shepherd, denying Herrick. Editor and Publisher. 48:401. Oct. 2, 1915

Irwin, William Henry
A reporter at Armageddon. 354p. New York, London: D. Appleton, 1918
> Letters from the Front and behind the lines of the Great War.

James, Lionel
Times of stress. 320p. London: J. Murray, 1932

Jesse, F. Tennyson
The trials of a war correspondent. Collier's. 55:19-21. Mar. 20, 1915

Journalists and peace. New Republic. 60:311-12. Nov. 6, 1929

Kellogg, Paul U.
How news of a great battle is gathered. New York Evening Post Magazine. p.2. Mar. 30, 1918

McCormick, Robert R.
With the Russian army. Being the experiences of a National Guardsman. 306p. London, New York: Macmillan, 1915

McCutcheon, John T.
With Davis in Vera Cruz, Brussels, and Salonika. Scribner's. 60:91-7. July 1916

Mason, Gregory
American war correspondents at the front. Bookman. 40:63-7. Sept. 1914
Efforts of military authorities to restrict the war correspondents.

Meet war emergency. Editor and Publisher. 14:154. Aug. 8, 1914
Press associations of the country well prepared for situation abroad.

Mott, Thomas Bentley
Myron T. Herrick, friend of France. 399p. Garden City, N.Y.: Doubleday, Doran, 1929
Ambassador Herrick was frequently helpful to American war correspondents in France.

Nafziger, Ralph O.
World war correspondents and censorship of the belligerents. Journalism Quarterly. 14:226-43. Sept. 1937

Nevinson, Henry W.
Battle-scribes, it's your turn again! World's Press News. 14:2. Oct. 10, 1935

Newspapers in war time. Public. 21:334-7. Mar. 16, 1918

Palmer, Frederick
My second year of the war. 404p. New York: Dodd, Mead, 1917

My year of the Great War. 464p. New York: Dodd, Mead, 1915

Things you don't know about the War. Collier's. 55:5-6, 29-32. Apr. 17, 1915

With my own eyes. 396p. Indianapolis: Bobbs-Merrill, 1933
The most informative of Mr. Palmer's books regarding war and press. It explains how he was selected early in the war to represent the whole American press at British army headquarters in France.

Powell, E. Alexander
Fighting in Flanders. 227p. New York: C. Scribner's Sons, 1914

Slanting lines of steel. 307p. New York: Macmillan, 1933
Powell, colorful American war correspondent, describes his activities and biases during the World War.

Reed, John
The War in Eastern Europe. 335p. New York: C. Scribner's Sons, 1917
John Reed was eventually expelled from Russia after attempting to report events on the Eastern Front independently of the authorities.

Rice, Wallace
Eye-witnesses at the shambles. Dial. 58:208-11. Mar. 18, 1915

Robert Herrick's indictment of American war correspondents. Current Opinion. 59:265. Oct. 1915
Many of the "famous war correspondents" never saw the scenes they wrote about, but got the reports in bars and in cafés.

Robinson, H. Perry
A war correspondent on his work. Nineteenth Century. 82:1205-15. Dec. 1917

Romantic days in war reporting. Literary Digest. 49:910-11, 13-14, 17. Nov. 7, 1914

Ruhl, Arthur
Antwerp to Gallipoli. 304p. New York, London: C. Scribner's Sons, 1916
A year of war correspondence on many fronts and behind them, with illustrations from photographs.

A war correspondents' village. Collier's. 56:10-11, 26. Feb. 5, 1916

White nights, and other Russian impressions. 248p. New York: C. Scribner's Sons, 1917

With the invader. Collier's. 55:13-14. Aug. 14, 1915

Schreiner, George Abel
The craft sinister. 422p. New York City: G. Albert Geyer, 1920
An American correspondent in Central Europe describes his vain efforts to evade censorships and to report his observations to the American people.

Should the war correspondent be resurrected? Editor and Publisher. 48:1, 25. June 17, 1916
Describes qualifications.

Shaw, Albert
Our foremost war writer. Review of Reviews. 53:424-5. Apr. 1916
Concerning Frank H. Simonds.

Shepherd, William Gunn
Confessions of a war correspondent. 210p. New York, London: Harper, 1917
Picturesque narrative of a war correspondent's daily life. The chapter entitled "The Forty-two Centimeter Blue Pencil" discusses the censorship.

Confessions of a war correspondent. Everybody's. 36:168-81. Feb. 1917
One of a series of revealing articles by an American war correspondent on the super-human task of reporting the World War independently and objectively.

Forty-two centimeter blue pencil. Everybody's. 36:470-82. Apr. 1917

The free lance and the faker. Everybody's. 36:337-49. Mar. 1917

Simms, William Philip
Covering the War from the French capital. Editor and Publisher. 48:1101. Feb. 12, 1916
By a United Press war correspondent.

Simonds, Frank H.
About
Our foremost war writer. Albert Shaw. Review of Reviews. 53:424-5. Apr. 1916

Sweetser, Arthur
A diary from the Front. World's Work. 29:350-6, 475-80, 544-5. Jan.-Mar. 1915
Account of the World War by an American press correspondent.

Swope, Herbert Bayard
Inside the German Empire in the third year of the War. 366p. New York: Century, 1917

Tompkins, Raymond S.
First page stuff: 1918. American Mercury. 20:469-77. Aug. 1930
A war correspondent ridicules the manner in which World War news was gathered and published.

Van Loon, Hendrik Willem
Tricks of newspaper correspondents. Nation. 100:77-8. Jan. 21, 1915

War as viewed by a correspondent. Editor and Publisher. 47:182. July 31, 1915

A War correspondent of the new dispensation. Literary Digest. 54:129. Jan. 20, 1917

A War-correspondent's job was not a soft snap. Literary Digest. 62:67-70. July 19, 1919

War correspondents not fakes says Shepherd, denying Herrick. Editor and Publisher. 48:401. Oct. 2, 1915

Washburn, Stanley
Field notes from the Russian front. 291p. London: Andrew Melrose, 1915
By an American war correspondent.

The Russian campaign, April to August 1915. 347p. (His Field notes from the Russian campaign, v.2) New York: C. Scribner's Sons; London: Andrew Melrose, Ltd., 1915

The Russian offensive. 193p. (His Field notes from the Russian campaign, v.3) London: Constable, 1917

Victory in defeat; the agony of Warsaw and the Russian retreat. 180p. Garden City, N.Y.: Doubleday, Page, 1916

Williams, Wythe
Passed by the censor. 270p. New York: E. P. Dutton, 1916
The experience of an American newspaper man in France; with an introduction by Myron T. Herrick.

(2) OTHER WAR CORRESPONDENTS

Amy, W. Lacey
Confidences of a war correspondent. Canadian Magazine. 56:39-52. Nov. 1920

De Beaufort, J. M.
Behind the German veil; a record of a journalistic war pilgrimage. 367p. London: Hutchinson, 1917

Fox, Edward Lyell
Behind the scenes in warring Germany. 333p. New York: McBride Nast, 1915
By a special correspondent with the Kaiser's armies and in Berlin.

Gibbs, Sir Philip Hamilton
More that must be told. 407p. New York, London: Harper, 1921

The street of adventure. 437p. New York: E. P. Dutton, 1919

Hedin, Sven Anders
With the German armies in the West. Tr. from the Swedish by H. G. de Walterstorff. 402p. London, New York: John Lane, 1915
About
War correspondence de luxe. Nation. 100: 686-7. June 17, 1915
Review of Hedin's *With the German Armies in the West.*

Hutcheon, William
Gentlemen of the press. Memories and friendships of forty years. 238p. London: John Murray, 1933

James, Lionel
High pressure. 314p. London: John Murray, 1929
Record of activities in the service of *The Times*; primarily the record of a war correspondent.

Jeffries, J. M. N.
Front everywhere. 298p. London: Hutchinson, 1935
A British war correspondent's story of experiences during the World War and in other campaigns.

Powell, Lyman Pierson
At the front in Indiana. Outlook. 118: 577-9. Apr. 10, 1918

Slocombe, George E.
The tumult and the shouting. 437p. London, Toronto: W. H. Heinemann, 1936
Memoirs of a reporter and war correspondent.

Tomlinson, Henry M.
Mars, his idiot. Harper's. 171:298-307. Aug. 1935

Villiers, Frederic
Villiers: his five decades of adventure. 2v. New York: Harper, 1920
The War correspondent. Nation (London) 26:768-9. Mar. 6, 1920

3. APRIL 1917-1918

a. THE AMERICAN PRESS

(1) PRESS REGULATION

Aids correspondents in getting news. Editor and Publisher. 51:31. June 15, 1918
Secretary Baker gave Marlen E. Pew an office in the War Department with authority to organize his own staff and to get the facts.

American censorship in France. Review of Reviews. 57:205-6. Feb. 1918

Americans now censor German newspapers. Editor and Publisher. 51:10. Feb. 8, 1919
<blockquote>The military officials in charge of occupation of German territory were compelled to check German propaganda and criticism.</blockquote>

Barry, Richard
"Freedom" of the press. North American Review. 208:702-9. Nov. 1918
<blockquote>Author questions whether the control of the press and suppression of vital public discussion during World War was actually used for the purpose of preventing disloyalty in the United States.</blockquote>

Barry, Robert T.
Charge plan to censor news of great peace conference. Editor and Publisher. 51:33. Nov. 23, 1918
<blockquote>Seizure of cables by administration arouses newspapers.</blockquote>

Blankenhorn, Heber
Adventures in propaganda: letters from an intelligence officer in France. 166p. Boston, New York: Houghton Mifflin, 1919

War of morale; how America shelled the German lines with paper. Harper's. 139:510-24. Sept. 1919

Borah denounces censorship features of Espionage Law in hot Senate debate. Editor and Publisher. 51:9. Feb. 15, 1919

Brisbane to testify at Senate hearing. Editor and Publisher. 51:31. Oct. 5, 1918
<blockquote>Arthur Brisbane asserts he is "100 per cent American and 500 per cent anti-German."</blockquote>

Burleson, Albert Sidney
Postmaster General explains to editor purpose and operation of new law. Editor and Publisher. 50:5. Oct. 6, 1917

Callwell, Charles E.
The press censorship. Nineteenth Century. 85:1132-45. June 1919

Censorship as finally enacted. Survey. 38:245-6. June 9, 1917
<blockquote>Official demand for some form of press control during the War is rejected by the House of Representatives.</blockquote>

Censorship needed in war times. Editor and Publisher. 50:9. Mar. 30, 1918
<blockquote>Address by Melville E. Stone, general manager of the Associated Press.</blockquote>

Charles Evans Hughes defines functions of newspaper criticism in war times. Editor and Publisher. 50:8. May 4, 1918
<blockquote>Address at annual banquet of A.N.P.A.</blockquote>

Cobb, Frank I.
The press and public opinion. New Republic. 21:144-7. Dec. 31, 1919
<blockquote>Manipulation of public opinion by means of propaganda during wartime. It is futile for a government to endeavor to protect the people from propaganda.</blockquote>

Control of press was bitterly fought by Senators Norris and Cummins. Editor and Publisher. 50:7, 26. Oct. 6, 1917
<blockquote>Denounced grant of arbitrary power to Postmaster-General as a menace to our traditional freedom of speech and of the press.</blockquote>

Corwin, Edward S.
Constitutional law in 1919-1920; decisions of the Supreme Court on freedom of speech and press. American Political Science Review. 14:655-8. Nov. 1920
<blockquote>The Espionage Act of 1917 and the right of Congress to suppress efforts to control public opinion.</blockquote>

Daniels to centralize all naval publicity. Editor and Publisher. 50:9. Oct. 20, 1917

Deny German control charge against Pueblo Chieftain. Editor and Publisher. 51:44. Jan. 18, 1919

Disloyal publications continue to disappear. Editor and Publisher. 50:9. Oct. 13, 1917
<blockquote>Post Office Department quietly causes decline of newspapers and magazines whose policies are held to be detrimental to best interests of nation.</blockquote>

Disloyalty in print serious offence. Editor and Publisher. 50:18. Apr. 6, 1918
<blockquote>Senate amends Espionage Law to place heavy penalties upon those convicted of interfering with war's progress.</blockquote>

Espionage Act awaits Wilson's signature to become law. Editor and Publisher. 50:12. May 11, 1918

Evening Mail in Stoddard's charge pending final disposition by U.S. Government. Editor and Publisher. 51:5-6, 38-9. July 13, 1918
<blockquote>Charges and disclosures regarding schemes of German government to buy or subsidize American newspapers in effort to influence public opinion. See also Editor and Publisher. 51:7. July 20, 1918; 51:16. July 27, 1918; also Dr. Rumely's answer to indictments, 51:34. Aug. 10, 1918.</blockquote>

Government takes over all wires on July 31. Editor and Publisher. 51:12. July 27, 1918
<blockquote>Postmaster Burleson promised not to interfere with press wire service.</blockquote>

The **Government's** control of the press. Nation. 105:283. Sept. 13, 1917

Hard, William
Mr. Burleson, espionagent. New Republic. 19:42-5. May 10, 1919
<blockquote>Instances of press censorship by Postmaster-General Burleson.</blockquote>

Independence for editors. New Republic. 16:61-3. Aug. 17, 1918

Johnson, Thomas M.
Without censor; new light on our greatest World War battles. 411p. Indianapolis: Bobbs-Merrill, 1928

Leaders stand pat on Postal Law. Editor and Publisher. 50:6. Jan. 5, 1918

Lee, Ivy L.
Fighting German propaganda by organized publicity. Editor and Publisher. 50:14. May 25, 1918

Licenses for journalists. Literary Digest. 54:1021-2. Apr. 7, 1917

Martin, Frederick R.
A plea for an uncensored press. American Academy of Political Science, Proceedings. 7:360-4. July 1917

Melville, Lewis
German propagandist societies. Quarterly Review. 230:70-88. July 1918; *reprint* Living Age. 298:513-25. Aug. 31, 1918

Mr. Burleson throws further light on his attitude toward disloyal papers. Editor and Publisher. 50:17. Nov. 3, 1917
> Postmaster-General explains in detail the "trading-with-the-enemy act" of Oct. 6, 1917.

Mr. Burleson to rule the press. Literary Digest. 55:12. Oct. 6, 1917
> Limitations on press freedom in wartime are discussed, with special reference to the foreign language newspapers; and also censorship of cable and mail communications with foreign countries.

Must we go to jail? North American Review. 206:673-7. Nov. 1917
> The editor of the *North American Review* criticizes Postmaster-General Burleson's restrictions on the press in wartime.

Newspaper correspondence. Army and Navy Journal. 76:113. Oct. 1, 1938
> Major General W. C. Sweeney, chief of the A.E.F. Censorship Division, believes that war correspondents are an important part of an army, and can do much to assist in a military effort.

Newspapers classed as war industry. Editor and Publisher. 50:25. Apr. 25, 1918
> Revised Priority Regulations issued by War Industries Board classify newspapers and periodicals as necessary to winning the war.

Palmer, Frederick
America in France. 479p. New York: Dodd, Mead, 1918
> By the press relations officer of the American Expeditionary Forces, who had previously served as a war correspondent.

Frederick Palmer explains "mysteries" of the American censorship in France. Editor and Publisher. 50:5-6, 27-8. Feb. 16, 1918
> Text of address before the National Press Club in Washington.

About

Col. Palmer knows war, has seen all since '97. Editor and Publisher. 72:8. Sept. 9, 1939
> Biographical sketch of noted correspondent who served as press censor with the A.E.F. in 1917-18.

Patriotism, East and West. Literary Digest. 54:1486. May 19, 1917

Pew, Marlen E.

About

Aids correspondents in getting news. Editor and Publisher. 51:31. June 15, 1918
> Secretary Baker gave Marlen E. Pew an office in the War Department with authority to organize his own staff and to get the facts.

Post office department given power to suppress all disloyal publications. Editor and Publisher. 50:5-6. Sept. 29, 1917

Press holds Peace League's fate in its hand, says Palmer. Editor and Publisher. 51:10. Mar. 1, 1919
> Frederick Palmer, war correspondent and observer for General Pershing, says reporters are the best news censors.

The **Press** under Post Office censorship. Current History. 7, pt. 1:235-6. Nov. 1917
> The far-reaching powers conferred on the Postmaster-General by a clause in the Trading with the Enemy Act of 1917.

Protest against a muzzled press. Survey. 38:358. July 21, 1917
> Socialist newspapers denied the second-class mail privilege by Secretary Burleson during the War stage a protest. Press censorship is futile.

Stone, Donald L.
Press and mail censorship in war-time. Editor and Publisher. 59:5-6, 41. Aug. 14, 1926
> The operation of the American Army's censors under Pershing in France, and rules that governed the press.

Too dangerous for us to read. Literary Digest. 54:1413. May 21, 1917

Treason's twilight zone. Literary Digest. 54:1763-5. June 9, 1917

Untold tales of the A.E.F. censorship. Editor and Publisher. 60:9. Nov. 26, 1927

U.S. exposed Germany's effort to control newspapers. Editor and Publisher. 51:10. Dec. 14, 1918

War and a free press. Outlook. 116:56-7. May 9, 1917

Warning; relations of the government and the press. Spectator. 120:368-9. Apr. 6, 1918

Watterson, Henry
Henry Watterson sees menace to republic in servility of press in war time. Editor and Publisher. 50:5, 28-9. Mar. 9, 1918

Williams, Walter, ed.
U.S.A. war time censorship regulations. (Press Congress of the World in Switzerland. 1926, Proceedings) Columbia, Mo.: Univ. of Missouri, E. W. Stephens Pub. Co., 1926

Would wipe Berlin off U.S. map. Editor and Publisher. 51:25. Oct. 5, 1919
> An example of hysterical feelings toward references to Germany during the World War.

(2) COMMITTEE ON PUBLIC INFORMATION

A.N.P.A. accepts Creel challenge to investigate news bureau. Editor and Publisher. 50:12. May 4, 1918

Blankenhorn, Heber
War of morale; how America shelled the German lines with paper. Harper's Monthly Magazine. 139:510-24. Sept. 1919
    Planes and toy balloons were enlisted in the propaganda campaign directed at the German soldiers.

Creel, George
Aid and comfort to the enemy. Independent. 93:446-7. Mar. 16, 1918

How we advertised America. 466p. New York: Harper, 1920
    Head of the United States Department of Information tells the story of America's efforts to sell the World War to the public.

About

Creel announces abolition of news censorship. Editor and Publisher. 51:10. Nov. 16, 1918

George Creel sounds call to unselfish national service to newspapermen. Editor and Publisher. 51:5-6. Aug. 17, 1918
    Part of an address by the chairman of the Committee on Public Information.

Tributes paid to George Creel on retirement. Editor and Publisher. 51:34. Dec. 7, 1918

Irwin, William Henry
Propaganda and the news, or, what makes you think so? 325p. New York, London: McGraw-Hill, Whittlesey House, 1936
    The development of propaganda technique and the methods applied by various countries, by a seasoned reporter and former member of the Creel Committee.

Keeps whole world in touch daily with American news. Editor and Publisher. 51:24. July 20, 1918
    A description of the work of the Division of Foreign Press Service of the Committee on Public Information.

Larson, Cedric and Mock, James R.
The lost files of the Creel Committee of 1917-1919. Public Opinion Quarterly. 3:5-29. Jan. 1939
    Preliminary analysis of papers of the Committee on Public Information, United States propaganda agency during the World War.
——See Mock, James R. jt. auth.

Marlen E. Pew's work in War Department. Editor and Publisher. 50:14. May 18, 1918
    Secretary of War Baker appointed Mr. Pew as his personal publicity representative. Mr. Pew continued to act on the Creel Committee.

Mock, James R. and Larson, Cedric
Words that won the war. Princeton, N.J.: Princeton University Press, 1939
    An analysis of records of the Creel Committee of 1917-1919.
——See Larson, Cedric, jt. auth.

New voluntary censorship rules issued by George Creel. Editor and Publisher. 50:24-5. Jan. 5, 1918

Plans for censorship. Editor and Publisher. 48:871. Jan. 8, 1916
    Major General Scott submits plan for dealing with press in time of war.

Preciado, A. A.
Chilean newspapers equal to best in South America. Editor and Publisher. 51:34. Mar. 22, 1919
    The writer, a Pacific coast newspaperman, represented the Creel Committee on Public Information in Chile.

Stone, Isidor F.
Creel's crusade. Nation. 149:647-9. Dec. 9, 1939
    Committee on Public Information during the World War.

Winning the war with news bombs. Current Opinion. 64:346. May 1918

Work of the Foreign Press Service as a successor to the Creel Committee. Current Opinion. 67:132-3. Aug. 1919

(3) FOREIGN LANGUAGE PRESS IN THE UNITED STATES

Adams, Samuel Hopkins
Invaded America. Everybody's. 37:9-16, 86; 38:28-33, 82-4; 30-2, 74-6, 78, 80-3; 55-6, 60, 62, 64. Dec. 1917—Mar. 1918
    The attitudes of the German-American press during the World War, with particular reference to the Middle West.

Editor Lucius W. Nieman fights Germanism in its chief American stronghold. Editor and Publisher. 50:5. May 25, 1918
    Founder and owner of the *Milwaukee Journal* led relentless campaigns against German-language newspapers.

Enemy speech must go. North American Review. 207:811-14. June 1918

Frank, Glenn
Our foreign language press. Century. 99:636-8. Mar. 1920

German paper foes press the fight. Editor and Publisher. 50:26. May 25, 1918
    Petition President to forbid publication in German language.

German-language newspapers are passing. Editor and Publisher. 50:24. May 11, 1918

German-language newspapers face growing resentment of American people. Editor and Publisher. 50:11. May 11, 1918

Growing demand for the suppression of the German-American press. Current Opinion 63:151-2. Sept. 1917

Hagedorn, Hermann
Menace of the German-language press. Outlook. 116:579-81. Aug. 15, 1917

The Language of the Hun. Editor and Publisher. 51:30. Aug. 3, 1918
    This vitriolic editorial opposed waiting for a gradual elimination of the German language in the United States.

May ban all German papers from U.S. Editor and Publisher. 50:xix. Apr. 27, 1918

Papers in the enemy tongue. Literary Digest. 55:16. Sept. 22, 1917

Stop publication of German language newspapers in the United States. Editor and Publisher. 50:34. Apr. 27, 1918

To kill or use our German press. Literary Digest. 57:12. May 11, 1918

The **Trail** of German propaganda in the American press. Current Opinion. 65:139-41. Sept. 1918

War started on the German press. Editor and Publisher. 51:28. June 15, 1918

Will not tolerate disloyal press. Editor and Publisher. 50:xix. Apr. 27, 1918

(4) War News

Admiral Sims' challenge to our press. Nation. 116:458. Apr. 18, 1923

Claff, Julian B.
"Thirty" sounded for Amaroc News, most unique of American dailies. Editor and Publisher. 55:11, 31. Mar. 17, 1923
<small>Journal of the American Army of Occupation on the Rhine.</small>

Cost of war news takes big jump. Editor and Publisher. 50:6 Apr. 6, 1918

Durant, William J.
The war within the War. Dial. 65:5-7. June 20, 1918
"Elaborating" war news. Nation. 105:30. July 12, 1917

Germans print weekly paper for U.S. soldiers' reading. Editor and Publisher. 51:14. Sept. 28, 1918
<small>Toy balloons carry papers to American soldiers telling how to get to amusements in Frankfort on time.</small>

Historic war editorials which won for Henry Watterson the Pulitzer Prize. Editor and Publisher. 50:11-12. June 29, 1918
<small>These two emotionally charged editorials by the Louisville editor are reproduced in full.</small>

Kauffman, Ruth Wright
News embargo. North American Review. 208:831-41. Dec. 1918

Nation's war heads plead for criticism that will help, not hinder, war work. Editor and Publisher. 50:v-vii. Apr. 27, 1918
<small>Speeches of Secretary of the Navy Daniels, Secretary of War Baker, Justice Hughes and Stéphane Lauzanne, editor of Le Matin, before the American Newspaper Publishers Association.</small>

Not for editors only. Outlook. 118:130-1. Jan. 23, 1918

Paul, Edward
The newspaper versus President Wilson on the question of Japanese intervention in Siberia. Public. 21:532-6. Apr. 27, 1918

The newspapers and a just peace. Public. 21:664-7. May 25, 1918

Publish trench papers in shadow of death. Editor and Publisher. 51:14. Oct. 9, 1918

Rathom articles on plots suppressed. Editor and Publisher. 50:12, 26. Mar. 2, 1918
<small>World's Work ceases publication of Providence Journal editor's exposé of German intrigue in this country. See editorial comment, 50:24.</small>

Stone, Donald L.
Amazing adventures of "Stars and Stripes." Editor and Publisher. 59:20. Apr. 23, 1927
<small>Founding and publishing the doughboy's newspaper in wartime France.</small>

Understanding war news. Independent. 85:146. Jan. 31, 1916

The **WGN.** 302p. Chicago: Chicago Tribune, 1922
<small>Contains a brief account of the Chicago Tribune's efforts to report the World War.</small>

War lies. Nation. 128:335. Mar. 20, 1929

(5) War Correspondents

Cobb, Irvin S.
Speaking of Prussians. 80p. New York: Geo. H. Doran, 1917
<small>Cobb's viewpoint after the United States entered the War.</small>

Correspondents give war news despite drastic censors. Editor and Publisher. 51:18, 27. Aug. 3, 1918
<small>A few of Frederic Villiers' experiences during the World War.</small>

Correspondents in Paris air raid. Editor and Publisher. 50:17. Mar. 9, 1918

Cost of war news takes big jump. Editor and Publisher. 50:6. Apr. 6, 1918
<small>Full cable rates used for all messages concerning Hindenburg drive; number of American war correspondents doubled.</small>

Curtin, D. Thomas
How I helped bring the United States into the last war. Liberty. 12:5-7. Oct. 26, 1935
<small>A sensationally written article by a former war correspondent, who asserts that he used his position in Germany to gather information for the Allies.</small>

Floyd Gibbons describes conditions under which U.S. war correspondents work. Editor and Publisher. 51:5-6. Sept. 7, 1918

Hazen, David W.
Giants and ghosts of central Europe. 197p. Portland, Oregon: Metropolitan Press, 1934

Heddle, James
Going to press under fire of the air-raiding gun. Editor and Publisher. 51:18. Oct. 5, 1918

News-gathering troubles. Nation. 106:7. Jan. 3, 1918

Payne, Philip
A scribe in France. Editor and Publisher. 51:12, 26. Dec. 7, 1918

Reporter wounded with U.S. troops. Editor and Publisher. 51:18. June 15, 1918
Floyd Gibbons lost one eye at Chateau-Thierry two hours after filing dispatch to the *Chicago Tribune*.

Schlesinger, Arthur Meier
The khaki journalists, 1917-1919. Mississippi Valley Historical Review. 6:350-9. Dec. 1919

Seven men who are the "eyes of the world" at the Front. Literary Digest. 57:54-60. May 11, 1918
How the World War news was handled by the headquarters correspondents, seven in number. Daily routine of the newsmen.

A **War-correspondent's** indictment of war. Current Opinion. 71:772-4. Dec. 1921

The **Work** of the war-censor on the field and at home. Literary Digest. 57:46-53. Apr. 20, 1918
America's treatment of correspondents with the Army was more liberal than that of our allies. The author describes the great difficulties which face the news censor during wartime.

b. THE PRESS OF OTHER COUNTRIES

Bombardment fails to stop paper. Editor and Publisher. 50:6. Apr. 13, 1918
Story of a plucky newspaper, *L'Est Républicain*, published at Nancy.

Canadian censorship rules amended. Editor and Publisher. 50:33. Apr. 27, 1918
Drastic changes in regulations made to prohibit publication of statements tending to prevent united public support of the War.

Censor should give news of deeds. Editor and Publisher. 50:21. Jan. 5, 1918
Sir Frederick E. Smith, Attorney-General of England, says public is entitled to whatever will not give enemy useful information.

Clark, Victor S.
The German press and German opinion. Atlantic. 122:1-9. July 1918

Colles, W. Morris
Germany and the neutral press. Fortnightly Review. 111:925-36. June 1919

5,000 censors at work in England. Editor and Publisher. 50:14. Apr. 13, 1918

France will now censor all ads. Editor and Publisher. 51:30. June 15, 1918
Mysterious and unintelligible groups of letters and figures suspected of carrying information to the enemy.

French censorship more liberal. Editor and Publisher. 50:16. Jan. 5, 1918
Clemenceau's attitude toward press.

German press dare not print news. Editor and Publisher. 50:24. Jan. 12, 1918

Lauzanne, Stéphane J. V.
"First newspaperman of France" is now Prime Minister of the Republic. Editor and Publisher. 50:5. May 4, 1918
Georges Clemenceau, dean of French newspapermen, is associated with other distinguished journalists in high government positions.

Pacher, Gustav von
Die Dreiverbandspresse, ihr Anteil an der Kriegsentfachung und ein Weg zur ihrer Bekämpfung. 79p. Leipzig: S. Hirzel, 1915
A German view of the press of the Allies, and suggestions for fighting its tendencies.

Paris journalists in union against free competitors. Editor and Publisher. 51:16. Oct. 26, 1918
Organize to do away with unfair competition by senators and other public men who furnish free matter to newspapers.

Playne, Caroline E.
Britain holds on, 1917-18. 440p. London: G. Allen and Unwin, 1933
A record of the social history of Britain during the last two years of the War, continuing the author's book *Society at War*.

Posse, Ernst
Presse. 513p. (Der Weltkrieg in seiner Einwirkung auf das Deutsche Volk, VIII) Leipzig: Quelle und Meyer, 1918
Ed. by Max Schwarte.
The World War press and its influence on Germany.

Rheims L'Éclaireur de l'Est looks like a handbill but appears regularly. Editor and Publisher. 50:26. Jan. 26, 1918
Facsimile of first two pages of the paper published under fire of German guns.

Running a newspaper in Russia isn't exactly a soft job. Editor and Publisher. 50:12. Jan. 5, 1918

South American newspapers are prospering in spite of war. Editor and Publisher. 50:30. Feb. 9, 1918

c. THE PEACE CONFERENCE

Admit press representatives to Peace Conference. Editor and Publisher. 51:5. Jan. 25, 1919

American newspaper men at peace gathering were from every part of States. Editor and Publisher. 51:8. Mar. 9, 1919
A list of nearly 200 special representatives who registered at the Press Bureau of the American Commission to Negotiate Peace at the Hotel Crillon in Paris.

Baker, Ray Stannard
Statement of Peace Conference on publicity, January 17, 1919, and meeting of press representatives. p.47-54. *In* his Woodrow Wilson and world settlement, v.3. Garden City, N.Y.: Doubleday, Page, 1922
Statement adopted by the Council of Ten, January 17, for presentation to the press representatives at Paris explaining policies of publicity.

Text of resolutions adopted by delegates of the Allied and American press at the Hotel Ritz, January 16, 1919.

Record of protests and resolutions adopted by American press correspondents April 23, 1919, regarding admission to meeting of Allied and German delegates at Versailles, May 7, at which the Treaty was formally presented to the Germans.

Capehart, Charles
Newspapers of Britain and United States stand together for press freedom. Editor and Publisher. 51:7-8. Jan. 25, 1919
Achieve modification of order for censorship and secrecy at Peace Conference.

Censorship and the Peace Conference. New Republic. 17:61-3. Nov. 16, 1918
Abuse and dangers of censorship. Is war censorship to be continued through the period of peace negotiation?

Close intimacy of press and world rulers planned by French government. Editor and Publisher. 51:7-8. Mar. 15, 1919
By Henry Wood, chief of staff of the United Press in Rome and war correspondent.

Coggeshall, Reginald
"Was there censorship at the Paris Peace Conference?" Journalism Quarterly. 16: 125-35. June 1939
Rare instances of censorship, the importance of which was generally exaggerated, are examined critically in this study.

Democratizing the press. Nation. 108:727. May 10, 1919

Essary, J. Frederick
Covering Washington. 280p. Boston, New York: Houghton Mifflin, 1927
Includes experiences during the World War and the Press Conference.

Lincoln, Charles M.
Peace reporting hardest task ever before United States press. Editor and Publisher. 51:30. Mar. 8, 1919
Managing editor of New York *World* says only about forty correspondents remained of the vast number who attended opening of Conference.

Noble, George Bernard
Policies and opinions at Paris, 1919; Wilsonian diplomacy, the Versailles peace, and French public opinion. 465p. New York: Macmillan, 1935

Roy W. Howard tells full story of premature peace rumor. Editor and Publisher. 51:18. Nov. 23, 1918

Thompson, Charles T.
The Peace Conference day by day; a presidential pilgrimage leading to the discovery of Europe, by Charles T. Thompson; with an introductory letter by Colonel E. M. House. 423p. New York: Brentano's, 1920
By an American newspaper correspondent.

4. CARICATURES AND CARTOONS

See also
Public Opinion and the Press—Caricatures and Cartoons, p.57.

Abbott, Lyman
Cartoons and caricatures in wartime. Outlook. 114:561-5 Nov. 8, 1916

European war cartoons—chiefly German. Review of Reviews. 52:418-24. Oct. 1915

Fox, Fontaine
Fontaine Fox tell his wife how war helped cartoonists. Editor and Publisher. 51:7. Jan. 11, 1919

Fuchs, Eduard
Der Weltkrieg in der Karikatur. Munich: A. Langen, 1916
Cartoons and the World War.

Germany's martial spirit as shown in German and Austrian cartoons. Review of Reviews. 50:547-60. Nov. 1914

Olszewski, Karl Ewald
Der Kriegs-Struwwelpeter; lustige Bilder und Verse. 24p. Munich: Holbein Verlag, 1915
German political and war caricatures of the World War period. Colored illustrations.

Raemaekers, Louis
Kultur in cartoons. 219p. New York: Century, 1917
Dutch cartoonist whose vitriolic sketches of Germany at war won him worldwide fame.

The "Land and Water" edition of Raemaekers' cartoons. 25pts. in 1v. London: Pub. by Land and Water, 1917

About
The War's greatest cartoonist. Literary Digest. 51:526. Sept. 11, 1915
The part played by Louis Raemaekers, Dutch cartoonist, during the World War.

Schulz-Besser, Ernst
Die Karikatur im Weltkriege. 108p. Leipzig: E. A. Seemann, 1915

K. RECENT MILITARY CAMPAIGNS, 1919-1939

1. GENERAL DISCUSSIONS

Ackerman, Carl William
The prelude to war: controlled public opinion. Annals of the American Academy of Political and Social Science. 192:38-41. July 1937
War makers still have respect for public opinion of the world, as evidenced by the amount of propaganda emitted over shortwave channels to other nations.

Allen, Devere
News for peace. World Tomorrow. 16: 595-6. Oct. 26, 1933
Nofrontier News Service, a periodical for editors which will ferret out and assemble important data on current events that are not ordinarily available.

Baillie, Hugh
News-gathering in a frenzied era. Quill. 25:3ff. Dec. 1937

China and Spain wars have given new "break" to foreign correspondents. Newspaper World. 41:88, 91. Jan. 22, 1938
Reviews Boer War, Russo-Japanese War, and recent campaigns.

Churchill, Winston Leonard Spencer
The world crisis. 866p. New York: C. Scribner's Sons, 1931

Coverage of future war will be much like the last says Simms. Editor and Publisher. 70:9. Apr. 10, 1937
Author says that during World War correspondents enjoyed freedom of movement and relatively little censorship, at least with the Allies on Western Front. Expects conditions to be same in future war.

Covering the War where rumor was thicker than fleas. Newsweek. 6:19-20. Oct. 12, 1935

Delafons, Allan
Correspondents will have no place in future wars, Nevinson says. Editor and Publisher. 63:78. Mar. 14, 1931

Gunther, John
Inside Europe. 470p. New York, London: Harper, 1936
A survey of European affairs by a former correspondent of the Chicago Daily News.

Hubbard, Wynant Davis
Mislaid: a war. Harper's. 172:700-9. May 1936

In the driftway; war censorship. Nation. 134:702. June 22, 1932

Manning, George H.
Swope urges strict censorship of press in time of war. Editor and Publisher. 64:14. May 30, 1931
Former executive editor of New York World advocates suppression of bad news and active propagandizing, in testimony before War Policies Commission.

Manuel, Frank E.
Mr. Carney and the Times. Nation. 143:743. Dec. 19, 1936

Miller, Webb
I found no peace. 332p. New York: Simon and Schuster, 1936
United Press foreign news editor sketches the hectic life of a foreign correspondent.

Monchak, Stephen J.
U.S. European press corps alert in war crisis. Editor and Publisher. 71:3, 38-9. Sept. 24, 1938

Nevinson, Henry W.
Battle-scribes, it's your turn again! World's Press News. 14:2. Oct. 10, 1935

Perry, John W.
Writers mobilize for war coverage. Editor and Publisher. 68:9, 12. Aug. 31, 1935

Topping, Thomas T.
Dodging bullets and censorship adds zest to reporting abroad. Editor and Publisher. 59:10. Mar. 19, 1927
Topping covered Riff warfare and fierce fighting in Syria for the A.P.

Villari, Luigi
Press prejudice. Saturday Review. 162:654-5. Nov. 21, 1936

Wells, Linton
Blood on the moon. 418p. Boston, New York: Houghton Mifflin, 1937
The autobiography of Linton Wells, Chicago Tribune correspondent.

Whitaker, John T.
And fear came. 273p. New York: Macmillan, 1936
An American foreign correspondent discusses European politics and asks for international cooperation to dispel fear gripping Europe and the world.

2. ITALO-ETHIOPIAN CAMPAIGN

Addis Ababa has Hollywood aura. Editor and Publisher. 68:9. Oct. 26, 1935

Chaplin, William Watts
Blood and ink: an Italo-Ethiopian war diary. 206p. Harrisburg, Pa.: Telegraph Press, 1936
Incidents during four months on the Italo-Ethiopian war front.

Clark, Eleanor. See Werth, Alexander, jt. auth.

Clemow, Bice
Strictest war censorship is imposed to silence many wild rumors. Editor and Publisher. 68:5-6. Oct. 12, 1935
Hectic days, especially in Addis Ababa, during the Italo-Ethiopian campaign. Correspondents forced to rely on unconfirmed reports.

Correspondents trek to Africa. Literary Digest. 120:24-5. Aug. 24, 1935
"Terrific handicaps face news-men assigned to cover Italo-Ethiopian imbroglio in getting dispatches out of the country."

Defeat of the press, Ethiopia. Time. 27:21. Jan. 27, 1936

Garratt, Geoffrey Theodore
News-hunting in Ethiopia. New Statesman and Nation. 11:378-9. Mar. 14, 1936
Only 20 of the original 120 correspondents remained in Ethiopia owing to unusual difficulties encountered in that country.

Italy denounces British press and news agencies. World's Press News. 14:3. Oct. 10, 1935
Italy charges that pro-Ethiopian news is going to British newspapers; correspondents denied privilege of going to the front in the Italo-Ethiopian conflict.

Miller, Webb
Webb Miller tells of hardships of news men in Ethiopia. Editor and Publisher. 68:11. Nov. 9, 1935

Perry, John W.
Webb Miller tells war experiences. Editor and Publisher. 69:7. Jan. 11, 1936
Correspondents in Ethiopia suffered numerous hardships.

Steer, George L.
Caesar in Abyssinia. 411p. Boston: Little, Brown, 1937
  A caustic portrayal of Mussolini by an American foreign correspondent.

War in Ethiopia will test reporters. Editor and Publisher. 68:26. July 27, 1937

War—propaganda—and the press. Christian Science Monitor. Dec. 4, 1935
  Symposium by correspondents in Rome, Ethiopia, Paris, Berlin, Austria, and the United States on the manner in which the press in those countries—foreign language newspapers in the case of the United States—are handling the Italo-Ethiopian conflict.

Werth, Alexander and Clark, Eleanor
The press goes to war. New Republic. 84:355-7. Nov. 6, 1935
  Contents: I. What France reads. II. The Italian press, New York.

3. SPANISH CIVIL WAR

Brown, Robert U.
Smuggling undoes Spain's censors. Editor and Publisher. 69:11. Aug. 29, 1936

Carney, William P.
Fighting the censor. Scribner's. 101:33-8. June 1937
  A description of the struggle between American correspondents intent on giving their readers unbiased news, and censors who suppress unfavorable reports, particularly during the Spanish Civil War.

Dies, Douglas
Rebel phone censors have a sense of humor (sometimes), says U.P. man. Editor and Publisher. 69:16. Sept. 26, 1936

Faking the Spanish news. Nation. 143:322. Sept. 19, 1936

Fernsworth, Lawrence A.
Correspondents in Spain. Current History. 48:31-4. Mar. 1938
  Government censorship in Civil War not so black as it has been painted.

Foreign journalists under Franco's terror. London: United Editorial Limited, 1938

Franco issues press decree. Newsdom. 9:5. May 21, 1938

Gorrell, Henry T.
War reporter's own story of facing death in Spain. Editor and Publisher. 70:7, 32. Sept. 25, 1937

It's a Richard Harding Davis war; correspondents in Spain work amid danger and glamour. Literary Digest. 122:33-5. Oct. 3, 1936

Jerrold, Douglas
Red propaganda from Spain. American Review. 9:129-51. May 1937

Jones, Robert L.
So I went to Spain. Quill. 25:3-4, 14. Sept. 1937

Knoblaugh, H. Edward
Correspondent in Spain. 233p. London, New York: Sheed and Ward, 1937
  An Associated Press correspondent with the Loyalist forces.

Loyalist propaganda machine. Catholic World. 146:479-81. Jan. 1938

Matthews, Herbert L.
Two wars, and more to come. 311p. New York: Carrick and Evans, 1938
  New York Times war correspondent in Ethiopia and Spain relates the experiences of a conscientious reporter.

Miller pictures Civil War horror. Editor and Publisher. 70:26. Apr. 24, 1937

Ortega y Gasset, Eduardo
La presse espagnole pendant la Guerre Civile. Cahiers de la Presse. 3:247-56. July-Sept. 1939
  The Spanish press during the Civil War.

Powell, Anthony
Marginal comments; what writers think about the Spanish war. Spectator. 159: 991. Dec. 3, 1937

Pratt, Fletcher
Hot-air castles in Spain. American Mercury. 43:450-61. Apr. 1938

Propaganda from Spain. American Mercury. 41:409-22. Aug. 1937
  Discussion: 42:251-3. Oct. 1937

Seeley, Evelyn
Hearst fights the Spanish Republic. New Republic. 88:217-20. Sept. 30, 1936

Spain's revolt draws newsmen; some receive baptism of fire. Editor and Publisher. 69:6. July 25, 1936
  Swiftness of revolution caught correspondents and State Department unprepared; veterans of Ethiopian front flew to new war zones.

Thorning, Joseph Francis
Why the press failed on Spain. Catholic World. 146:289-91. Dec. 1937

Treatment of correspondents in insurgent Spain. Newspaper World. 41:2. Feb. 19, 1938

Von Wiegand, Karl H.
I cover the Spanish front. Cosmopolitan. p. 26-7, 174-7. Dec. 1936
  A veteran among war correspondents contributes details of gathering and forwarding news from Madrid during the early days of the Spanish Civil War.

Von Wiegand tells difficulties of covering Spain's Civil War. Editor and Publisher. 69:6. Aug. 15, 1936

4. SINO-JAPANESE WAR

American papers echoed resentment of people over bombing of Panay. China Weekly Review. 83:184-5. Jan. 15, 1938

Anti-British campaign and suppression of Chinese newspapers. China Weekly Review 88:399-401. May 27, 1939

Army dictating to Japanese press on war reporting. World's Press News. 18:17. Sept. 2, 1937

Booker, Edna Lee
News is my job: a reporter in war-torn China. New York: Macmillan, 1938

British editors rebel against press censorship. China Weekly Review. 89:39. June 10, 1939

China war is heavy expense to newspapers. Newspaper World. 41:1-2. Jan. 1, 1938
Cable rate Tokio to London, "press" about 26.5c, "urgent press" about $1.10 a word. Hong Kong or Shanghai to London "press" 24c, "urgent press" $1.10.

Chinese newspapers move to colony of Hongkong. China Weekly Review. 89: 327. Aug. 12, 1939

Ekins, H. R.
China war "toughest news job in years," H. R. Ekins declares. Editor and Publisher. 71:5, 33. Jan. 1, 1938

English journalism also goes west in war time China! China Weekly Review. 88:292. May 6, 1939

Gould, Randall
Recruits drifting in add to China staffs. Editor and Publisher. 70:14. Oct. 16, 1937

Great Britain, United States protest against mail censorship. China Weekly Review. 84:48. Mar. 12, 1938

Heads fall, grenades explode as terrorists attack newspapers. China Weekly Review. 83:320-1. Feb. 19, 1938

Japanese press conference at Shanghai where the atmosphere is belligerent. China Weekly Review. 88:287-8. May 6, 1939

Japanese propaganda pamphlets reveal anxieties about world opinion on army's actions. China Weekly Review. 83:286-9. Feb. 12, 1938

Japan's thought control in North China. China Weekly Review. 84:346-7. May 21, 1938

Kao, George
What America is reading about the Far East. China Weekly Review. 84:248. Apr. 30, 1938

Koito, Chugo
Japan. Journalism Quarterly. 15:423-5. Dec. 1938
The Japanese press and the Sino-Japanese conflict.

Kuh, Frederick
Censorship, wire delays, sub-zero weather vex Manchuria writers. Editor and Publisher. 64:20. Jan. 9, 1932

Kurth, Karl
Die japanische Propaganda in Nordchina. Zeitungswissenschaft. 13:31-2. Jan. 1, 1938
Japanese propaganda in Northern China.

Der japanische Propagandakampf im chinesische Kriege. Zeitungswissenschaft. 13:339-40. May 1, 1938
Instances of Japanese propaganda during the Sino-Japanese conflict.

Die Masznahmen der Japaner in Schanghai auf dem Press- und Propagandagebiet. Zeitungswissenschaft. 13:137. Feb. 1, 1938
Japanese measures to assure control of the press and propaganda in Shanghai.

Lindt, A. R.
Special correspondent: with bandit and general in Manchuria. 292p. London: Cobden-Sanderson, 1933

Manchester Guardian Shanghai correspondent "invited" to Japanese censor's office. World's Press News. 18:11. Jan. 20, 1938

Martin, Kingsley
British opinion and the proposed boycott of Japan. Political Quarterly. 9:106-12. Jan. 1938

Monchak, Stephen J.
Chinese Japanese situation reviewed by two U.S. foreign correspondents. Editor and Publisher. 72:3, 30. July 8, 1939
Wilfred Fleisher, *New York Herald Tribune,* and Hallett E. Abend, *New York Times,* discuss censorships and trouble spots in China.

Moore, Horatio Booth
Soviet press and Japan's war on China. Pacific Affairs. 11:44-51. Mar. 1938

Nanking government stresses regulations for foreign photographers in interior of China; text. China Weekly Review. 76:216. Apr. 11, 1936

Norins, Martin R.
War in China and the Soviet press. Pacific Affairs. 12:157-68. June 1939

Oestreicher, J. C.
Shanghai's still sending. Quill. 25:12-14. Sept. 1937

Parker, William
Shanghai press conference. American Mercury. 44:156-61. June 1938
Difficulty of getting news from official Japanese sources during Sino-Japanese conflict.

Perry, John W.
Manchurian war costly to newspapers; far flung area hard to cover. Editor and Publisher. 64:5-6. Nov. 14, 1931

War-time reporting returns in China. Editor and Publisher. 64:9, 45. Feb. 6, 1932

Pew, Marlen E.
Shop talk at thirty. Editor and Publisher. 64:48. Apr. 16, 1932
Karl von Wiegand covers the Manchurian war.

Powell, John Benjamin
British press regulations and the newspaper situation at Shanghai. China Weekly Review. 87:140-3. Dec. 31, 1938

Puppets publish twenty-eight newspapers. China Weekly Review. 88:105. Mar. 25, 1939

Raine, David N.
Japanese propaganda in North China. Public Opinion Quarterly. 3:564-80. Oct. 1939

Rea, George Bronson
Great Pacific war; an indictment of military alarmists. Living Age. 329:439-47. May 29, 1926

Rubens, Doris
Japanese propaganda efforts in Shanghai. China Weekly Review. 89:332-6. Aug. 12, 1939

Samson, Gerald L. G.
Burma and India and the Sino-Japanese conflict. China Weekly Review. 88:132. Apr. 1, 1939

U.S. newsmen dodge death in Shanghai war. Editor and Publisher. 70:12. Aug. 21, 1937

Vaughn, Miles W.
Covering the Far East. 408p. New York: Covici-Friede, 1936
    Reminiscences of an observant United Press foreign correspondent in Japan and China.

Wild rumors hamper China war coverage. Editor and Publisher. 62:12. Sept. 14, 1929

Violent anti-British campaign being conducted by Japanese puppets. China Weekly Review. 88:212. Apr. 15, 1939

Why so many Japanese newspapermen have been killed. China Weekly Review. 83:284-5. Feb. 12, 1938

Widespread Japanese propaganda drive against Chinese unity. China Weekly Review. 83:31. Dec. 11, 1937

Writer dies, 2 others hurt in bombing of Panay. Editor and Publisher. 70:51. Dec. 18, 1937
    The Panay incident, involving the bombing of a United States Navy vessel, opened up a fertile field for anti-Japanese propaganda in connection with the Sino-Japanese warfare.

L. SECOND WORLD WAR, 1939

1. GENERAL DISCUSSIONS

Australian newspapers in conference. Newspaper News (Sydney) 12:1-2. Dec. 1, 1939
    Delegates discussed war and press, censorship, broadcasting.

Casey, Ralph D.
America's press and the war. The Ohio Newspaper. 20:3, 11-15. Nov. 1939
    A thought-provoking challenge to editors during wartime, presented to Ohio editors at a symposium on propaganda.

Censorship and muddling continue to harry U.S. press in coverage of the war. Newsweek. 14:36-7. Sept. 18, 1939

Fortune survey: credibility of foreign news. Fortune. 20:120. Dec. 1939

Limpus, Lowell M.
It's a military impossibility; how to read the war news. Forum. 102:253-7. Dec. 1939

Monchak, Stephen J. and Schneider, Walter E.
Censorship, secrecy hamper U.S. writers' war coverage. Editor and Publisher. 72:3-4, 36-7. Sept. 9, 1939
    Correspondents seriously restricted immediately after war opens.

Parker, William
Holland is important war news relay point. Editor and Publisher. 72:14. Nov. 11, 1939

Passion v. reason. Time. 34:59-60. Sept. 18, 1939
    Details of censorship machinery in countries at war.

Plenty of German but lack of British pictures. Newspaper World. 42:2. Sept. 16, 1939
    War Office order restricts photography.

Premier on responsibility of the press. Newspaper World. 42:3. Sept. 2, 1939

Schneider, Walter E. See Monchak, Stephen J. jt. auth.

2. PRESS OF BELLIGERENTS; OFFICIAL PRESS BUREAUS

a. FRANCE

Censorship of French press. Newspaper World. 42:26. Sept. 2, 1939
    Papers restricted to six pages; correspondents must use censored telegraph rather than telephone.

French press under censorship. World's Press News. 22:10. Aug. 31, 1939
    News censorship began August 28; six Communist newspapers suspended.

b. GERMANY

Whiteleather, Melvin K.
Germany. Journalism Quarterly. 16:395-8. Dec. 1939
    Associated Press correspondent in Berlin describes censorship, war reporting, and German press in war time.

c. GREAT BRITAIN

Anderson, Russell F.
Britain's censorship now covers diplomatic stories. Editor and Publisher. 72:8. Dec. 9, 1939

Back to the old system for war news, says Prime Minister. World's Press News. 22:1. Oct. 5, 1939
    Ministry of Information decentralized.

d. OTHER COUNTRIES

3. PROPAGANDA

Miller, Clyde Raymond and Minsky, Louis
Newspaper and propaganda. Survey Graphic. 28:713-16. Nov. 1939
    Part of a study on propaganda as discussed at the Williamstown Institute of Human Relations, 1939.
Propaganda, good and bad, for democracy. Survey Graphic. 28:705-20. Nov. 1939
    An analysis and discussion, fully illustrated.

Minsky, Louis. See Miller, Clyde Raymond, jt. auth.

Muller, Edwin
Waging war with words. Current History. 50:24-7. Aug. 1939
    Radio propaganda.

Powell, Robert
Warfare by leaflet. Living Age. 357:326-9. Dec. 1939

Propaganda is found ineffective when minds are not ready. Science News Letter. 36:334. Nov. 18, 1939

Propaganda need not lie, may succeed with part truths. Science News Letter. 36:367. Dec. 2, 1939

4. WAR CORRESPONDENCE

Difficulties of war coverage told by Hugh Baillee. Editor and Publisher. 72:5. Sept. 30, 1939
    United Press official describes obstacles to effective war reporting, following survey in Europe.

Gallagher, O'Dowd
Out of the Blue H.Q. World's Press News. 22:4. Nov. 16, 1939
    London Daily Express correspondent describes experiences with the British army in France.

Green felt and gold C. Time. 34:58. Oct. 16, 1939
    Twelve American correspondents authorized to go to the Western Front with the British army.

Kontrolle des Nachrichtenwesens in der Schweiz. Zeitungswissenschaft. 14:665. Oct.-Nov. 1939
    As a security and neutrality measure the Swiss government has taken over the control of the news agencies and delegated the general in command of the army to enforce these measures.

Monchak, Stephen J. See Schneider, Walter E. jt. auth.

Names of British and American war correspondents. Newspaper World. 42:1. Sept. 23, 1939
    Group of officially accredited correspondents selected to report activities of British army in France. French restrict British press to representative of one news agency and three newspapers.

Reporters live in hotels at war front. Editor and Publisher. 72:9. Nov. 18, 1939
    Diary of an International News Service correspondent.

Schneider, Walter E.
U. S. war writers join British army in France. Editor and Publisher. 72:10. Oct. 14, 1939

United Press levies 12½% war assessment. Editor and Publisher. 72:4. Oct. 14, 1939

War in Europe doubles cost of United, States foreign news services. Editor and Publisher. 72:5, 32. Sept. 23, 1939

—and Monchak, Stephen J.
U.S. press geared for coverage of war as crisis sets new pace. Editor and Publisher. 72:3-5, 29, 33. Sept. 2, 1939
    Descriptions of American correspondents in Europe who will serve as war reporters.

Western front tour made by 10 U.S. writers. Editor and Publisher. 72:10. Oct. 7, 1939
    First officially conducted visit to French side of the Front.

5. COMMUNICATIONS

See also
Communications, p.1; Germany—Censorship and Propaganda, p.132.

À l'écoute de la diplomatie européenne; les émissions de trois radios allemande, russe et italienne. L'Europe Nouvelle. 22:1049-50, 1087-9, 1109-10, 1135-6. Sept. 23, Oct. 14, 1939
    Listening in on European diplomatic affairs and radio broadcasts from Germany, Russia and Italy.

British news by wireless. Round Table. 29:719-32. Sept. 1939
    Outlines a plan by which the British government could aid British news broadcasting, bringing a return in defensive value out of all proportion to its cost.

Chains limit newscasts; WMCA is "on the mat." Editor and Publisher. 72:8. Sept. 16, 1939

Communications: the fourth front. Fortune. 20:90-6. Nov. 1939
    News communications during the early period of the European War, supplemented by a map showing international communications channels in most of the world.

Macaulay, Rose
War and the B.B.C. Spectator. 163:538-9. Oct. 20, 1939

Muller, Edwin
Waging war with words. Current History. 50:24-7. Aug. 1939
    Radio propaganda.

Radio censorship in Europe described; German system called most efficient. Broadcasting. 17:17. Oct. 15, 1939

Rigid censorship of communications in Europe impedes radio reporters. Broadcasting. 17:22. Sept. 15, 1939

Saerchinger, César
Radio, censorship and neutrality. Foreign Affairs. 18:337-49. Jan. 1940

Schneider, Walter E.
Radio poor war news source for wire services, dailies. Editor and Publisher. 72:5-6. Nov. 4, 1939

Urgent press rates reduced. Newspaper World. 42:3. Sept. 1939
British Empire rates reduced to no more than 7½d.

Voluntary plan for war news is adopted. Broadcasting. 17:11, 88. Sept. 15, 1939
Major networks agree on war coverage.

White, William L.
Short wave war. Current History. 51:43-4. Nov. 1939

Wright, Basil
Films and the war. Spectator. 163:498. Oct. 13, 1939

PART II. THE FOREIGN PRESS

I. GENERAL REFERENCES

A. GENERAL AND MISCEL-LANEOUS

Angell, Sir Norman
The problem of the press. Nineteenth Century. 125:184-93. Feb. 1939
It is difficult to get the public to buy a paper that tells the truth impartially, free of bias and sensationalism; quotes from the P.E.P. *Report on the British Press.*

Bibliographie historique de la presse: Vorarbeiten zu der historischen Bibliographie der Presse. 113p. (Bulletin of the International Committee of Historical Sciences. v. 6, pt. 1, no. 22) Paris: Les Presses Universitaires de France, Mar. 1934
A guide to historical source material on the press. In French and German.

Bömer, Karl
Bibliographisches Handbuch. 344p. Leipzig: O. Harrassowitz, 1929

Handbuch der Weltpresse. 340p. Berlin: C. Duncker, 1934
3rd ed., 1937.
A comprehensive handbook and directory of newspapers in all countries of the world.

Das internationale Zeitungswesen. 134p. Berlin, Leipzig: Walter de Gruyter, 1934

——and Rochlin, Raphall
Internationale Bibliographie des Zeitungswesens. 373p. Leipzig: O. Harrassowitz, 1932

Groth, Otto
Die Zeitung. Ein System der Zeitungskunde (Journalistik). 4v. Mannheim: J. Bensheimer, 1928-30
Handbook on journalism.
Public opinion: v.1, p.91-111. The relations of press and public: v.1, p.111-67. The telegraph agencies: v.1, p.482-547. Government and the press: v.2, p.3-333. The publisher: v.4, p.3-51. The journalist: v.4, p.51-320.
Bibliography: v.4, p.343-549.

Handbuch der Auslandpresse, 1918. 270p. Berlin: E. S. Mittler und Sohn, 1918

Handbuch der Weltpresse. 340p. Berlin: C. Duncker, 1937
An inclusive directory of leading newspapers throughout the world.

International year book. New York: Editor and Publisher, 1938
Annual. First edition 1920-21.
Newspaper lists of the United States and foreign countries.

Is a press dictatorship possible? Saturday Review. 149:810-11. June 28, 1930

Kellogg, Paul Underwood
Ring in the news. il., facsims. Survey. 61:276-84. Dec. 1, 1928
Pressa, the International Journalistic Exposition, Cologne.

Muller, Edwin
America through the looking glass; the eyes of the European press. Christian Century. 55:788-90. June 22, 1938

Parsons, Henry S., comp.
A check list of foreign newspapers in the Library of Congress. 209p. Washington: Government Printing Office, 1929
Listed alphabetically according to countries.

Publisher's International Congress at Brussels. Athenæum (London) 2:67. July 10, 1897

Rochlin, Raphall. See Bömer, Karl, jt. auth.

Sell's World's press. London: Henry Sell, 1938-39
Annual. First edition 1883-84.
A newspaper directory.

Silver, Ann R.
Subsidies help European press to continue despite depression. Editor and Publisher. 65:13. Dec. 24, 1932

United States. Library of Congress. Periodical Division
A check list of foreign newspapers in the Library of Congress, newly compiled by Henry S. Parsons, chief, Periodical Division. 209p. Washington: Government Printing Office, 1929

Wade, George A.
Famous foreign newspapers. Pall Mall. 19:375-86. Sept.-Dec. 1899
Relative importance of news and literature in the foreign press. More news in British and American newspapers, less in continental.

Williams, Walter
The world's journalism. 44p. (Univ. of Missouri Bulletin, v.16. Journalism Series, no.6) Columbia, Mo.: Univ. of Missouri, 1915
Briefly summarizes some observations made in visiting nearly 2,000 newspaper offices in a world tour, 1913-1914.

B. OWNERSHIP AND FINANCIAL CONCENTRATION

Bell, Sam
Radio corporation holds wireless monopoly, U.S. report charges. Editor and Publisher. 56:14. Dec. 8, 1923

Bömer, Karl, ed.
Handbuch der Weltpresse. 340p. Berlin: C. Duncker, 1934

British United Press deny M.P.'s "ninety-nine per cent American" statement. Newspaper World. 41:1. Jan. 15, 1938
Purports to prove that the British United Press is entirely in British hands; started 1924 and owned solely by Charles F. Crandall, formerly editor of *Montreal Star.* Herbert Bailey, formerly *Daily Express, Daily Mail,* is now managing editor. 51 per cent of shares are held in Canada and voting control is in Crandall's hands. Merely exchange agreement with U.P.

Cannon, Carl L., comp.
Journalism: a list of references in English. 360p. New York: New York Public Library, 1924
Bibliography.

Hayes, A. J.
Cooperative journalism; summary. Consumers' Cooperation. 21:13-14. Jan. 1935

Hearst's London activities. Editor and Publisher. 13:609. Jan. 17, 1914
Hearst buys *Vanity Fair* and *Hearth and Home* and merges them with London *Budget.*

Hopkins, Roy, ed.
Newspaper finance annual. 130p. London: World's Press News and London General Press, 1930

Lord Beaverbrook pays £6,000,000 for Hulton publication. Editor and Publisher. 56:24. Oct. 13, 1923
Sharp fight for supremacy precedes British deal; Beaverbrook to keep London *Evening Standard,* remainder of 15 publications go to Lord Rothermere.

Magazine king: Seiji Noma owns 80 per cent of all Japan's periodicals. Literary Digest. 122:16. Sept. 12, 1936

Mallory, Walter H., ed.
Political handbook of the world, 1938. New York: Harper, for Council on Foreign Relations, Inc., 1938
Annual.
Information on parties, parliaments and the press. In the press section the emphasis is on those papers most likely to be quoted abroad.

O'Brien, Terence H.
Experiments in public ownership and control. 304p. New York: W. W. Norton, 1938

Pall Mall Gazette. Editor and Publisher. 10:7. Nov. 19, 1910
Astor plans to make it an influential newspaper.

Robb, Arthur T.
British chains battle in provinces. Editor and Publisher. 62:9, 42. Sept. 21, 1929
Powerful groups establishing zone dailies.

C. RACE AND THE PRESS

Detweiler, F. G.
Negro press today. American Journal of Sociology. 44:391-400. Nov. 1938

Gist, N. P.
Negro in the daily press. tables Social Forces. 10:405-11. Mar. 1932
A quantitative study of Negro news as it appeared in 17 white daily newspapers over a 60-day period.
Racial attitudes in the press. Sociology and Social Research. 17:25-36, Sept. 1932

Meacham, W. S.
Newspaper and race relations. Social Forces. 15:268-71. Dec. 1936

D. EDUCATION AND RESEARCH IN JOURNALISM

Barlow, Reuel R.
Journalistic education under the Third Reich. Journalism Quarterly. 12:357. Dec. 1935
A systematic plan, adopted by the German schools of journalism, for supplying young men to the press who are properly and rigorously trained to serve the nation.

First journalism school of France now in its second year. Editor and Publisher. 59:F 48. June 19, 1926
Catholic University of Lille giving three-year course.

Monroe, Paul
What can formal education contribute to the solution of world conflicts? School and Society. 48:1-7. July 2, 1938

Schöne, Walter
Zeitungswissenschaftliche Grundbegriffe. Zeitungswissenschaft. 9:473-83. Nov. 1, 1934
A discussion of the relation of journalism to publicity and of the fundamental concepts of journalism as discussed by several contemporaneous writers.

Striefler, Heiner
Statistisches zu der Auslandsberichterstattung deutscher Tageszeitungen. Zeitungswissenschaft. 5:262-75. Sept. 15, 1930
A study on the reporting of foreign news in German daily newspapers supplemented by a discussion of research method.

Valot, Stephen
Y a-t'il une science de la presse? Cahiers de la Presse. 1:12-16. Jan.-Mar. 1938
Journalism, in higher education, takes its place as a science in its own right.

II. AFRICA

A. GENERAL DISCUSSION

Ester, Karl d'
Die Presse Afrikas. Zeitungswissenschaft. 12:297-307. May 1, 1937
An excellent survey which discusses means of communications among the natives; the native press; the colonial press; influences exerted by the press of agencies and countries outside of the African continent; the problem of language difficulties.

Fischaleck, Lorenz
Die französische Kolonialpresse. Zeitungswissenschaft. 12:433-46. July 1, 1937
The French colonial press.

James, Lionel
High pressure; being some record of activities in the service of The Times newspaper. 314p. London: J. Murray, 1929

B. ABYSSINIA

Abyssinian Emperor is country's press cable censor. World's Press News. 14:5. Oct. 29, 1935
Abyssinia has but one newspaper, a weekly, with Emperor as editor-in-chief.

Clemow, Bice
Strictest war censorship is imposed to silence many wild rumors. Editor and Publisher. 68:5-6. Oct. 12, 1935
Travel and communications difficulties pile up in Ethiopian war situation. War dispatches limited to 100 words each.

Correspondents' stories from East Africa must pass censor before transmission. World's Press News. 14:13. Sept. 5, 1935
Brief news note.

Nevinson, Henry W.
Battle-scribes, it's your turn again! World's Press News. 14:2. Oct. 10, 1935
The reporting of the Italo-Ethiopian conflict.

Newshawks, seals. Time. 26:40-2. Oct. 14, 1935
The problem of getting news on Ethiopian war.

Perry, John W.
Writers mobilize for war coverage. Editor and Publisher. 68:9, 12. Aug. 31, 1936

Seeley, Evelyn
Sentimental attitude is absent in reporting of Ethiopian war. Guild Reporter. 2:6. Oct. 15, 1935

War will have cost Fleet Street £250,000 by Christmas. World's Press News. 14:1. Oct. 17, 1935
"Thousands a week for correspondents and cables." Hundreds of special war editions are published.

C. EGYPT

Crabites, Pierre
Journalism along the Nile. Asia. 27:992-7. Dec. 1927
Egypt's many newspapers are chiefly party organs, devoted to political propaganda.

L'Égypte indépendante. 456p. (Collection du Monde Islamique, t. I, Travaux des groupes d'études, publication no. 7) Paris: Hartmann, 1938
Pt. IV includes a discussion of the Egyptian press.

Egyptian newspapers. Great Britain and the East. 49:870. Dec. 30, 1937

Elder, E. E.
America in the Cairo press. Moslem World. 21:282-6. July 1931
Egyptian press has become highly "America conscious" and periodicals glorify American culture and merchandise.

Hartmann, Martin
The Arabic press of Egypt. 94p. London: Luzac, 1899

Hay, Lady Drummond
The press in Egypt. Near East. 26:195. Aug. 21, 1924
The influence of Egyptian press is paramount despite 98% illiteracy of the natives.

Die **Heutige** Press Ägyptens. Zeitungswissenschaft. 8:46. Jan. 15, 1933
The contemporary Egyptian press.

Khemiri, T.
The Egyptian press today. Moslem World. 18:399-401. Oct. 1928
The author discusses literary journalism of Egypt and the diffusion of culture by the press.

Kittredge, D. W.
Native journalism in Egypt. Nation. 92:498-9. May 18, 1911
Egypt's press opposes introduction of English language.

Mikhail, Kyriakos
The freedom of the press in Egypt. 20p. London: Hutchinson, 1914

Parlament und Press (Ägypten). Zeitungswissenschaft. 2:23. Feb. 15, 1927

The **Printed** word—popularity of periodicals. Special tabloid section. The Times (London) [Egypt number]. p.xv. Jan. 26, 1937
Contains remarks on reader interest and circulation among newspapers in Egypt.

Rae, W. F.
The Egyptian newspaper press. Nineteenth Century. 32:213-23. Aug. 1892
A survey of press conditions in Egypt in early 90's: many newspapers and high degree of news suppression.

D. SOUTH AFRICA

Cutten, T. E. G.
A history of the press in South Africa. 160p. London: Central News Agency, 1936

Hennegin, M.
How the Newspaper Press Union protects member. World's Press News. 17: 38. July 15, 1937
Story of South Africa newspaper employers' association.

Stonehouse, Ken
South African newspapers have become increasingly "overseas conscious." Newspaper World. 41:30. Jan. 29, 1938

Van Den Heever, C. M.
Afrikaans, an established and growing language. World's Press News. 20:498 suppl. p. vii. Sept. 15, 1938

E. OTHER COUNTRIES

Allen, D. A.
Government education programme is aiding West African press. World's Press News. 19:19. Oct. 21, 1937

René-Leclerc, Charles
La presse quotidienne française au Maroc. Presse Publicité. 37:3-4. May 7, 1938
Growth of the daily press of Morocco.

III. EUROPE

A. GENERAL DISCUSSION

Arbouin, Gabriel
Les nations d'après leurs journaux. 104p. Paris: Bossard, 1917

Bullard, Arthur
The breakdown of Europe's news services. Our World. 5:15-21. May 1924
Pooling of information by news agencies is killed by dictatorship press. Geneva is best European news source, writer says.

Butcher, Harold
All Europe is breaking intellectually. Editor and Publisher. 56:5. Aug. 18, 1923
Newspapers of all countries abroad have ceased to influence public opinion.

What Europe wants in U.S. news told by De Sales. Editor and Publisher. 70:16. Oct. 16, 1937

Censorship-ridden Europe. Literary Digest. 121:17. Mar. 21, 1936
A brief article showing that the press is muzzled in 24 European nations.

Chamberlain, H. R.
The newspaper press of Europe. Chautauquan. 20:39-43. Oct. 1894
Lack of enterprise among British newsmongers is scored. Hot news is shunned until it cools off, then published.

Crawford, T. C.
The newspapers of Europe. Munsey's Magazine. 8:376-80. Jan. 1893

Cressey, Kendall B.
Misunderstandings hold Europe from reorganization progress. Editor and Publisher. 54:7, 32. Mar. 25, 1922
Lack of communications prevents unity of thought by people and press.

Europe imitating our journalism. Literary Digest. 46:76. Jan. 11, 1913
Influence of American journalism on European press. Evolutionary trends are cited.

Europe's declining freedom of the press. Literary Digest. 117:15. Apr. 14, 1934
Press casualties in totalitarian states are described.

Europe's widespread censorship of press. Literary Digest. 119:13, 29. June 29, 1935
Mussolini expels David Darrah, *Chicago Tribune* correspondent, from Italy as the press gag tightens.

Foreign papers shun 'average' reader. Editor and Publisher. 59:16. Mar. 12, 1927
Press of Central Europe handicapped by conservative news attitude.

How the continental European censors wield their blue pencils. China Weekly Review. 73:189-90. July 6, 1935
Walter Duranty discusses the muzzling of the press in Germany and Russia.

Irwin, Will
The press in Europe. Collier's. 54:13. Nov. 7, 1914
Press camp followers excluded by belligerents early in World War. Rumors raged where press was throttled.

Johnson, Harold B.
Politics slows progress of European press. Editor and Publisher. 60:11. Oct. 1, 1927
Newspapers generally, except in Britain, are small party organs ignoring news for partisan propaganda.

Krassovsky, Dimitry M.
New bibliographical periodical; Gazetnafâ Letopis (Newspaper Annals). Library Journal. 61:516. July 1936

Lee, James Melvin
Cologne exhibition traced history of press. Editor and Publisher. 61:8. Dec. 15, 1928
Place of journalism in economic and political life linked with cultural and intellectual background at German exposition.

Lively life, sudden death, for ye editor in Europe. Literary Digest. 81:47, 49. Apr. 26, 1924
Subscribers protest with bombs and shooting in Europe. German press censorship before Hitler's regime is described.

McKenzie, Vernon
Press and propaganda in Europe. p15-23. *In* Institute of World Affairs. Proceedings, 1934. Los Angeles: Univ. of Southern California, 1935

News barriers in Europe. Living Age. 315:619-20. Dec. 16, 1922
European news facilities crack up in World War aftermath. Report of a disaster was delayed for an entire week.

Schuyler, Philip
Europe is progressing on Pacific wings. Editor and Publisher. 58:9. Sept. 5, 1925
Europe turns to newspapers of America. Editor and Publisher. 58:7. Jan. 16, 1926
Interested in technical methods of United States dailies.

Smith, Neville
Finds European papers lag behind those of New World. Editor and Publisher. 59:14. July 31, 1926
Intimate picture of continental journalism presented by Australian writer.

Stowe, Leland
Propaganda over Europe. Scribner's. 96: 99-101. Aug. 1934
Totalitarians control public opinion through press, radio and movies. French press corrupt, too.

Swift, Otis Peabody
Jail, duels, bombs, fate of Europe's editors. Editor and Publisher. 56:5. July 14, 1923
Journalism on the Continent is not a pastime.

Waples, Douglas
What is Europe reading? Publishers' Weekly. 121:1872-3. Apr. 30, 1932

Watson, A. H.
Origin and growth of journalism among Europeans. Annals of the American Academy. 145(2):169-74. Sept. 1929
Freedom of the press in India is stifled by Britain.

B. AUSTRIA, TO 1938

Änderung in der Ostmark-Presse. Zeitungswissenschaft. 13:642. Oct. 1, 1938
Changes made in the press of Austria following the occupation by Germany.

Best. of U.P., heads Vienna press corps. Editor and Publisher. 67:24. Mar. 9, 1935

Censorship; new Vienna gag chokes off another news area. News Week. 8: 24-5. July 25, 1936

Dopf, Karl
Die Presse der Stadt Wien. Zeitungswissenschaft. 7:45-6. Jan. 15, 1932
A study of the press in Vienna.

Die sozialdemokratische Presse in Oesterreich, 1930. Zeitungswissenschaft. 7:46-7. Jan. 15, 1932
Statistics on the Social Democratic press in Austria, taken from yearbook of the Austrian labor movement, 1930.

Dresler, Adolf
Östreichisch-italienische Pressebeziehungen des 16.-18. Jahrhunderts. Zeitungswissenschaft. 3:44-5. Mar. 15, 1928
Factors in Austro-Italian press relations from the 16th to the 18th century.

Evans, Arthur J.
The Austrian war against publicity. Contemporary Review. 42:383-99. Sept. 1882

Gedye, George Eric Rowe
Vienna waltz. p.29-73. *In* Baldwin, H. W. and Stone, S., eds. We saw it happen. New York: Simon and Schuster, 1938
Experiences of a foreign correspondent in Vienna and the Balkans.

Gugitz, Gustav
W. L. Wekhrlins Aufenthalt in Wien und die Wiener handschriftlichen Zeitungen. Zeitungswissenschaft. 9:49-62, 104-19. Feb.-Mar. 1934
An interesting account of the talented adventurer Wekhrlin and his connection with the handwritten newspapers of Vienna. Facsimiles.

Gunther, John
Dateline Vienna. Harper's. 171:198-208. July 1935
Censorship of the press in quasi-Fascist Austria, and the news-gathering methods used by foreign correspondents.

Keeping Hitler out of Austria. Nation. 138:180-1. Feb. 14, 1934
A foreign correspondent's diagnosis of the causes leading up to the Nazi conquest of Austria: the economic crisis, internal and external aggression, popular apathy and treason.

Hartl, Franz
Die Neuordnung der Presse in Oesterreich. Zeitungswissenschaft. 13:472-5. July 1, 1938
Reorganization of the press after Germany took over Austria in March 1938. New press law.

Hirschfeld, Gerhard
Austrian press now dominated by German language papers. Editor and Publisher. 64:22. Nov. 28, 1931

Hofmann. Wilhelm
Das Presserecht der Ostmark im Lichte der Reichskulturkammergesetzgebung. Zeitungswissenschaft. 14:55-63. Jan. 1, 1939
A discussion of the difficulties of adjusting the press laws of Greater Germany to Austria.

Johnson, Albin E.
Professional aspects of journalism highly developed in Austria. Editor and Publisher. 61:30. May 18, 1929

Journalism in Austria. Nation. 64:306. Apr. 22, 1897

Kraus, René
Glanz und Elend der Österreichischen Presse. Nord und Süd. 53:818-26. Sept. 1930
The Austrian press.

Limedorfer, Eugene
Great newspapers of continental Europe. IV. Austrian and Hungarian newspapers. Bookman. 11:149-57. Apr. 1900

News censor in Vienna is termed myth. Newsdom. 5:5. Mar. 3, 1934

Restrictions on journalism in Austria. Nation. 64:306 Apr. 22, 1897

Steed, Henry Wickham
Through thirty years, 1892-1922. 2v. Garden City, N.Y.: Doubleday, Page, 1924.
A story of international public life in the past thirty years in the form of a personal narrative, by the London *Times* correspondent and editor.

The **Vienna** press. Appleton's Journal. 7: 319-20. Mar. 23, 1872

What the people read in Austria and Bohemia. Review of Reviews. 31:84-5. Jan. 1905

Wittner, Otto
Die Presse vor, während und nach der Revolution (von 1848 in Oesterreich). Kampf. 5:280-6. Dec. 1911

C. BALKANS

Andreeff, Boris M.
Die bulgarischen Zeitschriften und die Presseverhältnisse Bulgariens, 1844-1925. 137p. Sofia: Hermann Pohle, 1927
Bulgarian press from 1844 to 1925.

La presse bulgare. Son développement et ses traits caractéristiques. Sofia: L'Essor Bulgare, 1937
A brief view of the development of the Bulgarian press from its origins to the present day.

Arrests correspondents. Editor and Publisher. 60:28. May 19, 1928
Rumanian government smothers press as reign of terror begins.

Bulgarien. Internationale Pressegesetzgebung. Zeitungswissenschaft. 2:168. Nov. 11, 1927
Account of press conditions under Turkish rule to 1878 when Bulgaria received its freedom and its constitution. Also brief survey of its press laws from May 30, 1881 to June 9, 1923.

Burnett, Whit
Hunting headlines in the Balkans. American Mercury. 30:42-9. Sept. 1933

Chumarevich, Svetislav
La presse yougoslave. 71p. Belgrade: Bureau Central de Presse, 1937
In this brochure M. Chumarevich, a Jugoslavian journalist, traces the evolution of the press of the southern Slavic peoples from its earliest manuscripts to its present development.

Drastic press law planned in Rumania. Editor and Publisher. 59:13. Dec. 25, 1926
Carries four years' imprisonment and $100 fine for writers who send news offending King or Queen.

Das **Eingreifen** der Konstantinopler bulgarischen Presse in die bulgarische Freiheitsbewegung 1860-1879. Zeitungswissenschaft. 4:92-93. Mar. 15, 1929
The influence of the press in Constantinople on the Bulgarian struggle for freedom.

Folly of Balkan censorships. Great Britain and the East. 49:799. Dec. 16, 1937

Foreign press curbed. Editor and Publisher. 65:12. Aug. 6, 1932
The Yugoslav government created a monopoly for the importation of foreign newspapers, thereby strengthening its dictatorship.

Germann, John
Zur Entwicklung der Balkanpresse. Zeitungswissenschaft. 7:83-90. Mar. 15, 1932
The development of the press in the Balkans.

Hamburger, Ernest
Chronique constitutionelle et législative de la presse: Bulgarie; décret-loi bulgare du avril 1938 sur le contrôle temporaire de la presse. Cahiers de la Presse. 1:459, 507-9. July-Sept. 1938
Summary of recent codification of Bulgarian press laws, with text.

Chronique constitutionelle et législative de la presse: Roumanie, Lettonie, Grèce. Cahiers de la Presse. 1:283-6, 317-22. Apr.-June 1938
Reviews with accompanying extracts of new press laws in Rumania, Latvia and Greece.

Heizler, Rudolf
Neues Presserecht in Rumänien. Zeitungswissenschaft. 13:701-2. Oct. 1, 1938
A press law designed to prevent financial control of a newspaper by foreign capital.

Johnson, Albin E.
Government safe from censure by press in Yugoslavia. Editor and Publisher. 62:22. Sept. 7, 1929
Publishers voluntarily comply with monarch's decree not to criticize regime.

Kurth, Karl
Rede des rumänischen Propaganda Staatssekretärs Titeanu über die Presse. Zeitungswissenschaft. 13:819-20. Dec. 1, 1938
Titeanu discusses the necessity of press reorganization and commends the conduct of the minority press in recent international events.

Leonard, O.
What the people read in the Balkans. Review of Reviews. 31:341-3. Mar. 1905

Levenson, Heinrich
Stand und Bedeutung der bulgarischen Presse von heute. Zeitungswissenschaft. 1:26-7. Feb. 15, 1926
The contemporary Bulgarian press.

Lias, Godfrey A.
British prestige in the Balkans. Spectator. 163:210-11. Aug. 11, 1939

Petrovitch, Mihailo S.
La presse yougoslave. Cahiers de la Presse. (3):285-97. July-Sept. 1939
In this study of the Jugoslavian press the Paris correspondent of the *Politika* brings out some of the important points of difference between the press of that country and others.

Political parties and the censor in Macedonia. Review of Reviews. 31:351-3. Mar. 1905

Das **Presserecht** und das öffentliche Kritik. Zeitungswissenschaft. 5:355. Nov. 15, 1930
Discussion of new restrictive press laws in Jugoslavia.

Pressezensur in Rumänien. Zeitungswissenschaft. 1:31. Feb. 15, 1926
Law applying to the press in Rumania.

Ravry, André
La presse albanaise. Cahiers de la Presse. p. 337-43. July-Sept. 1939
Chronological history of the Albanian press.

Rumania. Laws, Statutes, etc.
Codul presei. Legiuri române in Legătură cu presa. 227p. Bucuresti: Tipografia Romaneascâ Timisoara, 1937
Ed. by Serbescu, Pompiliu and Bânciulescu.
A useful and conveniently classified collection of Rumanian laws and codes concerning the press, compiled by reputable journalists.

Sadoveanu, Mihai
Freedom of the Roumanian press is guarded by law. World's Press News. 18:suppl. p.xxix. Dec. 9, 1937

Slavic darkness. Editor and Publisher. 65: 18. Sept. 10, 1932
Censorship and government monopoly of the press in Jugoslavia.

Streit, of Times, exiled from Rumania, protests rigid censorship rules. Editor and Publisher. 59:1. May 29, 1926

Über die Entwicklung der preszgesetzlichen Bestimmungen in Bulgarien. Zeitungswissenschaft. 2:168. Nov. 15, 1927
A sketch of the development of Bulgarian press laws.

Wallish, Friedrich
Bulgarien und seine Zeitungen. Zeitungswissenschaft. 9:159-64. Apr. 1, 1934
Intellectual renaissance of Bulgaria starting about the middle of the nineteenth century. Individual newspapers and periodicals.

Wessely, Franz
Zur Geschichte der albanischen Presse. Zeitungswissenschaft. 13:643-9. Oct. 1, 1938
A short history of the press of Albania.

What are they reading in the Balkans? Review of Reviews. 47:113. Jan. 1913

Yalman, Ahmet Emin
The Inter-Balkanic Press League. Public Opinion Quarterly. 3:688-93. Oct. 1939
Journalists of Turkey, Rumania, Yugoslavia and Greece cooperate to promote pacification in the Balkans.

D. BALTIC

Bihlmans, Alfred
Das lettische Zeitungswesen. Zeitungswissenschaft. 7:1-29. Jan. 15, 1932
Journalism in Latvia.

Der **Estnische** Ministerpräsident über das Verhältnis von Staat und Press. Zeitungswissenschaft. 14:318. May 1, 1939
Understanding existing between press and government in Estonia.

Helisse, N.
Les chambres culturelles lettones. Cahiers de la Presse. 1:495. July-Sept. 1938
New Latvian law looks to the press to do its part in helping Latvia to appreciate its own culture and heritage.

Kurth, Karl
Propagandaamt in Litauen. Zeitungswissenschaft. 13:340. May 1, 1938
The creation of a bureau of press and propaganda in Lithuania.

Lezius, Hellmuth
Die estländische Presse. Zeitungswissenschaft.. 12:797-806. Dec. 1, 1937
A thorough-going survey of the Estonian press.

Die **Litauische** Presse im Jahre 1936. Zeitungswissenschaft. 12:814. Dec. 1, 1937
Statistics on new press organs in Lithuania.

Neue Presseverordnung in Estland. Zeitungswissenschaft. 10:187-90. Apr. 1, 1935
Discussion and the text of the new decree relating to newspapers and periodicals in Estonia.

Die **Pressebeziehungen** Polens zu Litauen und Lettland. Zeitungswissenschaft. 14: 40. Jan. 1, 1939
Agreement between Poland and Lithuania to preserve friendly relations by avoiding unfriendly references in the newspapers. The report of the meeting of a commission in Riga representing Polish and Lettish newspapermen.

Schönemann, Ad.
Die litauische Presse. Zeitungswissenschaft. 13:353-62. June 1, 1938
An interesting survey of the Lithuanian press: press history, press laws, official government propaganda and analysis.

E. BELGIUM

Annuaire officiel de la presse belge. 1937-1938 ed. Brussels: Belgian General Press Association, 1938
An annual directory of the Belgian press.

Belgium's clandestine journalism. Literary Digest. 54:625. Mar. 10, 1917

Dons, Herman
L'Institut pour Journalistes de Belgique. Cahiers de la Presse. 3:464-6. July-Sept. 1938
M. Dons, president of the administrative council of the Belgian Institute of Journalists, reviews the work and ideals of the Institute during the past 16 years.

La liberté de la presse en Belgique. Cahiers de la Presse. 1:81-7. Jan.-Mar. 1939
Freedom of press is guaranteed in Belgium but there is ample provision for control of libel and protection against political rumours. The writer was formerly president of the International Federation of Journalists.

A **Furtive** newspaper. Literary Digest. 52: 176-7. Jan. 22, 1915

Hamburger, Ernest
Un projet de réforme du régime de la presse en Belgique. Cahiers de la Presse. 1:96-104. Jan.-Mar. 1938
Projected reforms of the Belgian government as they affect the liberty of the press.

How "La Libre Belgique" defied death and the Kaiser. Literary Digest. 60:66, 68. Mar. 1, 1919

Kistemaeckers, Henry, sr.
Mes procès littéraires: souvenirs d'un éditeur. Mercure de France. 166:670-92. Sept. 15, 1923
Belgian publisher, recounts his successful resistance against law suits purporting to suppress pornographic literature but which were in reality a subtle attack on freedom of expression in art and literature as well as the press.

"La Libre Belgique." Outlook. 113:241-2. May 31, 1916
Concerning a secretly published newspaper in Belgium during the German occupation of that country.

Mansvelt, F.
Before you advertise in Belgium. World's Press News. 17:418. suppl. p.5. Mar. 4, 1937
A review of the Belgian press, pointing out divergence among newspapers appealing to different ethnic and language groups.

Massart, Jean
La presse clandestine dans la Belgique occupée. 318p. Paris: Berger-Levrault, 1917
The secret Belgian press during the German occupation. 26 facsimiles of World War periodicals.

Millard, Oscar E.
The secret press in Belgium. 96p. London: T. F. Unwin, 1918
Translation of the first chapter of La Presse Clandestine dans la Belgique Occupée. It shows the secret methods resorted to by Belgians in obtaining and circulating news during the World War. Illustrated. Translated by Bernard Mall.

Uncensored! 287p. London: Hale, 1937
The true story of the clandestine newspaper, La Libre Belgique, published in Brussels during the German occupation.

Newspapers of Belgium. Editor and Publisher. 53:96, 98. Jan. 22, 1921
Directory.

Press of Brussels. Literary Digest. 58:20. Sept. 14, 1918

Secret journalism in Belgium. Current History. 6:136-7. Apr. 1917
Belgium's clever, efficient La Libre Belgique and other publications during the German occupation in the World War.

Sint-Jan, R. van
Die ältesten Zeitungen in Flandern. Zeitungswissenschaft. 3:80-3. May 15, 1928
The oldest papers in Flanders.

Die politische Presse Belgiens. Zeitungswissenschaft. 4:1-24. Jan. 15, 1929
Abraham Verhoeven and the Niewe Tijdingen. 4:7-13. Die Presse bis zur Mittel des 18. Jahrhunderts. 4:13-16. Die Wallonei und der französische Philosophismus. 4:16-21. Die Brabantische Revolution und die ersten politischen Parteien.

4:65-73. Mar. 15, 1929. Die französische Herrschaft. 4:73-81. Das Reich der Niederlande. 4:81-7; 129-55. Mar. 15, May 15, 1929. Die französische Presse von 1830-1914. 4:139-55; 193-7. May, July 15, 1929. Die flämische Presse bis 1914. 4:197-205. Die Kriegspresse. 4:205-12; 257-8. July 15, Sept. 1929. Statistisches. 4:258-65. Sept. 15, 1929. Der belgische Durlismus und die Romanisierung. 4:265-71. Politik und Presse seit dem Kriege. 4:271-4. Nachrichtwesen. 4:274-7. Der belgische Redakteur; die berufliche Vorbildungen und Organisation. 4:321-5. Nov. 15, 1929.

Statistisches von der belgischen Presse. Zeitungswissenschaft. 12:812. Dec. 1, 1937
Total number papers in Belgium classified as dailies, weeklies and others, together with languages in which they appear.

Vienne, Antony
En Belgique, la presse politique connaît un important développement. Presse Publicité. no. 33, p.15. Mar. 7, 1938
Increase in the socialist press of Belgium.

F. CZECHOSLOVAKIA TO DECEMBER 1938

Bass, Éduard
The Czech reads his papers in cafés. World's Press News. 20:xxix. July 21, 1938

Chmelař, Josef
Political parties in Czechoslovakia. 102p. Prague: Orbis, 1926

Crha, V.
Czechs are the biggest readers in Europe. World's Press News. 20:xxv. July 21, 1938

Czechoslovakia warns foreign journalists. Newspaper World. 41:1. Mar. 26, 1938
Government will not tolerate tendentious reporting.

Czechoslovakia's oldest paper is Sudeten-German organ. World's Press News. 20:xxix. July 21, 1938

Dresler, Adolf
Die Anfänge der Zeitungspresse in Böhmen. Zeitungswissenschaft. 4:34-5. Jan. 15, 1929
The beginnings of the press in Bohemia.

Economic and racial divisions affect Czechoslovak press. World's Press News. 20:xxvii. July 21, 1938

German propaganda ministry against Czechoslovakia. Living Age. 352:98-9. Apr. 1937

Give them what they want; newspaper coverage of Czechoslovakian crisis. American Mercury. 45:458-63. Dec. 1938

Heide, Walter
Der Pressekampf um das Sudetendeutschtum. Eine Rückschau auf die deutschsprachige Presse der früheren Tschechoslowakei. Zeitungswissenschaft. 13:705-11. Nov. 11, 1938
An insight into the propaganda organizations in Czechoslovakia involved in the fight for Sudeten Germany.

Johnson, Albin E.
Czech journalism encouraged by government expenditures. Editor and Publisher. 62:24. Aug. 17, 1929
Country has 2,000 papers.

Kocourek, Franta
Die Tagespresse in der Tschechoslowakei. Nord und Süd. 53:827-30. Sept. 1930
The daily press in Czechoslovakia.

Lesko, John
Press censorship in Czechoslovakia. Editor and Publisher. 67:38. July 14, 1934

Naschér, Arthur
Die geschichtliche Entwicklung des tschechoslowakischen Pressgerichts. Zeitungswissenschaft. 8:320-2. Sept. 15, 1933
Historical development of press laws in Czechoslovakia.

Das tschechische Zeitungswesen. Zeitungswissenschaft. 1:105-6. July 15, 1926
The situation of the press in Czechoslovakia.

Neue Maulkorbvorschriften für die Presse. Zeitungswissenschaft. 13:75. Jan. 1, 1938
New press decree by the Ministry of Interior of Czechoslovakia under National Defense Law.

Osusky, Stefan
T. G. Masaryk, journaliste. Cahiers de la Presse. 1:17-20. Jan.-Mar. 1938
A short summary of the public life of this eminent Czechoslovakian statesman, scrupulous and indefatigable journalist.

Panofsky, Walter
Der Pressekampf um Böhmen 1914-1919. Zeitungswissenschaft. 13:418-28. July 1, 1938
The Czechoslovakia propaganda activities for independence in the World War and those of the Sudeten and Bohemian Germans in favor of Austria, 1918-19.

Das **Pressekammergesetz.** Zeitungswissenschaft. 5:355-6. Nov. 15, 1930
A new law in Czechoslovakia sought to set up a press chamber charged with the task of raising journalistic ethics and recommending disciplinary actions when necessary.

Rossipaul, Lother
Die Haltung der tschechischen Presse zur Errichtung des Protektorats. Zeitungswissenschaft. 14:309-11. May 1939
Attitude of the Czech press during March 1939 following the occupation by the Germans.

Roubik, Frant.
Bibliographie časopisectva v Čechach z let 1863-1895. 322p. Praha: Čheska Akademie Ved a Umeni, 1936
A bibliography of journalism in Bohemia from 1863 to 1895.

Schaurek, Rudolph
Das tschechoslowakische Presserecht. v.1. 286p. Reichenberg: Sudetendeutscher Verlag Franz Kraus, 1937
The press of Czechoslovakia.

Das **Tschechoslowakische** Journalistengesetz. Zeitungswissenschaft. 1:173-4. Nov. 15, 1926
A new Czechoslovakian press law.

Die **Umschichtung** in der Presse der Tschecho-Slowakei. Zeitungswissenschaft. 14: 183-5. Mar. 1, 1939
Changes in the press of Czechoslovakia since October 1938.

Volf, Joseph
Zur Geschichte des Zeitungswesen in der Tschecho-Slowakei bis 1848. Zeitungswissenschaft. 4:235-40; 291-7. July 15, Sept. 15, 1929
A history of journalism in Czechoslovakia to 1848 with special attention to official supervision of the press.

Von der tschechischen Preszpropaganda. Zeitungswissenschaft. 2:9. Jan. 15, 1927
Plans for the establishment of a Czechoslovakian school of journalism and the further development of the official press bureau.

What the people read in Austria and Bohemia. Review of Reviews. 31:84-5. Jan. 1905

G. FINLAND

Akseli, Toutavaara
Suomen sanomalehdistö, 1771-1932: bibliografinen esitys. 145p. Helsinki: Suomalaisen Kirjallisuuden Seura, 1935
The only bibliographic account of the press of Finland since 1871. Complete alphabetical list of 702 Finnish journals, with important data concerning each.

Gruenbeck, Max
Die Presse Finnlands. Zeitungswissenschaft. 7:192-3. May 15, 1932
The press of Finland and the part which it played in the movement for freedom and political development.

Hamburger, Ernest
La presse finlandaise. Cahiers de la Presse. 1:311-13. Apr.-June 1938
The struggle for an ideal, rather than pecuniary gain, characterizes the press of Finland.

Lauren, Georg
Finland's daily and periodical newspapers. World's Press News (Marketing Supp. on Finland) 16:v. Dec. 24, 1936

Silander, A.
Le développement de la presse finlandaise. International Committee of Historical Sciences, Bulletin: Historical Bibliography of the Press. 6:78-84. Mar. 1934
A short history of the press of Finland including some statistics on its growth.

Torne, P. O. von
Bibliography of the Finnish press. International Committee of Historical Sciences, Bulletin: Historical Bibliography of the Press. 6:26. Mar. 1934
The period 1771-1900, during which 300 newspapers appeared in Finland.

Törnudd, Allan
The press of Finland. Newspaper World. 39:54, 58. July 11, 1936

H. FRANCE

1. HISTORY AND ANALYSIS

a. GENERAL DISCUSSION

L'Activité de l'Accueil Français. L'Europe Nouvelle. 19:1237. Dec. 12, 1936
A statement of the purposes of the organization of journalists: to strengthen the bonds of friendship between the foreign journalist and the French press; to aid the foreign journalist in his work in Paris; and to facilitate the contact of foreign press representatives with political men, artists and French writers.

Alengry, F.
La vérité et l'équité dans la presse. Cahiers de la Presse. 1:609-11. Oct.-Dec. 1938
Truth for the journalist; equity and impartiality of criticisms.

Annuaire de la presse française et étrangère et du monde politique. Paris: Ch. Lorilleux, 1938
Annual. Founded in 1882.

Argus de la presse. 7.éd. 271p. Paris: Argus, 1917
Founded in 1879.

Avenel, Henri
Histoire de la presse française depuis 1789 jusqu'à nos jours. 884p. Paris: E. Flammarion, 1900
A history of the French press from 1789 to 1900.

La presse française au vingtième siècle. 631p. Paris: E. Flammarion, 1901
A history of the French press to the twentieth century.

Blum, André
Les origines du livre à gravures en France, les incunables typographiques. 99p. Paris, Brussels: G. Van Oest, 1928

Chambure, A. de
À travers la presse. 687p. Paris: Th. Fert, Albouy, 1914
History, growth and development of journalism from early times, with lists of the most important newspapers in each country.

Datz, P.
Histoire de la publicité depuis les temps les plus reculées jusqu'à nos jours. 231p. Paris: J. Rothschild, 1894
The author finds elements in ancient methods of publicity which were the roots from which modern ideas of advertising evolved.

Dubief, Eugène
Le journalisme. 313p. Paris: Hachette, 1892

French journalistic associations. Editor and Publisher. 53:100, 101, 102, 105. Jan. 22, 1921

Ginisty, Paul
Anthologie du journalisme, du XVIIe siècle à nos jours. 455p. Paris: Librairie Delagrave, 1817
An anthology of French journalism which discusses chronologically the press activities of famous literary and other public figures, showing how they influenced public opinion and contributed to the growth of journalism as a power.

Green, Frederick C.
Eighteenth-century France; six essays. 221p. New York: D. Appleton, 1931

Hatin, L. Eugène
Histoire du journal en France. 128p. Paris: Gustave Havard, 1846
A short history of the French press showing mainly how it related itself to the world of ideas.

Histoire politique et littéraire de la presse en France. 8v. Paris: Poulet-Malassis et De Broise, 1859-61
An old but complete political and literary history of the periodical press in France, with an introduction giving the origins of the newspaper. A bibliography of newspapers is appended.

Janmart de Brouillant, Léonce
La liberté de la presse en France au XVIIe et XVIIIe siècles. 324p. Paris: Maison Quantin, 1888

Kleinpaul, Johannes
Zur Frühgeschichte der periodischen Presse in Frankreich. Zeitungswissenschaft. 1:40-1. Mar. 15, 1926
Early history of the periodical press in France.

Koszmann, Egon
Auf den Anfängen des Anzeigenwesens. Zeitungswissenschaft. 13:200-7. Mar. 1, 1938
Origin of advertising in France through Renaudot and, briefly, early advertising in Germany.

Peignot, Gabriel
Dictionnaire critique, littéraire et bibliographique des principaux livres condamnés au feu supprimés ou censurés. 2v. Paris: A. A. Renouard, 1806

Schwob, Marcel
Mœurs des diurnales—traité de journalisme. 221p. Paris: Mercure de France, 1918
A satire on journalism with ribald observations as to its origins.

b. PRE-REVOLUTION

Azam, Denise Aimé
Le Ministère des Affaires Étrangères et la presse à la fin de l'Ancien Régime. Cahiers de la Presse. III:428-38. July-Sept. 1938
Quotations from original documents showing the methods by which the French press obtained news from the Minister of Foreign Affairs during the Old Regime.

Bachman, Albert
Censorship in France from 1715 to 1750: Voltaire's opposition. 206p. New York: Columbia University Press, 1934

Belin, Jean Paul
Le commerce des livres prohibés à Paris de 1750 à 1789. 129p. Paris: Belin Frères, 1913

Chauchat, A.-M.
La curieuse et grande figure de Théophraste Renaudot. 155p. Paris: Messageries Hachette, 1937
This sketch on a founder of French journalism is the first of a series by the same author entitled: *Histoire de la Presse en Dix Portraits.*

Dauphin, V.
Les origines de la presse en Anjou aux XVIIe et XVIIIe siècles. Cahiers de la Presse. II:230-6. Apr.-June 1938
An account of early Angevin journalism.

Dickie, Francis
Renaudot, founder of the first newspaper with paid ads. Inland Printer. 86:94-6. Dec. 1930

Ester, Karl d'
Aus den Kindheitstagen der französischen Presse. Zeitungswissenschaft. 1: 69-72. May 15, 1926
Beginnings of the French press with special reference to Renaudot's *Gazette.*

Estrée, Paul d'. See Funck-Brentano, Franz, jt. auth.

Funck-Brentano, Franz and d'Estrée, Paul
Figaro et ses devancières. 338p. Paris: Hachette, 1909
Pre-revolutionary methods of gathering news in France, which, though usually clandestine, developed into the modern press.

MacPherson, Harriet Dorothea
Censorship under Louis XIV, 1661-1715. 176p. New York: Institute of French Studies, 1929

Menz, Gerhard
Colbert und die fransösische Press seiner Zeit. Zeitungswissenschaft. 12:750-9. Nov. 1, 1937
Colbert as a propagandist, his connections with the early newspapers of his time and with the founding of the learned periodical *Journal des Savants.*

Sée, Henri
Note sur la presse provinciale à la fin de l'Ancien Régime: les Affiches de Revues, 1784-1790. Annales Historiques de la Révolution Française. 4:18-25. Jan. 1927
Some notes on the French provincial press at the close of the Old Regime; the *Affiches de Revues* as an example of how commercial and advertising publications came to occupy themselves with news on the eve of the Revolution.

Vallée, Arthur
Théophraste Renaudot et la troisième centenaire du journalisme en France. Royal Society of Canada, Transactions. s3, 25(sec. 1):41-6. 1931

Weil, Georges
Le journal. Origines, évolution et rôle de la presse périodique. 450p. Paris: La Renaissance du Livre, 1934

Wright, C. Hagberg
Renaudot, father of French journalism. Nineteenth Century. 108:770-6. Dec. 1930
Born 1586; obtained patronage of Cardinal Richelieu; published the *Gazette* May 31, 1631; died 1653.

c. FRENCH REVOLUTION AND NAPOLEONIC ERA

Bourgin, Georges
Les journaux à Paris en l'an VII. Cahiers de la Presse. 2:137-44. Apr.-June 1939
New material on the Paris press in 1799 is yielded by the French national archives. Deals especially with the difficulties of the Directory in running down the authors of unpalatable and reactionary articles.

Cardenal, L. de
La liberté de la presse sous la Constituante. Cahiers de la Presse. 1:52-80. Jan.-Mar. 1939
The liberty of the press as it existed at the time of the Constituent Assembly (1789).

Carnahan, D. H.
The attitude of the French Royalist press towards romanticism during the restoration. Romanic Review. 23:1-8. Jan. 1932

Chapin, Howard Millar
Calendrier français pour l'année 1781 and the printing press of the French fleet in American waters during the Revolutionary War. Providence, R.I.: Preston and Rounds, 1914

Coffin, Victor
Censorship and literature under Napoleon I. American Historical Review. 22:288-308. Jan. 1917
Formal censorship instituted in 1810 by the Direction Générale de l'Imprimerie et de la Librairie, from the point of view of the administrative attitude towards literature and public opinion.

Cunow, Heinrich
Die Parteien der grossen Französischen Revolution und ihre Presse. 394p. Berlin: Buchhandlung Vorwärts Paul Ginger, 1912
A discussion of the history of French class and party conflicts and the press at the end of the 18th century.

Delmas, Gaëtan
Curiosités révolutionnaires; les journaux rouges. 158p. Paris: Giraud, 1848

Delsaux, Hélène
Condorcet journaliste (1790-1794). 354p. Paris: Librairie Ancienne Honoré Champion, 1931

Dufay, Pierre
Comment le "Mercure de France" devint "Mercure Français" et ce qu'il en advint. Mercure de France. 212:467-73, 718-26. June 1, 15, 1929
The *Mercure de France* was originally a privileged monthly which furnished news of the court and city to the cultivated class.
During the Revolution it changed its name, was published daily, and dealt with political problems, without entirely losing its Old Régime flavor.

Ebbinghaus, Therese
Napoleon, England und die Presse, 1800-1803. 211p. Munich, Berlin: R. Oldenbourgh, 1914

Gaston, Martin
Un procès de presse en 1791: Estienne contre "l'ami du peuple." Cahiers de la Presse. 2:267-70. Apr.-June 1938
On the manner in which a libel suit against Marat was conducted in revolutionary times.

Green, Frederick C.
Eighteenth-century France; six essays. 221p. New York: D. Appleton, 1931
"The Censorship," p. 194-221. A history of 18th century censorship in France as exercised by the University of Paris.

Huddleston, Sisley
L'ami du peuple. New Statesman. 31: 474-6. July 21, 1928

Le Poittevin, Gustav
La liberté de la presse depuis la Révolution, 1789-1815. 330p. Paris: A. Rousseau, 1901
A history of the liberty of the press from the French Revolution to the fall of Napoleon.

Lhéritier, Michel
La presse française pendant la Revolution. International Committee of Historical Sciences, Bulletin. v.10, no.38: 114-23. Jan. 1938

Locré, Jean G.
Discussions sur la liberté de la presse, la censure, la propriété littéraire. 300p. Paris: Garnery-Nicolle, 1819

Mirabeau sur la liberté de la presse. 62p. Paris: L'Office Technique de Presse de l'Université de Paris, 1939
Annotated reprint of Mirabeau's famous essay; published on the occasion of the 150th anniversary of the French Revolution.

Napoleon and the press. Spectator. 123: 9-10. July 5, 1919

Neményi, Ambros
Journale und Journalisten der französischen Revolutionszeit. 63p. Berlin, Carl Habel, 1880
The press during the French Revolution.

Pens and ink in the Reign of Terror. Temple Bar. 5:287-95. May 1862

Perrin, Bernard
La liberté de la presse au Club des Jacobins. (1790-9 thermidor an II) Cahiers de la Presse. 2:183-208. Apr.-June 1939
A study of press freedom during the time the famous Jacobin Club took control of the government at Paris.

Le **Régime** de la presse pendant la Révolution Française. Athenæum (London) no. 3824:168-9. Feb. 9, 1901
A review of vol I. of Le Régime de la Presse Pendant la Révolution Française. 2v. by Alma Söderhjelm. Helsingfors: Hufvudstadsbladet, 1900-1901. The book summarizes the events of the fierce struggle for freedom of the press during the French Revolution.

Robison, Georgia
Molding public opinion under the French Directory. Public Opinion Quarterly. 2:281-6. Apr. 1938
Miss Robison, lecturer in history at Barnard College, points out the resemblance between methods and techniques for social control used in Italy, Russia, and Germany today, and those advocated by a member of the French Directory.

Söderhjelm, Alma
Press during the French Revolution. Athenæum. 1:168-9. Feb. 9, 1901
Newly won liberty of the press in the French Revolution led to many evils, but caused newspapers to multiply rapidly.

Le régime de la presse pendant la Révolution Française. 2v. Helsingfors: Hufvudstadsbladet, 1900-01
Government administration of the press and the fight for freedom of the press during the French Revolution.

Welschinger, Henri
La censure sous le Premier Empire, avec documents inédits. 400p. Paris: Charavay Frères, 1882
Censorship under the First Empire. The first four chapters discuss censorship and the press; the rest of the book deals with the censorship of the theater. Documented.

d. TO 1870

Audedrand, Philibert
Un café de journalistes sous Napoléon III. Paris: E. Dentu, 1888

Biré, Edmond
La presse royaliste de 1830 à 1852; Alfred Nettement, sa vie et ses œuvres. 567p. Paris: V. Lecoffre, 1901

Brisson, Jules. See Ribeyre, Félix, jt. auth.

Burnet, William
The early days of French newspapers. Living Age. 193:572-5. May 28, 1892

Bury, Y. Blaze de
French journalism before the 2nd Empire. Time (London) 19:44. 1888

French journalism from 1852 to 1888. Time (London) 19:402. 1888
Relations of the French press to the changing governments of this era. Popular press in opposition to the Empire was subjected to various threats.

Case, Lynn Marshall
New sources for the study of French opinion during the Second Empire; reports of the procureurs généraux. Southwestern Social Science Quarterly. 18:161-70. Sept. 1937
Bibliographical footnotes.

Castille, Charles Hippolyte
Les journaux et les journalistes sous l'Empire et sous la Restauration. 50, 62, 56p. Paris: F. Sartorius, 1858
The struggle of the French press for freedom from government control.

Chateaubriand, François Auguste René, vicomte de
The censorship of the press. Pamphleteer. 24:59-72. 1824

Crémieux, Albert
La censure en 1820 et 1821. 195p. Paris: É. Cornély, 1912

Fourcauld, Max de
Les procès de presse à la fin du règne de Charles x. Revue des Deux Mondes. 17:198-217. Aug. 1, 1933
Lawsuits between press and government involving articles protesting against certain appointments by the King.

French newspapers. Chambers's Journal. 8:365-7. Dec. 4, 1847

The French press. Chambers's Edinburgh Journal. 16:169-70. Sept. 13, 1851

The French press. New Monthly Magazine and Humorist. 61:371-81. Mar. 1841

Germain, A.
Martyrologe de la presse. 297p. Paris: H. Dumineray, 1861

Giraudeau, Fernand
La presse périodique de 1789 à 1867. 313p. Paris: E. Dentu, 1867

Hudson, Nora E.
The circulation of the ultra-royalist press under the French Restoration. English Historical Review. 49:687-97. Oct. 1934

Izambard, Henry
La presse parisienne. 203p. Paris: P. H. Krabbe, 1853

Journalism in France. British Quarterly Review. 3:468-524. May 1, 1846
First regular journal in France published in 1605. Description of various journals and journalists, and the Société Générale des Annonces, an advertising agency.

Le Livre du centenaire du Journal des Débats. 630p. Paris: E. Plon, Nourrit, 1889

Maury, Lucien
Émile de Girardin: le créateur de la presse moderne, de M. Reclus. Review in Revue Politique et Littéraire. 72:306-8. Apr. 21, 1934

Mélia, Jean
Stendhal et le journalisme. Mercure de France. 238:573-90. Sept. 15, 1932

Montenon, Jean de
La France et la presse étrangère en 1816. Nouvelle Revue. 119-120:241-56 ff. 1932
France and the foreign press in 1816.

The Newspaper press of France. Foreign Quarterly Review. 30:466-98. Jan. 1843

The Newspaper press of Paris. (I-II) Fraser's Magazine. 17:50-61, 208-29. Jan.-Feb. 1838
An examination of the newspaper press of Paris with a view to ascertaining whether it is, as claimed, "the fourth power of the state." The author concludes its importance has been exaggerated.

Newspapers in France. Chambers' Edinburgh Journal. 8:365-7. Dec. 4, 1847

Ribeyre, Félix and Brisson, Jules
Les grands journaux de France. Paris: Jouaust Père et Fils, 1862

Vandam, Albert D.
The king of the journalists. Fortnightly. 68:304-13. Aug. 1, 1897
Émile de Girardin; his duel with Armand Carrel, which cost Carrel's life.

Vingtain, Jean Thomas Léon
De la liberté de la presse. 432p. Paris: M. Levy Frères, 1860

Wallon, Henri A.
La presse de 1848. 138p. Paris: Pillet Fils, Sr., 1849

Weill, Georges
Les tribulations des journalistes de province au xixe siècle. Cahiers de la Presse. (3):241-6. July-Sept. 1939
The tribulations of French journalists in the provinces during the 19th century.

e. TO 1918

American and French caricature. Literary Digest. 46:948-9. Apr. 26, 1913

Arbouin, Gabriel
Les nations d'après leurs journaux. 104p. Paris: Bossard, 1917

Caillaux again active. Literary Digest. 55: 19. Aug. 18, 1917

Carroll, Eber Malcolm
French public opinion and foreign affairs, 1870-1914. 348p. New York, London: Century, 1931
Development of public opinion in its relation to foreign affairs, quoting a large number of newspapers.

Changes in the French press. Nation. 83: 432-3. Nov. 22, 1906

Child, Theodore
The Paris newspaper press. Fortnightly. 44:149-65. 1885
A discussion of a period in Parisian journalism when Paris had 50 newspapers—few of which prospered.

Clemenceau a power as a journalist. Editor and Publisher. 51:18. Feb. 8, 1919

Cohn, Adolphe
Great newspapers of Continental Europe. II and III. French newspapers. Bookman. 10:540-7; 11:39-45. Feb.-Mar. 1900

Conner, Edward
French advertising. Editor and Publisher. 11:22. Dec. 23, 1911

Modern French newspaper world. Editor and Publisher. 12:21. May 17, 1913
A discussion of French journalists and their functions, method of launching a paper, sources of income, circulation and advertising policies.

Danthesse, Émile
Cinquante-sept ans de journalisme. Presse Publicité. 37:5; 38:25; 39:9; 41:7-8; 42: 9-10; 44:11-12; 48:11-12; 49:7-8; 50:11-12. May 7, 21, June 7, July 15, Aug. 15, Sept. 21, Nov. 21, Dec. 7, 21, 1938
Memoirs of 57 years in journalism; anecdotes concerning famous French journalists and statesmen.

Davies, Thomas Robert
French romanticism and the press: the Globe. 224p. Cambridge: University Press, 1906

Delille, Edward
The French newspaper press. Nineteenth Century. 31:474-86. Mar. 1892

Erwin, J. M.
Master French journalists. Editor and Publisher. 48:1060-1, 1064. Feb. 12, 1916
Description of Paris newspapers of the day.

The **Father** of cheap newspapers. Nation. 82:338-9. Apr. 26, 1906

The **Father** of the French bar. Temple Bar. 1:38-44. Mar. 1861

Fonsegrive, Georges
Comment lire les journaux? 230p. Paris: Librairie Victor Lecoffre, 1903

The French newspaper press. Cornhill. 48: 124-35; 243-54. Aug.-Sept. 1883
A critical discussion of the French newspaper press.

The **French** press. Cornhill. 27:703-31; 28: 411-30; 29:154-71, 535-52. June, Oct. 1873; Feb., May 1874

The **French** press. Cornhill. 84:239-48. Aug. 1901

The **French** press and Russia. Nation. 34: 659-60. Feb. 9, 1924

French press and Tsarist Russia. Labour Monthly. 6:36-45. Jan. 1924

Friend, Emil
The Paris press. Cosmopolitan. 30:260-8. Jan. 1901

Garçon, Maurice
La justice et la presse sous la III⁰ République. Mercure de France. 244:51-75. May 15, 1933
Observations on the operations and character of press laws under the Third Republic.

The **Hard** lot of the French journalist. Review of Reviews. 29:233. Feb. 1904

Hartmann, Charles L.
Die russischen Archive und die französische Presse. Deutsche Rundschau. 199:1-13, 225-40; 200:1-17, 113-34. Apr., June, Aug. 1924
A selection of secret transactions between France and Russia intending to show the irresponsibility and suppressive activity of the French press in connection with the expected advent of a World War.

Hornblow, Arthur
French journalists and journalism. Cosmopolitan. 14:153-62. Dec. 1892

Jamati, Vincent
Pour devenir journaliste, comment se rédige, et s'administre un journal. Paris: Victorion, 1906

MacDonald, William
The press and the censorship in England and France. Nation. 105:287-9. Sept. 13, 1917

Maillard, Firmin
Histoire des journaux publiés à Paris pendant le Siège et sous la Commune, 4 septembre 1870 au 28 mai 1871. 267p. Paris: E. Dentu, 1871
Descriptions of numerous publications which appeared in Paris during the Franco-Prussian war, showing how opinions and emotions of the people found expression in the utterances of the press.

Martyring a newspaper. Literary Digest. 54:1782-3. June 9, 1917

Matthews, Brander
Notes on Parisian newspapers. Century. 13:200-12. Dec. 1887

Mirkine-Guetzévitch, B. (Boris Sergieievich)
Le centenaire de Gambetta. Cahiers de la Presse. 1:211-15. Apr.-June 1938
A tribute to this great statesman who founded La République Française.

The **Paris** press. Saturday Review. 53:170-1. Feb. 11, 1882

Parisian journalism. Nation. 14:286-7. May 2, 1872

Parisian journalists of to-day. Cornhill. 28: 715-32. Dec. 1873

Preston, Thomas B.
The newspaper and periodical press of France. Chautauquan. 24:415-19. Jan. 1897

Reinach, Joseph
Parisian newspapers. Nineteenth Century. 12:347-60. Sept. 1882

Stewart, Charles P.
French censorship. Editor and Publisher. 10:1, 4. Nov. 12, 1910
American correspondent arrested for sending out true reports of floods and railroad strikes.

The **Temper** of French newspapers. Literary Digest. 51:114. July 17, 1915

Troubles of the French press. Nation. 66: 24-5. Jan. 13, 1898

Wallis, J. P.
Liberty of the press in France. Nineteenth Century. 45:315-26. Feb. 1899

Warner, Arthur H.
Sainte-Anastasie: the censorship in France. Outlook. 116:258. June 13, 1917

Weill, Georges
"La République Française" au temps de Gambetta. Cahiers de la Presse. 1:525-32. Oct.-Dec. 1938
Great political and social issues in the time of Gambetta and how they were met by the journal which he founded.

What the people read in France. Review of Reviews. 29:337-8. Mar. 1904

Women journalists of Paris. Review of Reviews. 43:627-8. May 1911

THE FOREIGN PRESS

2. RECENT PRESS

a. GENERAL DISCUSSION

Hayes, Carlton J. H.
France, a nation of patriots. 487p. New York: Columbia Univ. Press, 1930
Ch. VI, p.124-71. The press: newspapers and magazines. General description of the French press. Appendix C, p.409-30. Select list of French periodicals. Appendix D, p.430-59. Guide to daily newspapers of Paris. Appendix E, p.460-70. Daily newspapers of provincial France.

Huddleston, Sisley
A correspondent in Paris. Blackwood's. 216:321-31. Sept. 1924

Lauzanne, Stéphane J. V.
Sa majesté la presse. 253p. Paris: A. Fayard, 1925
A retrospect of the romantic career of the press, expressing its traditions, progress, dangers, and hopes.

Léautaud, Paul
Gazette d'hier et d'aujourd'hui. Mercure de France. 247:747-9. Nov. 1, 1933
Press of yesterday and today.

b. PRESS AND GOVERNMENT

Barber, Wilfred
On the firing line in Paris riots. Editor and Publisher. 66:22. Mar. 17, 1934

Barlow, Reuel R.
The government and the press in France. Journalism Quarterly. 6:13-22. June 1929

Bourdon, Georges
Les étapes de l'organisation du journalisme français. Cahiers de la Presse. 1:23-30. Jan.-Mar. 1938
Stages in the development of French journalists' organizations and their great strides toward social security.

Chance, Wade
Censorship at Paris. New Outlook. 128:478. July 20, 1921

Les **Comités** de coopération européenne à l'Accueil Français. L'Europe Nouvelle. 20:550. June 5, 1937

Dell, Robert
The French police and the foreign press. Nation and Athenæum. 44:101-2. Oct. 20, 1928

The Paris press scandal. Nation. 128:129-31. Jan. 30, 1929
The Gazette du Franc and other Paris newspapers became involved in Mme. Hanau's promotional schemes which resulted in financial and legal difficulties.

France gets U.S. news from other nations. Editor and Publisher. 56:18. June 23, 1923
Poincaré to ask increased subsidies for agencies in order to eliminate second-hand information.

France orders U.S. correspondent expelled. Editor and Publisher. 61:5, 52. Oct. 13, 1928
Harold J. T. Horan expelled because he cabled to American newspapers France's explanation to its diplomats of the Anglo-French naval compromise.

France's "yellow dog fund." Editor and Publisher. 67:26. Aug. 11, 1934
Editorial.
During Stavisky inquiry in Paris M. Tardieu was interrogated about a secret fund which the French government was said to maintain to subsidize or bribe newspapers.

Mévil, André
Parlementarisme et journalisme. Journal des Débats. 40(2):894. Dec. 1, 1933

Middleton, W. L.
The French political system. 296p. New York: E. P. Dutton, 1933

M. Camille Chautemps à l'Accueil Français. L'Europe Nouvelle. 21:599. June 4, 1938
One of a series of addresses by distinguished public men delivered before this organization of French journalists.

M. Georges Bonnet à l'Accueil Français. L'Europe Nouvelle. 20:1129. Nov. 20, 1937

M. Georges Bonnet à l'Accueil Français. L'Europe Nouvelle. 21:668. June 25, 1938

M. Jean Zay à l'Accueil Français. L'Europe Nouvelle. 21:540. May 21, 1938

M. Paul Reynaud à l'Accueil Français. L'Europe Nouvelle. 20:1187. Dec. 4, 1937

M. Yvon Delbos à l'Accueil Français. L'Europe Nouvelle. 21:368. Apr. 9, 1938

Paris censors foreign news. Newsdom. 6:2. May 11, 1935

Paris embassy restricts news. Editor and Publisher. 67:40. June 9, 1934

Paris press-scandal gossip. Living Age. 320:535-6. Mar. 22, 1924

Perry, John W.
France plans propaganda drive in U.S. Editor and Publisher. 65:7, 34. Apr. 15, 1933
Budget called for $1,320,000 to influence Americans; Associated Press denies that it will serve as channel for disseminating French propaganda.

Le **Président** de la République à l'Accueil Français. L'Europe Nouvelle. 20:430-1. May 1, 1937

Terrou, F.
L'information du gouvernement par la presse. Cahiers de la Presse. 3:462-4. July-Sept. 1938
Note on a more efficient method of government documentation of the press in France.

Werth, Alexander
Laval and the French press. New Statesman and Nation. 10:365-6. Sept. 21, 1935
For fear of Hitler, Laval temporized with Mussolini's ambitions in Abyssinia, thereby giving incentive to the French press to be bought off in Italy's favor.

c. PRESS LAWS

Auréjac, J.
Un projet de loi sur la presse en 1789. Revue Politique et Littéraire. 76:184-6. May 1938

Dappigny, Roger
French law strengthens news men. Guild Reporter. 2:2. May 1, 1935
<small>Security of tenure, minimum wages, registration of journalists, and arbitration of disputes are provided for in the new legislation.</small>

Garçon, Maurice
Le droit de réponse. Mercure de France. 172:622-39. June 15, 1924

Gruber, Walter
Die Entwicklung des französischen Presserechts. Zeitungswissenschaft. 11:198-203. Apr. 1, 1936
<small>A brief review of French press laws from the time of the Revolution, centering chiefly on the freedom of the press.</small>

Grunebaum-Ballin, P.
Le statut social du journalisme français. Cahiers de la Presse. 1:31-42. Jan.-Mar. 1938
<small>A discussion of recent forward-looking French social legislation affecting journalists.</small>

Mathews, Joseph J.
Death of press reform in France. Public Opinion Quarterly. 3:409-19. July 1939

Sevareid, A. Eric
French press. Journalism Quarterly. 16:203-6. June 1939
<small>Restrictions imposed on the extremist French press by the Daladier government.</small>

Six-day week in France. Editor and Publisher. 53:22. Apr. 9, 1921

Teipel, H.
Das Problem der Verantwortlichkeit in der französischen Presse. Zeitungswissenschaft. 13:480-5. July 1, 1938
<small>A discussion of a proposed press law for placing responsibility in law suits because of the inadequacy in this regard of the present French press laws.</small>

Théry, José
La loi sur la liberté de la presse. Mercure de France. 212:257-76. June 1, 1929
<small>Discussions evoked by a proposed modification of a press law of 1881 concerning defamatory matter.</small>

d. NEWSPAPERS AND NEWSPAPERMEN

Archambault, G. H.
Le journal français de demain. Mercure de France. 231:554-72. Nov. 1, 1931

So passes the polémiste. Quill. 21:3, 13. Feb. 1933
<small>Léon Daudet alone remains as standardization of the press brings an era of personal journalism in France to a close.</small>

Armstrong, Hamilton Fish
Newsless France. Independent. 108:183-4. Feb. 25, 1922

Bacourt, Pierre D.
French of today. 342p. New York: Macmillan, 1927

Billy, André and Piot, Jean
Comment se fait un journal. Mercure de France. 171:630-66. May 1, 1924
<small>A popular description of the technique in publishing a daily paper in France.</small>

Newspaper-making à la française. Living Age. 321: I. 1130-4; II. 1191-3. June 14-21, 1924

Bourdon, Georges and others
Le journalisme d'aujourd'hui. 162p. Paris: Librairie Delagrave, 1931

Brogan, D. W.
Charles Maurras and the Action Française. Living Age. 350:231-4. May 1936

Burnett, Whit and Foley, Martha
Your home-town paper: Paris. American Mercury. 22:24-31. Jan. 1931

Carr, Philip
French journalism. Contemporary Review. 137:760-4. June 1930

Daily newspapers of France. Editor and Publisher. 53:92, 94, 96. Jan. 22, 1921
<small>List of newspapers and addresses.</small>

De Lanzac de Laborie, Léon
Centenaire du "Correspondant." Journal des Débats. 36(1):637-9. Apr. 19, 1929

Demaison, André
Visites à la presse de province. Revue des Deux Mondes. 7: 48:874-93; 49:623-38; 50:394-407; 51:826-39; 53:866-82; 54: 394-405; 55:608-22; 56:432-54; 59:390-401; 8: 1:622-45; 2:597-619. Dec. 15, 1928; Feb. 1, Mar. 15, June 15, Oct. 15, Nov. 15, 1929; Feb. 1, Mar. 15, Sept. 15, 1930; Feb. 1, Apr. 1, 1931
<small>A series of eleven articles describing the press throughout the provinces of France. In the first article the author contrasts the freedom of the individually-owned French provincial press with the standardized newspaper monopolies of other nations.</small>

Dietz, Jean
Notre maison. Journal des Débats. 36(1):531-2. Apr. 5, 1929

Duplessy, Lucien
Le journal et la crise du français. Mercure de France. 214:23-41; 215:474-80. Aug. 15, Oct. 15, 1929
<small>The author blames the decadence of the French language upon the State and the press.</small>

Foley, Martha. See Burnett, Whit, jt. auth.

Forest, H. U.
"Réalisme." Journal de Duranty. Modern Philology. 24:463-79. May 1927

French and American newspapers. Review of Reviews. 69:547-8. May 1924

French freedom of press upheld by C. K. Streit in letter to Ackerman. Editor and Publisher. 67:9, 38. Sept. 29, 1934

French newspaper press. Economist. 108:617-18; 674-5. Mar. 23-30, 1929

The **French** press. Spectator. 149:7-8. July 2, 1932

French press profusion bewilders visitor. Editor and Publisher. 61:F3. July 7, 1928
    Discusses the large number of French newspapers and the great increase in readers.

French regional press is powerful. Editor and Publisher. 61:F6. July 7, 1928

Galtier-Boissière, Jean and Lefebvre, René
The Paris post-war press. Living Age. 348:116-25. Apr. 1935
    Events which throw light on the occult resources of the Paris post-war press; the tremendous power and growth of the Havas agency.

Gwynn, Denis
The Catholic press in France. Catholic World. 118:1-12. Oct. 1923

Huddleston, Sisley
A French Hearst. Living Age. 335:124-5, 158. Oct. 1928
A survey of the press. p.88-98. *In his* France and the French. New York: C. Scribner's Sons, 1925
    A short sketch of the Paris and regional press by a noted foreign correspondent.

Johnson, Albin E.
Strong trade union movement now noticeable in French journalism. Editor and Publisher. 62:24. Aug. 24, 1929

Journalism in Paris discussed by Hills. Editor and Publisher. 63:11. Jan. 24, 1931

Jubin, Georges
Journalism in France: 1933. Journalism Quarterly. 10:273-82. Dec. 1933

Keeffe, Grace M.
French newspapers have gained circulation during the depression. Editor and Publisher. 65:16. Nov. 19, 1932

Klein, Felix
One hundred years of success. Commonweal. 10:38-9. May 1929
    A résumé of activities of the French Catholic review *Correspondant* on the occasion of its first centennial celebration.

Kühn, Joachim
The French daily press. Living Age. 317:528-33. June 2, 1923

Lefebvre, René. See Galtier-Boissière, Jean, jt. auth.

Lefranc, Georges
La presse syndicate ouvrière (C.G.T.). Cahiers de la Presse. (3):270-84. July-Sept. 1939
    A study of the labor press syndicate of France, with tables.

Legendre, Maurice
La situation de la presse. Journal des Débats. 31(2):877-8. Nov. 21, 1924

Levy, Raphael
The daily press in France. Modern Language Journal. 13:294-303. Jan. 1929
    A review of the origin, development, ideology, make-up and circulation of the French daily press. Contrasts American and French press practices.

Liesse, André
Le journalisme en France. Journal des Débats. 37(1):910-13. June 6, 1930

L'Intransigeant (Paris) offers novel telephone service. Business Week. p.30. Dec. 28, 1935

Paris' most popular daily. Editor and Publisher. 13:582. Jan. 10, 1914
    Le Journal, of Paris, founded 20 years ago, has circulation of over million copies a day.

Paris muckraker. Time. 26:52-4. Dec. 2, 1935

The **Paris** press. Living Age. 316:375-6. Feb. 17, 1923

Piot, Jean. See Billy, André, jt. auth.

The **Press** and France. Saturday Review. 154:37. July 9, 1932

The **Press** of Paris. Literary Digest. 72:73. Feb. 11, 1922

Reporting in France told by Taylor. Editor and Publisher. 67:16. Sept. 8, 1934

Rise to power of French trade press a postwar development. Editor and Publisher. 59:F32. June 19, 1926
    More than 150 technical journals now being published under 39 classifications.

Ruhl, Arthur
A Paris news-stand. New Republic. 18:84-7. Feb. 15, 1919

Schinz, Albert
French newspapers and periodicals. Library Journal. 45:927-30. Nov. 15, 1920

Tixier, Georges
Writing on the wall; Paris inscriptions now political. Living Age. 354:352-4. June 1938

Train, Arthur, jr.
François Coty and the war of words and ink. World's Work. 59:89-92. Feb. 1930

Two American Paris papers merge. News Week. 4:23. Nov. 10, 1934

The **Unique** newspaper of Paris. Literary Digest. 63:32-3. Dec. 13, 1919

La **Vie** et les origines de la presse du Nord et d' l'Est. Presse Publicité. no. 31, p.1-3, 27-8. Feb. 7, 1938
    A cross-section of the press in the north and east parts of France. Facsimiles and historical notes.

Willson, Beckles
The Paris press and French public opinion. Contemporary Review. 128:574-83. Nov. 1925
    The Paris press is a century behind the English press in its respect for public opinion. Propaganda dissemination seems to be the purpose of the Paris journalists.

e. PROPAGANDA AND PUBLIC OPINION

Boris, Georges
The French press. Foreign Affairs. 13: 319-27. Jan. 1935
A discussion of factors which predispose the French press to undue influence from known and unknown subsidies.

Bribing the French press. New Republic. 37:273-4. Feb. 6, 1924

Brown, Harrison
Who calls the French tune? Living Age. 342:16-19. Mar. 1932

A Chapter in propaganda. Living Age. 320:151-6. Jan. 26, 1924

Dell, Robert
The corruption of the French press. Current History. 35:193-7. Nov. 1931
A brief account of the French press with emphasis on the unreliability of its political news.

Gannett, Lewis S.
The secret corruption of the French press. Nation. 118:136-8. Feb. 6, 1924

Kurth, Karl
Organisation der französischen Auslandpropaganda. Zeitungswissenschaft. 13: 31. Jan. 1, 1938
Funds spent by France for cultural propaganda in foreign countries.

Lang, André
La science du journalisme; ou, Comment on fait l'opinion. Annales Politiques et Littéraires. 85:597-9. Dec. 6, 1925
Attainments of the press; treatment of the news article in efforts to form public opinion.

Lebas, M. J.
Il n'existe pas, en France, d'organisme de contrôle des télégrammes de presse. Presse Publicité. no.20, p.3. Jan. 21, 1938
Government communications official denies charge that press telegrams are censored.

Propaganda plans denied. Editor and Publisher. 66:39. May 20, 1933

Topping, Thomas T.
France establishes propaganda bureau. Editor and Publisher. 65:16. Mar. 25, 1933
Formation of a new press bureau for explaining to foreign nations the French point of view.

Werth, Alexander
The press goes to war; what France reads. New Republic. 84:355. Nov. 6, 1935
Pro-Italian propaganda in the French press is paid for by Italy, the writer charges.

Wood, Ellery
How France uses press of America. American Press. 51:3. May 1933

Zentralisierung der amtlichen französischen Propaganda und Nachrichtendienste. Zeitungswissenschaft. 14:349-50. May 1, 1939
The history and formation of a centralized bureau for propaganda and information in France.

f. THE PRESS AND FOREIGN AFFAIRS

Gauvin, Auguste
L'affaire Horan. Journal des Débats. 35(2):619-20. Oct. 19, 1928
Horan and his superior, W. R. Hearst, were punished for overreaching themselves in their effort to get the text of the Anglo-French naval compromise.

Huddleston, Sisley
French nationalism and the Vatican. New Statesman. 28:529-31. Feb. 12, 1927

Hull hits inaccuracy in Havas story—Says would build ill-will for U.S. Editor and Publisher. 67:4. Oct. 13, 1934

Lengyel, Emil
Hitler and the French press. Nation. 138: 216-17. Feb. 21, 1934

New Franco-American press relations. Review of Reviews. 60:90. July 1919

Price, Julius M.
The influence of Paris on the comity of nations. Fortnightly. 117:977-85. June 1, 1922

Une "Propagande de presse" italienne en Corse? Presse Publicité. no.32, p.1. Feb. 21, 1938
Comment on unwelcomed Italian influence in the press of Corsica.

Severeid, A. Eric
Notes on the French press and the Czech crisis. Journalism Quarterly. 15:379-82. Dec. 1938
How the French press handled the crisis news of September and October 1938, by the city editor of the Paris edition, *New York Herald*.

g. MISCELLANEOUS REFERENCES

Alexander's slaying throws all correspondents into action. Editor and Publisher. 67:8. Oct. 13, 1934

Antoine, Jean
Un spécialiste de la presse parlée défend la radio. Presse Publicité. no.23, p.3. Oct. 24, 1937
Youthful director of Radio City defends the dissemination of news by radio.

Billy, André and Piot, Jean
Le monde des journaux. 239p. Paris: G. Crès, 1924

Bourson, Paul
Les statistiques de la "Pressa." Journal des Débats. 35(2):585-6. Oct. 12, 1928

Les Cahiers de la Presse. L'Europe Nouvelle. 21:178. Feb. 19, 1938

Champeaux, Georges
En lisant la presse au tour de France. Annales Politiques et Littéraires. 101: 90. July 28, 1933

Clair-Guyot, Ernest
Un demi-siècle à L'Illustration. L'Illustration. 185:325-32. July 1, 1933

Control of Inquirer formally transferred to Patenotre, statesman and publisher. Editor and Publisher. 67:38. Oct. 20, 1934

De la mission éducatrice de la presse. L'Europe Nouvelle. 21:1040-1. Sept. 24, 1938

Fay, Bernard
French news from France. Commonweal. 23:285-7. Jan. 10, 1936

Fischaleck, Lorenz
Die französische Kolonialpresse. Zeitungswissenschaft. 12:433-46. July 1, 1937
The French colonial press.

France now teaches journalism. Editor and Publisher. 53:50. Apr. 30, 1921
Department of journalism organized.

Gombault, Georges
L'école de journalisme de Paris. Cahiers de la Presse. 1:126-8. Jan.-Mar. 1938
How the Paris School of Journalism (L'École de Journalisme de Paris) meets the need for adequate training of journalists.

Hachette, Frankreichs größtes Verlags- und Vertriebsunternehmen. Zeitungswissenschaft. 7:359-60. Nov. 16, 1932
An analysis of Hachette, the huge publishing, sales and newspaper distributing agency of France.

Hémardinquer, Pierre
Les progrès du radio-reportage. La Nature. 63(2):397-401. Nov. 1, 1935
Les progrès et les transformations du radio-reportage. La Nature. 60(2):204-9. Sept. 1, 1932

Jaryc, Marc
Problèmes et méthodes de la science de la presse. Cahiers de la Presse. 1:62-82. Jan.-Mar. 1938
Notes on the problems and methods involved in a study of the press, to which is appended an excellent classified list of source material.

Jouvenel, Robert de
Le journalisme en vingt leçons. 109p. Paris: Payot, 1920

Keeffe, Grace M.
Radio and the press are partners in France, Mme. Dupuy says. Editor and Publisher. 65:12. Feb. 11, 1933

Lanux, Pierre de
French magazines. Bookman. 55:208-10. Apr. 1922

Le Verrier, Madeleine
Un centre d'accueil pour les journalistes étrangers à Paris. L'Europe Nouvelle. 19:561-3. May 30, 1936
Announcement of organization of L'Accueil Français as a means of welcoming foreign newspapermen, guiding them to research facilities, and otherwise offering assistance and fellowship.

La Mise en marche de la nouvelle imprimerie de L'Illustration. L'Illustration. 184:216-17. Feb. 25, 1933

La Nouvelle usine de L'Illustration. L'Illustration. 181:xix, suppl. Mar. 26, 1932

Piot, Jean. See Billy, André, jt. auth.

Quelques mots, quelques chiffres sur L'Illustration. L'Illustration. 87(2):ix. Aug. 31, 1929

Radio keen competitor of French press. Newspaper World. 41:6. Apr. 9, 1938

Ragner, Bernhard
"Grads" mourn Paris Tribune passing. Editor and Publisher. 67:10, 39. Nov. 24, 1934

Schinz, Albert
French literary journals. Saturday Review of Literature. 1:417. Dec. 27, 1924

Schneider, Carl, ed.
Die Messageries Hachette, das französische Großzunternehmen für Zeitungsvertrieb. Zeitungswissenschaft. 13:20-3. Jan. 1, 1938
The ramifications of the vast interests of Hachette, newspaper distributing agency.

Spender, Constance
French children's magazines. Contemporary Review. 132:362-7. Sept. 1927

Susini, M. A. de
Le Corse aime la polémique et les quotidiens de combat. Presse Publicité. no.23, p.1-2, 5. Oct. 24, 1937
Characteristics of the Corsican, and descriptions of the problems of newspaper publishing on the island.

Westling, Arvid
Chicago Tribune forged plough from sword. Editor and Publisher. 59:F22. June 19, 1926
Describes the founding of the Paris edition of The Chicago Tribune.

Zur Geschichte der Pariser deutschen Zeitungen. Zeitungswissenschaft. 1:185-6. Dec. 15, 1926
The story of German newspapers in Paris.

I. GERMANY

1. GENERAL DISCUSSION

Die Älteste Berliner Zeitung. Berlin: Preuszische Staatsbibliothek, 1928

Ala Vereinigte Anzeigen-Gesellschaften. Zeitungs-Katalog. Berlin: Haasenstein und Vogler A.-G.; Daube und Co., m.b.H., 1925-39
Annual.

Bauer, Wilhelm
Die öffentliche Meinung in der Weltgeschichte.   402p.   Wildpark-Potsdam: Akademische Verlagsgesellschaft Athenaion, 1930
An interesting, fully illustrated history of the development of public opinion, including the rise of the press, cartoons and other media of mass impression.

Biedermann-Detlev, W. von
Das Zeitungswesen sonst und jetzt. 108p. Leipzig: W. Friedrich, 1882

Bömer, Karl
Bibliographisches Handbuch der Zeitungswissenschaft. 344p. Leipzig: O. Harrassowitz, 1929
A bibliography of journalism.

Das internationale Zeitungswesen. 134p. Berlin, Leipzig: Walter de Gruyter, 1934
——ed.
Handbuch der Weltpresse. 632p. Leipzig, Frankfort a.M.: Armanen, 1937
——and Rochlin, Raphall
Internationale Bibliographie des Zeitungswesens. 373p. Leipzig: O. Harrassowitz, 1932

Ester, Karl d'
Die geschichtliche Entwicklung der Zeitungsforschung in Deutschland von ihren ersten Anfängen bis zur Gegenwart. Zeitungswissenschaft. 3:69-72. May 15, 1928
A historical survey of newspaper research in Germany.

Freund, Cajetan, ed.
Die München-Augsburger Abendzeitung. 90p. Munich: F. Bruckman, 1914
A short abstract of the 300-year history of this newspaper, 1609-1914.

Geschichte der Frankfurter Zeitung, 1856-1906. 977p. Frankfurt a.M.: August Osterrieth, 1906

Groth, Otto
Die Zeitung; ein System der Zeitungskunde. 4v. Mannheim: J. Bensheimer, 1928-30

Houben, Heinrich H.
Verbotene Literatur von der klassischen Zeit bis zur Gegenwart. 2v. Berlin: E. Rowohlt, 1925-28

Hundert Jahre Hamburger Fremdenblatt. Zeitungswissenschaft. 3:152. Oct. 15, 1928
A sketch of the noted Hamburg newspaper on the occasion of its 100th anniversary.

Krüdener, Olaf, baron von
Die Zensur im deutschen Verwaltungsrecht unter Berücksichtigung des kanonischen Rechts. 189p. Berlin: Emil Ebering, 1938

Rochlin, Raphall. See Bömer, Karl, jt. auth.

2. HISTORY AND ANALYSIS

a. TO 1870

Asher, C. W.
Handelspolitische Briefe; deutsche Handelspolitik und deutsche Presse. 48p. Berlin: Hermann Schultze, 1848

Bandmann, Otto
Die deutsche Presse und die Entwicklung der deutschen Frage 1864-1866. 193p. Leipzig: Quelle und Meyer, 1910

Bergsträsser, Ludwig
Entstehung und Entwicklung der Parteikorrespondenzen in Deutschland im Jahre 1848 and 49. Zeitungswissenschaft. 8:12-25. Jan. 15, 1933
Origin of parliamentary political correspondence; how it developed in Vienna, Berlin and Frankfort a.M. Each faction came to issue its own organ, and this correspondence as a whole permeated all German newspapers, even those in the provinces.

Consentius, Ernst
Die Berliner Zeitungen bis zur Regierung Friedrichs des Grossen. 127p. Berlin: Haude und Spener, 1904
History of the early newspapers in Berlin.

Dopf, Karl
Das Flugblatt und seine Geschichte. Zeitungswissenschaft. 3:165-6. Nov. 15, 1928
A short history of pamphlets and pamphleteering.

Dresler, Adolf
Die Anfänge des Augsburger Presse und der Zeitungsdrucker Andreas Asperger. Zeitungswissenschaft. 5:275-95; 336-47. Sept. 15; Nov. 15, 1930
A discussion of the early printers and publishers in Augsburg and the beginnings of the press in this important center of commercial activities in the 15th, 16th and 17th centuries.

Zur Geschichte unserer älteste Zeitungen. Eine Erwiderung an Dr. Günther Ost. Zeitungswissenschaft. 6:96-8. Mar. 15, 1931
A reply to Dr. Ost's article on the same subject.

Ehrentreich, Hans
Die freie Presse in Sachsen-Weimar, von den Freiheitskriegen bis zu den Karlsbader Beschlüssen. 87p. Halle a.S.: Max Niemeyer, 1907
Early history of press freedom in Saxe-Weimar.

Ester, Karl d'
Das Zeitungswesen in Westfalen von seinen ersten Anfängen bis zum Jahre 1813. 240p. Münster i. W.: Heinrich Schöningh, 1907

Fischer, Helmut
Die ältesten Zeitungen und ihre Verleger. Nach archivalischen und sonstigen Quellen dargestellt von Helmut Fischer. 152p. Munich: 1936

Gebhardt, Walter
Die deutsche Politik der Augsburger allgemeinen Zeitung, 1859-1866. 97p. Dillingen-Donau: G. J. Manz, 1935

Geiger, Ludwig
Das junge Deutschland und die Preussische Zensur. 250p. Berlin: Gebr. Paetel, 1900
Early Prussian censorship.

Grasshoff, Richard
Die briefliche Zeitung des XVI. Jahrhunderts. Leipzig: C. Q. Vollrath, 1877
News-letters of the 16th century.

Grosse-Freese, K. H.
Die rheinische liberale Presse im Jahre 1859. 66p. Bonn: 1914

Heide, Walter
Die älteste gedruckte Zeitung. 35p. Mainz: Gutenberg Gesellschaft, 1931
Die älteste gedruckte Zeitung. Zeitungswissenschaft. 11:62-70. Feb. 1936
An interesting and lucid account of what the author contends is the oldest known printed newspaper in the world.

Hermanns, Wilhelm
Josef Görres und Franz Dautzenberg. Berlin: B. Behr, 1906. 1909
Two advocates of human rights during the late 18th and early 19th centuries.

Houben, Heinrich H.
Zeitschriften des jungen Deutschlands. 2v. Berlin: B. Behr, 1906, 1909

Jessen, Hans
Die Nachrichtenpolitik Friedrichs des Groszen und die erste Teilung Polens. Zeitungswissenschaft. 14:587-94. Sept. 1939
An insight into the political and journalistic activities of Frederick the Great through the press in his policy attending the first partition of Poland.

Kleinpaul, Johannes
Die ältesten deutschen Zeitungen. Preussische Jahrbücher. 198:89-92. Oct.-Dec. 1924
Der Nachrichtendienst des sächsischen Hofes vom 15.-18. Jahrhundert. 43p. Tübingen: H. Laupp, 1927

Lahne, Werner
Die ersten Zeitungsschreiber im Urteil ihrer Zeitgenossen. Zeitungswissenschaft. 11:70-3. Feb. 1936
Views of the first newspaper writers during the 17th century, with rhymes showing these views; they are written in the colloquial German of that time.

Mentz, George
Die deutsche Publizistik im 17. Jahrhundert. 31p. Hamburg: Verlagsanstalt und Druck, 1897

Meyer, Dora H.
Die Weserzeitung von 1844 bis zur Reichsgründung. 265p. Bremen: Carl Schünemann, 1932

Müller, Leonhard
Die Breslauer politische Presse von 1742-1861. Nebst einer Übersicht über die Dekade 1861-1871. 443p. Breslau: Goerlich u. Coch, 1908
The political press of Breslau.

Neefe, Fritz
Geschichte der Leipziger Allgemeinen Zeitung, 1837 bis 1843. 192p. Leipzig: Voigtländer, 1914

News service of long ago: Fugger newsletters. Mentor. 15:63. Dec. 1927

Newspaper writers in Germany. Cornhill Magazine. 7:748-55. June 1863

Ost, Günther
Die Staatszeitung als Geschaftszeitung. Zeitungswissenschaft. 7:294-8. Sept. 15, 1932
A discussion of official government newspapers in Germany, particularly during the 18th and early 19th centuries.
Über Legenden und Legendenbildung in der Zeitungsgeschichte. Zeitungswissenschaft. 6:284-8. Sept. 15, 1931
The legends which have grown up in the history of the press; for example, the news activities of the House of Fugger and the development of news correspondence in Hamburg and other cities.
Unbekannte Zeitung aus der Epoche des Dreizigjährigen Krieges. Zeitungswissenschaft. 7:183-7. May 15, 1932
Obscure newspapers during the Thirty Years' War.
Zur Geschichte unserer ältesten Zeitungen. Zeitungswissenschaft. 6:28-32. Jan. 15, 1931
A controversial discussion on the oldest German newspaper; papers in Nürnberg and Augsburg are presented as rivals for the distinction.

Prutz, Robert Eduard
Geschichte des deutschen Journalismus. 436p. Hannover: Kius, 1845

Raumer, Kurt von
Eine preussische Zeitungsgründung in München 1859. Deutsche Rundschau. 203:150-8. Apr.-June, 1925

Rebmann, G. F.
Censur oder Pressfreiheit? 30p. Leipzig: Weller, 1847
Censorship or freedom of the press, written during a period in which these questions were being heatedly discussed.

Remppis, Hermann
Die Wurttembergischen Intelligenzblätter von 1736-1849. 108p. Stuttgart: W. Kohlhammer, 1922

Schöne, Walter
Drei Jahrhunderte Leipziger Presse. Zeitungswissenschaft. 11:506-68. Nov. 1, 1936
The beginnings of the earliest Leipzig press.

Vehse, Otto
Die amtliche Propaganda in der Staatskunst Kaiser Friedrichs II. Berlin, 1924; Munich: Verlag der Münchener Drucke, 1929
Dissertation.

Wehle, J. H., ed.
Das Toleranz-Buch; Aufsätze und Aussprüche über die Freiheit der Meinungsäusserung aus dem 17., 18. and 19. Jahrhundert. 242p. Vienna: Waldheim, 1879

Widdecke, Erich
Die Berliner Pressezenzur bis zur Einsetzung des Oberzenzurkollegiums (1819). Zeitungswissenschaft. 1:102, 117-20, 134-7, 150-2. July 15, Aug. 15, Sept. 15, Oct. 15, 1926
Censorship of the press in Berlin to 1819.

Zimmermann, Walter
Alte Würzburger und Nürnberger Zeitungen. Zeitungswissenschaft. 7:29-36. Jan. 15, 1932
A study of the oldest newspapers in Würzburg and Nürnberg.

Entwicklungsgeschichte des Nürnberger Friedens- und Kriegskuriers, (Nurnberger Kurier) von seinen ersten Anfängen bis zum Übergang an den Fränkschen Kurier, 1663-1865. Nürnberg: W. Tümmel, 1930
The story of an early newspaper in Nürnberg.

b. THE FIRST REICH (TO 1918)

Bamberger, Ludwig
The German daily press. Nineteenth Century. 27:24-37. Jan. 1890

Berlin rebels seize newspaper plant. Editor and Publisher. 51:48. Jan. 18, 1918

Bigelow, Poultney
The German press and the United States. North American Review. 164:12-23. Jan. 1897
Because of the subservience of the German press to the Imperial Government after 1871, it could only reflect the mistrust felt by that government toward the republic.

Blos, Wilhelm
Unsere Presszustände. 40p. Leipzig: Genossenschaftsdruckerei, 1875

Brooks, Robert C.
Lèse majesté in Germany. Bookman. 40: 68-82. Sept. 1914

Bunting, P. W. See Low, Sidney, jt. auth.

Busch, Moritz
Bismarck: some secret pages of his history. 2v. London, New York: Macmillan, 1898
How Bismarck used the press to further his aims.

Calder, W. M. and Sutton, C. W. H.
Memoirs of Prince Max of Baden. 2v. (Authorized translation.) London: Constable, 1928

Carroll, Eber Malcolm
Germany and the Great Powers, 1866-1914. 852p. New York: Prentice-Hall, 1938
Documented study of public opinion and foreign relations.

The **Change** of government in Germany. Fortnightly Review. 48 n.s.:282-304. Aug. 1, 1890

Choisy, Gaston and Vergnet, Paul
La presse allemande. Revue Politique et Littéraire. 56:463-9. Aug. 3-10, 1918

Collier, Price
German political parties and the press. Scribner's. 52:662-76. Dec. 1912

Curti, Theodor
Der Literatenstand und die Presse. 20p. Leipzig: B. G. Teubner, 1911

Dernburg, Friedrich
The visit of the English journalists. Contemporary Review. 91:761-6. June 1907

Diez, Hermann
Das Zeitungswesen. 145p. Leipzig: Teubner, 1910

Eltzbacher, Paul
Die Presse als Werkzeug der auswärtigen Politik. 161p. Jena: E. Diederich, 1918
The press and foreign politics.

Falkenhayn, Erich G. A. S. von
The German General Staff and its decisions, 1914-1916. 333p. New York: Dodd, Mead, 1920

Fest-Schrift zur Feier des fünfzigjährigen Bestehens der Annoncen-Expedition Rudolf Mosse. 147p. Berlin: Rudolf Mosse, 1916

Fischer, Henry W.
Great newspapers of continental Europe. I. German newspapers. Bookman. 10: 444-54. Jan. 1900

Foreign complications and the German press campaign. Contemporary Review. 85: 592-5, 598. Apr. 1904
The writer contends that the German press convinced Russia that England rather than Japan was her real enemy during the Russo-Japanese war.

Freytag, Gustav
Die Journalisten. 152p. Leipzig, S. Hirzel, 1905

Garr, Max
Parliament und Presse. 75p. (Wiener Staatswissenschaftliche Studien, Bd. 8) Vienna, Leipzig: Franz Deuticke, 1908
Explains rights of the press relative to parliamentary (government) procedure; traces their development in various constitutional countries.

Die wirtschaftlichen Grundlagen des modernen Zeitungswesen. 79p. Vienna, Leipzig: Franz Deuticke, 1912

Die **Geschichte** des Formellen und Materiellen deutschen Presserechts 1874-1914. Zeitungswissenschaft. 8:249. July 15, 1933
A discussion of vain attempts by law makers to hem in and muzzle the German press for political ends, 1874-1914.

Haas, Albert
Das moderne Zeitungswesen in Deutschland. 35p. Berlin: L. Simion, 1914

Hale, Oron James
Germany and the diplomatic revolution. 233p. Philadelphia: Univ. of Pennsylvania Press, 1931

Handbuch deutscher Zeitungen. 440p. Berlin: Otto Eisner, 1917

Harrison, Austin
The German press. North American Review. 185:724-36. Aug. 1907

Hedin, Sven Anders
With the German armies in the West. (Translated from the Swedish by H. G. de Walterstorff.) 402p. London, New York: John Lane, 1915

Held, Adolf
Die deutsche Arbeiterpresse der Gegenwart. 196p. Leipzig: Duncker und Humblot, 1873

Hirsch, Carl
Die Parteipresse und ihre Organisation. 24p. Leipzig: Vorwärts, 1876
The party press and its organization.

How Bismarck used the press. Spectator. 102:489-90. Mar. 27, 1909

Keeping out German newspapers. Nation. 106:670-1. June 8, 1918

Kellen, Tony
Das Zeitungswesen. 212p. Munich: Jos. Kösel, 1908

Krumbharr, Herbert
Die Häufigkeit des Erscheinens der Zeitungen. Breslau: 1919; Liegnitz: H. Krumbhaar, 1920
Dissertation.

Kürschner, Joseph
Handbuch der Presse. 1594p. Berlin: Hermann Hillger, 1902

Lehmann, Hans
Die Nachrichtenpolitik der deutschen Presse gegenüber der Einkreisung vor dem Weltkrieg (1902-1909). Zeitungswissenschaft. 14:523-37. Aug. 1939
The attitude of the German press toward encirclement before the World War, 1902-1909. Chancellor Bülow's policy is severely criticized.

Löbl, Emil
Kultur und Presse. 291p. Leipzig: Duncker und Humblot, 1903

Low, Sidney and Bunting, P. W.
The journalistic tour in Germany. Contemporary Review. 92:1-15. July 1907

Lowe, Charles
The German newspaper press. Nineteenth Century. 30:853-71. Dec. 1891
Criticism of the German press law which makes the press subservient.

Meister, Alois
Die deutsche Presse im Kriege und später. 91p. Münster: Borgmeyer, 1916

Muser, Gerhard
Statistische Untersuchung über die Zeitungen Deutschlands, 1885-1914. 173p. Leipzig: E. Reinicke, 1918
A statistical study of the German newspapers.

Naschér, Arthur
Das Berliner Deutsche Tageblatt. Zeitungswissenschaft. 1:153-4. Oct. 15, 1926
A brief historical sketch of the Berlin Deutsche Tageblatt.

Oberholtzer, Ellis Paxson
Die Beziehungen zwischen dem Staat und der Zeitungspresse im Deutschen Reich. 180p. Berlin: Mayer und Müller, 1895

Osborn, Max, ed.
50 Jahre Ullstein 1877-1927. 411p. Berlin: Ullstein, 1927
The story of the famous publishing house in Berlin, which the National Socialists forced into new hands.

A Police daily. Editor and Publisher. 10: 5. Oct. 22, 1910
New German paper will keep police officers informed.

The Political press in Germany. Review of Reviews. 42:109-10. July 1910

Die "Pressa" und die deutsche Weltpolitik. 88p. Zurich: Zürcher and Furrer, 1906

Preston, Thomas B.
Newspaper and periodical press of Germany. Chautauquan. 27:231-7. June 1898

Die Publicistik der Gegenwart. 6pts. in 1v. Würzburg: Leo Woerl, 1879-81

Reaction in Germany. Spectator. 62:422-3. Mar. 30, 1889

Rodenberg, Julius
Deutsche Presse; eine Bibliographie. 550p. Zürich: Amaltheaverlag, 1925

Salomon, Ludwig
Geschichte des deutschen Zeitungswesens von den ersten Anfängen bis zur Wiederaufrichtung des Deutschen Reiches. 3v. Oldenburg und Leipzig: A. Schwartz, 1906
A standard work on the history of journalism in Germany.

Schulz, Eduard
Bismarcks Einfluss auf die deutsche Presse. 109p. Leipzig: Gustav Fock, 1910
Dissertation—Halle.
Bismarck's influence on the German press.

Scott, James Brown
A survey of the international relations between the United States and Germany, 1914-1917. 390p. London, New York: Oxford Univ. Press, 1917

Staedler, E.
Der deutsche Postzeitungsvertrieb in Recht und Geschichte. Zeitungswissenschaft. 6:129-49. May 15, 1931
A study of the close relationship between newspaper circulations in Germany and the postal service which guarantees the delivery of newspapers and also serves as a clearinghouse for getting subscribers.

Sturminger, Alfred
Politische Propaganda in der Weltgeschichte. 320p. Salzburg, Vienna, Leipzig: Bergland, 1938
A historical survey of political propaganda.

Sutton, C. W. H. See Calder, W. M. jt. auth.

Tower, Charles
The history of the "inspired" press in Germany. Spectator. 101:729. Nov. 7, 1908

Traub, Hans K. T.
Grundbegriffe des Zeitungswesens. 184p. Stuttgart: C. E. Poeschel, 1933

Vergnet, Paul. See Choisy, Gaston, jt. auth.

Wehle, J. H.
Die Zeitung, ihre Organization und Technik. 234p. Vienna: Hartleben, 1878

Wehrmann, Martin
Die pommerschen Zeitungen und Zeitschriften in alter und neuer Zeit. 111p. Von der Gesellschaft für Zeitungskunde und Buchdrück in Pommern, 1936
Succinct and carefully collected data on the history of the press in Pomerania.

What the people read in Germany. Review of Reviews. 30:210-12. Aug. 1904

Williams, G. Valentine
The German press bureau. Contemporary Review. 97:315-25. Mar. 1910
The inner workings of the "German Press Bureau," news outlet of the German Foreign Office.

Wolfframm, Peter
Die deutsche Aussenpolitik und die grossen deutschen Tageszeitungen 1871-1890. 76p. Zeulenroda: Bernhard Sporn, 1926
German foreign policy and the leading German daily newspapers.

c. THE REPUBLIC (TO 1933)

Baumert, Dieter Paul
Die Entstehung des deutschen Journalismus. 101p. Munich, Leipzig: Duncker und Humblot, 1928

Blau, Albrecht
Der Inseratenmarkt der deutschen Tageszeitungen. 198p. Berlin: Junker und Dünnhaupt, 1932

Böhmer, Joachim
Die Norddeutsche Allgemeine Zeitung. Zeitungswissenschaft. 1:56-8; 73-5; 92-4; 103-5. Apr. 15, May 15, June 15, July 15, 1926
The story of the *Norddeutsche Allgemeine Zeitung* of Berlin.

Bouton, Stephen Miles
False news from Germany. American Mercury. 27:30-7. Sept. 1932
Newspaper reporting has created for Americans a picture of a Germany which does not exist.

Bücher, Karl
Abhandlungen aus dem Institut für Zeitungskunde an der Universität Leipzig. Leipzig: E. Reinicke, 1918. 1921
Gesammelte Aufsätze zur Zeitungskunde. 429p. Tübingen: H. Laupp, 1926
Ten instructive articles upon the various departments of the German newspaper by a noted student of the press.

Censorship in Germany. Living Age. 337: 157-8. Oct. 1, 1929

Cohnstaedt, Wilhelm
German newspapers before Hitler. Journalism Quarterly. 12:157-63. June 1935
Newspapers of a foreign country must be viewed and appreciated in light of their own national environment and tradition. In that perspective the German newspapers before Hitler fulfilled their purpose well. Freedom of the press was limited by negative direction, not by positive regimentation.

Daniels, Emil
Traditionen und Richtlinien. Preussische Jahrbücher. 231:1-3. Jan.-Mar. 1933

Dewall, Wolf von
The German press. Spectator. 148:892-3. June 25, 1932

Dovifat, Emil
Der amerikanische Journalismus. 255p. Stuttgart: Deutsche Verlagsanstalt, 1927
Zeitungswissenschaft. Berlin, Leipzig: W. de Gruyter, 1931

Edwards, W. H.
Der Auslandsdienst der deutschen Presse. Archiv für Exakte Wirtschaftsforschung. 9:15-51. 1919

Eltzbacher, Paul
Die Presse als Werkzeug der auswärtigen Politik. 161p. Jena: E. Diederich, 1918
Technical questions on the use of the press in influencing world politics.

Ester, Karl d'
Zeitungswesen. 152p. Breslau: F. Hirt, 1928

Florent-Matter, Eugène
De Bismarck à Stresemann; comment l'Allemagne fait l'opinion publique. 218p. Paris: J. Tallandrier, 1932

Galtier-Boissière, Jean; Zimmer, Bernard; and Salten, Felix
Germany inside out. Living Age. 340: 46-61. Mar. 1931

Gauvain, Auguste
Le Chancelier Müller, la presse et les négociations. Journal des Débats. 35(2): 582-4. Oct. 12, 1928
Misleading news was fed to German people in spite of Müller's speech to the press representatives in which he asked them to use correct information.

German newspaper press. Economist. 108: 279-80. Feb. 9, 1929

German newspaper publisher seeks to form Fascist dictatorship. Editor and Publisher. 58:46. Apr. 3, 1926
Dr. Alfred Hugenberg owns newspaper chain.

A German paper preparing for the deluge. Literary Digest. 60:26-7. Jan. 25, 1919

German press faces serious problems. Editor and Publisher. 65:28. Aug. 13, 1932

German press prefers "bias" to U.S. news style. Editor and Publisher. 64:44. Nov. 28, 1931

Germans protect editorial convictions. Editor and Publisher. 58:13. May 15, 1926
Opinions and convictions of German journalists to be safeguarded by legal contract against business office tyranny.

Germany will not obstruct flow of news, Frederick Kuh says. Editor and Publisher. 65:22. Dec. 10, 1932

Greenburger, Sanford J.
Harden, fighting editor of royal Germany, dies in 66th year. Editor and Publisher. 60:36. Nov. 5, 1927

Heerdegen, Ernst
Der Nachrichtendienst der Presse. 128p. Leipzig: Reinicke, 1920
News agencies and Germany's special problems of world-wide news gathering and dissemination.

Heide, Walter
Julius Ferdinand Wolff. Zeitungswissenschaft. 3:121. Aug. 15, 1928
Life sketch of the former editor-in-chief of the Dresden Neuesten Nachrichten.

Heinke, Hans
Die Heimatblätter der deutschen Tageszeitungen. 111p. Linz a.D.: F. Winkler, 1931

Hirschfeld, Gerhard
Press of Germany sharply divided by political affiliations. Editor and Publisher. 64:24. May 23, 1931
Trend toward neutrality more marked, but largest dailies are those vigorously allied with a political faction. The country has 3,350 papers.

Jaeger, Karl
Von der Zeitungskunde zur publizistischen Wissenschaft. 126p. Jena: Fischer, 1926

Jaeger-Essen, Karl
Zeitungswissenschaft. Preussische Jahrbücher. 206:63-72. Oct.-Dec. 1926

Jöhlinger, Otto
Probleme der Tagespresse. Schmollers Jahrbuch. 44:215-40. 1920
Attempts to socialize the daily press. Criticisms, questions about advertising, journalism as a course of study.
Zeitungswesen und Hochschulstudium. 179p. Jena: G. Fischer, 1919

Johnson, Albin E.
German papers highly organized with full protection for writers. Editor and Publisher. 62:11. Aug. 3, 1929

Kantorowicz, Ludwig
Die sozialdemokratische Presse Deutschlands. 27p. Berlin: J. H. W. Dietz, 1928

Merrill, W. S.
The new German check-list of periodical holdings. Library Journal. 52:816-17. Sept. 1, 1927

Meynen, Otto and Reuter, Franz
Die deutsche Zeitung, Wesen und Wertung. 202p. Munich: Duncker und Humblot, 1928

A Model news-trust. New Statesman (London) 30:786-8. Mar. 31, 1928

News men well treated in Germany returning correspondents say. Editor and Publisher. 57:10. May 23, 1925
Dispatches from Republic uncensored.

Peters, Alfred
Die Zeitung und ihr Publikum. 174p. Dortmund: F. W. Ruhfus, 1930

Plieninger, Martin
Die Kampfpresse. Zeitungswissenschaft. 8:65-75. Mar. 15, 1933
The writer predicts that because of high pressure methods and because of its service to a movement, the violently partisan press will cease to exist when the cause actuating it loses its force.

Reuter, Franz. See Meynen, Otto, jt. auth.

Rippler, Heinrich
Das Journalistengesetz. Deutsche Rundschau. 201:253-7. Oct.-Dec. 1924
A proposed law sought to safeguard economic security for journalists following a change in policy by publisher.

Salten, Felix. See Galtier-Boissière, Jean, jt. auth.

Schacht, Hjalmar
Wirtschaft und Presse. Zeitungswissenschaft. 2:177-9. Dec. 15, 1927
The German economist and financier discusses his views on newspaper management.

Schöne, Walter
Die Zeitung und ihre Wissenschaft. 235p. Leipzig: H. F. A. Timme, 1928

Socialization of the press in Munich. Nation. 108:1031. June 28, 1919

State of journalism in Germany a grotesque picture to American eyes. Editor and Publisher. 64:1. May 23, 1931
Editorial.

Stein, Wolfgang C. Ludwig
Vorlesungen für die Presse. Preussische Jahrbücher. 204:1-24. Apr.-June 1926

Troeltsh, Ernst
Public opinion in Germany. Contemporary Review. 123:578-83. May 1923

Trust idea dominant in growth of German newspaper chain. Editor and Publisher. 60:24. Oct. 1, 1927
Hugenberg influences entire country.

Villard, Oswald Garrison
The German phoenix; the story of the Republic. 358p. New York: H. Smith and R. Haas, 1933
The press today; X. Hugenberg and the German dailies. Nation. 131:197-8. Aug. 20, 1930
The capitalist Hugenberg established an important chain of daily newspapers and organized a news-gathering organization.

Williams, Walter
Some observations on the German press. (Univ. of Missouri Bulletin, v.33. Journalism Series, no. 67) Columbia, Mo: Univ. of Missouri, Nov. 10, 1932

Würfel, Gotthard
Kritisches über die Zeitung von heute. 255p. Leipzig, Cologne: Kommissionsverlag Schulze, 1930

Zeitungs-Katalog der Annoncen-Expedition. Leipzig: Annoncen-Expedition Rudolf Mosse, 1922
Annual. First edition, 1867.
A German newspaper directory.

Zeitungsstatistik (Deutschland). Zeitungswissenschaft. 2:54. Apr. 15, 1927
Contemporary statistics on the German press.

Zimmer, Bernard. See Galtier-Boissière, Jean, jt. auth.

Zur Reform des Presserechts. Deutsche Rundschau. 186:289-97. Mar. 1921

3. RECENT PRESS: THIRD REICH

a. GENERAL DISCUSSION

Amann, Max
Es gibt nur eine deutsche Presse. Zeitungsverlag. 36:279. 1935
National-sozialistische deutsche Volkspresse. Zeitungsverlag. 37:572. 1936
Die Presse im zweiten Jahre des nationalsozialistischen Staates. Zeitungsverlag. 36:87. 1935

Barlow, Reuel R.
Journalistic education under the Third Reich. Journalism Quarterly. 12:357. Dec. 1935
A systematic plan, adopted by the German schools of journalism, for supplying young men to the press who are properly and rigorously trained to serve the nation.

Bömer, Karl
Das Dritte Reich im Spiegel der Weltpresse. 173p. Leipzig: Armanen-Verlag, 1934

Dresler, Adolf
Aus der Geschichte des "Völkischen Beobachter" und des Zentral-Verlages der N.S.D.A.P. Franz Eher Nachf. Zeitungswissenschaft. 11:433-7; 12:569-80. Oct. 1, Dec. 1, 1936
This account is an abridgment of the Geschichte des Völkischen Beobachter und des Zentral-Verlages der NSDAP. München: Franz Eher Nachf. An interesting article dealing with the history of the newspaper and of the publishing house which eventually was taken over by Hitler, and which served as a sounding board for the National Socialists for a decade before the accession of the party to power.

Die Reichspressestelle der NSDAP. 15p. Berlin: Walter de Gruyter, 1937
A discussion of the Press Bureau of the National Socialist party.

Die Reichspressestelle der NSDAP. Zeitungswissenschaft. 11:149-53. Apr. 1, 1936
The organization and services of the press of the National Socialists in Germany.

Goebbels, Joseph
My part in Germany's fight. 253p. London: Hurst and Blackett, 1938

Hands across the Rhine. Living Age. 349: 458-9. Jan. 1936

Henri, Ernst
Revolutionary movement in Germany. I-II. New Statesman and Nation. 6:153-4, 207-8. Aug. 5, 19, 1933

Hitler, Adolf
Ist die Errichtung einer die breiten Masses erfassenden völkischen Zeitung eine nationale Notwendigkeit? Zeitungswissenschaft. 12:145-9. Mar. 3, 1937
Lest the German people suffer the same fate as the people of Russia, Hitler urges a rebirth of nationalism with a press for the people, one that shall penetrate all parts of the nation, and lash the people into an awareness of national necessities. An important discussion by Hitler in the early days of the National Socialist movement.

Mein Kampf. 2v. in 1. New York: Stackpole Sons, 1939
See p. 177-86 and 560-76.
Profiting by what he felt to be the superior propaganda methods of the Allies during the World War, Hitler expounds his ideas on that subject, giving both his aims and methods. This is a new and unexpurgated English translation.

Hoover, Calvin B.
Germany enters the Third Reich. 243p. New York: Macmillan, 1933

Johnson, Albin E.
Fight for free speech and press fiercely fought in Saar, Danzig. Editor and Publisher. 66:31. Mar. 17, 1934

Kosok, Paul
Modern Germany; a study of conflicting loyalties. 348p. Chicago: Univ. of Chicago Press, 1933

Krumbach, Josef H.
Grundfragen der Publizistik. 256p. Berlin: Walter de Gruyter, 1935

Lehmann, Ernst Herbert
Einführung in die Zeitschriftenkunde. 253p. Leipzig: K. W. Hiersemann, 1936

Lore, Ludwig
Nazi politics in America. Nation. 137: 615-17. Nov. 29, 1933

Monroe, Elizabeth
Germans and Morocco. Spectator. 158: 465-6. Mar. 12, 1937

Münster, Hans A.
Zeitung und Zeitungswissenschaft im neuen Staat. Zeitungswissenschaft. 8: 273-88. Sept. 15, 1933
Compares public opinion in the old state with that in the new and sets forth problems yet to be solved by research work in journalism.

Nations cannot afford war, says Cooper. Editor and Publisher. 67:8. Sept. 15, 1934

Neuberger, Richard
Germany under the choke bit. New Republic. 77:13-15. Nov. 15, 1933

Die Presse der nationalsozialistischen deutschen Arbeiterpartei im Überblick. Zeitungswissenschaft. 7:176-83. May 15, 1932
An analysis of the National Socialist press in Germany prior to the accession to power of Adolf Hitler.

Die Presse im neuen Staat. Zeitungswissenschaft. 8:193-201. July 15, 1933
Excerpts from addresses of German national leaders giving the ideals and aims for the new German nation and the integration of the press.

Schaeffer, Wolfgang
Faschistische Pressegestaltung — neue deutsche Presse. Preussische Jahrbücher. 233:26-41. July-Sept. 1933

Schiller, Heinrich L.
Prize journalism under Hitler. Nation. 141:12-13. July 3, 1935

Schoenstedt, Walter
Illegal periodicals in Germany. American Mercury. 34:40-3. Jan. 1935
Anti-fascist literature and methods of distribution.

Seminar des Instituts für Zeitungswissenschaft. Zeitungswissenschaft. v.11,no.5. May 1, 1936
Selected articles on development of technical journals: philosophy, history, philology, the theatre, motion pictures, military science, sports, labor, agriculture, paper.

Traub, Hans K. T.
Sinn und Aufgabe der Zeitungswissenschaft. Preussische Jahrbücher. 240: 44-53. Apr. 1935

Von der deutschen Presse. Spectator. 151: 216-17. Aug. 18, 1933

Waldkirch, Wilhelm
Weltpresse und Weltkrise. 228p. Ludwigshafen a.R.: Waldkirchdruck; Berlin: Geo. Neuner, 1936

Die zeitungspolitische Aufgabe. 3v. Ludwigshafen a.R.: J. Waldkirch, 1935
The worth, the work, and the influence on culture of the newspapers.

b. PRESS AND GOVERNMENT; PRESS LAW

A. Hitler, publisher: Führer and his war sergeant gobble up Reich press. Newsweek. 13:28. Jan. 23, 1939

Controlled German newspapers—Ministry's instructions to the press. Manchester Guardian Weekly. 32:430. May 31, 1935
Excerpts from official instructions pointing out to editors how the news of the day shall be handled.

Desmond, Robert William
200 dailies are suppressed by Hitler. Editor and Publisher. 65:8, 38. Apr. 1, 1933
Prohibition of all publications not in the public interest and those not published for the welfare of the German nation.

Dietrich, Otto
Nazi press chief spanks "agitators" in world press. Current History. 50:49. July 1939
The Reich press chief in a round-robin to the German press.

Dresler, Adolf
Der Führer und die Presse. Zeitungswissenschaft. 14:297-305. May 1, 1939
Hitler's close connections with the German press and his stand toward the foreign press.

Fay, Sidney Bradshaw
The German press today. Current History. 40:100-2. Apr. 1934
Dr. Goebbels criticizes the tameness of the press and urges it to tell the world frankly what Germany is aiming to accomplish.

German press slaughter. Editor and Publisher. 66:24. Mar. 24, 1934
In less than a year 600 daily newspapers have been swept out of existence by Nazis.

Greenwood, Harry Powys
Public opinion in Germany. Spectator. 162:407. Mar. 10, 1939

Herr Hitler and the press. Spectator. 160: 417. Mar. 11, 1938
Reply by N. D. Cliff: Spectator. 160:522. Mar. 25, 1938.

Hitler copying Mussolini's press regime—iron censorship relaxed; editorial responsibility revived. World's Press News. 13:9. Apr. 18, 1935

How German government restricts editor's work. World's Press News. 14:15. Oct. 10, 1935

Die Kongreszreden der Reichsleiter Amann und Dr. Dietrich auf dem Reichsparteitag 1936. Zeitungswissenschaft. 11: 443-5. Oct. 1, 1936

Kornev, N.
Persons and personages: the man who made Hitler rich. Living Age. 355: 337-41. Dec. 1938
Financial shrewdness of Max Amann in the unification, centralization and management of the Nazi press.

Larson, Cedric
The German press chamber. Public Opinion Quarterly. 1:53-70. Oct. 1937
A concise outline of the official organizations through which the German press is integrated and supervised.

Das Lebengesetz der deutschen Zeitung. Zeitungswissenschaft. 13:638-42. Oct. 1, 1938
The place and concepts of the German press under the National Socialistic regime, presented in an address by the Nazi press chief, Max Amann.

La **Législation** sur la presse en Allemagne. Texte des documents. L'Europe Nouvelle. 17:443-7. Apr. 28, 1934
Text of the German law affecting editors put in force Jan. 1, 1934, and an explanation by the German Minister of Education before the representatives of the German press on the reasons for its enactment.

Lengyel, Emil
Hitler and the French press. Nation. 138: 216-17. Feb. 21, 1934

Lowe, Charles
The German newspaper press. Nineteenth Century. 30:853-71. Dec. 1891
Criticism of the German press law which makes the press subservient.

Nazi instructions to press cited. Editor and Publisher. 66:37. Sept. 23, 1933
German newspaper in Paris outlines methods of Hitler government for controlling news, and quotes official orders.

Nazi press in training. Editor and Publisher. 66:36. Apr. 21, 1934

Nazi slew thousand German papers. Editor and Publisher. 67:33. Sept. 1, 1934

Pew, Marlen
Shop talk at thirty. Editor and Publisher. 66:44. Nov. 25, 1933
The German "Editor's Law" established under the Hitler regime is outlined.

Press purge. Time. 25:25-6. May 6, 1935

Rentrop, Oswald
Die Reichspropagandaämter. Zeitungswissenschaft. 13:1-8. Jan. 1, 1938
The construction and duties of the branch offices of the Ministry of National Political Enlightenment and Propaganda in the Third Reich.

Spiecker, Karl
Das deutsche Reichspresseamt. Zeitungswissenschaft. 1:133-4. Sept. 15, 1926
The German official press bureau.

Sunk without trace. Editor and Publisher. 66:22. Apr. 7, 1934

Waldkirch, Wilhelm
Auf dem Wege zur Zeitungswissenschaft. Zeitungswissenschaft. 9:29-32. Jan. 1, 1934
Journalism will attain the status of a science only through the proper evaluation of its relationship to laws governing the state and public opinion.

The **Week.** New Republic. 83:152-3. June 19, 1935
Instructions to the Nazi-controlled press by the German Ministry of Propaganda, reprinted from the *Manchester Guardian*.

Williams, J. Emlyn
Journalism in Germany: 1933. Journalism Quarterly. 10:283-8. Dec. 1933
Abolition of freedom of the press by the Nazi party. Special qualifications are required of newspaper men, who must belong to the official German press associations.

Zur Reform der Presserechts. Deutsche Rundschau. 186:289-97. Mar. 1921

c. CENSORSHIP AND PROPAGANDA

Bertaux, Pierre
La propagande allemande. L'Europe Nouvelle. 22:735-7. July 8, 1939

Birchall, F. T.
Where heroes can be made to order. New York Times. Section 6, p. 6-7. May 6, 1934

Ethridge, Mark F.
Reich press defeat held "degrading." Editor and Publisher. 65:13, 78. Apr. 22, 1933

Fay, Sidney Bradshaw
The German press today. Current History. 40:100-2. Apr. 1934
Germany illustrates how curtailment of freedom of expression undermines the influence of the press.

Fog of propaganda covers Germany. Editor and Publisher. 67:10. July 21, 1934

Fry, Varian
The German press—in exile. Review of Reviews. 93:57. Feb. 1936

Germany spending £20,000,000 yearly on propaganda. World's Press News. 14: 11. Oct. 24, 1935

Hamburger, Ernest
Le ministère allemand de la propagande. Cahiers de la Presse. (3):298-315. July-Sept. 1939
A study of the administrative organization of the German ministry of propaganda and public information by the associate general secretary of the Institut de Science de la Presse of the Univ. of Paris. Contains useful chart.

Henderson, Arthur
Nazi news service. Nation. 145:599. Nov. 27, 1937

Kurth, Karl
Die Rede Reichsleiter Dr. Dietrichs auf dem Reichsparteitag der Arbeit in ihren zeitungswissenschaftlichen Bedeutung. Zeitungswissenschaft. 12:762-4. Nov. 1, 1937
Dr. Dietrich, Nazi party press chief, discusses the need for research into press propaganda.

McKenzie, Vernon
Press and propaganda in Europe. p.15-23. *In* Institute of World Affairs. Proceedings, 1934. Los Angeles: Univ. of Southern California, 1935

Marx, Fritz Morstein
Propaganda and dictatorship. Annals of the American Academy. 179:211-18. May 1935
Methods which have been adopted to meet the chief problem of propaganda in a dictatorship: how to win public opinion.

Meyer, I. S.
History into propaganda; how Nazi scholars are rewriting Jewish history. Menorah Journal. 26:51-74. Jan. 1938
Bibliographical footnotes.

Nazi journalism and the British Home Office. Nation. 145:213. Aug. 28, 1937

Nazi papers regret "doctoring" dispatch. Editor and Publisher. 68:24. July 27, 1935

Nazi purging story blurred by censors; officials admit misstatements. Editor and Publisher. 67:3-4. July 7, 1934

Reich gives warning to foreign writers. Editor and Publisher. 65:6. Mar. 4, 1933
Newspapers in Germany are completely gagged as Chancellor Hitler abolishes constitutional rights.

Rentrop, Oswald
Die Reichspropagandaämter. Zeitungswissenschaft. 13:1-8. Jan. 1, 1938
An explanation of the branch offices of the German Propaganda Ministry.

Vermeil, Edmond
Les thèmes de la propagande allemande. L'Europe Nouvelle. 22:770-2. July 15, 1939

Wagner, Eugene
Saarpresse im Kampf gegen Frankreichs Propaganda, 1918-1925. 144p. Saarbrücken: Saarbrücker Drückerei, 1933
The press in the Saar Basin during French occupation.

d. NEWSPAPERS AND NEWSPAPERMEN

Decline and extinction of many German newspapers once proud and powerful. Nation. 138:170. Feb. 14, 1934

Exiled Reich editor visiting in U.S. Editor and Publisher. 67:18. Sept. 8, 1934

Germany bans 36 foreign newspapers. World's Press News. 14:11. Aug. 1, 1935
A short announcement listing well-known publications which have been suppressed.

The German press. World Tomorrow. 17: 156. Mar. 29, 1934
Statistics on the quantitative decline of the German press through suppression since 1932.

German press: a barren desert of conformity. China Weekly Review. 88:43. Mar. 11, 1939

Germany's secret newspapers have biggest circulations. World's Press News. 14:13. Aug. 15, 1935
The experience of 50 years of clandestine activity in pre-Soviet Russia and Poland has been drawn upon in the distribution of anti-Nazi propaganda among the German masses under the eyes of the German secret police.

Guthrie, F. M.
Der Stürmer. New Statesman and Nation. 10:934. Dec. 14, 1935
A correspondent's letter to the editor protesting misrepresentation of Der Stürmer's policies. Der Stürmer is a Nazi and violently anti-Semitic newspaper.

Heizler, Rudolf. See Kurth, Karl, jt. auth.

Hollering, Franz
I was an editor in Germany. Nation. 142:151-2; 182-4. Feb. 5, 12, 1936
By an exile.

Kurth, Karl and Heizler, Rudolf
Veränderung in der Berliner Presse. Zeitungswissenschaft. 14:103-4. Feb. 1, 1939
A brief account of the end of three old Berlin newspapers.

Straws in the wind: Germany's moribund press. Living Age. 347:497-8. Feb. 1935
Translated from the Neues Wiener Tageblatt, Vienna conservative daily. Article holds that the National-Socialist party, in stifling the press, defeats its own purpose, for many refuse to read the repetitious articles in the newspapers.

Tante Voss ist tot! Spectator. 152:573. Apr. 13, 1934
After 230 years the Vossische Zeitung of Berlin ceased publication because of "undernourishment."

Die Vossin. Neue Rundschau. 45:589-90. Jan.-June 1934

Wilkens, Josef
Die Kongreszrede von Reichsleiter Amann auf dem Parteitag, 1937. Zeitungswissenschaft. 12:760-2. Nov. 1, 1937
Statistics on the German press following the rise to power of the NSDAP.

Wolff, Theodor
Epitaph of a newspaper. Living Age. 356:84-5. Mar. 1939
Obituary on the passing of the Berliner Tageblatt, pillar of Germany's democratic past.

Zankl, L.
Die Gesamtauflage der deutschen Zeitungen. Zeitungswissenschaft. 12:621-3. Sept. 1, 1937

e. FOREIGN CORRESPONDENTS IN GERMANY

Berlin correspondents protest against Nazi attack. Newspaper World. 40:13. Aug. 21, 1937

German scene; complaints of a foreign newsgatherer. Living Age. 353:208-10. Nov. 1937

Lochner, Louis P.
News gathering in Nazi Germany. Quill. 27:5-6. Aug. 1939
By the head of the Associated Press Bureau in Berlin.

Mowrer, Edgar Ansel
Germany puts the clock back. 325p. New York: W. Morrow, 1933
By a correspondent of the Chicago Daily News.

Pew, Marlen
Shop talk at thirty. Editor and Publisher. 67:44. Sept. 15, 1934
Dorothy Thompson describes her expulsion from Germany.

27 correspondents leave Germany under pressure of Nazi regime. Editor and Publisher. 67:10. Apr. 6, 1935
Contains complete list with the probable causes for ejection.

Whiteleather, Melvin K.
German press. Journalism Quarterly. 16:
207-9. June 1939
    Relations between German government
    and the foreign correspondents improved
    greatly.

f. MISCELLANEOUS REFERENCES

Broadcasts in German. Spectator. 160:1147.
June 24, 1938

Gower, Francis
Broadcasting in Germany. Spectator. 162:
294-5. Feb. 24, 1939
    The set-up, control, activity and propa-
    gandistic nature of German broadcasting.

Kittel, Erick Kurt
Das Nachrichtenwesen der Wehrmacht.
Zeitungswissenschaft. 12:782-6. Nov. 1,
1937
    Reviews the news organization of the
    army; means of news transmission and the
    training of news and press sections as an
    integral part of the army.

Die "Pressa" in Köln. Westermanns Monatshefte. 144:489-95. July 1928

J. GREAT BRITAIN

1. HISTORY AND ANALYSIS

a. GENERAL DISCUSSION

Andrews, Alexander
The history of British journalism from
the foundation of the newspaper press
in England, to the repeal of the Stamp
Act in 1855; with sketches of press
celebrities. 2v. London: R. Bentley,
1859

The **Beginnings** of English journalism.
p. 389-415. (Cambridge History of English Literature. v. 7) New York: Macmillan; Cambridge, England: University Press, 1932

Belloc, Hilaire
English revolution and the press. Harper's
Monthly. 151:367-73. Aug. 1925
    Revolution in newspaper publishing
    brought about by (a) popularization of
    press; (b) ownership by the wealthy; (c)
    dependence upon advertising.

Blumenfeld, Ralph D.
The press in my time. 253p. London:
Rich and Gowan, 1933
    The growth of the press, newspapers
    and public opinion, law and libels, the Sun-
    day Press, the future. By the editor for
    three decades of the London Daily Express.

Bourne, Henry R. F.
English newspapers: chapters in the history of journalism. 2v. London: Chatto
and Windus, 1887

Bowman, William Dodgson
The story of The Times. il. 342p. London: George Routledge and Sons, 1931
    A concise history of The Times (London)
    from the early feuds between authority
    and the press to recent times.

The **British** literary year book. Editor and
Publisher. 53:13. May 28, 1921
    Reference book concerning British jour-
    nalistic and literary conditions.

Cockburn, James D.
Beginnings of the Scottish newspaper
press. Scottish Review. 18:366-77; 21:
399-419. Oct. 1891; Apr. 1893

Day-to-day record of Empire's Press Conference. Newspaper World. 40:9-12.
May 29, 1937

Delafons, Allan
A concise survey of British publications.
Editor and Publisher. 61:98. July 7,
1928
    Great Britain and Ireland have total of
    2,150 newspapers and 3,500 periodicals of
    all kinds.

Donald, Robert
The Imperial Press Conference in Canada.
295p. London, New York, etc.: Hodder
and Stoughton, 1921

The **English** newspaper. Catalogue of an
exhibition illustrating the history of the
English newspaper through three centuries, from the library of the Press
Club, London, May 25, to June 18,
the old Court House, Messrs. J. and E.
Bumpus, Ltd. 57p. Cambridge: University press, by W. Lewis, 1932

Englishman's ideal of a newspaper. Review
of Reviews. 21:607-8. May 1900

Essays from the London Times; a collection of personal and historical sketches.
2v. London: 1851-54

First English paper. Editor and Publisher.
13:196-7. Aug. 23, 1913
    Collector of Hungaria accidentally finds
    copy of Corant or Weekly Newes, dated
    London, Oct. 11, 1621.

Historical and personal history of the Scottish press. II-III. Fraser's Magazine.
18:75-85, 201-9. July-Aug. 1838

Leeds Intelligencer—Yorkshire Post. Newspaper World. 42:5. Aug. 19, 1939
    Nineteenth of a series on Britain's oldest
    newspapers.

London Gazette. Editor and Publisher. 10:
7. Oct. 12, 1910
    Oldest English newspaper; has smallest
    circulation, no editor, no editorial staff.

Macaulay, Thomas Babington
The News Letter. Editor and Publisher.
9:22. Apr. 30, 1910
    A quotation from Macaulay's History of
    England treating the source from which
    the great body of gentry and clergy of
    England in early times learned the history
    of their own period.

Mackintosh, Sir Alexander
Fifty-seven years in the press gallery.
World's Press News. 19:2. Apr. 7,
1938

Maitland, Francis H.
One hundred years of headlines, 1837-1937.
251p. London: Wright and Brown,
1938
    An illustrated chronological panorama of
    English newspaper headlines, articles, trade
    and private advertisements.

Mackower, Stanley V.
Some notes upon the history of the Times, 1785-1904. 35p. Edinburgh: Morrison and Gibb, 1904

May's British and Irish press guide. London: F. L. May, 1938
Annual. First issued in 1873.

Meynell, Wilfrid (John Oldcastle, pseud.)
Journals and journalism, with a guide for literary beginners. 151p. London: Field and Tuer, 1880

Morison, Stanley
The English newspaper. 335p. Cambridge: University Press, 1932

Muddiman, J. G.
Tercentenary handlist of English and Welsh newspapers, magazines and reviews. 212p. London: The Times, 1920

A Newspaper history, 1785-1935. 213p. London: The Times Publishing Co., 1935
Reprinted from the 150th anniversary number of The Times (London), January 1, 1935.

The Newspaper press directory. London: Mitchell, 1938
Annual. Established 1846.

Postgate, Raymond and Vallance, Almer
England goes to press. 337p. Indianapolis: Bobbs-Merrill, 1937

Sell's World's press. London: Henry Sell, 1938
Annual. First issued in 1880.

Symon, James David
The press and its story. 327p. London: Seeley, Service, 1914
An account of the processes that go into the making of the daily or weekly newspaper in England.

The Times, London
The history of The Times. v. 1-2. New York: Macmillan, 1935-39
Contents: v.1.The Thunderer in the making, 1785-1841. v.2. The tradition established, 1841-1884.
The foundation of the paper by the first John Walter; the changes wrought by his successor, not only in influence on The Times but in the whole standing of English journalism.
The third and last volume is in preparation.

The Times, London: a newspaper history, 1785-1935. 213p. London: Times Pub. Co., 1935

Vallance, Almer. See Postgate, Raymond, jt. auth.

Williams, J. B.
A history of English journalism to the foundation of the Gazette. 293p. New York, London: Longmans, Green, 1908

Willing's Press guide. 1938 edition. 498p. London: 1938
Annual. First edition 1884.

b. TO 1800

Bilainkin, George
Front page news—once (from 1642-1815). 288p. London: Methuen, 1937

Clyde, William M.
Parliament and the press, 1643-1647. Library (London) 13:399-424; 14:39-58. Mar.-June, 1933
The working of the licensing system imposed by Parliament on the press in 1643.

Crane, Ronald Salmon; Pryor, M. E.; and Kaye, F. B.
A census of British newspapers and periodicals, 1620-1800. 206p. Chapel Hill, N.C.: Univ. of North Carolina Press, 1927

Editors and newspaper writers of the last generation. Fraser's Magazine. 65:169-83; 595-609; 66:32-49. Feb., May, July 1862

Gabler, Anthony J., comp.
Check list of English newspapers and periodicals before 1801 in the Huntington library. Huntington Library Bulletin. no. 2, p. 1-66. Cambridge, Mass.: Harvard Univ. Press, Nov. 1931
A convenient list restricted to publications of England, Scotland and Ireland. Includes the early corantos and newsbooks.

Graham, Walter
The beginnings of English literary periodicals, 1665-1715. 91p. London: Oxford Univ. Press, 1926

Defoe's Review and Steele's Tatler—the question of influence. English and German Philology. 33:250-4. Apr. 1934
Bibliographical footnotes.

Hanson, Laurence
English newsbooks, 1620-1641. Library. s4, 18:355-84. Mar. 1938
Bibliographical footnotes.

Government and the press, 1695-1763. 149p. London: Oxford Univ. Press, H. Milford, 1936

Junius, pseud.
The letters of Junius. Ed. by Charles W. Everett. 410p. London: Faber and Gwyer, 1927
Letters written under the pseudonym of "Junius" on various public and personal topics in the English Public Advertiser between 1769 and 1772.

Kaye, F. B. See Crane, Ronald Salmon, jt. auth.

Laprade, William Thomas
Power of the English press in the eighteenth century. South Atlantic Quarterly. 27:426-34. Oct. 1928

Public opinion and politics in eighteenth century England to the fall of Walpole. 463p. New York: Macmillan, 1936
Coffeehouses, orators, the press and other factors in the development of public opinion. An interesting study including a survey of public opinion during the 18th century wars and of regulatory laws.

Lee, James Melvin
Month of May recalls cradle days of English journalism. Editor and Publisher. 54:7-8. May 20, 1922
In 1622 news sheets underwent peculiar transformation whereby they appeared as news books.

Lee, William
Daniel Defoe. 3v. London: J. C. Hotten, 1869

Lindsay, W. B.
Defoe's review—forerunner of modern journalism. English Journal. 16:359-63. May 1927

London newspapers of 1776 and the Declaration of Independence. Nation. 66:127-8. Feb. 17, 1898

Madan, Falconer
The Oxford press, 1650-1675: the struggle for a place in the sun. 147p. London: The Library, 1926

Muddiman, J. G.
The King's journalist, 1659-1689. 294p. London: John Lane, Bodley Head, 1923

Newton, Theodore Francis Moorehouse
William Pittis and Queen Anne journalism. Modern Philology. 33:169-86, 279-302. Nov. 1935-Feb. 1936
Bibliographical footnotes.

Oldmixon, John
Memoirs of the press, historical and political, 1710-1740. 64p. London: Printed for T. Cox, 1742

Remarks on Fog's Journal, of February 10, 1732-1733; exciting the people to an assassination. 23p. London: Printed for J. Wilford, 1733

Rosenfeld, Sybil Marion
Restoration stage in newspapers and journal, 1660-1700. Modern Language Review. 30:445-59. Oct. 1935
Bibliographical footnotes.

Shaaber, Matthias A.
History of the first English newspaper. Studies in Philology. 29:551-87. Oct. 1932
The series of quarto news-books started in London in May, 1622; news-gathering methods and treatment.
Some forerunners of the newspaper in England, 1476-1622. 368p. Philadelphia: Univ. of Pennsylvania Press, 1929

Stearns, Bertha Monica
Early English periodicals for ladies, 1700-1760. Modern Language Association Publications. 48:38-60. Mar. 1933
Bibliographical footnotes.
First English periodical for women: Ladies Mercury. Modern Philology. 28:45-59. Aug. 1930
Bibliographical footnotes.

Stevens, David H.
Party politics and English journalism, 1702-1742. 156p. Menasha, Wis.: George Banta Pub. Co., 1916

Watts, Thomas
A letter to Antonio Panizzi, Esq., keeper of the printed books in the British Museum, on the reputed earliest printed newspaper, The English Mercurie, 1588. 16p. London: W. Pickering, 1839

Wead, Eunice
A packet of news from eighteenth century England. Colophon. n.s. 1:441-52. Feb. 1936

c. 19th CENTURY

Alexander, Helen (Cadbury)
Richard Cadbury of Birmingham. 448p. London: Hodder and Stoughton, 1906

Beckett, A. W. à
The A'Becketts of "Punch." 333p. New York: E. P. Dutton; London: Constable, 1903

Bell, E. H. C. Moberly
The life and letters of C. F. Moberly Bell. 326p. London: Richards Press, 1927
A biography of this famous editor of the London *Times*, written by his daughter. The influence exerted by the paper on domestic and foreign policy.

Blunden, Edmund C.
Leigh Hunt's Examiner examined. London: Cobden-Sanderson, 1928

The British press: its growth, liberty, and power. North British Review. 30:367-402. May 1859

China and the Times. Outlook (London) 1:177. Mar. 12, 1898

Cook, Edward T.
Delane of the Times. 319p. London: Constable, 1916

Dasent, Arthur Irwin
John Thadeus Delane, editor of the Times, his life and correspondence. 2v. London: J. Murray, 1908

Dawson, John
Practical journalism: how to enter thereon and succeed. 124p. London: L. U. Gill, 1885

Death of Labouchere. Editor and Publisher. 11:11. Jan. 20, 1912
Obituary notice of Henry ("Labby") Labouchere giving highlights in the career of one of England's most colorful journalists.

Early Victorian England, 1830-1865. 2v. London: Oxford Univ. Press, H. Milford, 1934
See also Kellett, E. E. *The Press.*

English newspapers. Nation. 46:223-4. Mar. 15, 1888
A review of English Newspapers, by H. R. Fox Bourne. 2v. London: Chatto and Windus, 1887.

Escott, Thomas H. S.
The evolution of the leader. Living Age. 236:596-606. Mar. 7, 1903
Early historical sources of the "leader" or editorial, its function, subsequent development, literary aspects and influence.

The Father of "dailies." Living Age. 233:507-9. May 24, 1902

Fox, William
Morality of the press, a lecture. London: 1835

Grant, James
The newspaper press: its origin, progress, and present position. 3v. London: Tinsley Bros., 1871-72
The leading events in the history of the English and Scottish newspaper press to 1871.

Greenwood, Frederick
Forty years of journalism. English Illus-
trated Magazine. 17:493-8. July 1897
"The newspaper press: half a century's
survey. Blackwood's. 161:704-20. May
1897
The press and government. Nineteenth
Century. 28:108-18. July 1890

Hatton, Joseph
Journalistic London. 249p. London: S.
Low, Marston, Searle, and Rivington,
1882

Holtzendorff, Franz von
Englands Presse. 32p. Berlin: Luderitz-
sche Verlagsbuchhandlung, 1870

Hume, Abraham
The learned societies and printing clubs of
the United Kingdom. 307p. London:
Longman, Brown, Green, and Longmans, 1853

Hunt, F. Knight
The fourth estate. 2v. London: David
Bogue, 1850

Jackson, Mason
The pictorial press, its origin and progress.
363p. London: Hurst and Blackett,
1885

Jourdan, Henry D.
Daily and weekly press of England in
1861. South Atlantic Quarterly. 28:
302-17. July 1929

Kellett, E. E.
Early Victorian England, 1830-1865. p. 3-
97. (*His* The press, v.2) London: Oxford Univ. Press, 1934

Kitchin, F. Harcourt
The London Times under the managership
of Moberly Bell: an unofficial narrative.
298p. New York, London: G. P. Putnam's Sons, 1925

Lucy, Henry William
The power of the British press. North
American Review. 163:168-74. Aug.
1896
Sixty years in the wilderness. 450p. Lon-
don, New York: E. P. Dutton, 1909

MacDonagh, Michael
The reporters' gallery. 452p. London,
New York, Toronto: Hodder and
Stoughton, 1913
How the reporting of Parliamentary debates, at first looked upon as inimical to
the authority and independence of Parliament, was later reluctantly tolerated. The
reporters' gallery came to be fully recognized as an essential part of free representative government.

Mackie, John B.
Modern journalism; a handbook of instruc-
tion and counsel for the young journalist. 144p. London: C. Lockwood and
Son, 1894

The **Newspaper** press of Scotland. Fraser's
Magazine. 17:559-71. May 1838

Oliphant, Mrs. Margaret (Wilson)
Annals of a publishing house. William
Blackwood and his sons, their magazine
and friends. 3v. New York: Scrib-
ners, 1897-8

Pendleton, John
Newspaper reporting in old time and today. 246p. London: Elliot Stock, 1890
The newspaper reporter, pointing out
how and under what conditions he does
his work as the daily historian of his
time.

Porritt, Edward
The government and the newspaper press
in England. Political Science Quarterly. 12:666-83. Dec. 1897
Traces the change in the government's
relations with the press which took place
after George III came to the throne (1760-
1820) in which government rewards to
editors gave way to a new order in which
newspapers became financially and politically independent.

Private history of the London newspaper
press. Tait's Edinburgh Magazine (suppl.
for 1834). 1:788-92. 1834

Ralph, Julian
London journalists. Harper's Weekly.
43:1283. Dec. 16, 1899

Reid, Arnot
The English and the American press.
Nineteenth Century. 22:219-33. Aug.
1887

Reid, William Alfred
Some reminiscences of English journalism.
Nineteenth Century. 42:55-66. July
1897

Robinson, Sir John R.
Fifty years of Fleet Street. Comp. and
ed. by Frederick Moy Thomas. 418p.
London; Macmillan, 1904
Memoirs of distinguished journalist of
Queen Victoria's reign.

Rose, J. Holland
The unstamped press, 1815-1836. English
Historical Review. 12:711-26. Oct.
1897

Saintsbury, George
Journalism fifty years ago. Nineteenth
Century. 107:426-36. Mar. 1930

d. 1900-1918

Austen-Leigh, Richard Arthur
The story of a printing house, being a
short account of the Strahans and Spot-
tiswoodes. 61p. London: Spottiswoode,
1912

Belloc, Hilaire
The free press. 102p. London: G. Allen
and Unwin, 1918
Evils of the modern capitalist press, its
tendency to vitiate and misinform public
opinion. Mr. Belloc suggests the formation
of small independent organs.

Brookes, Sydney
The English press. Harper's Weekly. 47:
570. Apr. 4, 1903

Carson, William E.
Northcliffe, Britain's man of power. 456p.
New York: Dodge, 1918

Chancellor, E. Beresford
The annals of Fleet Street: its traditions
and associations. 358p. London: Chapman Hall, 1912

Courlander, Alphonse
Mightier than the sword. 352p. London:
Unwin, 1913

English red tape. Editor and Publisher. 11:
1-2. Feb. 17, 1912
The difficulties encountered by an
American journalist in England.

Escott, Thomas H. S.
Masters of English journalism, a study
of personal forces. 368p. London: T. F.
Unwin, 1911
Brief biographies of prominent English
journalists and their journalistic work.
Submerged profession. London Quarterly
Review. 131:73-83. Jan. 1919
Two epochs behind the Fleet Street scenes.
Living Age. 284:281-91. Jan. 30, 1915

Foreign affairs: a chronique. Fortnightly
Review. 89:743-9. Apr. 1908

Government by newspaper. Spectator. 114:
738-9. May 29, 1915

Halewyck, Michel
Le régime légal de la presse en Angleterre. 142p. Louvain: Ch. Peeters;
Paris: Larose et Forcel, 1899

Harmsworth, Alfred
Simultaneous newspapers of the 20th century. North American Review. 172:72-
90. Jan. 1901

Hayward, F. H. and Langdon-Davies, B. N.
Democracy and the press. 88p. Manchester: National Labour Press, 1919

International hatred and the press. Nation.
86:276. Mar. 26, 1908

Jones, Kennedy
Fleet Street and Downing Street. 363p.
London: Hutchinson, 1920

The **King** in yellow. Bellman. 22:175. Feb.
17, 1917
Concentration of power in the hands of
Northcliffe is the greatest in the history
of journalism, says Sir Norman Angell.

Koch, Theodore Wesley
War libraries and allied studies. 287p.
New York: G. E. Stechert, 1918

Langdon-Davies, B. N. See Hayward, F.
H., jt. auth.

Loeb, Sophie Irene
Tea in a London newspaper office. Editor and Publisher. 12:4. Feb. 22, 1913

Lorenz, Theodor
Die englische Presse. 136p. Halle: Gebauer-Schwetschke, 1907

Lucy, Henry William
Nearing Jordan. 453p. London: Smith,
Elder, 1916

Mackail, J. W., ed.
Modern essays. (From the London
Times). 291p. London: Longmans,
Green, 1915

McKenzie, Fred A.
The mystery of the Daily Mail, 1896-1921.
128p. London: Associated Newspapers,
1921

Maurice, Arthur Bartlett
"The Thunderer." Bookman. 19:505-8.
July 1904
Review of Mackower, S. V. Some Notes
upon the History of The Times, 1785-1904.

Mr. Chesterton on anonymous journalism.
Spectator. 100:1020-1. June 27, 1908

News values. Editor and Publisher. 10:5.
Nov. 12, 1910
American and English standards of journalism compared by British writer.

Progress of British journalism. Editor and
Publisher. 13:63, 75. July 12, 1913

Rees, J. D.
The Times and India. Fortnightly Review. 88:857-65. Nov. 1910

Scott-James, R. A.
The influence of the press. 320p. London:
S. W. Partridge, 1913
Essential facts about the condition, influence and function of the press, especially
in England and America.

Stead, W. T.
Lord Cromer and government by journalism. Contemporary Review. 93:436-49.
Apr. 1908
A defense by the author of his attempts
as a journalist to influence government
policy, as in the Soudan case.

Stephen, Leslie
Journalism. Atlantic Monthly. 92:611-22.
Nov. 1903

Times printing number. The Times (London) Sept. 10, 1912

Walbrook, H. M.
Under four editors. Nineteenth Century.
78:1161-73. Nov. 1915

Walston, Charles
Truth, an essay in moral reconstruction.
233p. New York: Putnam's, 1919

Ward, Wilfrid
Journalism of great Englishmen. Dublin
Review. 156:288-310. Apr. 1915

The **Week**: English journalism. Outlook.
67:186. Jan. 26, 1901
Editorial.

Wrench, John E. L.
Struggle, 1914-20. 504p. London: Ivor
Nicholson and Watson, 1935

Yellow journalism. Editor and Publisher.
12:15. May 17, 1913
Comment on the novel The Preposterous
Yankee, written by a London editor, in
which the author, (signed Ponsonby), arraigns yellow journalism.

Zimmerman, Walter
Die englische Presse zum Ausbruch des Weltkrieges. 269p. Charlottenburg: "Hochschule und Ausland," 1928
A German study of the British press before the World War.

2. RECENT PRESS

a. PRESS AND GOVERNMENT

The **Attempt** to suppress Lord Stanhope's speech. Newspaper World. 42:1. Apr. 8, 1939
Prime Minister Chamberlain takes responsibility for effort to suppress a speech made by the First Lord of the Admiralty.

Attitude of army to press should be one of "complete frankness." Newspaper World. 42:7. Apr. 22, 1939
Excerpts from a speech by the Director of Public Relations at the British War Office.

Blumenfeld, Ralph D.
How labor censored and gagged press told by London newspaper editor. Editor and Publisher. 58:3, 38. May 8, 1926

Brailsford, Henry N.
The British press and British policy. New Republic. 85:221-2. Jan. 1, 1935

Britain's D (danger) notices: hitherto meek editors start rebellion against curbs. Newsweek. 13:39-40. May 15, 1939

Brittain, Sir Henry
Ministry of Information would be an excellent thing if—. World's Press News. 21:4. June 8, 1939
Must rely strongly on news, not propaganda, and the staff must represent a wide range of special qualifications.

Casey, Ralph D.
The national publicity bureau and British party propaganda. Public Opinion Quarterly. 3:623-34. Oct. 1939
Results of a study describing in detail the propaganda activities of the national government.

Cheaper Empire press rates. World's Press News. 19:5. Apr. 14, 1938
Lower rates from London to various points in Empire. Thus press rates to Australia down from 6d to 4d cable or wireless, and deferred press down to 3d from 4½d.

Craick, W. A.
More news to cement British Empire ties. Editor and Publisher. 58:12. Nov. 7, 1925
New cables and lower radio rates between United Kingdom and dominions sought by Empire Press Union.

Editors' views on "D" notices. Newspaper World. 42:1. Apr. 22, 1939
Example of the controversy in British newspaper circles centering in a new system for requesting the press not to publish, in the national interest, certain "dangerous" news items.

Fewer "D" notices the better, says War Office chief. World's Press News. 21:5. Apr. 20, 1939
Major-General J. H. Beith, public relations officer, recounts arrangements made for British war correspondents in 1914.

Gardiner, Alfred G.
The press and the state. Nation (London) 33:736-7. Sept. 15, 1923

Government press. Nation (London) 28: 155-6. Oct. 30, 1920

Government prohibits radio news in British Malaya. World's Press News. 18:15. Nov. 4, 1937
How radio news comes to Far East, some free, and how Dutch Islands get good radio news reports.

Government sets up foreign publicity department. Newspaper World. 42:1. June 17, 1939
Lord Perth to head Ministry of Information, planned for war time "to coordinate overseas publicity about Britain."

Home Secretary's strong attack on censorship. World's Press News. 21:3. May 4, 1939
Sir Samuel Hoare addressed Newspaper Society dinner.

Hopkins, G. S.
Foreign news—an increasingly important market. How the Foreign Office News Department helps. World's Press News. 13:14. Mar. 14, 1935

Information Ministry is essential to national safety. World's Press News. 21: 532, p. 25. May 11, 1939
Advertising Association's general secretary advocates "fourth line defense."

It's that ministry again. World's Press News. 21:2. May 18, 1939
R. A. Scott-James and Trevor Fenwick recount experiences of World War propaganda ministry.

Journalists' vain vigil at Whitehall. World's Press News. 22:3. Aug. 31, 1939
Premier Chamberlain warns press to exercise "utmost restraint" in reporting foreign affairs.

Mansfield, F. J.
Royal interest in the press. Newspaper World. 40:53-4, 56-7. May 8, 1937

Martin, Kingsley
The press in Britain: is it subject to censorship? New Republic. 98:183-5. Mar. 22, 1939

Mr. Baldwin and Lord Rothermere. New Statesman and Nation. 1:136. Mar. 21, 1931

More imperial news in Britain's press. World's Press News. 13:24. Apr. 11, 1935

Morgan, William Thomas
Recent British politics and the newspaper barons, 1929-1935. South Atlantic Quarterly. 34:419-43. Oct. 1935

National government launches propagandist picture paper. World's Press News. 13:3. May 16, 1935

Press and the election. Spectator. 131:833. Dec. 1, 1923

The **Prime Minister** and the press. Nation (London) 25:41-2. Oct. 12, 1918

Ramsay MacDonald and the press. Newspaper World. 40:4. Nov. 13, 1937

Shape of things; efforts made by British government to suppress opinions and news it dislikes. Nation. 147:577-8. Dec. 3, 1938

Spender, John Alfred
The public life. 2v. London, New York: Cassell, 1925
Vol. II, Book VI, The Press and Public Life. p. 95-141. Old and new journalism; the making of opinion; journalists and politicians; the press and foreign affairs. By the editor of the liberal *Westminster Gazette.*

Steed, Henry Wickham
The press. 250p. Harmondsworth: Penguin, 1938
A critical survey of the British press, and a consideration of its freedom by the former editor of the London *Times.*

Tell the public at once why Information Ministry is vital now. World's Press News. 21:17. May 4, 1939

Turner, H. E., comp.
The Fourth Imperial Press Conference (Britain), 1930. 390p. London: Empire Press Union, 1931

Will Italian pact affect government attitude to press? World's Press News. 19:1. Apr. 21, 1938
Clause in Anglo-Italian pact rules out injurious publicity or propaganda against each other.

Willert, Sir Arthur
British news controls. Foreign Affairs. 17:712-22. July 1939
Relations of press and the British government; inadequacy of official propaganda in Britain.

Wilson, Philip Whitwell
Reporting Parliament and Congress. North American Review. 214:326-33. Sept. 1921
Contrasting methods of releasing news.

Winterton, Earl
The press and Parliament. Fortnightly. 135:325-35. Mar. 1931
The clash of ambitions to influence and guide the nation is the main cause of the contest between the politicians and the press.

b. PRESS LAWS

Blumenfeld, Elliot
Fleet Street. Bookman. 59:32-6. Mar. 1924

British ban on divorce news not binding on U.S. writers in London. Editor and Publisher. 60:14. Dec. 31, 1927
Unless paper circulates in Britain.

Camrose denies laws or courts limit British press freedom. Editor and Publisher. 72:47, 52. June 3, 1939
Letter from *London Daily Telegraph* and *Morning Post* proprietor disputes Col. R. R. McCormick's appraisal of British law and the press.

Dicey, Albert V.
Lectures on the relation between law and public opinion in England during the 19th century. 506p. London: Macmillan, 1905. 1930

Laski, Harold J.
Sedition; the case of the Daily Worker. New Statesman and Nation. 2:743. Dec. 12, 1931

Martin, Kingsley
Press in Britain, is it subject to censorship? New Republic. 98:183-5. Mar. 22, 1939
Libel laws are severe in Britain but the press is independent.

Official secrets. New Statesman and Nation. 16:4-5. July 2, 1938

Robson, Norman
The Official Secrets Act and the British press. Journalism Quarterly. 15:253-8. Sept. 1938

Siebert, Frederick S.
Contemporary regulations of the British press. Journalism Quarterly. 8:235-56. June 1931
Regulations of the British press which were in effect on January 1, 1931 regarding libel, advertising, use of the mails and other matters. By a capable student of press laws.

c. NEWSPAPERS

Belloc, Hilaire
Prophets of the press. Outlook (London) 51:49-52. Jan. 20, 1923

Bennett, Rodney. See Gordon, H. S., jt. ed.

Bowman, William Dodgson
The story of The Times. 342p. New York: Dial Press; London: C. Routledge and Sons, 1931

British newspapers' circulation and rates. Editor and Publisher. 53:67-8, 70, 76, 78, 80, 82, 87. Jan. 22, 1921
Statistics.

Callender, Harold
Britain's old "Thunderer" rounds out 150 years. New York Times Magazine. p. 6, 14. Jan. 2, 1938

Casey, Ralph D.
Britain. Journalism Quarterly. 14:387-94; 15:73-7, 224-8. Dec., Mar., June 1938
This series, written while the author was studying in London on a Guggenheim fellowship, presents a concise and critical picture of the British—particularly the London—press.

Cobbett, Walter Willson and Dark, Sidney
Fleet Street, an anthology of modern
journalism. London: Eyre and Spottiswoode, 1932

Collins, John Philip
Cult of the hyena. Nineteenth Century.
123:535-49. May 1938

Dark, Sidney. See Cobbett, Walter Willson, jt. auth.

Delafons, Allan
London Times in modern plant. Editor
and Publisher. 71:suppl. v-vii. Feb. 12,
1938

Desmond, Robert William
Journalism in England: 1933. Journalism
Quarterly. 10:266-72. Dec. 1933

Each Reporter has his own room, big arm-
chair, desk and typewriter. Newspaper
World. 40:4. Sept. 4, 1937

End of the "Morning Post." Newspaper
World. 40:1. Oct. 2, 1937

Ensor, R. C. K.
Coronation milestones: news and communications. Spectator. 158:801-2. Apr.
30, 1937

Fifty years, memories and contrasts; a
composite picture of the period, 1882-
1932. 223p. London: T. Butterworth,
1932

Fox, George
Reception of Lord Durham's report on
the English press. Canadian Historical
Review. 16:276-88. Sept. 1935
Bibliographical footnotes.

Fyfe, Hamilton
Pestering by the press. Fortnightly. 147
(n.s. 141):304-11. Mar. 1937

Gardiner, Alfred G.
Policy of the Daily Mail. Nation (London) 34:111. Oct. 20, 1923

Gordon, George S., ed.
Third leaders. (Reprinted from The
London Times). 256p. London, 1928

Gordon, H. S. and Bennett, Rodney, eds.
Through the eyes of The Times. 182p.
London: University of London Press,
1937

Grasty, C. H.
British and American newspapers. Atlantic Monthly. 124:577-91. Nov. 1919
The differences between American,
British and French newspapers are due
largely to the differences among the peoples
of these nations; the American press leads
in news-gathering enterprise, and is inferior in expressing editorial opinion.

Hart, Albert Bushnell
America in the British press. Current
History. 30:305-7. May 1929
Comments on the lack of articles on vital
American institutions and affairs in the
English press.

Herd, Harold
The making of modern journalism. 118p.
London: G. Allen and Unwin, 1927

Hindle, Wilfrid H.
The Morning Post, 1772-1937; portrait of
a newspaper. 260p. London: G. Routledge and Sons, 1937

Hood, Peter
Ourselves and the press. London: Lane,
1939
A social study and criticism of news,
advertising and propaganda.

Independence of the British press. Spectator. 140:216-17. Feb. 18, 1928

Journalism more dignified. Editor and Publisher. 67:11. Nov. 10, 1934

Lansbury, George
The miracle of Fleet Street: the story of
the Daily Herald. 166p. London: Victoria House Printing Co., Labour Pub.
Co., 1925

London Post is sold to Lord Camrose.
Editor and Publisher. 70:42. July 31,
1937

MacGuiggan, George
Great Britain's advertising bill reaches
$500,000,000 annually. Editor and Pub-
lisher. 53:9. Jan. 1, 1921

Massingham, Henry William
Journalism as a dangerous trade. Spectator. 131:839-40. Dec. 1, 1923
Reply: Spectator. 131:1029-31. Dec. 29,
1923.

Mills, J. Saxon
The press and communications of the
Empire. 289p. (The British Empire,
v.6) New York: Henry Holt, 1924
See especially ch. vi, p. 103-31: "Newspapers of the Empire." Surveys the press,
its extent, influence, accomplishments of
the Imperial press conferences, the Empire
Press Union and Reuter's news agency.

Morning Post. National Review. 109:
352-6. Sept. 1937

Moseley, Sydney Alexander
The truth about a journalist. 352p. London: I. Pitman and Sons, 1935

Ownership of London newspapers. Newspaper World. 42:7. June 17, 1939
Taken from an analysis by Lord Camrose
in the Daily Telegraph.

Oxford and Asquith, Margot Asquith, count-
ess of
U.S. journalism more "restful" than
British. World's Press News. 13:9.
May 16, 1935

Political and Economic Planning. News
from America. 16p. (Pamphlet no. 148)
London: PEP, May 30, 1939
A PEP survey, supplementing the comprehensive Report on the British Press,
1938, and revealing "the weaknesses in the
service of the American news supplied to
British readers."

Ratcliffe, S. K.
Revolution in Fleet Street. Nineteenth
Century. 108:15-24. July 1930
The transition of newspaper ownership
from private families to financial syndicates. Newspapers under this system have
gained in circulation and popular appeal
but editors have become subordinate to
owners.

Les Réactions de la presse Anglo-Saxonne.
L'Europe Nouvelle. 21:1042-4. Sept.
24, 1938

Roche, John F.
British press becoming "sensational."
Editor and Publisher. 63:7. Nov. 22,
1930

Roebuck, C. M.
Daily Herald: a worker's daily? Labour
Monthly. 4:201-18. Apr. 1923

Scarborough, Harold E.
The British press. Foreign Affairs. 12:
508-19. Apr. 1934
An evaluation of English newspapers:
make-up, policy, circulation, influence on
public opinion.

Smith, Ernest
Fields of adventure. 319p. London:
Hutchinson, 1923; Boston: Small,
Maynard, 1924

Soames, Jane
The English daily press. English Review.
61:195-201. Aug. 1935
Author complains of too great uniformity
in reporting of news in the English press.
Opposition is needed to present all sides
of a news story. "News not views" is not
the best policy.
English press. American Review. 8:578-
89. Mar. 1937

Some of the leading Welsh newspapers.
Newspaper World. 42:35. May 13, 1939
Supplemented by other articles on the
press of Wales.

Spender, Hugh
Press octopus. Contemporary Review.
124:701-8. Dec. 1923

Stong, Phil D.
Rothermere masses millions to expand
chain. Editor and Publisher. 60:11, 45.
Mar. 24, 1928
Will establish evening paper in five key
cities and acquire others in adjacent towns.
$15,000,000 stock issue oversubscribed.

Strachey, John St. Loe
British press. Living Age. 320:199-205.
Feb. 2, 1924
The editor of the Spectator expresses
concern over increasing newspaper mon-
opoly.

Stutterheim, Kurt von
The press in England. 223p. London:
G. Allen and Unwin, 1934

Tracey, Herbert, ed.
The British press, a survey, a newspaper
directory and a who's who in journalism. 139p. London: Europa Publications, 1929

Twenty-six years of "Nash's-Pall Mall."
World's Press News. 13:17. May 16,
1935

Warren, Low
Journalism. 352p. London: C. Palmer,
1922
A British textbook on journalism. Ch. 27.
Newspapers and war; ch. 28. The news-
paper of the future.

What is the readership of Britain's weeklies? World's Press News. 13:25.
May 16, 1935

d. BIOGRAPHY

Baxter, Arthur Beverley
Strange street. 296p. New York, London: D. Appleton-Century, 1935
The lively autobiography of the Canadian
piano salesman who became editor-in-chief
of the London Daily Express. His reminiscences include stories of significant
events and famous statesmen.

Beaverbrook and Rothermere unlimited;
latest phases of the personal press.
World Today. 55:430-3. Apr. 1930

Blumenfeld, Ralph D.
R.D.B.'s procession. 285p. New York:
Macmillan, 1935
Famous people whom the author has
known during his editorship of the London
Daily Express, including Lloyd George,
Gladstone, Buffalo Bill, Kitchener, P. T.
Barnum, Sarah Bernhardt, prime ministers
and presidents.

Bottomley, Horatio
About
Colorful British journalist wielded great
power over masses; dies in London.
Editor and Publisher. 66:33. June 3,
1933

Carson, William E.
Northcliffe—genius of a hundred successes.
Editor and Publisher. 55:5-10. Aug.
19, 1922

Clarke, Tom
My Northcliffe diary. 304p. London:
V. Gollancz; New York: Cosmopolitan,
1931

Curious fellow: Lord Beaverbrook. Time.
32:44-50. Nov. 28, 1938

Gardiner, A. G.
Two journalists: C. P. Scott and Northcliffe, a contrast. Nineteenth Century.
111:247-56. Feb. 1932

H. W. Massingham. New Republic. 40:
32-3. Sept. 10, 1924

Hammond, John L.
C. P. Scott of the Manchester Guardian.
364p. New York: Harcourt, Brace,
1934

Hutcheon, William
Gentlemen of the press. 238p. London:
John Murray, 1933

Memory, F. W.
Memory's. 311p. London: Cassell, 1932
The adventures of a newspaper man.

Mills, J. Saxon
Sir Edward Cook, K.B.E. 304p. London: Constable, 1921
Cook was connected with the *Pall Mall Gazette*, first editor of the *Westminster Gazette*, leader writer of the *Daily Chronicle*. His strong political convictions toward the Boer War led him to sever from the *Daily News*. During the World War he was closely identified with the official press bureau.

Odhams, W. J. B.
The business and I. 193p. London: Martin Secker, 1935

Ridout, Herbert C.
Berry brothers effect combination of big British interests. Editor and Publisher. 53:9. Jan. 1, 1921
Gives them control of publishing and printing properties valued at $8,500,000.

Sammis, Walter
Northcliffe a surprise to reporters. Editor and Publisher. 54:5. July 30, 1921

Wrench, Evelyn
New controller of the Daily Mail. Spectator. 129:427-8. Sept. 20, 1922

e. THE PRESS AND FOREIGN AFFAIRS

British press rebuked for depicting U.S. as land of gangs and violence. Newsweek. 11:28. May 9, 1938

Bullen, Percy S.
Journalistic ethics and world affairs: British and American journalism. p. 13-19. (Univ. of Missouri Bulletin, v. 25. Journalism Series, no. 32) Columbia, Mo.: Univ. of Missouri, Nov. 10, 1924
Observations of a British journalist after serving 20 years as a correspondent in the United States for the London *Daily Telegraph*.

"The Daily Herald" and Bolshevik money. Spectator. 125:357-9. Sept. 18, 1920

Ffoulks, Harold
Behind the scenes at the foreign office. Institute of Journalists' Journal. 27: 108. May 1939
London editor of *Daily Dispatch* tells how the Foreign Office is reported.

Fuller, Edward
The Times and the Russian famine. Nation (London) 31:52. Apr. 8, 1922

Hodson, H. V. See Willert, Sir Arthur, jt. auth.

Is Lord Rothermere right? Saturday Review. 156:512. Nov. 18, 1933
Lord Rothermere, in 1933, favored arming against the threat of Hitler, forecasting the drift of events which shook Europe in 1938.

Long, B. K. See Willert, Sir Arthur, jt. auth.

Martin, Kingsley
British opinion and the Abyssinian dispute: a survey of the daily papers during the second half of August, 1935. Political Quarterly. 6:583-90. Oct. 1935

British opinion and the proposed boycott of Japan. Political Quarterly. 9:106-12. Jan.-Mar. 1938

The British press and foreign affairs. Political Quarterly. 2:115-20. Jan. 1931
British newspapers reflect a decline in the interest of the British people in extra-insular affairs. Cynicism, party maneuvering and indifference have taken the place of a tendency in the past toward tolerance, constitutional methods, and revulsion against repression, arbitrary government and deliberate cruelty.

Fascism and the "Daily Mail". Political Quarterly. 5:273-6. Apr. 1934

Foreign policy of the Daily Express. Political Quarterly. 4:438-41. July 1933

Nicolson, Harold
British public opinion and foreign affairs. Journal of the British Institute of Journalists. 25:84-5. May 1937

British public opinion and foreign policy. Public Opinion Quarterly. 1:53-63. Jan. 1937
An excellent analysis of British public opinion and of post-war influences that have temporarily upset the traditional British calm.

Pares, Bernard
English news on Russia. Contemporary Review. 142:282-91. Sept. 1932

Phayre, Ignatius
The British press and the United States. Quarterly Review. 259:229-44. Oct. 1932
Too much pro-Americanism in the British press.

Hitler and the British press. Saturday Review. 161:396-7. Mar. 28, 1936

Rogerson, Sidney
Propaganda and truth. Spectator. 162: 535. Mar. 31, 1939
British are not being told the truth relative to foreign politics.

Rothermere press and France. Nation (London) 33:567-9. Aug. 4, 1923

Scott-James, R. A.
British press finds need for vigilance. Christian Science Monitor. Weekly Magazine Section. p. 4. Nov. 30, 1938

Willert, Sir Arthur; Long, B. K.; and Hodson, H. V.
The Empire in the world. 334p. London: Oxford Univ. Press, 1937
A discussion by the former Foreign Office press official of the political and economic status of the British Empire overseas, past and present.

f. THE PRESS AND PUBLIC OPINION

Angell, Sir Norman
"The Daily Blackmail": how much longer? Nation and Athenæum. 35:684. Sept. 6, 1924
The *Daily Mail* blacklisted all financial institutions that handled subscription for a German loan.

Place of the press. Spectator. 143:758-9. Nov. 23, 1929
The real problem of the press is to secure freedom from the pressure of an emotional and excitable public in times of excitement and prejudice.

Baily, Herbert
British newspapers and foreign propaganda. Living Age. 311:548-51. Nov. 26, 1921

Belloc, Hilaire
Few kind words on the press. Nineteenth Century. 120:438-51. Oct. 1936

British news abroad. The Round Table. 27:533-46. June 1937
Contents: I. War over the air. II. News in the Far East. III. Fact or sensation.

British public opinion and foreign affairs. Journal of the British Institute of Journalists. 25:84-5. May 1937

British self-advertisement. Spectator. 160: 5. Jan. 7, 1938

Donald, Robert
Influence of the press. Outlook (London) 57:309-10. Apr. 24, 1926

German and English censorship. Living Age. 332:270-1. Feb. 1927

Heindel, Richard H.
Some predecessors of "Anglo-American News". Anglo-American News (American Chamber of Commerce in London) 4:481, 513. Dec. 1937
Forgotten journalistic efforts that throw light on social history.

Limits of press power. Spectator. 124:297-8. Mar. 6, 1920

The Misrepresentation of news. Saturday Review. 151:329. Mar. 7, 1931

Morgan, William Thomas
British general election of 1935; study of British public opinion as expressed in ten daily newspapers. South Atlantic Quarterly. 37:108-31. Apr. 1938

The Moscow trial. Spectator. 150:867-8. June 16, 1933
The author of this letter upbraids the London Times for its failure to send a correspondent to report the Moscow trial, and for the inaccurate and fantastic tales about the trial which the Times did publish.

News from America. Spectator. 160:457. Mar. 18, 1938
Discussion, 160:517-18, 677. Mar. 25, Apr. 15, 1938.

No news from America. Reader's Digest. 33:106-7. Nov. 1938

Rothermere or Mosley. Saturday Review. 157(2):879-80. July 28, 1934
Was fascist leader, Sir Oswald Mosley, receiving support of the Rothermere newspapers?

Sitwell, Osbert
Press dictators; excerpts from triple fugue. Nation (London) 47:402. June 28, 1930

Truth and news. Review of Reviews. (London) 86:19-21; 22-4. Feb.; Mar. 1935
Bibliographical footnotes.

Wilson, Reginald
"The Daily Herald" and "compulsory propaganda." Spectator. 128:620-1. May 20, 1922

g. MISCELLANEOUS REFERENCES

Amery, Leopold Stennett
The era of the press Caesars. Nineteenth Century. 109:521-8. May 23, 1931
A fantasy visualizing the British Empire being governed by powerful press lords in the year 2231.

Book and a newspaper. New Statesman. (London) 34:370-1. Dec. 8, 1923

Griggs, Earl Leslie
Robert Southey and the Edinburgh Review. Modern Philology. 30:100-3. Aug. 1932

Marsh, G. L. and White, N. I.
Keats and the periodicals of his time. Modern Philology. 32:37-53. Aug. 1934
Bibliographical footnotes.

Thomas, William Beach
The story of the "Spectator" 1828-1928. 260p. London: Methuen, 1928
A general review of the Spectator's 100 years of existence (founded 1828); its editors and various collaborators.

Training for journalism at the University of London. School and Society. 43:144. Feb. 1, 1936

Wessely, Franz
Die Anfänge der Presse auf Malta. Zeitungswissenschaft. 13:429-34. July 1, 1938
History of journalism in Malta from 1644 to the present time.

White, N. I. See Marsh, G. L., jt. auth.

K. GREECE

Bach, Julian, jr.
The mailed fist in Greece. Nation. 145: 197-8. Aug. 21, 1937

Control of press news and views in Greece. Newspaper World. 21:2120, p. 8. Aug. 27, 1938
Excerpts from a confidential circular, Instructions for the Supervision of the Daily and Periodical Press.

Gaedicke, Herbert
Eine Statistik der griechischen Presse. Zeitungswissenschaft. 7:101-3. Mar. 15, 1932
Official statistics regarding the press of Greece, submitted to the Greek government under a ruling of March 22, 1928.

Heizler, Rudolf
Ein neues griechisches Pressegesetz. Zeitungswissenschaft. 14:79-81. Jan. 1, 1939
A detailed account of a new Greek press law limiting freedom of the press.

Huybers, John A.
The venal press in Athens—the incident at the French legation. Nation. 103: 391-2. Oct. 26, 1916

Meissel, H. E.
Das "Presse-Büro" der phanariotischen Prinzen. Zeitungswissenschaft. 3:186-7. Dec. 15, 1928

Mirkine-Guetzevitch, B. (Boris Sergieie-vich)
Recent developments in laws. Political Quarterly. 3:591-7. Oct. 1932
Survey of legislation curtailing freedom of the press in Turkey, Egypt, and Greece.

Politis, M. A. G.
Greek journalism and its influence; abstract. Great Britain and the East. 48:886. June 17, 1937

Short-lived Greek revolution taxed ingenuity of reporters. Editor and Publisher. 67:34. Mar. 16, 1935

L. HOLLAND

Blokzijl, Max
Die Presse in Holland und Holländisch-Indien. I–II. Wirtschaftsdienst. 14: 1669-72, 1712-14. Sept. 27, Oct. 4, 1929
The press in Holland and the Dutch East Indies.

Boskamp, M. A.-J.
Faire sérieux: telle est la formule des journaux hollandais. Presse Publicité. no. 32, p. 3. Feb. 21, 1938
The press of Holland tends to be more serious and substantial in tone than that of other countries.

Hamburger, Maurice
Le délit d'outrage à un groupe de la population. Cahiers de la Presse. 1: 27-42. Jan.-Mar. 1939
Discussion of new Dutch law prohibiting publication of matter offensive to one section of the population, also possibilities of its application in French law.

Hatin, L. Eugène
Les gazettes de Hollande et la presse clandestine aux XVIIe et XVIIIe siècles. 232p. Paris: R. Pincebourde, 1865
An old, but none the less valuable history of the gazettes of Holland and the clandestine press of the 17th and 18th centuries. The author's research on Holland seeks also to reveal roots of early French journalism.

Malssen, P. J. W. van
Louis XIV d'après des pamphlets répandus en Hollande. 226p. Paris, Amsterdam: 1936
Examination of 800 early pamphlets preserved in the libraries of Holland reveals an attitude of fear and bitterness toward Louis XIV.

Ninety dailies to reach 2,000,000 homes. World's Press News. 15:360 suppl. Jan. 23, 1936
A survey of the Dutch press.

Slewe, C.
How Dutch newspaper circulations compare abroad. World's Press News. 17:44. Mar. 18, 1937

What the people read in Holland, Belgium, and Switzerland. Review of Reviews. 32:185-8. Aug. 1905

M. HUNGARY

Csizmadia, Andreas
Die Presserechtsreform in Ungarn. Zeitungswissenschaft. 13:702-4. Oct. 1, 1938
A reform of press laws in Hungary, by creating a press department in the cabinet.

Johnson, Albin E.
Hard won rights of Hungarian news men scrapped in post war period. Editor and Publisher. 62:44. Oct. 26, 1929
A review of the newspaper situation in Hungary.

Kurth, Karl
Ungarn errichtet ein Presse- und Propagandaamt. Zeitungswissenschaft. 13: 548. Aug. 1, 1938
Hungary establishes a press and propaganda office.

Limedorfer, Eugene
Great newspapers of continental Europe. IV. Austrian and Hungarian newspapers. Bookman. 11:149-57. Apr. 1900

Polish and Hungarian governments are best censor-propagandists. World's Press News. 18:13. Dec. 9, 1937

Rossipaul, Lother
Von der ungarischen Pressekammer. Zeitungswissenschaft. 14:479. July 1, 1939
Hungary establishes a new official press bureau.

Skotthy, John
What the people read in Hungary. Review of Reviews. 30:590-1. Nov. 1904

Statistisches über das Zeitungswesen in Ungarn. Zeitungswissenschaft. 2:56. Apr. 15, 1927
Hungarian press statistics.

Szalai, T.
Beiträge zum ungarischen Zeitungswesen. Zeitungswissenschaft. 7:65-83. Mar. 15, 1932
Suggestions for a method of studying the Hungarian press.

Szasz, Menyhert
Newspapers unite Hungarians in all countries. World's Press News. 2-:499, suppl. p. xxxi, Sept. 22, 1938
——See Sziklay, J., jt. ed.

Sziklay, J. and Szasz, Menyhert, eds.
A Magyar sajto evkonyve 1937. Budapest: Hungaria Lloyd, 1937
Press handbook.

Über die Vergangenheit des ungarischen Zeitungswesen. Zeitungswissenschaft. 2:45. Mar. 15, 1927
A condensed report of a talk on the history of the Hungarian press by Dr. Emil Kumlik, librarian.

N. IRELAND

Book censorship in Ireland. Literary Digest. 100:23. Feb. 2, 1929

De Valera denies new constitution crushes press. Newspaper World. 40:4. June 12, 1937
> A press clause in the new Irish constitution was regarded by British newspapermen's journals as a threat to freedom of press.

De Valera modifies freedom threat in draft constitution. World's Press News. 17: 13. June 17, 1937

Dennigan, Joseph
Trade falls off, news is scanty as strike silences Dublin press. Editor and Publisher. 67:11. Sept. 29, 1934

Dublin's newspaper family. Newspaper World. 42:5. July 15, 1939
> The Murphys and the *Irish Independent*.

Eire appoints censorship chiefs. World's Press News. 22:11. Sept. 21, 1939

Fox, R. M.
Censorship in Ireland. Nation. 128:570-1. May 8, 1929
Censorship in the Irish Free State. Nation. 133:49-50. July 8, 1931
> Protests against suppression by the Irish Free State of books, plays and other printed matter dealing with sex and birth control.

Grene, David
Irish censorship. New Republic. 90:380-1. May 5, 1937

Grünbeck, Max
Die Presse Irlands. Zeitungswissenschaft. 11:393-403. Sept. 1, 1936
> An account of Irish newspapers including the part played by De Valera and his newspaper, the *Irish Press*. The rest of this survey recounts chiefly facts about the leading newspapers.
Von der Presse des Freistaats Irland. Zeitungswissenschaft. 11:127-8. Mar. 1936
> A brief review of the newspapers of Ireland and the incoming English papers and periodicals. Statistics.

Gwynn, Denis
Irish censors and English papers. Commonweal. 13:93-4. Nov. 26, 1930

I.F.S. government slashed for attacks on press. World's Press News. 13:2. May 23, 1935

I.F.S. government's silence on rumored press censorship. World's Press News. 13:2. May 23, 1935

Irish Free State government plans press censorship. World's Press News. 13:1. May 16, 1935

The Irish press is strongly entrenched. World's Press News. 4:49-51. Oct. 16, 1930

The Irish Republic speaks. Nation. 115: 132-4. Aug. 2, 1922

"The Irish Statesman." Freeman. 8:124-5. Oct. 17, 1923

Ordeal of the Irish press. Literary Digest. 68:22. Jan. 1, 1921

Passing of the Freeman's Journal. New Statesman. 24:356-7. Jan. 3, 1925
> Established as a daily paper in 1763, the *Freeman's Journal*, an Irish political paper, discontinued publication (1924), owing to armed violence by Irish Irregulars after a very stormy career of 150 years.

Powell, John Benjamin
Fighting Irish editor has seen "lost cause" become a reality. Editor and Publisher. 61:11. Aug. 18, 1928
> John Devoy, 86, has spent life in behalf of Irish freedom.

Press throttle alleged in new Irish constitution. Newspaper World. 40:1. May 22, 1937

Read, James Morgan
Atrocity propaganda and the Irish Rebellion. Public Opinion Quarterly. 2: 229-44. Apr. 1938
> A case study of the origin, circulation, and use of atrocity propaganda three centuries ago.

The Times and Ireland. Spectator. 123: 272. Aug. 30, 1919

Unknown persons with complete control over press. Newspaper World. 38:4. June 8, 1935

O. ITALY

1. HISTORY AND ANALYSIS

a. GENERAL DISCUSSION

Amicucci, Ermanno
Scuola di giornalismo. Nuova Antologia. 260:71-90. July 1, 1928
> Founding of the first school of journalism in 1927 at the University of Perugia.

Avanzi, Giannetto
La mostra storica del giornalismo italiano alla V Triennale di Milano. Nuova Antologia. 370:153-6. Nov. 1, 1933
> Journalistic exposition at Milan, May to October, 1933, showing the development of Italian journalism.

Boissier, Gaston
The Roman Journal. *In* Tacitus, and other Roman studies; tr. by W. G. Hutchinson. 227p. New York: G. P. Putnam's Sons; London: A. Constable, 1906
> In the original work (*Tacite*. 343p. Paris: Hachette, 1904) the chapter "Le Journal de Rome" appears on p. 239-78. It deals with publicity methods in ancient Rome which led to the establishment of *Acta Diurna Populi Romani*, the *Journal of Rome*.

Dresler, Adolf
Aus den Anfängen der italienischen Presse. Zeitungswissenschaft. 1:41-2. Mar. 15, 1926
> The beginnings of the Italian press.
Geschichte der italienischen Presse. 3v. Munich: R. Oldenbourg, 1933. 1934
> This comprehensive history of the Italian press includes a step-by-step story of Mussolini's activities as a journalist.

Kaffeehaus und Zeitung in Italien und Frankreich. Zeitungswissenschaft. 10: 313-18. July 1, 1935
An entertaining history of coffee houses and their relation to journalism in Italy and France.

Fattorello, Francesco
Il giornalismo italiano. 2v. Udine: Istituto delle Edizioni Accademiche, 1937
Il giornalismo veneto nel settecento. 2v. Udine: Istituto delle Edizioni Accademiche, 1937
Notizie per una bibliographia del giornalismo italiano. 2v. Udine: "Rivista Letteraria," 1936-37
First fruits of the author's forthcoming bibliography of Italian journalism.
Le origini del giornalismo moderno in Italia. 3. ed. 190p. Udine: Istituto delle Edizioni Accademiche, 1934

Levi, Cesare
La figura del "giornalista" nel teatro italiano. Nuova Antologia. 220:110-26. Sept. 16, 1922
The Italian theater considers journalists venal, servile and illiterate.

Östreichisch-italienische Pressebeziehungen des 16.-18. Jahrhunderts. Zeitungswissenschaft. 3:44-5. Mar. 15, 1928
Factors in Austro-Italian press relations from the 16th to the 18th century.

Piccioni, Luigi
Il giornalismo. 66p. Rome: Istituto per la Propaganda della Cultura Italiana, 1920
A bibliography of books, articles, and essays on journalism and journalists past and present.

Pompeati, Arturo
Sessantacinque anni di "Nuova Antologia." Nuova Antologia. 377:119-28. Jan. 1, 1935
Sixty-five years of Nuova Antologia and a review of its achievements.
Una storia della "Gazzetta ufficiale." Nuova Antologia. 369:317-19. Sept. 16, 1933
History of the *Gazzetta Ufficiale*. Official newspaper of the government of Italy; its vicissitudes and its influence on Italian culture.

Stein, Wolfgang C. Ludwig
Geschichte und Wesen der italienischen Presse. Preussische Jahrbücher. 200: 168-92, 287-392. Apr.-June 1925

b. TO 1870

Cavour und die Pressefreiheit. Zeitungswissenschaft. 3:88. May 15, 1928
The Italian patriot, Cavour, was a staunch advocate of political education through the press, and consequently fought to achieve freedom of expression in the press.

Cerro, Emilio del
Stampa e processi di stampa d'altri tempi. Rivista d'Italia. 16:93-112. 1913
The early struggles of the press in the Sicilies, about 1814.

Cironi, Piero
La stampa nazionale italiana, 1828-1860. Prato: Alberghetti, 1862
Story of the Italian press.
German translation by L. Assing. 155p. Leipzig: F. A. Brockhaus, 1863.

Claar, Maximilian
Die italienische Presse im Jahre 1850 nach handschriftlichen Aufzeichnungen eines Zensors. Zeitungswissenschaft. 11:311-16. July 1, 1936
An account of the stirring activity and censorship of the Italian press of 1850, from the impersonal handwritten notes of the jurist, Count Lorenzo Liverani.

The **Daily** press in Italy. Nation. 6:129-30. Feb. 13, 1868
Not less than 300 papers existed in Italy. They were decentralized, self supporting, and had few readers.

Dresler, Adolf
Cavour und die Presse. 72p. Würzburg-Aumühle: Konrad Triltsch, 1939
Cavour as a journalist, his influence on Italian press laws, news-gathering organizations and press politics.
Zur Frühgeschichte des Genueser Zeitungswesen. Zeitungswissenschaft. 9: 214-22, 256-64. May 1, June 1, 1934
A clear and entertaining account of the early written newspaper, and of the first printed newspaper of Michael Castellis that was printed, 1639-1646, and of the *Sincero* of Lucas Assarinos, 1646-1660. In 1682 all newspapers both written and printed were forbidden by law under punishment. An advertising sheet of about 1757 and the *Avvisi*, 1777-1779, are described.

Early Italian newspapers. Review of Reviews. 49:354-5. Mar. 1914

Fattorello, Francesco
Il giornalismo italiano dalle origini agli anni 1848-1849. 315p. Udine: Istituto delle Edizioni Accademiche, 1937

Greenfield, Kent Roberts
Economics and liberalism in the risorgimento; a study of nationalism in Lombardy, 1814-1848. 365p. Baltimore: Johns Hopkins Press, 1934

Italian journalism as seen in fiction. Blackwood's Edinburgh Magazine. 162:207-19. Aug. 1897

Manno, Antonio, ed.
Anèddoti documentati sulla censura in Piemonte dalla Restaurazione alla Costituzione. p. 1-199. *In* Biblioteca di storia italiana recente (1800-1850). Torino: 1907
Documented cases concerning the reaction of groups and individuals to press and book censorship in Piedmont from the Restoration (1815) to the Constitution (1848), the first period of the Risorgimento.

Thayer, W. R.
The life and times of Cavour. v.1. New York: Houghton Mifflin, 1911
Cavour was instrumental in the establishment of the leading Italian news-gathering organization, the Stefani agency.

c. TO 1922; THE MARCH ON ROME

Albertini gave Italy first modern daily. Editor and Publisher. 58:11. Dec. 26, 1925
> Managing director of Milan *Corriere della Sera*, deposed by Fascists, brought new life and methods to Italian press.

Cooper, Frederic Taber
Great newspapers of continental Europe. VI. Italian newspapers. Bookman. 11: 323-31. June 1900

Italian newspapers. Bookman. 11:323-31. June 1900
> The "clandestine" press of Italy and the obstacles to development of a political press.

Dieterich, Anton
Die Stellung Mussolini's in der Presse zum italienischen Kriegseintritt. Zeitungswissenschaft. 6:351-61. Dec. 11, 1931
> A chronicle of Mussolini's activity as a newspaperman before Italy entered the World War.

Dresler, Adolf
Mussolini's erste journalistische Tätigkeit. Zeitungswissenschaft. 13:81-100. Feb. 1, 1938
> A vivid portrayal of Mussolini as a journalist, to the World War, including excerpts from his newspaper writings.

Ferrero, F.
Free Italian press is still in its youth. Editor and Publisher. 51:98, 100. May 22, 1919

Guide to the foreign press: (II) Italy. New Europe. 7:19-24. Apr. 18, 1918

The **Italian** press and foreign policy. New Europe. 8:164-7. Aug. 29, 1918

The **Italian** press—its partial perversion. Catholic World. 85:721-7. Sept. 1907

Italy's new liberty of the press. Literary Digest. 78:20-1. Sept. 8, 1923

Piccioni, Luigi
Giornalismo italiano. Revista d'Italia. 17: 615-34. 1914

——and **Ugenti, Domenico**
Giornalismo italiano. Revista d'Italia. 17: 282-312. 1914

Thomas, A. V.
Newspaper control. Dial. 66:121-4. Feb. 8, 1919

Ugenti, Domenico. See Piccioni, Luigi, jt. auth.

Wood, Henry
Italy a press haven. Editor and Publisher. 13:331. Oct. 11, 1913

2. FASCIST REGIME

a. PRESS AND GOVERNMENT

Bertholz, Wolfgang
Press and dictatorships; abridgement. International Digest. 1:12-15. Apr. 1931

Buell, Raymond Leslie
New governments in Europe. 444p. New York: T. Nelson, 1935

Clough, Shepard B. See Schneider, Herbert W. jt. auth.

Darrah, David
Hail Caesar. 337p. Boston, New York: Hale, Cushman and Flint, 1936
> An indictment of Mussolini by an American correspondent who was expelled from Rome.

Dresler, Adolf
Mussolini als Journalist. 29p. Berlin: Walter de Gruyter, 1938

Mussolini und die Idee der Presse; die faschistische Presse 1922-1924. Zeitungswissenschaft. 13:561-70. Sept. 1, 1938
> Mussolini's concepts of journalism and what he expects of the party press in the Fascist programs for meeting the nation's problems.

"Fascistization" of Italian press. Nation. 117:305-6. Sept. 19, 1923

The **Fascists** roar—in print. Review of Reviews. 93:52. Jan. 1936

Guêze, André
Le régime de la presse en Italie fasciste. 260p. Paris: Sirey Collection, 1938
> The regime of the press in Fascist Italy.

The **Italian** press. Living Age. 320:205-8. Feb. 2, 1924
> A German correspondent in Italy warns readers against accepting at face value the quotations from the Italian newspapers that appear in dispatches, expressing hostility to France and friendship for Germany.

Johnson, Albin E.
Italy's press helpless in iron grip of Dictator Mussolini. Editor and Publisher. 61:24. May 11, 1929

Journalism under dictatorship. New Republic. 86:316. Apr. 22, 1936

Mussolini, Benito
My autobiography. 318p. New York: C. Scribner's Sons, 1928

Mussolini dignified journalism in Italy, Rome newspaper man says. Editor and Publisher. 61:24. Feb. 9, 1929
> Dictator cleaned up "blackmail press."

Mussolini outdoes himself. Nation. 120: 301-4. Mar. 18, 1925

Orth, Paul
Der Presseapparat der faschistischen National-partei. Zeitungswissenschaft. 10:145-7. Apr. 1, 1935
> An account of the workings of the "Partito Nazionale Fascista" (P.N.F.) propaganda and press.

Pew, Marlen
Shop talk at thirty. Editor and Publisher. 65:56. Sept. 24, 1932
> Mussolini an evil influence on Italian press.

Pierre, André
La main-mise du fascisme sur la presse italienne (1922-1927). Cahiers de la Presse. 2:271-8. Apr.-June 1938
A concise account of the manner in which the Italian press was gradually "fascisticized" and finally placed under the control of the Minister of Popular Culture, M. Dino Alfieri.

Salvemini, Gaetano
Mussolini chokes the press. Nation. 124:34-6. Jan. 12, 1927
Freedom of the press in Italy was guaranteed by the Constitution of 1848. Since 1923 this freedom has been nullified by the Fascist government.

The treatment of the press in Fascist Italy. New Statesman and Nation. 28:412-13. Jan. 15, 1927

Schneider, Herbert W. and Clough, Shepard B.
Making Fascists. 211p. Chicago: Univ. of Chicago Press, 1929

Schuyler, Philip
Only two anti-Fascist dailies survive Premier Mussolini's press gag. Editor and Publisher. 58:3. Feb. 6, 1926

Seldes, George
Sawdust Caesar. 459p. New York: Harper, 1935

Spencer, Henry Russell
Government and politics of Italy. New York: World Book Co., 1932

Swing, Raymond Gram
Only one truth. Vital Speeches. 4:78-80. Nov. 15, 1937

Villari, Luigi
Mussolini and the press. Saturday Review. 139:101. Jan. 31, 1925

b. OFFICIAL PRESS BUREAU

Cole, Taylor
The Italian Ministry of Popular Culture. Public Opinion Quarterly. 2:425-34. July 1938
A study of the organization, aims, and methods of the Ministry's six divisions.

Duce's orders to press disclosed in New York. Editor and Publisher. 70:20. June 12, 1937
27 decrees issued by the Minister of Press and Propaganda especially concerning the war in Spain.

Instructions to Italian press. Current History. 46:76. July 1937
Official instructions for handling news events covering the period Jan. 5 to May 10, (1937), secured from anti-Fascist paper, *Giustizia e Libertà*.

Das Pressbureau der Faschistischen Partei. Zeitungswissenschaft. 5:122. Mar. 15, 1930
The structure and development of the Fascist party press bureau.

Secret instructions to the press issued by Mussolini. New Republic. 91:142. June 16, 1937
A reprint from the *Manchester Guardian*.

Sereno, Renzo
Italian war propaganda at home. Public Opinion Quarterly. 3:468-72. July 1939

Servile press of fascism; instructions to Italian press. New Republic. 88:90. Sept. 2, 1936
List of instructions to the Italian press, showing the regimentation of news under fascism.

c. CENSORSHIP

Arbib-Costa, Alfonso
Journalism in Italy: 1933. Journalism Quarterly. 10:289-91. Dec. 1933
In political matters strict Fascist censorship prevails, although civic news is treated dispassionately.

Censorship in Italy. Living Age. 319:294. Nov. 17, 1923

Dell, Robert
Impressions of Italy. Nation. 138:670. June 13, 1934
British correspondent describes propaganda methods and press control in Germany and Italy.

European echoes: the Italian press. Living Age. 348:331-5. June 1935
Pt. 2 of a symposium. This article seeks to minimize the popular conception of rigid censorship in Italy, ascribing present regulations to growing pains of a newly born organism.

Gagging the press in Italy. Nation. 119:269. Sept. 10, 1924

Italian "immoral press censorship" denounced by U.S. newsman. Editor and Publisher. 58:10. Oct. 31, 1925

Johnson, Albin E.
"Wisecracks" about fascism barred by newest Italian censorship. Editor and Publisher. 62:24. Apr. 5, 1930

Seldes, George
The truth about Fascist censorship. Harper's. 155:732-43. Nov. 1927
This reporter, expelled from Italy, writes: "With the exception of Russia, Italy offers today the most flagrant example of journalistic terrorism in the civilized world."

d. PRESS LAW

A partir du 1er janvier, aucun journaliste italien ne pourra travailler pour la presse étrangère. Presse Publicité. no. 50, p. 8. Dec. 21, 1938
New Italian law (Jan. 1, 1939), forbids Italian journalists to collaborate with or be on the pay roll of foreign newspapers or news agencies.

Apolloni, Ettore
La nuova legge sul "diritto di stampa." Accademie e Biblioteche d' Italia. Annali. . . 5:453-64. 1932
The new law, "The regulation of the press," passed May 26, 1932, printed in full with favorable commentary.

Ascoli, Max
The press and the universities in Italy.
Annals of the American Academy. 200:
235-46. Nov. 1938
    A brief survey showing the passage of
the Italian press from a regime of legal
freedom to one of tight control, 1848-1924.

Assante, Arturo
Il giornale ed il giornalismo di stato.
58p. Napoli: Alberto Morano, 1937
    Seeks to show that the Italian people
are unwilling to relinquish to the state
the last traces of press freedom.

Fascism alters code of journalism. Editor
and Publisher. 65:40. July 30, 1932

"The **Fascisti** guarantee freedom of the
press." Nation. 116:280. Mar. 7, 1923

Geheimhaltung militärischer Nachrichten.
Zeitungswissenschaft. 10:27-8. Jan. 1,
1935
    Mussolini assures secrecy of military
news.

Naudeau, Ludovic
La liberté de la presse et le fascisme.
L'Illustration. 168:460-2. Oct. 30, 1926
    An examination of the reasons given by
Fascists for suppression of the liberty of
the press.

Press freedom in Italy. Living Age. 318:
340-1. Aug. 25, 1923

Veränderungen in der faschistischen Presse.
Zeitungswissenschaft. 5:31-2. Jan. 15,
1930
    Changes in the Fascist press following
the restrictions imposed by the press laws
of 1926-1927.

Verbot der Mitarbeit italienischer Journalisten an der Auslandspresse. Zeitungswissenschaft. 14:33. Jan. 1, 1939
    Decree forbidding Italian journalists to
represent foreign newspapers.

e. NEWSPAPERS AND NEWSPAPERMEN

Becker, May L.
The reader's guide. (Italian periodicals).
Saturday Review of Literature. 9:181.
Oct. 15, 1932

Murphy, James
The Italian newspaper press. Fortnightly
Review. 123:162-75. Feb. 1, 1925
    After the Matteotti assassination the
press of the whole country was put at the
mercy of the Fascist party. Description
and policies of various Italian journals.

Mussolini cuts size of Italian papers. Editor
and Publisher. 59:26. July 3, 1926
    Fascist economy plan limits newspapers
to six pages.

Robilant, Irene di
The Catholic press in Italy. Foreign
Affairs. 8:465-9. Apr. 1930
    Signing of the Lateran Treaty (1929) did
not bring expected relief to Catholic press
from Italian laws; Osservatore Romano
moved to Vatican City.

Stern, Robert L.
Political editorial is the heart of Italian
newspapers. Editor and Publisher. 58:
36. Aug. 15, 1925

f. FOREIGN CORRESPONDENTS IN ITALY

Brooklyn, Peter
Prison faces correspondents who violate
Mussolini's latest decrees. Editor and
Publisher. 59:12. Dec. 4, 1926
    With Italian press gagged, Premier using
every means to intimidate foreign corps.

Fascist government banishes Seldes for unfavorable news reports. Editor and
Publisher. 58:14. Aug. 1, 1925
    Chicago Tribune correspondent ordered
to leave Italy.

Johnson, Albin E.
Fascist dictator is snubbed by press.
Editor and Publisher. 58:11. Nov. 7,
1925
    Correspondents turn cold shoulder to
Mussolini who has terrorized press of
Italy.

Manning, George H.
Mussolini is barred from National Press
Club as enemy of free press. Editor and
Publisher. 61:16. June 9, 1928
    Expulsion of George Seldes, Chicago
Tribune correspondent, from Italy is cited
as one cause for rejecting Mussolini as
Press Club member.

Salvemini, Gaetano
Foreign correspondents in Italy. New
Republic. 86:369-70. May 6, 1936
    In a letter to the editor the writer ac-
cuses foreign newspaper correspondents of
being subservient to the Fascist government.

g. MISCELLANEOUS

Dresler, Adolf
Garibaldi und die Presse in der Tunisfrage.
Zeitungswissenschaft. 14:240-1. Apr. 1,
1939
    An account of the question of Tunis
taken from Garibaldi's letters on that subject to the press.

Il Giornalismo. Rassegna trimestrale di
studi sulla stampa periodica italiana
diretta da Francesco Fattorello; con-
direttore Antonio Galata. No. 1, Jan.-
Mar. 1939. Tolmezzo: Stabilimento
grafico Carnia
    Il Giornalismo is the name of the new
Italian quarterly on the press, the first
issue of which was dated Jan.-Feb.-Mar.,
1939. It is published under the direction
of Francesco Fattorello of the Univ. of
Rome and proposes to deal with the foreign as well as the Italian press. Its first
number is much on the order of the French
quarterly, Cahiers de la Presse, in form and
content.

Kaltofen, Rudolf
Die italienischen faschistischen Zeitschrif-
ten. Deutsche Rundschau. 222:55-7.
Jan.-Mar. 1930
    A brief comment on the periodicals of
Fascist Italy.

Migliore, Benedetto
Il diritto di cronaca e le esigenze della
morale. Nuova Antologia. 251:235-44.
Jan. 16, 1927
    The right to print the news is limited
by the right of the State to restrict the
press and by the right of the individual to
enjoy freedom of the press. Both parties
must contribute to an ultimate agreement.

Ott, Alfons
Italienische Kolonialzeitungen. Zeitungs-
wissenschaft. 12:308-11. May 1, 1937
  The press in the Italian colonies.

Wallisch, Friedrich
Das Zeitungswesen in Libyen. Zeitungs-
wissenschaft. 3:101-2. July 15, 1928
  The press in the Italian colony of Libya.

20 Jahre Popolo d'Italia. Zeitungswissenschaft. 10:26-7. Jan. 1, 1935
  A short account of this paper's attitude
  toward Germany during 1914-1915 and 1934.

P. POLAND (TO SEPTEMBER 1939)

Course of despotism. Editor and Publisher. 59:26. Nov. 20, 1926

Gustafson, David
Poland's fight for freedom helped by
hidden press. Inland Printer. 89:38.
Sept. 1932

Informator Prasowy, 1938-1939. 300p. Warsaw: Drukarnia Polska, 1938
  A Polish press directory containing much
  information regarding Polish press.

Jarkowski, Stanislaw
Die polnische Presse in Vergangenheit
und Gegenwart. Zeitungswissenschaft.
12:505-612. Aug. 1, 1937
  An exhaustive history of the Polish
  press, past and present, with correspond-
  ing statistics and an 8-page bibliography.

La presse, objet d'enseignement et
d'études en Pologne. Cahiers de la
Presse. p. 254-60, 289-92, 411-16. Apr.-
Sept. 1938
  In two parts.
  First attempt at establishing a center
  of study and research on the press were
  abortive in Poland for political reasons,
  but the past 20 years have witnessed the
  development of journalism into an important branch of higher education.
  The author tells of the achievements of
  L'École Supérieure de Journalisme at Warsaw. See p. 289-92 for a detailed program
  and list of courses offered at this school.

Johnson, Albin E.
Polish staff writers underpaid; free lances
take the cream. Editor and Publisher.
62:18. Aug. 31, 1929
  Criticism of government is taboo.

Muzzle is clamped on Polish press. Editor
and Publisher. 59:10. Nov. 20, 1926
  Dictator Pilsudski's decree penalizes
  publication of any news his government
  does not like.

Ein **Neues** polnisches Pressegesetz. Zeitungswissenschaft. 1:189-90. Dec. 15,
1926
  A new Polish press law.

Die **Neueste** Pressestatistik. (Poland).
Zeitungswissenschaft. 5:173-6. May
15, 1930
  Excerpts from official state statistics on
  the status of the Polish press.

Le **Nouveau** contrat collectif des rédacteurs
polonais. Cahiers de la Presse. 2:314,
327-32. Apr.-June 1938
  A translation into French of the principal articles of the new agreement of Jan.
  31, 1938 between publishers and journalists
  of Poland.

Olszyk, Edmund
Poland. Journalism Quarterly. 15:425-7;
16:78-81. Dec. 1938; Mar. 1939
  A survey of the Polish press and how it
  is organized.

Poles fight suppression. Editor and Publisher. 59:44. Jan. 1, 1927
  Editors hear new press law is being prepared.

Polish and Hungarian governments are
best censor-propagandists. World's
Press News. 18:13. Dec. 9, 1937

The **Polish Information Bulletin.** New
York, Washington: The Polish Information Service, 1930-39
  This fortnightly mimeographed bulletin,
  "sent free of charge to any institution or
  individual interested in Polish affairs," was
  first issued regularly in 1930, from New
  York to 1937 and from Washington, D.C.,
  to the issue of Dec. 1, 1939. It summarized
  and interpreted news concerning Poland,
  quoted and commented on news articles
  published throughout the world on Poland,
  and occasionally discussed the Polish press
  and press laws.

Polish Press Almanach. Katalog prasy
Polskieji obcej: Catalogue de la presse
en Pologne: Polnischer Zeitungskata-
log. 179p. Warsaw: Polska Agencja
Telegraficzna (Pat.), 1933
  Catalogue of Polish periodical publica-
  tions at home and abroad. In Polish,
  French, English and German.

Die **Polnische** Presse im ersten Jahrzehnt
des neuen selbständigen Staates. Zeitungswissenschaft. 3:183. Dec. 15, 1928
  The first decade of the new Polish press.

Das **Polnische** Zeitungswesen. Zeitungswissenschaft. 2:56. Apr. 15, 1927
  Polish press statistics.

Potulicki, Michel de
Le nouveau régime légal de la presse en
Pologne. Cahiers de la Presse. 2:
174-9. Apr.-June 1939
  Observations on the Polish press law of
  November 21, 1938. The author believes
  that the law seeks to reconcile two seem-
  ingly contrary principles: the authority of
  the state and the imprescriptable rights of
  the individual.

What the people read in Poland and Finland. Review of Reviews. 30:73-6. July
1904

Wrzos, Konrad
Poland's press. Independent Journal, Columbia University. 6:2. Feb. 17, 1939

Q. RUSSIA

1. HISTORY AND ANALYSIS

a. GENERAL DISCUSSION

Bauer, Erwin
Zeitungen und Zeitschriften in Russland.
p. 257-339. *In his* Naturalismus, Nihilis-
mus, Idealismus in der russischen
Dichtung. Berlin: Lüstenöder, 1890
  Newspapers and magazines in Russia.

Durland, Kellogg
The red reign: the true story of an adventurous year in Russia. 533p. New York: Century, 1907

Eckardt, Julius von
P.M. Leontjew und die russische Presse. p. 141-90. *In his* Russische und baltische Charakterbilder, aus Geschichte und Literatur. Leipzig: Duncker and Humblot, 1876
Condition of Russian press.

Fourth estate in Russia. Nation. 88:293-4. Mar. 25, 1909

Great Russian newspapers. Editor and Publisher. 13:682. Feb. 14, 1914
Russkoe Slovo, a Moscow daily, has circulation of 250,000 copies; *Retch* of St. Petersburg, 70,000.

The **Main** political school of the Russian people—the press. Review of Reviews. 48:95. July 1913
The provincial press in Russia is expanding despite severe administrative control.

Russian newspapers and magazines. Nation. 7:27-8. July 9, 1868
A general discussion of the newspaper press in Russia. Owing to lack of talent, the press did not take advantage of the measure of freedom it was given in St. Petersburg and Moscow.

Steveni, William Barnes
Petrograd, past and present. 319p. London: Grant Richards, 1915

Trench, F. Chenevix
The Russian journalistic press. Blackwood's. 148:115-26. July 1890
Russian journalistic press under censorship. List of newspapers and their policies.

What the people read in Russia. Review of Reviews. 29:457-8. Apr. 1904

Yarros, Victor S.
Great newspapers of continental Europe: Russian newspapers. Bookman. 11:235-43. May 1900
One of a series of seven articles on German, French, Austrian and Hungarian, Russian, Italian and Scandinavian newspapers. Describes the newspapers and their editors.

200 Jahre St. Petersburger Zeitung (Russland). Zeitungswissenschaft. 2:26. Feb. 2, 1927
200 years of the German newspaper in St. Petersburg.

b. TO NOVEMBER 1917

Edwards, Albert
The death and resurrection of the Russian press. Harper's Weekly. 50:424. Mar. 24, 1906

Rambaud, Alfred
History of Russia from the earliest times to 1882. Tr. by Leonora B. Lang. 3v. Boston: Page, n.d.
See v. 3, p. 271-4 on Russian periodicals during the reign of Alexander II (1856-1880).

Rochlin, Raphall
Die Anfänge der russischen Presse. Zeitungswissenschaft. 10:257-61. June 1, 1935
Interesting article on beginnings of the Russian press, including the contributions of Peter the Great and, later, of Catherine the Great.

The **Russian** bureaucracy. Spectator. 90:885-6. June 6, 1903

Russian newspapers have made great strides since the abolition of censorship. Editor and Publisher. 9:8. July 3, 1909

Sacke, George
Die Pressepolitik Katharinas II. von Ruszland. Zeitungswissenschaft. 13:570-9. Sept. 1, 1938
The interesting propaganda efforts of Catherine II in England, Poland and Austria.

Schierbrand, Wolf von
Conducting a Russian newspaper. World's Work. 5:2975-7. Jan. 1903
Government permission must be obtained; a "responsible editor" must be at the head of each newspaper; news is censored and infractions of censorship laws are promptly punished.

Scott, Leroy
The book and the revolution. New Outlook. 87:420-30. Oct. 26, 1907

Simmons, Ernest J.
English literature and culture in Russia, 1553-1840. p. 102-33. Cambridge: Harvard Univ. Press, 1935
The Russian press in the time of Catherine II.

Stepniak, Sergius (pseud.)
Russia under the Tzars. 2v. London: Ward and Downey, 1885
Vol. 2, ch. 29. The despotism and the press. ch. 30. The press under Alexander II. ch. 31. A sample from the bulk influence of the press despite suppressive governmental activities.

Villari, Luigi
Russia under the great shadow. 330p. London: T. F. Unwin, 1905

c. SOVIET PRESS, 1917-1925

See also
Newspapers and Newspapermen, p.155.

Beal, Fred E.
Proletarian journey. 352p. New York: Hillman-Curl, 1937
See chapters on censorship under Kerensky and the Bolshevist regime.

Bolshevik way with the press. Literary Digest. 64:25. Jan. 31, 1920

Bruck, Richard
The press of Soviet Russia. Living Age. 317:81-4. Apr. 14, 1923

Bryant, Louise
Six red months in Russia. 299p. New York: George H. Doran, 1918

Dean, Vera (Micheles)
Soviet Russia, 1917-1933. 40p. New York: Foreign Policy Association; Boston: World Peace Foundation, 1933

Education in Soviet Russia. Outlook (London) 51:124. Feb. 10, 1923

Ellis, William T.
How Lenin and Trotzky established an advertising monopoly in Russia. Editor and Publisher. 50:5. Jan. 5, 1918
  Writer, returning from adventurous trip through Russia, furnishes complete text of decree making advertising a state monopoly. All strong newspapers in country suppressed, including *Novoe Vremya* of *Petrograd* and the *Russki Slovoe.*

Faraut, Léon
The press under the Soviets. Living Age. 318:612-16. Sept. 29, 1923

Garry, Stephen
First Bolshevik worker's daily. Labour Monthly. 14:377-82. June 1932

Harris, F. T.
Russian press is slowly stifling under rigid Soviet control. Editor and Publisher. 56:30. Oct. 27, 1923
  Only 299 papers with aggregate circulation of 993,000 survive revolutionary chaos.

Kazarine, S. M.
The Soviet press. New Statesman (London) 21:260-1. June 9, 1923

Marcu, Valeriu
Lenin. 412p. New York: Macmillan, 1928
  Revolutionary paper founded by Lenin and fellow conspirators and published clandestinely.

Moravsky, Maria
Your newspapers and ours. Bookman. 48:584-90. Jan. 1919

The Press in the Soviet Republics. Nation. 118:748. June 25, 1924

Rise of the Soviet press in Russia. Literary Digest. 63:33. Oct. 25, 1919

Russian news bulletins. Nation. 107:604-5. Nov. 16, 1918

Russian newspapers since the revolution. New Statesman and Nation. 9:176-7. May 26, 1917

Russian papers red but not read. Literary Digest. 78:25-6. July 7, 1923

Says Russia's ugliest news not printed. Editor and Publisher. 57:34. Dec. 13, 1924
  Capt. McCullagh in *New York Herald Tribune.*

Soviet newspapers. Living Age. 318:476. Sept. 8, 1923

Talmy, L.
The Soviet press. Nation. 117:519-20. Nov. 7, 1923

2. RECENT PRESS

a. GENERAL DISCUSSION

Bolshevistskaja Pechat. (Bolshevist Press)
Moscow: Pravda
  This semi-monthly periodical, published in the Russian language in the *Pravda* plant in Moscow, is edited for newspaper-

men in the Soviet Union. It is essentially a trade journal which seeks to instruct and to inform the editors how they shall do their work and how to keep their efforts in line with the social, economic and political policies of the government.

Buchanan, Meriel
Moscow intrigues. Saturday Review. 161:712-13. June 6, 1936

Chamberlin, William Henry
Russia's iron age. 400p. Boston: Little, Brown, 1935

The Soviet press. Asia. 27:408-12. May 1927

Durant, Kenneth
Growth of the Soviet press. Journalism Quarterly. 14:83-5. Mar. 1937
  A brief sketch of the Soviet press by the manager of the New York office of Tass.

Durant, William J.
The tragedy of Russia; impressions from a brief visit. 164p. New York: Simon and Schuster, 1933

Farson, Negley
"Pacification" of the Ukraine. Nation. 132:14-15. Jan. 7, 1931

Fischer, Louis
Lies about Russia. New Republic. 67:94-6. Jan. 10, 1931
The Soviets in world affairs. 2v. New York: J. Cape and H. Smith, 1930

The Free press in Russia. Living Age. 345:267. Nov. 1933

Hill, A. V.
Foreign periodicals in the USSR. tables Science. n.s. 82:550. Dec. 6, 1935

Jaryc, Marc
Press and publishing in the Soviet Union. 24p. (Monograph, no. 6) London: London Univ. School of Slavonic and East European studies, 1935
  A useful synopsis.

Johnson, Albin E.
Russian newspaper men privileged workers under Soviet regime. Editor and Publisher. 62:32. Nov. 23, 1929

Just, Artur W.
Die wissenschaftlichen Zeitschriften. Zeitungswissenschaft. 1:72-3. May 15, 1926
  The science press of Soviet Russia.

Lee, Ivy L.
U.S.S.R. (Union of Socialist Soviet Republics). A world enigma. 158p. New York: Private Printing, 1927
  New ed. under title: *Present-day Russia.* 206p. New York: Macmillan, 1928.

Martin, Lawrence
Soviet press. Current History. 47:58-62. Oct. 1937

Morten, Lawrence
The Soviet press. Current History. 47:58-62. Oct. 1937

Passfield, Sidney James and Webb, Beatrice
Soviet communism. 2v. London, New York: Longmans, Green, 1935
Incidental references to the press.

Romm, Vladimir
The press in the U.S.S.R. Journalism Quarterly. 12:20-6. Mar. 1935
By the Washington correspondent of Izvestia, later removed from his post and recalled to the Soviet Union.

Soviet freedom for caricaturists. Literary Digest. 115:17. Jan. 28, 1933

Soviet lifts censorship. World's Press News. 21:3. May 11, 1939
London Times proposes to have Moscow correspondent, following announcement that outgoing messages from Soviet Union will not be censored but must not be "hostile or derogatory."

Stein, Gunther
What Moscow reads. Living Age. 341: 503-6. Feb. 1932

Strachey, John St. Loe
The Russian press. Spectator. 140:525. Apr. 7, 1928

Strong, Anna Louise
From Stalingrad to Kuzbas; sketches of the socialist construction in the U.S.S.R. 71p. New York: International Pamphlets, 1932

Webb, Beatrice. See Passfield, Sidney James, jt. auth.

b. PRESS AND GOVERNMENT

(1) GENERAL DISCUSSION

Butcher, Harold
Kerensky addresses foreign corps. Editor and Publisher. 59:8. Apr. 2, 1927
Attacks suppression of free press in Russia.

Chamberlin, William Henry
According to the press. Christian Science Monitor. Weekly Magazine Section. p. 6, 12. July 15, 1936
The Fourth Estate in Russia and Japan mirrors marked differences in public temperament and news emphasis, but both serve as object lessons regarding muzzled journalism.

Krassov, Vladimir
Journalism in Russia: 1933. Journalism Quarterly. 10:292-5. Dec. 1933
Editors may criticize flaws in the national program short of advocating revolution or criticizing government policy. The Soviet press handled news events frankly, and the readership increased enormously in contrast to pre-Revolutionary days.

Press and diplomacy in the Soviet Union. 24p. London: Univ. of London, 1935

(2) CENSORSHIP AND PROPAGANDA

Bertholz, Wolfgang
Press and dictatorships: abridgement. International Digest. 1:12-15. Apr. 1931

Bouroff, B. A.
Freedom of the press in Russia. World Today. 9:768-71. July 1905

Buchanan, Meriel
Red and black. Saturday Review. 161: 680-1. May 30, 1936
Soviet propaganda among the Negroes in the United States, Africa and elsewhere.

Chamberlin, William Henry
Russia is being seen through colored glasses. China Weekly Review. 71:41. Dec. 1934
Russia through colored glasses. Fortnightly. 142:385-97. Oct. 1934

Duranty, Walter
Russian news and Soviet censors. Spectator. 148:207-8. Feb. 13, 1932

Grady, Eve Garrette
Russian propaganda. Saturday Evening Post. 204:23, 80, 82. Aug. 15, 1931

Hullinger, Edwin W.
Battling for news in bolshevik Russia. Editor and Publisher. 54:5, 16. Jan. 7, 1922
Censor works in open but everything goes through his hands.

Literary censorship in Russia. Literary Digest. 94:27-8. Sept. 3, 1927

A **Real** reform of the Russian censorship. Review of Reviews. 31:608-9. May 1905

Russia and Italy press censorship described by United Press men. Editor and Publisher. 63:24. Mar. 28, 1931

The **Russian** censor and the Outlook. New Outlook. 73:351. Feb. 7, 1903

The **Russian** censor relents. Nation. 124: 218-20. Feb. 3, 1927

Russian censorship is fair, says Bickel. Editor and Publisher. 63:16. Aug. 9, 1930
An estimate by the general manager of the United Press.

The **Russian** press censorship. Outlook. 76:481-3. Feb. 27, 1904
Curious examples of Russian censorship.

Soviet lifts censorship. World's Press News. 21:532, p. 3. May 11, 1939
London Times proposes to have Moscow correspondent, following announcement that outgoing messages from Soviet Union will not be censored but must not be "hostile or derogatory."

Soviet's Izvestia demands end of censorship—but is forced to retract. World's Press News. 21:5. Mar. 23, 1939

Stone, Melville E.
The removal of the Russian censorship on foreign news. Century. 70:143-51. May 1905
The general manager of the Associated Press visited St. Petersburg and convinced the Russian government that official news sources should be opened to the American press.

Stoupnitzky, A.
La presse soviétique. Cahiers de la Presse. 1:88-103. Jan.-Mar. 1939
A critical discussion of the Soviet press, its role, organization and regulation, by the secretary of the *Revue Critique de Droit International.*

Tikhomirov, Lev A.
Russia, political and social. Tr. from the French by Edward Aveling. 2v. London: S. Sonnenschein, 1892
Vol. 2, Appendix C, p. 279-84: "Subjects forbidden by censorship."

Titus, E. K.
Soviet censorship becoming more reasonable, says Brooklyn writer. Editor and Publisher. 60:16. Aug. 20, 1927
Copy carefully scanned, but few deletions made.

Wales stories censored. Editor and Publisher. 63:10. Apr. 4, 1931
Soviet censors tampered with stories of Henry Wales, *Chicago Tribune* foreign staff correspondent.

Wollston, H.
Propaganda in Soviet Russia. American Journalistic Society. 38:32-40. July 1932

(3) PRESS LAWS

Lenin, V. Ilych
On the freedom of the press. Labour Monthly. 7:35-7. Jan. 1925

Maxwell, Bertram W.
The Soviet state. 383p. Topeka, Kansas: Steves and Wayburn, 1934
Ch. 15, p. 223-31, includes a discussion of the Soviet press and press laws.

No freedom of press in Russia. Editor and Publisher. 13:658. Feb. 7, 1914
Continual changes in regulations cause editors endless trouble.

Press censorship in Russia. Independent. 55:122. Jan. 15, 1903
Petition by Russian journalists for a revision of the press law was denied. Some paragraphs of this press law are cited.

Russia remuzzles press for 1914. Editor and Publisher. 13:568. Jan. 10, 1914
Issues a list of topics that may not be mentioned during 1914.

Throttling the Russian press. Literary Digest. 47:124-5. July 26, 1913

c. NEWSPAPERS AND NEWSPAPERMEN

See also
Soviet Press, 1917-1925, p.152.

The **Daily** press in Moscow. Nation. 114:578. May 10, 1922

Häntzschel, Kurt
Stellung der Presse in Sowjetrussland. Zeitschrift für die Gesamte Staatswissenschaft. 92:271-8. 1932

Jaryc, Marc
The press in Soviet Russia. Slavonic and East European Review. 11:530-42; 12:103-6. Apr., July 1933
Since 1932 a tremendous quantitative increase in newspapers accounted for 6,680 with a total circulation of 38 million. Newspapers are printed in 17 languages.

Just, Artur W.
Ausbau der Sowjetpresse. Zeitungswissenschaft. 11:385-93. Sept. 1, 1936
The various kinds of newspapers current in the Soviet Union, the production of machinery for newspaper plants and how the papers are sold. The activities of Tass, the Soviet news agency, are also taken up.

Die Presse der Sowjetunion; Methoden diktatorischer Massenführung. 304p. Berlin: C. Duncker, 1931
A German correspondent in Russia describes the Russian press and discusses propaganda methods.

Das Wesen der Sowjetpresse. Zeitungswissenschaft. 1:38-40. Mar. 15, 1926
Characteristics of the Soviet press by a German correspondent in Moscow.

Littell, Robert
Evening Moscow and Daily News. Living Age. 346:225-9. May 1934

McKenzie, Vernon
Soviet soldiers have own newspapers. Editor and Publisher. 62:13. Nov. 16, 1929
Fifteen strictly military dailies issued.

Pasvolsky, Leo
The Soviet newspapers. Forum. 68:736-46. Sept. 1922

Strong, Anna Louise
I change worlds. 422p. New York: H. Holt, 1935
In praise of the Soviet Union by American writer who organized the *Moscow News*, English language paper.

U.S.S.R. Handbook. London: Victor Gollancz, 1936

Walch, Erich
Zehn Jahre "Iswjestija". Zeitungswissenschaft. 2:72-4. May 15, 1927
Ten years of the Moscow newspaper *Izvestia.*

d. FOREIGN CORRESPONDENTS IN RUSSIA

Beal, Fred E.
Corrupted correspondents. Digest. 1:30. Oct. 2, 1937

Chamberlin, William Henry
Soviet taboos. Foreign Affairs. 13:431-40. Apr. 1935
The Soviet government forbids exportation of news of adverse conditions in Russia, such as famine, forced labor, religious persecution, or the depreciated ruble.

Durant, Kenneth
Soviet news in the American press. Journalism Quarterly. 13:148-56. June 1936
By the New York manager of the official Soviet news agency, Tass.

Duranty, Walter
I write as I please. 349p. New York: Simon and Schuster, 1935
How the correspondent in Moscow for *The New York Times* covers the news.

Griffin, Frederick
Soviet scene; a newspaper man's close-ups of new Russia. 279p. Toronto: Macmillan Co. 1932

High Soviet officials hard to interview. Editor and Publisher. 64:42. Nov. 7, 1931

Lippmann, Walter and Merz, Charles
More news from The Times. New Republic. 23:299-301. Aug. 11, 1920

A test of the news. New Republic. suppl. 23:1-42. Aug. 4, 1920
Examination of the news reports in *The New York Times* on aspects of the Russian Revolution, showing examples of newspaper bias and its causes.

Lyons, Eugene
Assignment in Utopia. 658p. New York: Harcourt, Brace, 1937
A former United Press correspondent in Moscow presents observations and opinions critical of the Soviet regime.

Reporting Russia; twenty years of books on the Soviet regime. Saturday Review of Literature. 17:3-4, 15-16. Dec. 25, 1937
Discussion, 17:9, 21-2. Jan. 22, 1938.

To tell or not to tell. Harper's. 171:98-112. June 1935

Mackenzie, Fred A.
Getting the news out of Soviet Russia. Editor and Publisher. 57:5. Mar. 7, 1925
Graphic story of reporter's life in Soviet Union.

Martin, Kingsley
The Russian press. Political Quarterly. 4:116-20. Jan. 1933
The Russian press openly criticises the Five-Year Plan.

Merz, Charles. See Lippmann, Walter, jt. auth.

Musgrave, Francis
Lenin, the "Times" and the Associated Press. Nation. 110:293-4. Mar. 6, 1920
The writer taunts the Associated Press and *The New York Times* for reporting several assassinations and many purported flights of Lenin.

Roche, John F.
Uninterpreted news of Russia puzzles prejudiced world, says Duranty. Editor and Publisher. 65:5-6. June 4, 1932

Sherwood, Harry S.
Freedom gained for Marguerite Harrison. Editor and Publisher. 54:5. Aug. 6, 1921
Baltimore *Sun* staff correspondent condemned to Russian prison as spy is freed.

Soviet government ousts Hullinger, U.P. correspondent, from Russia. Editor and Publisher. 54:24. May 20, 1922
Charged with having evaded censorship.

Tuckerman, Gustavus
Duranty reports Russia. 401p. New York: Viking Press, 1934
The work of the *New York Times* correspondent in Moscow.

e. MISCELLANEOUS REFERENCES

Fischer, Louis
The second Five year plan. Nation. 138: 182-4. Feb. 14, 1934

Krassovsky, Dimitry M.
New bibliographical periodical; Gazetnaîa Letopis (Newspaper Annals). Library Journal. 61:516. July 1936

Monroe, Paul
Observations on present day Russia: the culture program of Soviet Russia. 74p. Worcester, Mass., New York: Carnegie Endowment for International Peace, Division of Intercourse and Education, 1929

Russian money and the Daily Herald. Spectator. 125:231-2. Aug. 21, 1920

Schuman, Frederick L.
American policy toward Russia since 1917. 400p. New York: International Publishers, 1928
The attitude of the press, antagonistic to bolshevism, is explained under "The Poisoning of the Press," p. 151-7. Also other scattered references to the press.

R. SCANDINAVIA

1. GENERAL DISCUSSION

Dodge, Daniel Kilham
Great newspapers of continental Europe. VII. Scandinavian newspapers. Bookman. 11:439-46. July 1900

Moritzen, Julius
What the people read in Scandinavia. Review of Reviews. 31:206-9. Feb. 1905

Olberg, Paul
Scandinavia and the Nazis. Contemporary Review. 156:27-34. July 1939

Roemisch, Bruno
Das deutsche Element in den Gründerjahren der dänischen und norwegischen Presse. Zeitungswissenschaft. 13:652-9. Oct. 1, 1938
A short history of the part played by Germans in the early newspaper history of Denmark and Norway.

Scandinavian newspapers and reviews. Nation. 6:449-51. June 4, 1868

Zeitungen und Zeitschriften in Skandinavien zu Beginn des 19 Jahrhunderts. Zeitungswissenschaft. 14:398-400. June 1, 1939
An interesting article on the newspapers of Denmark, Sweden and Norway at the beginning of the 19th century.

2. DENMARK

Cavling, Henrik
Journalist liv. 301p. Copenhagen: Gyldendal. 1930

Christiansen, Valdemar and Foss, Victor
Journalistforbundets 25 aars jubilaeum.
Copenhagen: Gyldendal, 1929
Anniversary book of a journalists' organization, containing material on the society and on personalities.

Copenhagen newspaper readership leaps 35 per cent in six years. World's Press News. 18:42. Jan. 27, 1938

Denant, Henry
La nouvelle loi sur la presse au Danemark. Cahiers de la Presse. 1:405-10. July-Sept. 1938
The new Danish press law of July 1, 1938 preserves the liberty of the press intact but fixes more definitely the responsibility for matter published.

Elberling, Victor E., ed.
Avis-Aarbogen 1936. 209p. Copenhagen: J. H. Schultz, 1936
Annual. First edition 1925.
The Danish year book, which contains materials on the press.

Foss, Victor. See Christiansen, Valdemar, jt. auth.

Friebel, Otto
Die dänische Presse im Lichte der Statisticks. Zeitungswissenschaft. 10:112-14. Mar. 1, 1935
A statistical report of newspapers in Denmark 1924-1934, giving numbers of newspapers, economic development in advertising and numbers in editions.

Joesten, Joachim
Nazis and North-Schleswig. Spectator. 156:930. May 22, 1936
Four principal lines on which the Nazis are conducting their reconquest of North Schleswig.

Kirkeby, Anker
Politikens billedbog. 192p. Copenhagen: "Politikens" Forlag, 1920
Politiken's news pictures of the year.

Redlich, Monica
Denmark and its papers. Spectator. 162:591. Apr. 7, 1939
Reply by C. C. Bekkevold: Spectator. 162:768. May 5, 1939.

Rode, O.
Den Danske presse. Gad's Danske Magasin. 24:337-52. 1930

Sonning, C. J.
Politikens levnedslöb. 174p. Copenhagen: Nationale Forfatteres Forlag, 1911
The life span of Politiken, noted Copenhagen newspaper.

Sorenson, N. and A.
Avisen. Copenhagen: August Olsen, 1935
The Danish Avisen.

Stolpe, Peter M.
Dagpressen i Danmark, dens wilkaar og personer indtil midten af det attende aarhundrede. 4v. Copenhagen: Samfundettil den Danske Literatursfremme, 1878-82.
The daily press in Denmark, its make-up and personalities in the mid-19th century.

Swenson, David F.
A Danish thinker's estimate of journalism. International Journal of Ethics. 38:70-87. Oct. 1927
Incorporates translation of scathing criticism of the journalistic press from Sören Kierkegaard's diaries (ca. 1850).

Trap, Cordt
Pressestatistiske undersøgelser. 38p. Copenhagen: Nielsen och Lydiche, 1902
Investigations of statistics of the press.

3. NORWAY

Aarnes, Hans
Bladdrift; den okonomiske sida. 28p. Kristiansand: Agder Tidends Prenteverk, 1928
The financial side of newspaper management.

Bladmannen. 44p. Kristiansand: Agder Tidends Prenteverk, 1927
The newspaperman of Norway.

Bladstyraren. 60p. Kristiansand: "Agder Tidends" Prenteverk, 1926
Newspaper publishers in Norway.

Comprehensive media available for advertisers. World's Press News. 18: suppl. Nov. 11, 1937

Grassmann, Paul
Die Anfänge der norwegischen Presse. Zeitungswissenschaft. 11:23-5. Jan. 1, 1936
A brief survey of the beginnings of the newspapers of Norway.

Holst, Jens
Efter 10 aar. Betraktninger av en provinsjournalist. 62p. Tønsberg: Tønsbergs Aktietrykkeri, 1929

Kirkvaag, Ole A. K.
Arbeiderpressen i Norge. 51p. Oslo: Tiden N. Forlag, 1935
Labor press in Norway.

Morgenbladet gjennem 100 aar. Jubliaeumsavis, 1919. Oslo: Morgenbladet, 1919
The Morgenbladet of Oslo through 100 years.

Newspaper competition is keen in Norway. Editor and Publisher. 53:62. Apr. 30, 1921
Oslo has eight newspapers of general circulation, each having great political appeal.

Petersen, K.
Den Konservative Presseforening 1892-1917. 78p. Christiania: Kirste och Sieberth, 1917
The Conservative Press Society, 1892 to 1917.

Syrrist, Asbjørn B.
7 norske journalister og et anhang om den amerikanske presse. 32p. Tonsberg: Tonsbergs Aktietrykkeri, 1926
Seven Norwegian journalists and their relations with the American press.

Waage, Hjalmar, ed.
Hovedorganet. 6p. Oslo: Arbeidernes Aktietrykkeriet, 1930
Labor paper.

Winsnes, Fredrik H.
Omrids av norsk presserett. 100p. Oslo: H. Aschehoug, 1930
A survey of Norwegian press rights.

4. SWEDEN

Arstad, Sverre
Svenska Tidningsutgivareföreningen. Zeitungswissenschaft. 11:142. Mar. 1936
A brief account of this Swedish news agency, its makeup and the organizations with which it is connected.

Auerbach, Walter
Die politische Arbeiterpresse Schwedens. Zeitungswissenschaft. 5:191-211. 1930

Beskow, Bernhard von
Har sverige publicitet och publicister? Upsala: Upsala Univ. Press, 1839

Bjurman, Gunnar
Den svenska pressen förr och nu. 45p. Stockholm: 1929
The Swedish press of yesterday and today.
Tredje statsmakten; tidningspressens utveckling och nutida ställning. 300p. Stockholm: A. Bonnier, 1935
The press as the third power of the State.

Ekman, Ernst L.
Svenska tidningskungar. 189p. Upsala: Almqvist och Wiksell, 1924
Swedish press lords.

Guide to the foreign press: (IV) Sweden. New Europe. 7:115-17. May 16, 1918

Hedlund, Henrik
S. A. Hedlund, hans liv och gärning. 2v. Gothenberg: Göteborgs Handelstidnings Aktiebolags Tryckeri, 1929-30
The life and works of S. A. Hedlund.

How Sweden's newspapers cover the country. World's Press News. 18:suppl. VII. Dec. 2, 1937

Johnson, Albin E.
Happy medium of organization features Swedish press. Editor and Publisher. 62:36. Aug. 10, 1929
Journalism a leisurely profession with a livable wage scale.

Key, Emil
Försök till svenska tidningspressens historia. 200p. Stockholm: Bonnier, 1883
A history of the early Swedish press.

Klass, Eberhard
Aus der Frühzeit der schwedischen Presse. Zeitungswissenschaft. 14:119-26. Feb. 1, 1939
An account of early Swedish newspapers.

Kuhlmann, Gerhard
Ivar Kreuger und die schwedische Presse; ein Beitrag zum liberalistischen Pressesystem. Zeitungswissenschaft. 12:446-54. July 1, 1937

Lundstedt, Bernhard W.
Svenska tidningar och tidskrifter utgifna inom Nord-Amerikas förenta stater. 53p. Stockholm: Kungliga Bibliotekets Handlingar, 1886
Swedish newspapers and magazines in the United States.

Sveriges periodiska litteratur. 3v. in 2. Stockholm: Iduns Tryckeri, 1895-1902
Bibliography.

Marteau, F. A.
How Sweden's newspapers cover the country. World's Press News (Swedish suppl.) 16:v-vi. Dec. 3, 1936

Olberg, Paul
La presse ouvrière suédoise. Cahiers de la Presse. 2:149-73. Apr.-June 1939
A review of the Swedish labor or Social Democratic press, with descriptions and statistics.

Statistisches—Schweden. Zeitungswissenschaft. 2:74. May 15, 1927

Statistisches über die Zeitungen Schwedens. Zeitungswissenschaft. 2:88-9. June 15, 1927

Sweden, international press exhibition. "Pressa," Cologne, 1928. 111p. Stockholm: Norstedt och Söner, 1928

Swedish newspapers learn from U.S. Editor and Publisher. 56:19. Nov. 24, 1923

Sylwan, Otto
Den moderna pressen. 164p. Stockholm: Albert Bonnier, 1906
The modern press.
Pressens utveckling under det nittonde århundradet. 213p. Stockholm: P. A. Morstedt och Söners, 1924
A volume of the author's series on the history of the Swedish press.
Svenska pressens historia till statshvälfningen 1772. 498p. Lund: Distrib. Gleerupska Univ., 1896

Varenius, Otto
Svensk tryckfrihet. Stockholm: Fritzes, 1931
Freedom of the press in Sweden.

Wassén, Torsten
Hur en modern tidning kommer till. Stockholm: P. A. Norstedt och Söners, 1930
How a modern newspaper is produced.

Wieselgren, Harald O.
Lars Johan Hierta. 87p. Stockholm: Aftonbladets Tryckeri, 1881
The life story of a Swedish publisher who was a noted champion of press freedom in the middle of the 19th century.

S. SPAIN AND PORTUGAL

Brenner, Anita
Spain: viva la republica! Nation. 138:149-52. Feb. 7, 1934

Carter, W. Horsfall
Dictatorship and press in Spain. Fortnightly Review. 131:320-9. Mar. 1, 1929
The dictatorship of Primo de Rivera not extreme; censorship mild. Although on a leash the Spanish press has never been in better state.

Chaves, Manuel
Historia y bibliografia de la prensa sevillana. 375p. Sevilla: Impr. de E. Basco, 1896
The press of Seville.

Control of press in Franco's Spain. Newspaper World. 41:8. Apr. 30, 1938

Costa, Alfonso
L'ancienne influence des partis politiques portugais sur les journaux. Cahiers de la Presse. 4:646-7. Oct.-Dec. 1938
The great influence that political parties of Portugal formerly exerted through the press.

Deakin, Frank B.
Spain today. 221p. London, New York: A. A. Knopf, 1924
The press of Spain, ch.9, p.177-87.

Dresler, Adolf
Von der spanischen Presse. Zeitungswissenschaft. 1:121-2. Aug. 15, 1926

Fernsworth, Lawrence A.
Spanish "gag" active under republic. Editor and Publisher. 64:109. Apr. 30, 1932

Gonzáles, Manuel Grane
La Escuela de Periodismo; programas y métodos. Madrid: Ibero-Americana de Publicaciones, 1930
The School of Journalism; programs and methods.

González-Blanco, Edmundo
Historia del periodismo. 296p. Madrid: Biblioteca Nueva, 1919
History of the development of the periodical press. Seven appendixes on journalistic matters.

Guide to the foreign press: (III) Spain. New Europe. 7:42-4. Apr. 25, 1918

Hamburger, Ernest
Chronique constitutionelle de la presse: l'Espagne Nationaliste. Cahiers de la Presse. 3:453-4, 500-3. July-Sept. 1938
Summary and text of a press law promulgated April 22, 1938 by General Franco. It shows characteristics of totalitarian regulation.

Johnson, Albin E.
Muzzled Spanish press was primed to expose evils of dictatorship. Editor and Publisher. 63:34. Dec. 27, 1930
Censorship permitted publication of news but visited swift punishment on newspapers which printed matter displeasing to King or to dictator Berenguer.
New censorship of Spanish press stricter than Primo de Rivera's. Editor and Publisher. 62:18. Mar. 22, 1930
Spain's press muzzled but surly under De Rivera dictatorship. Editor and Publisher. 62:15. July 20, 1929
Must donate news space daily to government, but each item is labeled "forced publication."
Spanish newspapers the plaything of political prejudices. Editor and Publisher. 62:16. June 1, 1929
Journalism is usually a sideline.

Journalism in Spain. Editor and Publisher. 14:99. July 18, 1914
Political newspapers overshadow all others in Peninsula.

Kaltofen, Rudolf
Die Presse Kataloniens. Zeitungswissenschaft. 5:240-2. July 15, 1930
Interpretation of the press in Catalonia.

Kästner, Alfred
Die spanische Presse. 196p. Leipzig: C. und M. Vogel, 1926

Lingelbach, William E.
Spain moves toward fascism. Current History. 41:492-3. Jan. 1935

McCullagh, Francis
Freedom in Portugal. Living Age. 268:629-31. Mar. 11, 1911
The Portuguese Republic and the press. Dublin Review. 154:314-29. Apr. 1914
A vigorous criticism of the violent repression of the press by the Republicans after the revolution of 1910.

Die **Madrider** Presse nach der Befreiung der Stadt. Zeitungswissenschaft. 14:330-1. May 1, 1939
How the Madrid national papers reestablished themselves following the Civil War.

Ein **Neues** Pressegesetz der Regierung Franco. Zeitungswissenschaft. 13:492-4. July 1, 1938
Spanish Insurgent leader's new press laws.

Newspaper press and political literature of Spain. British Quarterly Review. 6:315-32. Nov. 1, 1847

Ossorio, Angel
Les journaux madrilènes à la fin du xviii° siècle. Cahiers de la Presse. 3:377-82. July-Sept. 1938
The primitive methods of gathering and publishing news in Madrid during the time of Charles III, by the Spanish ambassador to France.

A **Pioneer** Spanish journalist and publicist. Review of Reviews. 30:106-7. July 1904
Don Andrés Borrego founded the *Español* in 1835, a newspaper comparable in excellence to any, even in England. He edited seven journals and wrote 31 books.

Pressezensur—Spanien. Zeitungswissenschaft. 2:169. Nov. 15, 1927

Sheean, Vincent
Personal history. p. 63-78. Garden City, N.Y.: Doubleday, Doran, 1935
The author, a former foreign correspondent, describes his experiences as a newspaperman in Spain.

Spain crushes final hope of freedom. Editor and Publisher. 67:33. Feb. 16, 1935

The **Spanish** government and the press. Spectator. 103:452-4. Sept. 25, 1909
Outright discrimination by government censors.

Spanish press through Spanish eyes. New Europe. 7:310-12. July 11, 1918

Von der spanischen Presse. Zeitungswissenschaft. 3:23-4. Feb. 15, 1928
A survey of the Spanish press.

What the people read in Spain and Portugal. Review of Reviews. 31:586-8. May 1905

Die **Wichtigsten** Tageszeitungen in Madrid. Zeitungswissenschaft. 9:561-4. Nov. 1, 1934
    The important facts concerning the five largest daily papers in Madrid in 1934.

Xammar, Eugenio
Die Presse Spaniens. Zeitungswissenschaft. 10:377-95. Aug. 1, 1935
    An appreciative review of the press of Spain.
    In German and Spanish.

T. SWITZERLAND

Chapuisat, Édouard
Coup d'œil sur la presse suisse. Cahiers de la Presse. 1:83-95. Jan.-Mar. 1938
    A glance at the press in Switzerland; its origins, professional organizations, present status.

Fascist press censorship reaches into Switzerland. Editor and Publisher. 59: 49. Apr. 23, 1927
    Two Italian journalists opposed to blackshirts asked to place large bonds to remain in Geneva.

The **"Freie Zeitung"**—a democratic political organ. Spectator. 120:616-17. June 15, 1918
    In praise of the fearlessness and lofty idealism of this paper in proclaiming the issues at stake in the World War. The paper was launched at Bern, Switzerland, April 14, 1917.

Fusion of the Swiss reviews. Review of Reviews. 71:92-3. Jan. 1925

Giovanoli, Friedrich
Vom schweizerischen Zeitungswesen. Zeitungswissenschaft. 1:137-8. Sept. 15, 1926
    Statistics on the Swiss press, including the political affiliations of the newspapers.

Gossin, Albert
La presse suisse. 124p. Neuchâtel: Delachaux et Niestlé, 1936
    The history and present status of the press in Switzerland; statistical information on the 507 Swiss publications.

Guttinger, Fritz
Distribution of space in British and Swiss newspapers. Political Quarterly. 10:428-41. July 1939
    Bibliography and tables.

The **Ideal** newspaper. Editor and Publisher. 13:547. Jan. 3, 1914
    Swiss journalists agree on what should not be printed.

Johnson, Albin E.
Independent writers dominate Switzerland newspaper field. Editor and Publisher. 62:22. June 8, 1929

Katin, Louis
Journalism at the Zürich exhibition. Newspaper World. 42:7. July 15, 1939
    Survey of the Swiss press.

Kluge, E. E.
Le journalisme, matière d'enseignement à l'Université de Zürich. Cahiers de la Presse. 1:466-8. July-Sept. 1938
    Briefly reviewing the growth of the journalism course in the University of Zürich.

Kootz, R.
Verhältungen der schweizerischen Presse. Zeitungsverlag. 14:753, 777. 1913-14

Muyden, Berthold van
Histoire de la nation suisse. 2v. Lausanne: H. Mignot, 1899

Uebelhör, Max
Die zürcherische Presse im Anfange des 19. Jahrhunderts. 143p. Zürich: Rankim, 1908
    The press of Zürich, 1802-1821.

Von der Presse der Schweiz. Zeitungswissenschaft. 10:274-82. June 1, 1935
    A brief review and evaluation of the newspapers and publishing houses in Switzerland.

Weber, Carl
Die schweizerische Presse im Jahre 1848. 236p. Basel: Frobenius A.G., 1927

Weber, S.
Das Korrespondenzwesen in der Schweiz. Zeitungswissenschaft. 13:256-7. Apr. 1, 1938
    A brief perspective on foreign correspondence organizations in Switzerland during the World War and in recent critical times.

Wettstein, Otto
Die schweizerische Presse. Ihre rechtlichen, moralischen und sozialen Verhältnisse. Zürich: J. Lecmann, 1902
    The Swiss press.

What the people read in Holland, Belgium, and Switzerland. Review of Reviews. 32:185-8. Aug. 1905

U. THE VATICAN AND THE CATHOLIC PRESS

L'Action Catholique et la presse. Cahiers de la Presse. p. 313-14. Apr.-June 1938
    Criticism and remarks concerning some books and articles on the Catholic Action, an agency for the advancement of Catholicism, and the press.

Antoniazzi, Antonio
La stampa cattolica italiana. 216p. (Guide Bibliographiche Cattoliche, 1) Milan: Institute of Propaganda Library, 1937
    A guide to the Catholic press of Italy.

Brown, F. Clement and Stewart, George
The Catholic question in Canada: I. A struggle for freedom. II. The Index Expurgatorius in Quebec. Arena. 17: 742-51. Apr. 1897
    Pt. I. by F. Clement Brown; pt. II. by George Stewart.
    The effectiveness of the "mandement" and the Index in banning a publication.

IV. THE NEAR AND MIDDLE EAST

A. GENERAL DISCUSSION

Arabic journalism. Moslem World. 26:409. Oct. 1936

Arabic newspapers and mission work in Syria. Moslem World. 21:409-10. Oct. 1931

Kurth, Karl
Regierung von Saudi-Arabien errichtet Propagandabüros. Zeitungswissenschaft. 13:259. Apr. 1, 1938
The establishment of political propaganda bureaus among the Arabs by King Ibn Saud.

Nielsen, Alfred
Moslem mentality in the Syrian press. Moslem World. 20:143-63. Apr. 1930

Sprengling, Martin
An Arab editor surveys Japan and us. Open Court. 49:93-106. Apr. 1935

B. AFGHANISTAN

Dangel, Rudolf
Die Presse in Afghanistan. Zeitungswissenschaft. 1:55-6. Apr. 15, 1926
The press of Afghanistan.

Wessely, Franz
Die Presse in Afghanistan. Zeitungswissenschaft. 14:108-9. Feb. 1, 1939
A brief history of the press of Afghanistan.

C. PALESTINE

Gaedicke, Herbert
Pressestatistiks für Palästina. Zeitungswissenschaft. 9:174-5. Apr. 1, 1934
Two tables classify the newspapers and periodicals of Palestine, Table I according to languages and periodicity, and Table II according to languages and cities in which they are printed.

Gottgetreu, Eric
Public opinion in Palestine. Menorah Journal. 27:85-91. Jan. 1939
A summary of the views of Jewish and Arab newspapers on the proposed partition of Palestine.

Jerusalem News, a new American paper, price one piaster. Literary Digest. 64: 62-5. Feb. 14, 1920

Oenro, F. W.
Aus der Presse Palastinas. Zeitungswissenschaft. 4:366-8. Nov. 15, 1929
A sketch of the main centers of journalistic activity in Palestine.

Palestine censorship delays press messages. Newspaper World. 41:1. Oct. 22, 1938

Secret censorship of press messages from Palestine. Newspaper World. 41:2117, p. 6. Aug. 6, 1938

Sheean, Vincent
Personal history. 403p. Garden City, N.Y.: Doubleday, Doran, 1935
Sheean describes his experiences as a correspondent during Jewish-Arab conflicts in Palestine.

Zeitungswesen in Palästina. Zeitungswissenschaft. 4:234. July 15, 1929
A brief sketch of the press among the various racial groups in Palestine.

D. PERSIA

Browne, Edward G.
The press and poetry of modern Persia. 357p. Cambridge: Cambridge Univ. Press, 1914

Collins, Henry Michael
From pigeon post to wireless. 312p. London: Hodder and Stoughton, 1925

Current Mohammedan newspapers and magazines in Persia. Moslem World. 17: 86-7. Jan. 1927

Gaedicke, Herbert
Von der iranischen Presse. Zeitungswissenschaft. 14:326-8. May 1, 1939
Largely statistics on the press of Persia.

Hajibeyli, Jeyhoun Bey
Origins of the national press in Azerbaijan. Asiatic Review. n.s. 26:757-65; 27:349-59, 552-7. Oct. 1930, Apr.-July 1931

Kurth, Karl
Zentralstelle für Volksaufklärung und Propaganda geschaffen. Zeitungswissenschaft. 14:261-2. Apr. 1, 1939
Persia makes extensive plans for the education of its people through press, schools, radio, and theater.

Vom Hofe, Klopp
Die Entwicklung der persischen Presse. Zeitungswissenschaft. 9:392-7. Sept. 1, 1934
An account of the history of the Persian press.

What journalism has done for Persia. Review of Reviews. 39:352. Mar. 1909

Young, Herrick Black
The modern press in Persia. Moslem World. 24:20-5. Jan. 1934

Zantke, Siegfried
Das Pressewesens Irans. Zeitungswissenschaft. 12:1-6. Jan. 1, 1937
Press of Persia and the part taken by the present ruler, Resa Shah, in the rebuilding of his country and its press.

E. TURKEY

Angora on trial. Near East. 27:510. May 14, 1925
Reply by Jennan, *Near East.* 27:533. May 21, 1925.

Baker, Robert L.
The new Turkish diplomacy. Current History. 40:250-2. May 1934

Bleyer, Willard Grosvenor
New English dailies in Near East. Editor and Publisher. 55:42. Apr. 21, 1923
Jerusalem and Constantinople now have newspapers for English and American readers.

Ellis, William T.
Turkey—world center of news interest. Editor and Publisher. 55:2. Dec. 2, 1922
King-Crane report on the Near East; Balfour declaration on Zionism.

Emin, Ahmed
The development of modern Turkey as measured by its press. 142p. New York: Columbia Univ. Press, 1914

A **German** view of the Turkish press. New Europe. 8:113-15. Aug. 15, 1918

Gueron, E.
Turkey tightens censorship grip. Christian Century. 52:585. May 1, 1935
Twelve categories of publications are laid under interdict.

Halid, Achmed Bey
Die Press der Türkei. Nord und Süd. 53: 690-708. Aug. 1930
The Turkish press.

Jahn, Ferdinand C. M.
Turkish censor bans sensationalism, suicides, and sex appeal in newspapers. Newsdom. 5:3. Aug. 25, 1934

Just, Artur W.
50 Jahre türkische sozialistische Presse in Russland. Zeitungswissenschaft. 1: 120-1. Aug. 15, 1926
The Turkish socialist press in Russia.

Kord-Ruwisch, Will
Die Arbeiterpresse in der Türkei. Zeitungswissenschaft. 1:53-5. Apr. 15, 1926
The labor press in Turkey.

Die Presse in der neuen Türkei. Zeitungswissenschaft. 1:23-4. Feb. 15, 1926
A comprehensive survey of the press in new Turkey.

Levonian, Lutfy, ed. and tr.
The Turkish press: selections from the Turkish press showing events and opinions, 1925-1932. 216p. Athens: School of Religion, 1932

McCullagh, Francis
The fall of Abdul Hamid. 316p. London: Methuen. 1910
Mr. McCullagh was a correspondent in Constantinople during the decline of the Sultan's reign. His book is composed largely of dispatches and articles which he sent to the papers he represented.

Massignon, Louis
L'étude de la presse musulmane et la valeur de ce témoignage social. Annales d' Hist. Econ. et Soc. 2:321-7. July 15, 1930
A study of the Mussulman press and the value of this social testimony.

Newspapers in Turkey. Harper's Weekly. 50:933. June 30, 1906

Pears, Sir Edwin
The life of Abdul Hamid. p. 194-9. London: Constable, 1917
Attempts to control local and foreign press, forbidden news, newspapers which received subventions.

Die **Presse** des Islam. Zeitungswissenschaft. 2:89. June 15, 1927

Reinartz, Hans Armin
Die Istanbuler Presseverhältnisse bis zum Weltkrieg. Zeitungswissenschaft. 13: 322-3. May 1, 1938
Brief survey of Istambul press with a few statistics.

The **Spectator.** Outlook. 74:974-6. Aug. 22, 1903
Censorship of the press in Turkey is described as being "conducted on picayune ideas." Supervision is also exercised over books and telegrams.

Turkey's fighting newspaper. Literary Digest. 105:18. May 17, 1930

Turkey's polyglot press. Literary Digest. 51:113-14. July 17, 1915

Turks suppress blackmail papers. Christian Century. 51:1217. Sept. 26, 1934

Über die Presse in der Türkei. Zeitungswissenschaft. 10:282-3. June 1, 1935
A list of the principal newspapers and periodicals in Turkey, a brief history of its journalism and an account of the largest daily, Tan.

Das **Zeitungswesen** der Turkei. Zeitungswissenschaft. 9:502-7. Nov. 1, 1934
The press in Turkey, and a list of the most important newspapers in European and Asiatic Turkey.

V. AUSTRALASIA AND THE FAR EAST

A. GENERAL DISCUSSION

Alden, Roy
Pacific is center for next decade for world news. Editor and Publisher. 54:8, 37. Aug. 20, 1921

Australian and New Zealand press directory. Sydney: Country Press, 1938
Also includes the Pacific Islands, Fiji, New Caledonia, New Guinea, Norfolk, Papua, Samoa.

Lattimore, Owen
Facts do not speak for themselves. Pacific Affairs. 7:202-5. June 1934
Foreign reporters should not only report news but be able to interpret truthfully.

Lillie, J. J.
Journalism in the Far East. Saturday Review. 86:8-9. July 2, 1898
Mr. Lillie, editor of the *Siam Free Press*, complains against the Siamese government following his summary expulsion from the country.

Mail copy, not cable matter, tells real conditions in Far East. Editor and Publisher. 59:8. Dec. 11, 1926
Japan Advertizer executive, Frank H. Hedges, cites necessity of thorough "translation" of news events. Bare facts are meaningless.

Martin, Dudley B.
Western races misunderstand East, Kaltenborn says after tour. Editor and Publisher. 60:50. Oct. 15, 1927

Palmer, Dean
News from Orient sifted by alien censors. Editor and Publisher. 53:7-8, 42. July 3, 1920

Peffer, Nathaniel
Why news from the Far East is often unreliable and misleading. Editor and Publisher. 54:28. Nov. 26, 1921
Failure of foreign correspondent to distinguish between the important and unimportant and tendency of American editors to misinterpret events.

Stead, Henry
What the people read in Australasia. Review of Reviews. 33:469-71. Apr. 1906

Timperley, H. J.
"Makers of public opinion about the Far East. Pacific Affairs. 9:221-30. June, 1936
Correspondents have difficulties with translations, telegraphic facilities and censorship. News from China, and to a lesser degree from Japan, is therefore incomplete.

Trevelyan, G. M.
The white peril. Nineteenth Century. 50: 1043-55. Dec. 1901
Evils of journalism, its effects and the remedy, especially as it affects the Orientals.

Vaughn, Miles W.
High press wire rates chief bar to Far Eastern newspapers. Editor and Publisher. 59:24, 44. Nov. 13, 1926

B. AUSTRALIA

Australia and the Labour Monthly. Labour Monthly. 10:215-16. Apr. 1928

Australia: its trade and press. Newspaper World. 41:35. Dec. 3, 1938

Australia: the censorship of books. Round Table. 25:614-17. June 1935

Australian dailies take American news. Editor and Publisher. 50:10. July 28, 1917

Buchanan, Alfred
The real Australia. 318p. London: T. F. Unwin, 1907

A Century of journalism. The Sydney Morning Herald and its record of Australian life, 1831-1931. Sydney: John Fairfax and Sons, 1931

Curthoys, Roy L.
Australian newspaper men work differently than here. Editor and Publisher. 55: 8. Aug. 5, 1922
Everything is up to the individual and teamwork is unknown.

Foxcroft, A. B., ed.
The Australian catalogue: a reference index to the books and periodicals published and still current in the commonwealth of Australia. 118p. Melbourne: Whitcome and Tombs, 1911

Higgins, E. M.
Censor in Australia. Labour Monthly. 11:57-8. Jan. 1929

Lath, David
Union reporters work only five days a week in Australia. Editor and Publisher. 58:12. Dec. 26, 1925

Pratt, Sydney E.
Australian News Union has doubled salaries. Guild Reporter. 2:8. Sept. 1, 1935

Ross, Charles G.
Newspaper work in Australia. Editor and Publisher. 50:3-4, 19; 50:9, 36; 50:14, 37; 50:10, 35. Feb. 2, 16, 23, Mar. 2, 1918

Ryan, James S.
Starting as "Bush Savage" Sydney Bulletin now sways Australia. Editor and Publisher. 56:9 Nov. 24, 1923

Where Sunday papers are banned by law. World's Press News. 14:5. Sept. 26, 1935

C. CHINA

1. HISTORY AND ANALYSIS

a. GENERAL DISCUSSION

Latourette, Kenneth Scott
The Chinese, their history and culture. 2v. New York: Macmillan, 1934
Brief references to printing, v.2, p.313.

Liang, Hubert S.
Development of modern Chinese press. 20p. (Information bulletin, 4:1) Nanking: Council of International Affairs, May 12, 1937

Lin Yu-t'ang
A history of the press and public opinion in China. 179p. Chicago: Univ. of Chicago Press, 1936
History of the struggle between public opinion and authority in China. Pt.1 treats of the ancient oral ballads, public criticism and party inquisitions in Han and student petitions in Sung, censors and scholars in Ming, as methods of recording and expressing public sentiment. Pt.2; The modern press (since 1815).

Patterson, Don D.
The journalism of China. 89p. (Univ. of Missouri Bulletin, v.23. Journalism Series, no. 26) Columbia, Mo.: Univ. of Missouri, Dec. 1922
The field of journalism and the press in China, its history, background, characteristics, foreign publications in China, legal aspects, journalistic education in China, technical equipment, press associations and agencies. List of Chinese newspapers.

Wang, Y. P.
The rise of the native press in China. New York: Columbia Univ. Press, 1924

b. TO 1911

Asia's fourth estate. Nation. 86:460-1. May 21, 1908

Better news service. Editor and Publisher. 10:3. Nov. 5, 1910
    Far East newspapers to carry more news of the British Isles.

Chang Yow Tong
What the people read in China. Review of Reviews. 30:464-6. Oct. 1904

Chinese journalism. Independent. 64:1224. June 4, 1908
    As a result of the Russo-Japanese war, modern ideas have penetrated China thus promoting the growth of journalism. Shanghai was expected to be the center of further journalistic development. Chinese government decreed closer censorship of the press.

The Chinese periodical press 1800-1912. 151p. Shanghai: Kelly and Walsh, 1933

Chinese press. Editor and Publisher. 9:6. Aug. 14, 1909

Christian press in China. Editor and Publisher. 10:5. Sept. 24, 1910

Colquhoun, Archibald R.
China in transformation. 397p. New York, London: Harper, 1898
    Chapters on "The Question of Communication" and "The Native Press."

The Chinese press of today. North American Review. 182:97-104. Jan. 1906
    The Chinese press as of 1906; style, ownership, Japanese domination, influence of English-speaking countries.

Curious phases of Chinese journalism. Scientific American. 69:315-16. May 14, 1910

Michener, Carroll K.
From Confucius to "The Daily News." Catholic World. 123:20-7. Apr. 1926

The Native press and Chinese crisis. New Outlook. 67:188-9. Jan. 26, 1901

Ohlinger, Franklin
New journalism in China. World's Work. 20:13529-34. Oct. 1910

Some peculiarities of Chinese journalism. Review of Reviews. 32:242-3. Aug. 1905

c. 1911-1927

Borrey, Francis
Le paradis des journalistes. Journal des Débats. 33(2):664. Oct. 22, 1926
    Arbitrary arrests of journalists in Pekin at behest of war lords is protested.

China a propagandist playground, Glass tells press congress. Editor and Publisher. 54:15. Apr. 22, 1922
    Japan keeps heavy hand on Korean press, fearing revolution.

Chinese newspapers poor but vital. Editor and Publisher. 58:38. Feb. 13, 1926
    More than 700 dailies in nation; no advertising, poor communication and cumbersome alphabet.

Die Chinesische Presse. Zeitungswissenschaft. 1:184. Dec. 15, 1926

Christianity's journalistic door in China. Literary Digest. 52:122. Jan. 15, 1916

Gagging the press in China. Literary Digest. 48:152. Jan. 24, 1914

Gould, Randall
Editing a Chinese paper an "extra-hazardous" occupation. Editor and Publisher. 59:34. Oct. 2, 1926
    Two editors shot by military authorities; 120 "news agencies" in China.

Hutchinson, Paul
New China and the printed page. National Geographic. 51:687-722. June 1927

Körner, Fritz
Das chinesische Zeitungswesen der Gegenwart etc. Zeitungswissenschaft. 1:76-7. May 15, 1926
    Statistics on the contemporary Chinese press.

Newspaper enterprise in China. Review of Reviews. 43:110-12. Jan. 1911

Peffer, Nathaniel
Why news from the Far East is often unreliable and misleading. Editor and Publisher. 54:28. Nov. 26, 1921
    Mr. Peffer states it is due to failure of foreign correspondents to distinguish between the important and unimportant news and the tendency of American editors to misinterpret events.

The Press in China. Chinese Weekly Review. 45:384, 402. Aug. 18, 1926

The Proposed American paper for Shanghai. China Weekly Review. 37:83-4. June 26, 1926

Red journalism. Far-Eastern Review. 21:538-9. Aug. 1925
    John A. Brailsford, Kobe correspondent of the London Daily Herald, is taken to task for attempting to report events in Shanghai as though he were there.

Rich, Raymond T.
How to read the news from China. New Outlook. 140:363-6. July 8, 1925

Tong, H. K.
New journalism in China. Living Age. 313:83-6. Apr. 8, 1922

2. RECENT PRESS

a. GENERAL DISCUSSION

Betts, T. J.
Chinese public opinion. Foreign Affairs. 11:470-7. Apr. 1933
    Chinese public opinion is badly informed, inadequately led, imperfectly organized; often unexpressed, yet dynamic on occasion.

Britton, Roswell S.
Chinese news interests. Pacific Affairs. 7:181-93. June 1934

Censorship, illiteracy, circulation racket, retard Chinese press. World's Press News. 18:17. Aug. 19, 1937
China had 358 dailies in 1925 and 910 papers in 1935, plus 200 to 300 "mosquito" papers stressing sex and crime. Long lists of restrictions.

Chang, T. B.
The Chinese press since 1925. China Weekly Review. 71:227-8. Jan. 12, 1935

Chen, K. S.
Chinese papers as advertising mediums. China Weekly Review. 46:15-20. Sept. 1, 1928

China's "mosquito" newspapers. Literary Digest. 114:10. July 9, 1932

Fang, Fu-an
"Mosquito papers" and public opinion in Shanghai. China Weekly Review. 51:250, 256. Jan. 18, 1930

Has Shanghai a free press? China Weekly Review. 41:331. Aug. 27, 1927

Has the Chinese press begun to retaliate? China Weekly Review. 55:180-2. Jan. 3, 1931

Heads fall, grenades explode as terrorists attack newspapers. China Weekly Review. 83:320-1. Feb. 19, 1938

Hwang, Ching-shu
Suspension of newspapers in China. China Weekly Review. 54:359-60. Nov. 8, 1930

Joint press manifesto issued by 157 Chinese newspapers expressing their views on the Siam revolt. China Weekly Review. 79:108. Dec. 19, 1936

Journalistic ethics. China Weekly Review. 47:192. Dec. 29, 1928

Lin Yu-t'ang
My experience in reading a Chinese daily. China Weekly Review. 52:178-81. Mar. 30, 1930

Löwenthal, Rudolf
Public communications in China before July 1937. Chinese Social and Political Science Review. 22:42-58. Apr.-June 1938

——, comp.
Western literature on Chinese journalism: a bibliography. 69p. Tientsin: Nankai Institute of Economics, 1937
By a close student of the Chinese press at Yenching University.

——See Nash, Vernon, jt. auth.

Ma, W. Y.
A criticism of the press in Shanghai. China Weekly Review. 51:68. Dec. 14, 1929

McKenzie, Vernon
Many employees of Chinese papers have their homes in plant. Editor and Publisher. 62:56. Oct. 5, 1929
The newspaper situation in China.

Mayer, Norbert
Die Presse in China. Zeitungswissenschaft. 10:589-606. Dec. 1, 1935
The Chinese press in 1935 and its historical development.

Moorad, G. L.
When China goes to press. China Journal (Shanghai) 27:22-8. July 1937

Nash, Vernon
Chinese journalism in 1931. Journalism Quarterly. 8:446-52. Dec. 1931
China has about 1000 dailies, but many of them are very small and their existence is transitory. The author is an American, who for several years taught journalism in Yenching University.

Journalism in China: 1933. Journalism Quarterly. 10:316-22. Dec. 1933

——and Löwenthal, Rudolf
Responsible factors in Chinese journalism. Chinese Social and Political Science Review. 20:420-6. Oct. 1936
A demonstration with available data of how well, in spite of many drawbacks, the Chinese press is serving its purpose.

Press corruption in China. Literary Digest. 114:12. Sept. 17, 1932

The Press in China. Literary Digest. 97:23-4. June 30, 1928

Smallwood, H. St. C.
Modern press in China. Great Britain and the East. 49:202-3. Aug. 5, 1937

Smedley, Agnes C.
Corrupt press in China. Nation. 141:8-10. July 3, 1935

Sun, J. C.
New trends in the Chinese press. Pacific Affairs. 8:56-65. Mar. 1935

Waddell, J. A. L.
Dissemination of current news, information concerning world progress, and general knowledge. Far Eastern Review. 25:253. June 1929

White, J. D.
Chinese press goes American. Editor and Publisher. 67:x. Apr. 13, 1935

Young, C. Kuangson
La presse en Chine et ses services étrangers. Presse Publicité. no. 42, p. 7-8. Aug. 15, 1938
The Chinese press and its methods of gathering information.

b. PRESS AND GOVERNMENT

(1) GENERAL DISCUSSION

Can there be a free press in China? Far-Eastern Review. 25:53. Feb. 1929

The Chinese control of the China press. China Weekly Review. 55:441-2. Feb. 28, 1931

Chu Chia-Hua
China's postal and other communication services. 259p. London: Kegan Paul, 1937

Colquhoun, Archibald R.
Chinese newspapers. Current Literature. 24:452-3. Nov. 1898
Chinese newspaper technique is at its worst when foreign affairs are involved.

Ginsbourg, Anna
Chinese press control. China Weekly Review. 74:24. Sept. 7, 1935

Press in China—no freedom of opinion. Pacific Affairs. 4:532-3. June 1931
Chinese newspapers have been converted into official organs of the Nationalist government.

(2) CENSORSHIP AND PROPAGANDA

"Censorship should be conducted intelligently or abolished entirely." China Weekly Review. 74:216-18. Oct. 19, 1935

Chinese editors defy censorship, preserve best traditions of free press. China Weekly Review. 85:214-17. July 16, 1938

Chinese official publicity. Far-Eastern Review. 27:206. Apr. 1931
Official publicity is tainted with Nationalist or Communist propaganda within the country and abroad.

Continuous censorship in China bars U.S. grasp of events. Editor and Publisher. 66:16. Mar. 10, 1934

Lee, E. B.
China's lack of international publicity. China Weekly Review. 56:231, 238. Apr. 18, 1931

The **Muzzle** in China. Nation. 129:185-6. Aug. 21, 1929

Mysterious plot against Ariyoshi and the censorship situation. China Weekly Review. 72:107-9. Mar. 23, 1935

Nanking abolishes press censorship. Pacific Affairs. 4:64. Jan. 1931

Paper bombs. Asia. 38:535. Sept. 1938

Schuyler, Philip
Nationalist party of China behind efficient propaganda bureau. Editor and Publisher. 59:10. Feb. 26, 1927
Informative dispatches now reaching American newspapers from Hankow and Canton.

Snow, Edgar
The ways of the Chinese censor. Current History. 42:381-6. July 1935
Indiscriminate, ignorant, and unjust press control of China's central publicity bureau.

"Ta Kung Pao" censorship case and Sung Cheh-yuan's attitude on independence. China Weekly Review. 75:38-40. Dec. 14, 1935

Thackrey, T. O.
Censorship in China has been temporarily relaxed but never discontinued. Editor and Publisher. 67:37. Apr. 6, 1935

(3) PRESS LAW

China's new press laws. Editor and Publisher. 13:858. Apr. 11, 1914
Editors and publishers must be more than 30 years of age; publications must be licensed by local police.

National government's new press law. China Weekly Review. 55:422-3. Feb. 21, 1931

Ein **Neues** Pressgesetz. Zeitungswissenschaft. 5:44-5. Jan. 15, 1930
New press laws originating in the Kuomintang in an attempt to prevent the spread of "undesirable" publications.

Whang, P. K.
The problem of the freedom of the press in China. China Weekly Review. 70:300. Oct. 27, 1934

Yuan, L. Z.
New Chinese press law prohibits attacks on Nationalist party. Editor and Publisher. 63:44. Feb. 21, 1931

c. NEWSPAPERS AND NEWSPAPERMEN

Dean Williams on Chinese journalism. China Weekly Review. 45:353. Aug. 11, 1928

How Manchuria Daily News and Kokutsu distort the news. China Weekly Review. 76:232. Apr. 18, 1936

Löwenthal, Rudolf
The Tientsin press: a technical survey. Chinese Social and Political Science Review. 19:543-58. Jan. 1936

McKenzie, Vernon
Chinese newspapers and the men who make them. China Weekly Review. 50:376. Nov. 9, 1929

Newspaper directory of China, 4th issue. Shanghai: The Commercial Press, C. Crow, 1936-37

Passing of the last diehard foreign editor. China Weekly Review. 69:208-9. July 7, 1934

Thomas, Horace E.
Canton's two million read 43 daily newspapers. Editor and Publisher. 53:41. Feb. 12, 1921

Tong, H. K.
Developing a modern Chinese newspaper in Shanghai. China Weekly Review. 43:147. Jan. 7, 1928

Woodhead, Henry G. W.
Shanghai red weekly protested by Chinese. Trans-Pacific. 20:6. Aug. 4, 1932

Woodhead, Henry G. W.—*Continued*

——, ed.

The China year book. p. 279-89, 559, 561. Shanghai: North China Daily News and Herald, 1938

The University of Chicago Press is the agent in the United States for this volume. General description of Chinese daily newspapers, to which is added a list of the principal foreign newspapers and periodicals in China. A short history and description of the status of communications in 1937 is given on p.279-89.

d. FOREIGN PRESS IN CHINA

American advertising and an American press in China. China Weekly Review. 44:85-7. Mar. 24, 1928

American journalists and their works in China. China Weekly Review. 77:76-8. June 20, 1936

First American paper, *The Chinese Repository*, was published in Canton in 1930. List of other journals to 1936. Americans aided in introducing courses in journalism in Chinese universities.

American papers everywhere except in Shanghai. China Weekly Review. 36: 243. May 8, 1926

Ch'en Tzu-Hsiang

The English-language daily press in China. Edited under the auspices of the Department of Journalism, Yenching University. 26p. (Collectanea Commiss. Synodal. v.10, no. 11) Peiping: November, 1937

China and the foreign press. Literary Digest. 75:20. Dec. 2, 1922

The **Departure** of Editor Green of the N.C.D.N. China Weekly Review. 53: 168-9. July 5, 1930

Despicable reporting by the Shanghai Times. China Weekly Review. 50:153-4. Sept. 28, 1929

Early American newspaper issued in Shanghai. China Weekly Review. 56:145-6. Apr. 4, 1931

Johnson, Albin E.

Journalism in China undeveloped; called mercenary and colorless. Editor and Publisher. 62:32. Sept. 14, 1929

Many papers "fly foreign flag" for political convenience.

Löwenthal, Rudolf

Russian daily press in China. tables Chinese Social and Political Science Review. 21:330-40. Oct. 1937

The Russian Orthodox press in China. 8p. (Collectanea Commiss. Synodal. v.10, no. 12) Peiping: Dec. 1937

Rea, George Bronson

Twenty-five years: the Americanism of the "Far-Eastern Review." Far-Eastern Review. 24:145-51. Apr. 1928

Status of the American newspaper situation at Shanghai. China Weekly Review. 36:215-16. May 1, 1926

T'ien-Hu Chang

The French press in China. Edited under the auspices of the Department of Journalism, Yenching University. 7p. (Collectanea Commiss. Synodal. v.10, no.9-10) Peiping: Sept.-Oct. 1937

Work of the foreign newspaper correspondent in China. China Weekly Review. 46:suppl. 50-4. Oct. 10, 1928

e. FOREIGN CORRESPONDENTS IN CHINA

The **Case** of Chinese Republic versus The New York Times. China Weekly Review. 56:453-5. May 30, 1931

Chinese chaos told by I.N.S. reporter. Editor and Publisher. 66:33. Feb. 3, 1934

Vast difficulties facing those who sought to report activities of warring factions, related by Dixon Hoste of I.N.S. Staff.

Cooke, George Wingrove

China: being The Times special correspondence from China in the years 1857-1858. 457p. New York, London: G. Routledge, 1858

Covering China war stories against odds. Editor and Publisher. 59:7. Apr. 2, 1927

Communications greatest problem; American newspapers spending $5,000 a day to get news.

Green, O. M.

The organization of news from the Far East. 12p. London: Royal Institute of International Affairs, 1933

Pamphlet of presentation at the 5th biannual conference of the Institute of Pacific Relations, Banff, Canada, Aug. 14-28, 1933.

Kuangson Young, M. C.

La presse en Chine et ses services étrangers. Presse Publicité. 2:7-8. Aug. 15, 1938

Mr. Moore's private war. New Republic. 50:210-12. Apr. 13, 1927

Article attacks the warmongering dispatches from China by foreign correspondent of *The New York Times*.

Oestreicher, J. C.

Shanghai's still sending. Quill. 25:12-14. Sept. 1937

Powell, John Benjamin

The American correspondent in China. Asia. 27:380-2. May 1927

Was China "saved" by the foreign newspaper correspondents? China Weekly Review. 41:106-7. July 2, 1927

What the American press thinks about it! Editor Powell and China. China Weekly Review. 41:6. June 4, 1927

f. JAPANESE CONTROL

Censorship in North China. Living Age. 354:346-8. June 1938

Chinese editors and the war. China Weekly Review. 83:suppl. 20-1. Dec. 4, 1937

How Japanese pressure and Chinese censorship are killing the Chinese press. China Weekly Review. 74:289-90. Nov. 2, 1935

Japanese attempt to "buy up" Shanghai newspapers. China Weekly Review. 60: 67-8. Mar. 19, 1932

Japan's subsidized press in China. China Weekly Review. 42:242-5. Nov. 5, 1927
Until the time of the Washington Conference the Japanese government supported eight English language publications and many Chinese and Japanese papers in North, Central and South China, Manchuria and Korea for propaganda purposes.

Japan's thought control in North China. China Weekly Review. 84:346-7. May 21, 1938

Lack of censorship on Jap cable cause of distorted news. China Weekly Review. 72:274-5. Apr. 27, 1935

More uncensored Japanese cables on Yunnan political situation. China Weekly Review. 72:343-4. May 11, 1935

Rea, George Bronson
Adventure in American journalism in the Far East. Far-Eastern Review. 27:335-7. June 1931
The editor of the Far-Eastern Review defends his publications against charges by the China Weekly Review of being pro-Japanese.

Our friendship for China: Review attacked in the People's Tribune as a pro-Japanese organ. Far-Eastern Review. 28:6-7. Jan. 1932

About

The case of Adviser Rea and his Far Eastern Review. China Weekly Review. 63:193-4. Dec. 31, 1932
Owing to his pro-Japanese activities, Rea's monthly journal, the Far-Eastern Review, was deprived of postal privileges by the Chinese government.

Recent significant newspaper developments in China. China Weekly Review. 76: 182. Apr. 11, 1936
Reorganization of Chezz Peo, leading newspaper in Peiping, and establishment of offices in Shanghai of Tientsin newspaper, Ta Kung Pao, under pressure of Japan.

Tokyo defies Nanking on news—commercial censorship. China Weekly Review. 72: 240-1. Apr. 20, 1935

Wholesale suspension of Chinese newspapers follows extension of Japanese rule. China Weekly Review. 83:2-5. Dec. 4, 1937

g. MISCELLANEOUS REFERENCES

Fifth Annual Journalism Institute held at Yenching University. China Weekly Review. 76:453. May 30, 1936

Kuo, Wei-hung
Let us organize. China Weekly Review. 73:295. July 27, 1935

Liang, Hubert S.
Journalistic education in China. China Quarterly (Shanghai) 1:65-9. Mar. 1936
Peiping-Tientsin journalists organize society. China Weekly Review. 75:202. Jan. 11, 1936

Moy, Ernest K.
A school of journalism for China in Peiping. China Weekly Review. 48:519, 524. May 1929

Russell, J. T. and Wright, Quincy
National attitudes on the Far Eastern controversy. American Political Science Review. 27:555-76. Aug. 1933

U.S. newspaper men underwrite journalism school in China. Editor and Publisher. 61:30. Mar. 23, 1929
$50,000 fund assured to finance 5 years' work.

Wang, C. C. S.
China holds its first Journalism Week. China Weekly Review. 56:230, 238. Apr. 18, 1931

Willyoung, A. K.
Chinese journalism. American Press. 52: 20. May 1934
American methods taught in Yenching University.

Wright, Quincy. See Russell, J. T. jt. auth.

D. INDIA

Abbas, Khwaja Ahmad
Fascism over India. Asia. 39:323-7. June 1939
Totalitarian ideology, in spite of subtle, varied, and persistent methods of propagation, has thus far failed to affect public opinion in India.

India listens. Living Age. 357:55-8. Sept. 1939

Another censored message from India. China Weekly Review. 54:128. Sept. 27, 1930

Arnot, Sandford
A sketch of the history of the Indian press, during the last ten years. 88p. London: W. Low, 1829

Ayi Ten Dulkar
Das Zeitungswesen in Indien. Nord und Süd. 53:857-64. Sept. 1930
The daily press in India.

Bhownaggree, M. M.
The present agitation in India and the vernacular press. Fortnightly. 68:304-13. Aug. 1, 1897
Vernacular journalism in India is for the most part a tool in the hands of agitators (British malcontents especially) against British rule. Author advises curbing the liberty of Hindu press.

Bolton, Guy Reginald
Freedom of the press in India; Sir Stanley Reed celebrates his journalistic jubilee. Great Britain and the East. 50:123. Feb. 3, 1938

Bose, P. N. and Moreno, H. W. B.
A hundred years of the Bengali press.
129p. London: Luzac, 1920

Chatterjee, Ramananda
Origin and growth of journalism among
Indians. Annals of the American Academy. 145:161-8. Sept. 1929
    A short history of journalism in India,
1780-1927.

Chesney, G. M.
Native press in India. Nineteenth Century.
43:266-76. Feb. 1898

Circulations may soon be numbered in millions. Newspaper World. 40:38. Oct.
20, 1937
    The press of India.

Crime and the press in India. Spectator.
104:171. Jan. 29, 1910

Dev, D. Y.
Book censorship in India. Spectator. 158:
950. May 21, 1937

Falk, Roger
"India first" is the policy of all news-
papers. World's Press News. 17:suppl.
XI. Feb. 25, 1937

Fraser, A. H. L.
The press law in India. Nineteenth Century. 67:227-37. Feb. 1910

Freeman, A. A.
A tabloid in Bangkok. Asia. 30:555-60;
650-5. Aug.-Sept. 1930

Hossain, Syud
Sources of American news on India. New
Republic. 64:260. Oct. 22, 1930

Indian journalist says press is gagged. Newspaper World. 38:11. Aug. 24, 1935

India's press today. Newspaper World. 41:
26. Oct. 29, 1938

Journalism in partibus. Saturday Review.
76:704-5. Dec. 23, 1893

Lethbridge, Roper
Government relations with the press: an
Indian precedent. Nineteenth Century.
83:403-11. Feb. 1918
The vernacular press in India. Contem-
porary Review. 37:459-73. Mar. 1880

Low, Francis
The press in the new India. Newspaper
World. 40:27. Oct. 30, 1937

Mitra, S. M.
The press in India, 1780-1908. Nineteenth
Century. 64:186-206. Aug. 1908
    Various regulations for censorship were
imposed until 1835 when press freedom was
restored. Since 1878 new regulations have
been enacted to control vernacular press
accused of seditious publications.

Moreno, H. W. B. See Bose, P. N. jt. auth.

The Native press in India. Blackwood's
Edinburgh Magazine. 162:579-86. Oct.
1897

The New Indian Press Act. Spectator.
100:924-6. June 13, 1908
    The stringency of the new Press Act is
justified, in the opinion of the author, because liberty of the press, like representative and democratic institutions, is not
suited to Indian soil.

Party journalism in India. Near East and
India. 28:285. Sept. 3, 1925

Philip, P. O.
Indian press loses freedom. Christian
Century. 52:1430. Nov. 6, 1935
    Viceroy imposes law taking last liberty
from Nationalist papers.

The Pioneer's celebration banquet; extracts
from the speeches. Asiatic Review. 29:
124-30. Jan. 1933

The Press Association of India. Inland
Printer. 57:483. July 1916

Propaganda in India. Near East. 28:499.
Oct. 22, 1925

Ratcliffe, S. K.
An incident of Curzonian India. New
Statesman and Nation. 36:329-30. Dec.
20, 1930
An Indian editor. New Statesman and
Nation. 20:9-10. Oct. 7, 1922

Rees, J. D.
The native Indian press. Nineteenth Century. 49:817-28. May 1901

Sams, H. A.
India's improving communications. Great
Britain and the East. 48:614-15. Apr.
29, 1937

Stanhope, Leicester
Sketch of the history and influence of
the press in British India. 194p. London: C. Chapple, 1823
    Contains remarks on the effects of a free
press on alliances, on the administration
of justice, and on agriculture. Dangers
of a free press and of censorship.

Vijaya-Tunga, J.
The press in Ceylon. Newspaper World.
41:36. Oct. 29, 1938

Watson, Alfred
Journalism in India. Asiatic Review. 29:
254-64. July 1933
    The history of the British-owned press
in India.

Wiltshire, H. Roy
Journalism in Ceylon. British Institute of
Journalists' Journal. 26:161. Aug. 1938

E. JAPAN

1. HISTORY AND ANALYSIS

a. GENERAL DISCUSSION

Hanazono, Kanesada
The development of Japanese journalism.
100p. Tokyo: Nichi-Nichi, 1934
    A review of newspaper history in Japan
by the foreign editor of Nichi-Nichi and
lecturer in journalism at Waseda University.

Martin, Frank L.
The journalism of Japan. 38p. (Univ. of Missouri Bulletin, v.19. Journalism Series, no. 16) Columbia, Mo.: Univ. of Missouri, Apr. 1918
    An illustrated, general description of the rise and progress of journalism in Japan, plant equipment, kinds of news, government regulation, press association, foreign language newspapers.

Sugimura, K.
Japanese press grew and changed with nation of last fifty years. Editor and Publisher. 55:7. June 24, 1922
    First press clipped foreign news; then came political papers; now features of human interest are found in all.

b. 1868-1931

Cooper, Kent
News facilities few in Japan's wreck. Editor and Publisher. 56:7. Sept. 8, 1923
    First news of earthquake and fire by radio.

Flowers, Montaville
The Japanese conquest of American opinion. 272p. New York: George H. Doran, 1917
    Discusses Japanese propaganda methods designed to eliminate restrictions in the United States against Japanese nationals.

Glimpses behind the scenes of Japanese diplomacy. Current Opinion. 67:142-4. Sept. 1919
    Official news controlled by Press Bureau attached to Foreign Office. Correspondents transmitting news against its wishes are subject to expulsion.

Green, Thomas E.
The making of a Japanese newspaper. National Geographic. 38:327-34. Oct. 1920

Hanazono, Kanesada
Development of Japanese journalism. Trans-Pacific. 13:22. Nov. 6, 1926

Holt, Hamilton
Journalism in Japan and America. Independent. 71:1452-5. Dec. 28, 1911

Japan gets more U.S. news as cable and radio rates are slashed. Editor and Publisher. 62:48. Oct. 26, 1929
    Reduction to nine cents a word.

The **Japanese** magazines. Review of Reviews. 77:654-5. June 1928

Japanese news agency sending ten journalists on world tour. Editor and Publisher. 59:44. July 31, 1926

Japanese press. Living Age. 347:217-21. Nov. 1934

Die **Japanische** Presse. Zeitungswissenschaft. 4:218-33. July 15, 1929
    The status of the Japanese press and the problems peculiar to journalism in that country.

Japan's adolescent press. Bellman. 26:624. June 7, 1919

Japan's official propaganda. Literary Digest. 71:16. Nov. 5, 1921

Japan's periodical literature. Living Age. 313:498-9. May 27, 1922

Japan's press barrage on America. Literary Digest. 61:18-19. May 24, 1919

Journalism in Japan. Review of Reviews. 49:752. June 1914

Journalistic ethics and world affairs. 31p. (Univ. of Missouri Bulletin, v.25. Journalism Series, no. 32) Columbia, Mo.: Univ. of Missouri, Nov. 10, 1924
    Six experienced newspaper men express their views, in a series of addresses, on the ethics of journalism here and abroad.

Kawabé, Kisaburō
The press and politics in Japan. 190p. Chicago: Univ. of Chicago Press, 1921
    Relation between newspapers and politics in modern Japan.

Kawakami, K. K.
The Japanese press. Asia. 27:795-801. Oct. 1927

Kennedy, Malcolm Duncan
The Japanese press and its influence. Nineteenth Century. 105:634-49. May 1929

Press has proved benefit to Japan in spite of faults. Trans-Pacific. 17:13-14. May 16, 1929

Kikuchi, Hiroshi
Newspaper novel. Trans-Pacific. 13:7. Aug. 7, 1926

Low, A. Maurice
The yellow press of Japan. North American Review. 185:837-47. Aug. 16, 1907

McKenzie, Vernon
Old, new mingle in Japan's journalism. Editor and Publisher. 62:50. Oct. 19, 1929

Morris, John R.
Japan's dailies like American cartoons. Editor and Publisher. 55:18. Dec. 2, 1922

Nakagawa, T. J.
Journalism in Japan. Forum. 29:370-6. May 1900
    Historical development of modern journalism in Japan. By 1900 there were 745 periodicals; 20 dailies in Tokyo alone.

Nakano, Suyeo
Japanese press progress. Trans-Pacific. 16:5. June 30, 1928

Newspapers in Japan. Literary Digest. 53: 494, 497, 500. Aug. 26, 1916

Noguchi, Yone
Journalism in Japan. Bookman. 19:150-4. Apr. 1904

Paul, William
Capitalism, labour and the press. Labour Monthly. 7:560-9. Sept. 1925

Sammis, Walter
Phonetics and easy communication Japan's greatest needs. Editor and Publisher. 54:17-33. Dec. 24, 1921

Washio, Shogoro
Black third page. Trans-Pacific. 13:10. Jan. 23, 1926
Japan's public opinions. Trans-Pacific. 13: 21. Oct. 9, 1926

What the people read in Japan. il. Review of Reviews. 29:577-8. May 1904

Wildes, Harry Emerson
The press and social currents in Japan. 390p. Philadelphia: Univ. of Pennsylvania, 1927
Thesis.

Wood, J. B.
"Thought control in Japan." Nation. 112: 290-1. Feb. 23, 1921

c. 1931-1939

Chamberlin, William Henry
Japan's busy press world. Christian Science Monitor. Weekly Magazine Section. p. 8-9. Nov. 24, 1937

Howard, Harry Paxton
Blind leaders of the blind. China Weekly Review. 64:374-5. May 6, 1933

Inada, Sannosuke
Public service of phototelegraphy in Japan. Far Eastern Review. 27:759-62. Dec. 1931

Japan hopes to beat Western circulations shortly. World's Press News. 14:19. Sept. 19, 1935

Kennedy, Malcolm Duncan
The Japanese press and its influence. p. 180-203. *In his* The changing fabric of Japan. New York: R. R. Smith, 1931
These two chapters give a candid appraisal of the Japanese press, its national characteristics, connection with foreign news-gathering agencies, its independence, influence and faults.

Kessel, Elizabeth
Was steht in japanischen Zeitungen? Westermann's Monatshefte. 158:469-70. July 1935

Mattice, H. A.
Japanese books in American libraries. Library Quarterly. 8:13-24. Jan. 1938
Bibliographical footnotes.

Mighty ancestor. Time. 24:26. Dec. 17, 1934

100 words on Hauptmann. Editor and Publisher. 67:10. Apr. 6, 1935

Ozawa, Masamoto
Printed food for the millions. Contemporary Japan. 6:60-8. June 1937

Pierson, D. L.
Good news in the Japanese press. Missionary Review of the World. 57:507-11. Nov. 1934

The **Press** in Japan. New Statesman and Nation. 36:486-7. Jan. 31, 1931

Sassa, Hiro-O
Our public opinion: voices heard and unheard. Contemporary Japan. 5:545-57. Mar. 1937
Public opinion exists in Japan and is expressed in ways proper to the spirit of the Japanese people.

Stein, Gunther
Through the eyes of a Japanese newspaper reader. Pacific Affairs. 9:177-90. June 1936

Through Japanese spectacles. New Statesman and Nation. 3:159-60. Feb. 6, 1932

Wildes, Harry Emerson
Japan in crisis. 300p. New York: Macmillan, 1934
Includes a discussion of the Japanese press.

2. RECENT PRESS

a. PRESS AND GOVERNMENT

(1) GENERAL DISCUSSION

Army dictating to Japanese press on war reporting. World's Press News. 18:17. Sept. 2, 1937

Nakano, Suyeo
Throne and press. Trans-Pacific. 13:22. Nov. 13, 1926

Perry, John W.
Rengo agency takes blame for dispatch causing Japan attack on Stimson. Editor and Publisher. 64:5-6. Dec. 5, 1931
How errors in transmitting news cause international "incidents."

Press survey reveals serious anti-Chinese attitude of Japanese officials and government. China Weekly Review. 78:146-9. Oct. 3, 1936

Young, Arthur Morgan
The press and Japanese thought. Pacific Affairs. 10:412-19. Dec. 1937
Technically modern in practically every respect, the press of Japan does not reflect the better elements of public opinion because it follows too much the bidding of officials.

(2) CENSORSHIP AND PROPAGANDA

Chamberlin, William Henry
According to the press. Christian Science Monitor. Weekly Magazine Section. p. 6, 12. July 15, 1936
The Fourth Estate in Russia and in Japan mirror marked differences in public temperament and news emphasis—but both are object lessons in censorship.

Hanazono, Kanesada
Journalism in Japan: 1933. Journalism Quarterly. 10:309-15. Dec. 1933
Censorship of news by Home Office is very rigid. The author is an historian of the Japanese press.

Hansen, N.
Japan's foreign news-service. Living Age. 311:163-5. Oct. 15, 1921

Howard, Harry Paxton
Japanese propaganda, journalism, and history. China Weekly Review. 62:338-41. Oct. 22, 1932

Japan bans papers containing reports of Tokyo rebellion. China Weekly Review. 76:145-7. Apr. 4, 1936

Japan seeks to aid press. Newsdom. 6:1. May 18, 1935

Japanese censor holds up all reports of atrocities. China Weekly Review. 83: 199-200. Jan. 22, 1938

Japanese censorship, propaganda and anti-bandit campaigns in Manchukuo. China Weekly Review. 65:261-5. July 15, 1933

Japanese editor here to explain war aims. Editor and Publisher. 70:4. Nov. 20, 1937

Japanese impose cable censorship. World's Press News. 18:18. Dec. 9, 1937
Japanese install censors in Shanghai offices during Sino-Japanese War.

Lack of censorship on Jap cable cause of distorted news. China Weekly Review. 72:274-5. Apr. 27, 1935

More uncensored Japanese cables on Yunnan political situation. China Weekly Review. 72:343-4. May 11, 1935

No left turn. Fortune. 14:95-100, 102, 104, 106. Sept. 1936
The secret of Japanese success: thought police; thought bureaus; thought control.

Pew, Marlen
Shop talk at thirty. Editor and Publisher. 68:44. May 18, 1935
Japan's press censorship, including evidence to prove that freedom of expression in Japan has not been completely extinguished.

Saito denies Japan wants censorship. Editor and Publisher. 69:11. May 18, 1935

Spending vast sums to influence world opinion. China Weekly Review. 60:383-5. May 21, 1932

Tokyo defies Nanking on news—commercial censorship. China Weekly Review. 72: 240-1. Apr. 20, 1935

Young, Arthur M.
Collisions with Japanese authority. Asia. 37:703-7, 753-6. Oct.-Nov. 1937
The editor of an English newspaper in Japan describes his troubles with official censorship.
Japanese press censorship. Asia. 35:474-7. Aug. 1936

(3) PRESS LAWS

Japan plans press law. Editor and Publisher. 53:16. Feb. 5, 1921
Eight classes of articles are taboo.

Japanese newspapers fighting censorship. Editor and Publisher. 59:16. May 21, 1927
Oppose drastic new publication bill which prohibits many types of stories.

Morris, John R.
Japanese editors protest against oppressive regulations. Editors and Publishers. 55: 12. July 29, 1922
Power of Government to censor newspapers has been practically unlimited since 1909.
Japanese publishers and editors renew fight for liberty of press. Editor and Publisher. 54:18. May 20, 1922
Fourth national conference in Tokio asks for revision of vague and oppressive censorship and police regulation.

Revolt of the Japanese press. Current Opinion. 73:167-8. Aug. 1922

Wildes, Harry Emerson
Press freedom in Japan. American Journal of Sociology. 32:601-14. Jan. 1927

b. NEWSPAPERS AND NEWSPAPERMEN

Akimoto, Shunkichi
Japan's lord of printer's ink. Nation's Business. 16:23-54. Aug. 1928
The story of Seiji Noma, Japanese publishing tycoon, owner of nine magazines, one having a circulation of 1,500,000.
Seiji Noma, magazine king of Japan. 36p. Tokyo: Dai Nippon Yubenkai Kodansha, 1927

Bell, Archie
Adventures in a Japanese newspaper office. World Outlook. 2:19-20. Dec. 1916

Magazine king: Seiji Noma owns 80 per cent of all Japan's periodicals. Literary Digest. 122:16. Sept. 12, 1936

Nakano, Suyeo
Asahi's Jubilee. Trans-Pacific. 17:7. Feb. 14, 1929
Japanese papers abroad. Trans-Pacific. 16:7. Nov. 10, 1928
Tokyo newspapers. Trans-Pacific. 17:8. Sept. 12, 1929

Ramming, M.
Japan. Pressewesen der Gegenwart. Ostasiatische Rundschau. 16:155-60. 1935

Sanger, J. W.
Principal publications in Japan. p. 104-5. (U.S. Bureau of Foreign and Domestic Commerce. Special Agent ser., no. 209) Washington: Government Printing Office, 1921

Sato, Ken
Japan extends the hand; Tokyo Nichi Nichi and the Osaka Mainichi. Christian Science Monitor. Weekly Magazine Section. p. 1-2. June 9, 1937

Walter, Rudolf
Das japanische Zeitungswesen. Zeitungswissenschaft. 14:153-70. Mar. 1, 1939
Japanese newspaper systems today and their methods of work.

Young, James R.
J. R. Young tells oddities of news work in Japan. Editor and Publisher. 72:14. May 27, 1939

c. FOREIGN CORRESPONDENTS IN JAPAN

Japan drops Powell from official list. Editor and Publisher. 64:8. Mar. 12, 1932
Chicago Tribune man's dispatches and articles in *China Weekly Review* cited as basis for action.

The **Japanese** threat to "kill" Reuters news service. China Weekly Review. 74:365-6. Nov. 16, 1935

Kuh, Frederick
Censorship, wire delays, sub-zero weather vex Manchuria writers. Editor and Publisher. 64:20. Jan. 9, 1932

McReynolds, George E. See Tupper, Eleanor, jt. auth.

Perry, John W.
Manchurian "war" costly to newspapers; far flung area hard to cover. Editor and Publisher. 64:5-6. Nov. 14, 1931

No pressure on writers in Japan, Hearst correspondent says. Editor and Publisher. 66:14. July 8, 1933

Stein, Gunther
News from Japan. Living Age. 350:12-14. Mar. 1936

Tupper, Eleanor and McReynolds, George E.
Japan in American public opinion. 465p. New York: Macmillan, 1937
An interesting study of the methods and techniques of influencing public opinion.

U.S. writer accused by Japanese. Editor and Publisher. 65:8. June 25, 1932

Woodhead, Henry G. W.
Adventures in Far Eastern journalism. 266p. Tokio: Hokuseido Press, 1935
Journalistic experiences in China. Author was editor of the *Peking & Tientsin Times.*

F. OTHER COUNTRIES

Alsagoff, Hussein A.
Vernacular press has gone ahead in past eight years. World's Press News. 17: Malaya suppl. xiii. May 13, 1937

English dailies in the Peninsula. World's Press News. 17:Malaya suppl. viii. May 13, 1937

Faber, G. H. von
A short history of journalism in the Dutch East Indies. 160p. Sourabaya, Java: G. Kolff, 1932

Freedom of the press in Korea. Nation. 130: 652-3. June 4, 1930

New Zealanders avid newspaper readers. Editor and Publisher. 59:12. Dec. 11, 1926
Islands now have 200 papers.

Standing, Percy Cross
Journalism in the Far East. Saturday Review. 86:79. July 16, 1898
In a letter to the editor this correspondent defends the action of Siamese authorities in expelling Mr. J. J. Lillie, editor of the *Siam Free Press* from their country because of persistent defamation of Siam.

Stong, Phil D.
King of Siam's daily Americanized by New York newspaper man. Editor and Publisher. 61:16. Aug. 11, 1928

Zwemer, Samuel Marinus
Native press of the Dutch East Indies. Moslem World. 13:39-49. Jan. 1923

VI. LATIN AMERICA

A. GENERAL DISCUSSION

Arbaiza, Genaro
Latin America falls in line. American Mercury. 14:28-37. May 1928
The Americanization of the Spanish American press.

Babcock, C. E.
Newspaper files in the library of the Pan-American union. Hispanic-American Historical Review. 6:288. Nov. 1926

Barbagelata, Hugo D.
La presse de l'Amérique Latine. 12p. (Cahiers de Politique Étrangère, no. 37) Paris: Institut des Études Américaines, 1937
A review of the press of the Latin-American republics.

Beals, Carleton
Fire on the Andes. 481p. Philadelphia: Lippincott, 1934

Behrendt, Richard F.
Foreign influences in Latin America. Annals of the American Academy. 204:1-8. July 1939
Dr. Behrendt, professor of economics and sociology at the University of Panama, makes an appraisal of the extent and efficacy of totalitarian influence in Latin America.

Benét, Stephen Vincent
The United Press. Fortune. 7:67-72, 94, 97-8, 100, 102, 104. May 1933
Includes a discussion of the successful invasion of South America by the United Press, beginning in 1916.

Bickel, Karl August
South American newspapers prospering. Editor and Publisher. 58:10. Dec. 19, 1925

British news in South America—government aid asked. World's Press News. 18:19. Oct. 21, 1937

Butcher, Harold
South America seen as future U.S. news field. Editor and Publisher. 70:48. Oct. 23, 1937

Cable communications with South America. Review. 4:455. May 14, 1921
A dispute over cable landings between the Western Union and the British Telegraph Company.

Campbell, J. Bart
U.S. welcomes Latin American editors. Editor and Publisher. 58:25. Apr. 10, 1926
Twenty-one South and Central American republics represented.

Cohen, Bernard
South American journalism in 1931. Journalism Quarterly. 8:429-34. Dec. 1931

Cruickshank, A. J.
International news in Central and South America. Pan-American Magazine. 39:217-19. Jan. 1927

Doyle, Henry Grattan
The press in the development of an inter-American educational program. Pan-American Magazine. 44:211-15. Mar. 1931

English newspapers in Latin America. Harper's Weekly. 52:33. Sept. 12, 1908

Gerald, J. Edward
Aspects of journalism in South America. Journalism Quarterly. 8:213-23. June 1931

Goldberg, Isaac
What South Americans read. Bookman. 41:478-89. July 1915

Goldsmith, Peter
Latin American periodicals, containing bibliographies. Library Journal. 45:558. June 15, 1920

Harbord, James G.
My visit to South America. Outlook. 141:351-2. Nov. 4, 1925

Hole, M. Cadwalader
The early Latin-American press. English and Spanish texts: bibliography. Bulletin of the Pan-American Union. 60:323-52. Apr. 1926; *reprint* Review of Reviews. 73:540-2. May 1926
A condensed survey of the history and development of the press, characteristics of various dailies and their fight for freedom. *See also* "The Press in Chile", p.177.
In Spanish and English.
Bibliography.
The early Latin American press and development of the press of the Argentine republic. (Pan-American Miscellany, no. 6) Washington: Government Printing Office, 1926

Jones, Joseph L.
Press services tell Americas about each other. Pan-American Magazine. 43:302-8. Nov. 1930

Kihss, Peter F.
Headline hunting in South America. Quill. 23:6-7. May 1935

Madden, M. R.
Latin America and propaganda. Commonweal. 14:316-18. July 29, 1931

Mitre, Jorge A.
Untilled international fields for press. Editor and Publisher. 58:27. Apr. 10, 1926
South America now well served with news but little news of Latin life moves northward.

Newspaper directory of Latin America. 38p.
Washington: International Bureau of the American Republics, Government Printing Office, 1892

Pan American Congress of Journalists, Washington, 1926
Proceedings of the First Pan-American Conference of Journalists. 229p. Washington: Pan American Union, 1926

Pan-American press good-will. Literary Digest. 89:10-11. May 8, 1926

Reciprocity of interest between North and South America. Editor and Publisher. 58:18. May 8, 1926

Rodriguez, Virgilio Beteta
Perils of inquisition threatened first Latin American editors. Editor and Publisher. 58:130. Apr. 30, 1926
Press in early days an organ of Church and State, and in fear of both when it began to break shackles of authority.

Shepherd, William R.
Latin America. 256p. New York: Henry Holt, 1914
Ch. 19, p. 215-27: Journalism. A general description of the various newspapers in Central and South America.

Simondetti, Ernest T.
South American newspaper notes. Editor and Publisher. 12:11, 14. Jan. 18, 1913
The characteristics of the Latin-American newspapers.

South American newspapers prospering. Editor and Publisher. 58:10. Dec. 19, 1925

Tannenbaum, Frank
Whither Latin America? 185p. New York: Thomas Y. Crowell, 1935

Thompson, Wallace
The American press in Latin America. Bulletin of the Pan-American Union. 59:5-12. Jan. 1925

Von der Presse Latein-Amerikas. Zeitungswissenschaft. 3:153. Oct. 15, 1928

Warshaw, Jacob
The new Latin-America. 415p. New York: Thomas Y. Crowell, 1922
Description of Latin America of today and its relation with the United States. Newspapers, p. 252.

B. ARGENTINE REPUBLIC

C. BOLIVIA

Reyes, Frederico Nielsen
Die bolivianische Presse. Zeitungswissenschaft. 10:464-73. Aug. 1, 1935
    Review of the history of Bolivian journalism from the time of Bolivar up to the present.

D. BRAZIL

Brandenburger, Clemens
Presse in Brasilien. Weltwirtschaftliches Archiv. 23:479. 1926

Brazil censorship raised. Editor and Publisher. 64:8. Aug. 15, 1931
    Direct governmental press censorship in Brazil was finally abolished by Provisional President Vargas. Responsibility for publication of sensational and inaccurate news concerning the government will be borne by the newspapers and the news agencies themselves in the future.

Brazil ousts writer on false charge. Editor and Publisher. 64:7. Jan. 2, 1932; American Press. 50:5. Jan. 1932
    George H. Corey, *New York Times* correspondent in Brazil, arrested and forced to leave the country for sending out news "prejudicial" to that country.

Brazil revolt hard story to cover. Editor and Publisher. 63:6. Oct. 18, 1930

Burton, Wilbur
Swastika and Sigma in Brazil. Spectator. 159:419. Sept. 10, 1937

Cooper, Clayton Sedgwick
The newspaper press of Rio de Janeiro. Editor and Publisher. 49:5-6. Jan. 20, 1917

Corey, George H.
Times man a victim of Brazil's censors. New York Times. Sec. 4, p. 8. Dec. 27, 1931

Corey, N.Y. Times, ousted by Brazil on false charge. Editor and Publisher. 64: 7. Jan. 2, 1932

Drastic press law. Editor and Publisher. 56:37. Nov. 3, 1923
    Brazilian Senate would prohibit statements injurious to President.

Freise, Fred. W.
Beiträge zum brasilianischen Zeitungswesen in Vergangenheit und Gegenwart. Zeitungswissenschaft. 5:228-32. July 15, 1930
    A discussion of the contemporary press of Brazil, and a sketch of historical backgrounds.

Vergangenheit und Gegenwart. Zeitungswissenschaft. 5:290-5. Sept. 15, 1930
    A discussion of past and present development of the press in Brazil.

Gehse, Hans
Die deutsche Presse in Brasilien von 1852 bis zur Gegenwart. 174p. Munster i. W.: Aschendorffsche Verlag, 1931
    The German press in Brazil from 1852 to 1930.

Montarroyos, E.
Brasilianische Presse. Nord und Süd. 53: 846-56. 1930

Neues Pressegesetz in Brazilien. Zeitungswissenschaft. 14:78-9. Jan. 1, 1939
    Details of a new press law, including a stipulation limiting a work day to five hours.

Quelle, O.
Materialien zum Studium der spanischen Presse. Ibero-Amerikanisches Archiv. 9:296-9. 1936

Wright, Marie (Robinson)
The new Brazil. 494p. Philadelphia: Geo. Barrie and Sons, 1908
    History of Brazil. Journalism p. 182-4.

E. CHILE

Anderson, Lola
Chilean newspapermen organize to raise professional status. Editor and Publisher. 66:32. Feb. 3, 1934

Early press history in Chile. Bulletin of the Pan-American Union. 69:540-51. July 1935
    First periodical in Chile appeared in Santiago in 1812. Other periodicals described to 1827.

Cruchaga Ossa, Miguel
Die Presse in Chile. Zeitungswissenschaft. 10:458-63. Aug. 1, 1935
    High lights of Chilean journalism. In Spanish and German.

Edwards, Agustín
Journalism in Chile. Journal of the British Institute of Journalists. 25:96-8. May 1937

My native land. 430p. London: E. Benn, 1928
    Descriptive and cultural history by a Chilean diplomat. "The National Journalism": ch. 21, p. 369-90.

Fusoni, Raphael
Chile first country to provide pension for newspapermen. Editor and Publisher. 59:20. July 31, 1926

A **Great** South American newspaper: the Mercurio of Chile. Pan-American Magazine. 27:81-5. June 1918
    Mercurio de Valparaiso founded in 1827. Controls five other daily newspapers in Chile. The story of their editors and owners.

Grünbeck, Max
Aus den Anfängen der chilenischen Presse. Zeitungswissenschaft. 5:101-4. Mar. 15, 1930
    Beginnings of the press in Chile.

The **Press** in Chile. Bulletin of the Pan-American Union. 60:353-8. Apr. 1926
    In Spanish and English.

Vega, Daniel de la
Graphic journalism in Chile. Pan-American Magazine. 25:255-6. Sept. 1917
    The rapid rise since 1904 of graphic arts and cartooning in Chile.

Wright, M. R.
El Mercurio, a great South American newspaper. Era. 12:147-54. Aug. 1903

F. COLOMBIA

Grosz, R. F.
Die Presse der Republik Kolumbien. Zeitungswissenschaft. 10:473-9. Aug. 1, 1935
A brief review of Colombia's press.

Otero Muñoz, Gustavo
Historia del periodismo en Colombia; de la imprenta hasta el fin de la reconqista española (1737-1819). Bogota: Editorial Minerva, 1925
History of journalism in Colombia; the press until the end of the Spanish conquest.

Reinartz, Hans Armin
Die Entwicklung der Presse in Kolumbien, Ecuador und Peru bis zum 19. Jahrhundert. Zeitungswissenschaft. 12:703-6. Oct. 1, 1937
Short historical sketches of journalism in these countries.

G. CUBA, CENTRAL AMERICA AND THE CARIBBEAN

Beals, Carleton
Censorship in Cuba. Nation. 140:601. May 22, 1935
In a letter to the editor this correspondent accuses Ambassador Caffery of influencing United States correspondents in Cuba to send only reports favorable to the Batista Mendieta regime.

Cuban censors active. Editor and Publisher. 64:4. Dec. 12, 1931

Cuban editor jailed. Editor and Publisher. 64:12. Dec. 19, 1931

Cuban "gag" lifted. Editor and Publisher. 64:8. Sept. 26, 1931

Cuban news governed with iron hand. Editor and Publisher. 64:10. Sept. 5, 1931
Military censorship lifted but recalcitrant writers face heavy penalties if they print news favorable to rebels.

Cuban Supreme Court voids press gag. Editor and Publisher. 63:6. Apr. 4, 1931

Diaz censoring news from Nicaragua. Editor and Publisher. 59:iv. Jan. 29, 1927

First Pan-American congress of journalists. Bulletin of the Pan-American Union. 60:128-30. Feb. 1926

Fundamentals in Cuba. Outlook. 157:519-20. Apr. 15, 1931

Havana newspapers. Editor and Publisher. 12:32. June 14, 1913

Lincoln, Waldo, comp.
List of newspapers of the West Indies and Bermuda in the library of the American Antiquarian Society. American Antiquarian Society, Proceedings. n.s. 36:130-55. Apr. 14, 1926

Montague, Sherman and Rayner, O. T.
The press laws of foreign countries. London: 1926

Newspapers of Porto Rico. Editor and Publisher. 53:110. Jan. 22, 1921

Newspapers of Virgin Islands. Editor and Publisher. 53:110. Jan. 22, 1921

Perry, John W.
Machado suppression policy continues. Editor and Publisher. 63:v. Jan. 31, 1931

The Press in Haiti. Nation. 125:166, 168. Aug. 17, 1927

Printers strike in Cuba. Editor and Publisher. 64:46. Oct. 10, 1931

Rayner, O. T. See Montague, Sherman, jt. auth.

Reinartz, Hans Armin
Die Entwicklung der Presse in Guatemala und Honduras bis 1900. Zeitungswissenschaft. 14:549-50. Aug. 1939
A short account of the history of journalism in Honduras and Guatemala.

Die Presse von Haiti, 1800-1850. Zeitungswissenschaft. 13:13-14. Jan. 1, 1938
An abbreviated history of the press of Haiti.

Die Presse von Salvador, 1824-1900. Zeitungswissenschaft. 12:814-15. Dec. 1, 1937
A list of the newspapers of Salvador, 1824-1900.

Rodriguez, Virgilio Beteta
Early Guatemala paper launched 200 years ago on Nov. 1. Editor and Publisher. 62:27. Nov. 2, 1929
Gazeta de Guatemala issued as monarchical and religious publication.

Ruhl, Arthur
Muzzling editors in Haiti. American Mercury. 5:468-71. Aug. 1925

Sentner, David P.
News reports strictly censored in Cuba during revolution. Editor and Publisher. 64:11. Aug. 22, 1931

Three Haitian editors arrested. Editor and Publisher. 64:56. June 6, 1931

Warner, Arthur
Bayonet rule for our colonial press. Nation. 116:267. Mar. 7, 1923
Protests high-handed methods of U.S. Navy, which administrates in the Virgin Islands, in dealing with editors and their editorial utterances.

H. ECUADOR

Editors of Ecuador suffer prison and exile for press freedom. Editor and Publisher. 58:18. Mar. 6, 1926

Die Presse Ecuadors. Zeitungswissenschaft. 3:153. Oct. 15, 1928

Reinartz, Hans Armin
Die Entwicklung der Presse in Kolumbien, Ecuador und Peru bis zum 19 Jahrhundert. Zeitungswissenschaft. 12:703-6. Oct. 1, 1937

Die Presse Ecuadors an der Wende des 19. und 20. Jahrhunderts. Zeitungswissenschaft. 14:113-15. Feb. 1, 1939
A short account of the press of Ecuador from the latter part of the 19th century to the present.

1. MEXICO

Anderson, Lola
Mexican women journalists. Bulletin of the Pan-American Union. 68:315-20. May 1934

Ariza, F. J.
News a-plenty and thrilling, but few newspaper men left in Mexico. Editor and Publisher. 48:1208. Mar. 11, 1916

Beals, Carleton
How the news is made. p. 302-7. *In his* Banana gold. Philadelphia: J. B. Lippincott, 1932
News gatherers and news sources in Mexico and the attitude of the American military leaders toward the press during the Sandino revolt.

Porfirio Diaz, dictator of Mexico. p. 267-73. Philadelphia: J. B. Lippincott, 1932
Persecution of the press during the second term of Porfirio Diaz, 1884-1911.

Daily newspapers of Mexico. Editor and Publisher. 53:110. Jan. 22, 1921

Distinguished Mexican editors visit the United States. Bulletin Pan American Union. 46:709-17. June 1918

Fife, George Buchanan
On the Mexico special. Harper's Weekly. 54:9. Oct. 15, 1910

Gutiérrez de Lara, Lazaro
The Mexican people: their struggle for freedom. Garden City, N.Y.: Doubleday, Page, 1914
A political history of Mexico. Only scattered references to newspapers.

Hodson, Charles E.
Mexican journalism. Catholic World. 47:450-8. July 1888
Description of the journals of Mexico City, with interesting quotations from each.

The **Kluckhohn** case. Nation. 148:109-10. Jan. 28, 1939
Expulsion from Mexico of *New York Times* correspondent followed provocative articles on Nazi oil deals.

Léon Sánchez, Manuel
La imprenta en México desde la independencia hasta nuestros días. El Libro Mexicano. 1:4-9. Nov. 1924
A brief history of the Mexican press.

Lepidus, Henry
The history of Mexican journalism. 87p. (Univ. of Missouri Bulletin, v.29. Journalism Series, no. 49) Columbia, Mo.: Univ. of Missouri, Jan. 21, 1928
A compact history tracing the origins and development of the Mexican press, its characteristics, handicaps under an unfriendly government and poverty; its outlook.
Bibliography.

Lid off: Mexico now claims membership in censor-free nations of world. map Literary Digest. 123:30. May 29, 1937

McCaleb, Walter F.
The press of Mexico. Hispanic American Historical Review. 3:443-50. Aug. 1920
No real press existed in Mexico prior to Diaz regime. Changes in regime are accompanied by changes in press policy. Press of Mexico is dependent on the favor of the ruling powers.

Magner, J. A.
Publicity for Mexico. Commonweal. 21:443-5. Feb. 15, 1935

Merz, Charles
Propaganda against Mexico. World Tomorrow. 10:152-5. Apr. 1927

Mexico and the press. Editor and Publisher. 60:26. Nov. 26, 1927
Press not informing the public concerning what is known about Mexico.

Mexico bars dailies opposing Church ban. Editor and Publisher. 59:22. Aug. 7, 1926
Spanish papers published in Texas forbidden to circulate after criticism of Calles' religious reform.

Mexico expels N. Y. Times correspondent. Editor and Publisher. 72:8. Jan. 21, 1939
Frank L. Kluckhohn's articles on oil export deals displeased the government.

Mexico is strong in craft spirit among its journalists. Editor and Publisher. 55:18. Nov. 4, 1922
Nearly every newspaper a member of Associated Press.

More freedom for press in Mexico. Editor and Publisher. 53:9. Feb. 5, 1921
Improved condition of the Mexican press under President Obregon.

Murray, Robert H.
Denies censorship suppresses Mexican news. Editor and Publisher. 61:15, 84. Sept. 29, 1928
No important story kept from United States dailies.

Organizes press bureau. Editor and Publisher. 10:1. July 30, 1910
Mexican government proposes to furnish press with news.

The **Press** in Mexico. Bulletin of the Pan-American Union. 33:147-9. 1911
First printing press in the Americas was set up in Mexico City in 1536; the first newspaper in Mexico appeared in 1693. General comment on the newspaper press in Mexico to 1911.

Saunders, William L.
Mexican conditions obscured by censorship. Editor and Publisher. 61:5. Sept. 15, 1928
Prompt exile faces local publisher or foreign correspondents who displease present administration, despite constitutional guarantee of press freedom.

Spell, L. M.
Anglo-Saxon press in Mexico, 1846-1848. American Historical Review. 38:20-31. Oct. 1932
Bibliographical footnotes.

Spell, L. M.—*Continued*
Mexican literary periodicals of the nineteenth century. Modern Language Association Pub. 52:272-312. Mar. 1937

Starr-Hunt, Jack
Press Congress meets in Mexico City. Editor and Publisher. 64:9. Aug. 15, 1931
President Rubio and other high Mexican officials address fourth international meeting of editors. Press as power for peace discussed.

Suppression of newspapers and the imprisonment of editors in Mexico. Editor and Publisher. 9:7. Feb. 5, 1910
Twenty publications were suppressed in two months, many editors and employees imprisoned for opposing President Diaz.

Teja Zabre, Alphonso
A guide to the history of Mexico. Tr. from Spanish by P. M. del Campo. 375p. Mexico City: Ministry of Foreign Affairs, 1935

Tellez, Manuel C.
Journalism and diplomacy. p. 8-10. (Univ. of Missouri Bulletin, v.30. Journalism Series, no. 56) Columbia, Mo.: Univ. of Missouri, Dec. 1, 1929
Address of Mexican Ambassador to United States on the professional sphere of each, their responsibilities and privileges in international affairs.

Toro, Alfonso
Compendio de historia de México. t.2. México, D.F.: Sociedad de Edición y Librería Franco-Americana, S.A., 1926

Torres, Teodoro
Periodismo. Mexico City: Ediciones Botas, 1937
Bibliography of newspapers founded in Mexico 1730-1934.

Turner, Timothy G.
Bullets, bottles and gardenias. 258p. Dallas, Texas: Southwest Press, 1936
By an American correspondent in Mexico.

Walker, Nell
The life and works of Manuel Gutierrez Najera. (Univ. of Missouri Studies, v. 2, p. 18-22) Columbia, Mo.: Univ. of Missouri, Apr. 1, 1927
Mexican poet and journalist who founded the *Revista Azul*, a weekly journal. Co-author of the Modernista movement in Spanish-American literature.
Ch. 3. The poet's journalistic career.

What the people read in Mexico. Review of Reviews. 31:687-8. 1905
An appraisal of the Mexican newspapers of that day, Spanish and English.

Wittich, Ernst
Die Entwicklung des Zeitungswesens in Mexiko. Zeitungswissenschaft. 10:479-515. Aug. 1, 1935
Development of the Mexican press. The article in German is supplemented by a version of the same subject matter in Spanish under the title *El Desarrolo del Periodismo en México*.

Wright, Chester M.
How the propagandists work for war with Mexico. American Federationist. 27:550-6. June 1920
American oil, timber and real estate interests are active in creating dissensions between the two nations in order to force American intervention.

L. OTHER COUNTRIES

Kihss, Peter F.
News was censored at Montevideo. Editor and Publisher. 66:11. Jan. 13, 1934

Martin, Gerald
Venezuela threatened with civil war; drastic censorship methods of the government. China Weekly Review. 50:346. Nov. 2, 1929

Reinartz, Hans Armin
Die Entwicklung der Presse in Kolumbien, Ecuador und Peru bis zum 19 Jahrhundert. Zeitungswissenschaft. 12:703-6. Oct. 1, 1937

Die Entwicklung der Presse in Paraguay bis zum Weltkrieg. Zeitungswissenschaft. 14:118-19. Feb. 1, 1939
A brief sketch of the press in Paraguay.

Die Tagespresse in Venezuela, 1808-1900. Zeitungswissenschaft. 13:323-4. May 1, 1938
A short account of the press of Venezuela.

Rodway, James
The press in British Guiana. American Antiquarian Society, Proceedings. n.s. 28:274-90. Oct. 1918

VII. OTHER AMERICAN COUNTRIES

A. CANADA AND NEW-FOUNDLAND

America "starving" Canada's press. Literary Digest. 64:27. Feb. 14, 1920

Audet, Francis J.
William Brown, 1737-1789, premier imprimeur, journaliste et libraire de Québec: sa vie et ses œuvres. Royal Society of Canada, Transactions. ser. 3, 26 (sec. 1):97-112. 1932
Sketch of the life and works of William Brown, pioneer journalist, printer, and publisher in Canada; his *Gazette*; encounter with the Stamp Act (1765). Bibliography.

Banks, William
Press censorship. Canadian Magazine. 46:152-5. Dec. 1915

Beder, E. A.
The Toronto press. Canadian Forum. 12:6-8. Oct. 1931

Black, Robson
Canadian journalism. Canadian Magazine. 32:434-40. Mar. 1909
A severe criticism of the Canadian newspapers and suggestions for improvement.

Brown, G. M. L.
An editorial rainbow. Canadian Magazine. 28:29-31. Nov. 1906

Campbell, Wilfred
Four early Canadian journalists. Canadian Magazine. 43:551-8. Oct. 1914

Canada's press association. Editor and Publisher. 13:748. Mar. 7, 1914

Canadian associations and clubs. Editor and Publisher. 53:105, 106. Jan. 22, 1921

Canadian censorship. Canadian Forum. 19: 72-3. June 1939
Editorial.
An expression of dissatisfaction over arbitrary confiscation of so-called "subversive" or "obscene" literature.

Canadian news: new telegraphic association in Dominion allied with United Press. Editor and Publisher. 9:1-2. Apr. 23, 1910
Movement designed to break the Canadian Pacific Railway's monopoly of news.

Canadian press association. A history of Canadian journalism. 242p. Toronto: Murray Printing Co., 1908
History of the Canadian Press Association and its various officers. "Membership Roll, 1908," p. 234.

Canadian press gets broader charter. Editor and Publisher. 55:18. Apr. 7, 1923
New Dominion act eliminates "limited." Leased wire with French language service proves a success .

Canadian readers and American periodicals. Outlook. 86:228-9. June 1, 1907

Card, Raymond
Daltons and the "Patriot." Canadian Historical Review. 16:176-8. June 1935

Charlesworth, Hector W.
Candid chronicles: leaves from the notebook of a Canadian journalist. 404p. Toronto: Macmillan, 1925
Personal reminiscences of a Canadian journalist. Ch. 10, p. 147-64, "Hobbled Journalism"; discusses a newspaper governed by a party machine.
More candid chronicles. Further leaves from the notebook of a Canadian journalist. 429p. Toronto: Macmillan, 1928

Chartier, C. Émile
L'éloquence parlementaire et les journaux, 1792-1867. Royal Society of Canada, Transactions. Ser. 3, 27 (sec. 1):49-61. 1933
The effectiveness of parliamentary eloquence and journalism in securing equitable government for the French Canadians.

Clark, A. J.
The newspaper of 1810. Canadian Magazine. 36:579-83. Apr. 1911

Clark, Joseph T.
The daily newspaper. Canadian Magazine. 7:101-4. June 1896

Coast co-operative; Vancouver News-Herald. Time. 28:49. Dec. 14, 1936

Colonial press. Canadian Magazine. 28:409-11. Feb. 1907

Colquhoun, Arthur H. U.
A century of Canadian magazines. Canadian Magazine. 17:141-9. June 1901
Journalism and the university. Canadian Magazine. 21:209-19. July 1903

Cordingley, Audrey. See Tod, Dorothea D. jt. comp.

Coup d'œil sur le Canada français. Presse Publicité. no. 23, p. 9-10, 23. Oct. 24, 1937
The French press in Canada, strongly influenced by the United States, remains Latin in temperament.

Davin, Nicholas Flood
The London and Canadian press. Canadian Monthly. 5:118-28. Feb. 1874
An evaluation of the London and Canadian newspapers; the Canadian press is inferior but promising.

Deacon, William Arthur
Poteen; a pot-pourri of Canadian essays. 241p. Ottawa: Graphic Publishers, 1926

Desilets, Alphonse
Revues et magazines de langue française au Canada. Revue Politique et Littéraire. 63:209-11. Mar. 21, 1925

Drastic press curb bill held up in Alberta. Editor and Publisher. 70:8. Oct. 9, 1937

Dunbar, Robert C.
Perils of eloquence. Canadian Magazine. 19:120-4. June 1902

Executives of Canadian daily newspapers. Editor and Publisher. 53:90, 155. Jan. 22, 1921
List of newspapers, publishers, etc.

Fairfax, John
Apology for the press. Canadian Forum. 16:7-9. Apr. 1936

Fawcett, J. F. Morris
The newspapers of Newfoundland. Canadian Magazine. 4:422-7. Mar. 1895

Ferguson, Bessie Gowan
Progress written between the lines. Canadian Magazine. 67:16-17. June 1927

Flaherty, Francis
Canada's no. 1 newspaperman. Quill. 27: 13-14. July 1939
A personality sketch of John W. Dafoe, editor-in-chief of the Winnipeg Free Press, and for 53 years a newspaperman.

Gérin, Elzéar
La presse canadienne, la Gazette de Québec. 65p. Quebec: J.-N. Duquet, 1864

Hopkins, J. Castell, ed.
Canadian literature and journalism. p. 117-238. In his Canada: an encyclopaedia of the country, v.5. Toronto: Linscott, 1898-1900
Six articles on Canadian journalism.

Labor journals and papers published in Canada. Monthly Labor Review. 32: 113-14. June 1931

Lucidus, pseud.
A people's press. Canadian Forum. 18:
77-9. June 1938
A plan to force the press from the influence of wealthy owners and big advertisers.

McCready, J. E. B.
Journalisme et conféderation. Canadian
Magazine. 29:211-15. July 1907

Special correspondent. Canadian Magazine. 29:548-52. Oct. 1907

McGrath, P. T.
What the people read in Canada. Review
of Reviews. 33:720-2. June 1906

MacKim, A.
MacKim's Directory of Canadian publications. 30th ed. 480p. Montreal: A.
MacKim, Ltd., 1908-37
A complete list of the newspapers and periodicals published in the Dominion of Canada and Newfoundland.

MacMechan, Archibald
The literature of Nova Scotia. Canadian
Magazine. 25:565-7. Oct. 1905

MacPherson, R. G.
Trio of early Western journals. Canadian
Magazine. 30:550-2. Apr. 1908

Martell, J. S.
Press of the Maritime provinces in the
1830's; with list of extant files and some
editorial opinions. Canadian Historical
Review. 19:24-56. Mar. 1938
Bibliographical footnotes.

Notes on Canadian magazines. Canadian
Bookman. 12:85. Apr. 1930

Our class-conscious newspapers. Canadian
Forum. 17:79-80. June 1937

Oxley, J. MacDonald
Periodical literature in Canada. North
American Review. 147:349-51. Sept.
1888

Porritt, Edward
A century-and-a-half of English journalism
in Canada. p. 119-50. In Sell's Dictionary of the world's press. London: H.
Sell, 1906

The value of political editorials. Atlantic.
105:62-7. Jan. 1910

Rivard, Adjutor
De la liberté de la presse. Royal Society
of Canada, Transactions. ser. 3, 17(sec.
1):33-104. 1923
Observations on the liberty of the press.

Rogers, David B.
Canadian papers praise new form of censorship in labor dispute. Editor and
Publisher. 58:12. Dec. 5, 1925

Rutledge, J. L.
Magazines and national unity. Canadian
Magazine. 85:14. Jan. 1936

Shortt, Adam
Personality in journalism. Canadian Magazine. 29:520-4. Oct. 1907

Stewart, George
Literary reminiscences. Canadian Magazine. 17:163-6. June 1901

Stokes, C. W.
American magazines in Canada. English
Review. 43:452-6. Oct. 1926

Talman, J. J.
Newspapers of upper Canada a century·
ago. Canadian Historical Review. 19:9-
23. Mar. 1938
Bibliographical footnotes.

Thomas, A. V.
Newspaper control. Dial. 66:121-4. Feb.
8, 1919
Inquires why in the conscription issue in Canada (1917) so many newspapers embraced the cause of the Union Government. Probable answer: they were spiritually coerced and yielded to influences which they found irresistible.

Tod, Dorothea D. and Cordingley, Audrey,
comps.
A bibliography of Canadian literary periodicals, 1789-1900. Royal Society Canada, Transactions. ser. 3, 26(sec. 2):87-
96. 1932
Briefly annotated. Pt. I is devoted to periodicals in the English language, pt. II to French.

Underhill, F. H.
J. W. Dafoe. Canadian Forum. 13:23-4.
Oct. 1932
An appreciative review of the work of J. W. Dafoe as the editor of the Winnipeg Free Press and the outstanding Canadian journalist.

Wallace, W. S.
The periodical literature of upper Canada.
Canadian Hist. Review. 12:4-22, 181-3.
Mar.-June, 1931

Willison, John Stephen
Journalism and public life in Canada. Canadian Magazine. 25:554-8. Oct. 1905
Criticizes excessive partisanship of the various molders of public opinion in Canadian public life.

Reminiscences, political and personal. Canadian Magazine. 51:3-17, 95-104, 229-
40, 321-32, 387-97, 491-501; 52:579-87,
665-75, 773-82, 873-82, 895-908, 1019-28;
53:55-66, 126-36. May, Nov. 1918; June
1919

B. GREENLAND

Wessely, Franz
Die Presse auf Grönland. Zeitungswissenschaft. 13:583-4. Sept. 1, 1938
An interesting history of the press of Greenland.

C. UNITED STATES
POSSESSIONS

For Puerto Rico and the Virgin Islands see
Cuba, Central America and the Caribbean,
p.178.

I. ALASKA

Mowat, Jean
Newspaper making in Alaska. Inland
Printer. 71:221-2. May, 1923

Nichols, Jeannette P.
Alaska, a history of its administration, exploitation, and industrial development during its first half century under the rule of the United States. p. 425-31. Cleveland: Arthur H. Clark, 1924
Development of public opinion, p. 165-70; list of periodicals published in Alaska, p. 425-8

Wessely, Franz
Die Presse in Alaska. Zeitungswissenschaft. 13:366-9. June 1, 1938
Statistics and facts regarding the press in Alaska.

Wickersham, James, comp.
A bibliography of Alaskan literature, 1724-1924. 635p. Cordova, Alaska: Cordova Daily Times, 1927
Contains titles of all histories, chronicles of travels and voyages, newspapers, periodicals, public documents, etc., printed in English, Russian, German, French, Spanish, 1724-1924.

Willoughby, Barrett
Man who invented the ice worm. American. 111:77-8. Feb. 1931

2. HAWAII

Die Älteste Zeitung Hawaiis. Zeitungswissenschaft. 3:56. Apr. 15, 1928
The oldest paper in Hawaii.

Case, Howard D.
Hawaii boasts of most diversified press in the world. Editor and Publisher. 54:15. Sept. 24, 1921
English, Japanese, Korean, Portuguese, Filipino readers must be catered to.

Hawaii claims front rank position in use of press for Congress. Editor and Publisher. 54:12. Dec. 3, 1921

Liang, William W. Y.
The Chinese press in the territory of Hawaii. Edited under the auspices of the Department of Journalism, Yenching University. 4p. (Collectanea Commiss. Synodal. v.10, no. 12) Peiping: Dec. 1937

Newspapers of Hawaii. Editor and Publisher. 53:110. Jan. 22, 1921

Press control in Hawaiian Islands. Editor and Publisher. 54:12. June 4, 1921
Aimed at seditious matter printed in foreign language papers.

3. PHILIPPINES

Bogardus, E. S.
Filipino press in the United States. Sociology and Social Research. 18:581-5. July 1934

News communications in the Philippines. Press Congress of the World in Geneva, Proceedings. Columbia, Mo.: Univ. of Missouri, 1928

Newspapers of the Philippine Islands. Editor and Publisher. 53:110. Jan. 22, 1921

Sanger, J. W.
Philippine publications. p. 106-7. (U.S. Bureau of Foreign and Domestic Commerce. Special Agent ser., no. 209) Washington: Government Printing Office, 1921

Valenzuela, Jesús Z.
History of journalism in the Philippine Islands. 217p. Manila: The Author, 1933

Wessely, Franz
Die Presse auf den Philippinen (Spanien). Zeitungswissenschaft. 6:237-41. July 15, 1931
A summary and review of The History of the Philippine Press by Carson Taylor of the Manila Daily Bulletin.

Die revolutionäre Presse auf den Philippinen in den Jahren 1898 und 1899. Zeitungswissenschaft. 13:784-8. Dec. 1, 1938
The character of the revolutionary press in the Philippine Islands, 1898-1899.

D. THE FOREIGN LANGUAGE PRESS IN THE UNITED STATES

See also
World War, 1914—The Foreign Language Press in the United States, p.94.

American by decree. New Republic. 22:262-3. Apr. 28, 1920

Ander, Oscar Fritiof
Swedish American press and the election of 1892. Mississippi Valley Historical Review. 23:533-54. Mar. 1937
Bibliographical footnotes.

Baensch, Emil
The German-American press. p. 144-9. (Wisconsin Historical Soc., Proceedings, 1898) Madison: Democrat Printing Co., 1899

Ban, Oscar
Death comes to the foreign press. New Outlook. 162:44-8. July 1933
Mr. Ban predicts the end of the immigrant press of America, but sheds no tears. He contends that this press has failed utterly, maintained Old World and bygone animosities, was unsatisfactory as an agency of news distribution and as a disseminator of popular education, and proved to be a false leader and a bad guide.

Beuick, Marshall D.
Declining immigrant press. Social Forces. 6:257-63. Dec. 1927
A general discussion of the foreign press in the United States. Its influence on immigrants was largely for the better; its present decline from a peak of 1350 periodicals to about 1000 resulted from a decrease in immigration.

Bierstadt, Edward H.
Dailies for new Americans. Our World. 4:62-70. Mar. 1924

Blegen, T. C.
Early Norwegian press in America. Minnesota Historical Bulletin. 3:506-18. Nov. 1920

Bogory, N. de
What seven million Americans are reading. Outlook. 133:354-5. Feb. 21, 1923

Built up big daily. Editor and Publisher. 13:642. Jan. 31, 1914
    Jacob Saphirstein, publisher of New York *Jewish Morning Journal*, is now recognized power in foreign language field.

Butcher, Harold
Foreign writers celebrate 21st year of U.S. "coverage" from abroad. Editor and Publisher. 58:40. Mar. 27, 1926

How one man made Europe want U.S. news. Editor and Publisher. 70:20. Sept. 25, 1937

Clemens, Howard
Alien newspapers of New York City. Bookman. 14:37-47. Sept. 1901
    An interesting account of our foreign— but essentially American—press in New York City.

Foreign language editors. Editor and Publisher. 10:2. Nov. 19, 1910
    Letter from President Taft received at anniversary dinner, commending editors and publishers of foreign language newspapers.

Foreign language papers organize. Editor and Publisher. 13:834. Apr. 4, 1914
    The Association of Foreign Language Newspapers formed in St. Louis to promote social and business relations among members.

Foreign language papers pleading for life. Literary Digest. 65:24-5. Apr. 3, 1920

Ham, E. B.
Journalism and the French survival in New England. New England Quarterly. 11:89-107. Mar. 1938
    Bibliographical footnotes.

Harris, G. W.
Foreign-language newspapers in the United States. Editor and Publisher. 48:1099, 1134. Feb. 19, 1916
    Critical evaluation of their influence upon American ideals.

Holder, C. F.
Chinese press in America. Scientific American. 87:241. Oct. 11, 1902

Influence of the German and other foreign press. Literary Digest. 64:31-2. Feb. 28, 1920

Italian press of New York. Editor and Publisher. 11:8. Jan. 20, 1912

Keeler, E. C.
Our polyglot press. World Outlook. 4:9. June 1918

Kuo, T. L.
Chinese vernacular press in San Francisco. China Weekly Review. 63:344. Jan. 21, 1933

Lundstedt, Bernhard W.
Svenska tidningar och tidskrifter utgifna inom Nord-Amerikas forenta stater. 53p. Stockholm: P. A. Norstedt och Söner, 1886
    Swedish press in North America.

Park, Robert E.
Foreign language press and social progress. p. 493-500. *In* National Conference of Social Work, Proceedings, 1920. Chicago: Univ. of Chicago Press, 1920

The immigrant press and its control. 487p. New York: Harper, 1922
    A careful study of the immigrant press and its effect upon the immigrant's efforts to adjust himself to a new cultural environment. Nationalities and statistics.

Parry, Albert
Goodbye to the immigrant press. American Mercury. 28:56-63. Jan. 1933
    Downward trend of immigrant press, due to lack of immigration and Americanization.

Parsons, Henry S., ed.
A check list of foreign newspapers in the Library of Congress. 209p. Washington: Government Printing Office, 1929

Pixley, Morrisson
A Chinese newspaper in America. World's Work. 3:1950-3. Apr. 1902

Polyglot papers. Editor and Publisher. 11:12. Sept. 30, 1911
    Some idea of the extent of the foreign language newspapers in America.

Polyzoides, Adamantios Th.
Greek editor discusses significance of foreign language press. Editor and Publisher. 57:25. July 26, 1924
    Declares it does not compete unduly with local English papers.

Robinson, Edna
Chinese journalism in America. Current Literature. 32:325-6. Mar. 1902

Slauson, Allen B., comp.
A check list of foreign newspapers in the Library of Congress. 292p. Washington: Government Printing Office, 1901

Soltes, Mordecai
The Yiddish press, an Americanizing agency. 242p. New York: Teachers College, Columbia Univ., 1924

Tinker, E. L., comp.
Bibliography of the French newspapers and periodicals of Louisiana. il., pl., facsims. American Antiquarian Society, Proceedings. n.s. 42 pt. 2:247-370. Oct. 19, 1932

Toksvig, Signe K.
Many-tongued America. New Republic. 27:190-2. July 13, 1921

Totals of all foreign language "A.B.C." dailies in the U.S. Editor and Publisher. 53:57. Jan. 22, 1921
    Statistics.

Wittke, Carl
Ohio's German-language press in the campaign of 1920. Mississippi Valley Historical Review. 10:468-80. Feb. 1923

INDEX

INTERNATIONAL PROPAGANDA AND COMMUNICATIONS

An Arno Press Collection

Bruntz, George G. **Allied Propaganda and the Collapse of the German Empire in 1918.** 1938

Childs, Harwood Lawrence, editor. **Propaganda and Dictatorship:** A Collection of Papers. 1936

Childs, Harwood L[awrence] and John B[oardman] Whitton, editors. **Propaganda By Short Wave** *including* C[harles] A. Rigby's **The War on the Short Waves.** 1942/1944

Codding, George Arthur, Jr. **The International Telecommunication Union:** An Experiment in International Cooperation. 1952

Creel, George. **How We Advertised America.** 1920

Desmond, Robert W. **The Press and World Affairs.** 1937

Farago, Ladislas, editor. **German Psychological Warfare.** 1942

Hadamovsky, Eugen. **Propaganda and National Power.** 1954

Huth, Arno. **La Radiodiffusion Puissance Mondiale.** 1937

International Propaganda/Communications: Selections from *The Public Opinion Quarterly,* 1943/1952/1956. 1972

International Press Institute Surveys, Nos. 1-6. 1952-1962

International Press Institute. **The Flow of News.** 1953

Lavine, Harold and James Wechsler. **War Propaganda and the United States.** 1940

Lerner, Daniel, editor. **Propaganda in War and Crisis.** 1951

Linebarger, Paul M. A. **Psychological Warfare.** 1954

Lockhart, Sir R[obert] H. Bruce. **Comes the Reckoning.** 1947

Macmahon, Arthur W. **Memorandum on the Postwar International Information Program of the United States.** 1945

de Mendelssohn, Peter. **Japan's Political Warfare.** 1944

Nafziger, Ralph O., compiler. **International News and the Press:** An Annotated Bibliography. 1940

Read, James Morgan. **Atrocity Propaganda, 1914-1919.** 1941

Riegel, O[scar] W. **Mobilizing for Chaos:** The Story of the New Propaganda. 1934

Rogerson, Sidney. **Propaganda in the Next War.** 1938

Summers, Robert E., editor. **America's Weapons of Psychological Warfare.** 1951

Terrou, Fernand and Lucien Solal. **Legislation for Press, Film and Radio:** Comparative Study of the Main Types of Regulations Governing the Information Media. 1951

Thomson, Charles A. H. **Overseas Information Service of the United States Government.** 1948

Tribolet, Leslie Bennett. **The International Aspects of Electrical Communications in the Pacific Area.** 1929

Unesco. **Press Film Radio,** Volumes I-V *including* Supplements. 1947-1951. 3 volumes.

Unesco. **Television:** A World Survey *including* Supplement. 1953/1955

White, Llewellyn and Robert D. Leigh. **Peoples Speaking to Peoples:** A Report on International Mass Communication from The Commission on Freedom of the Press. 1946

Williams, Francis. **Transmitting World News.** 1953

Wright, Quincy, editor. **Public Opinion and World-Politics.** 1933